WITHDRAWN

HARVARD LIBRARY

WITHDRAWN

CANADA'S BIG BIBLICAL

Canada's Big Biblical Bargain

How McGill University Bought the Dead Sea Scrolls

JASON KALMAN AND JAQUELINE S. DU TOIT

McGill-Queen's University Press
Montreal & Kingston • London • Ithaca

© McGill-Queen's University Press 2010
ISBN 978-0-7735-3688-3

Legal deposit second quarter 2010
Bibliothèque nationale du Québec

Printed in Canada on acid-free paper that is 100% ancient forest free (100% post-consumer recycled), processed chlorine free

This book has been published with the help of a grant from the Canadian Federation for the Humanities and Social Sciences, through the Aid to Scholarly Publications Programme, using funds provided by the Social Sciences and Humanities Research Council of Canada. Funding has also been received from Hebrew Union College – Jewish Institute of Religion and the University of the Free State.

McGill-Queen's University Press acknowledges the support of the Canada Council for the Arts for our publishing program. We also acknowledge the financial support of the Government of Canada through the Book Publishing Industry Development Program (BPIDP) for our publishing activities.

Library and Archives Canada Cataloguing in Publication Data

Kalman, Jason, 1974–
Canada's big biblical bargain / Jason Kalman, Jaqueline S. du Toit.

Includes bibliographical references and index.
ISBN 978-0-7735-3688-3

1. Dead Sea scrolls. 4Q. 2. Acquisition of manuscripts – Québec (Province) – Montréal – History – 20th century. 3. Scott, R. B. Y. (Robert Balgarnie Young), 1899– – Correspondence. 4. Cultural property – Protection – Jordan – History. 5. McGill University – History – 20th century. 6. McGill University. Archives. 7. McGill University. Faculty of Religious Studies – Archives. 8. Israel. Rashut ha-atikot. 9. Acquisition of manuscripts – Québec (Province) – Montréal – History – 20th century – Sources. I. Du Toit, Jacqueline S., 1970–. II. Title

BM487.K34 2010   296.1'55   C2010-900375-6

Typeset by Jay Tee Graphics Ltd. in 10/12 Sabon

To
DANA & PIERRE
and
B. BARRY LEVY
Friend, Teacher, and Mentor

Contents

Illustrations ix
Acknowledgments xi
Foreword xv
Preface xix
Abbreviations xxiii

PART ONE

1 Introduction: "I should perhaps recall to you ..." 3
2 "Telling tales of the early days": McGill Buys the Dead Sea Scrolls 21
3 "We must ride out the crisis": The Efforts to Bring the Dead Sea Scrolls to Montreal 79
4 The Real Question: The Nation, the Object, and Owning the Past 123

Postscript "The harvest of this patient waiting" 135

PART TWO

Annotated Correspondence 139

Appendix Transcription of R.B.Y. Scott's Handlist of Qumran Cave Four fragments purchased by McGill University as of May 1955 308

Notes 319
Bibliography 387
Index 407

Illustrations

R. B. Y. Scott   24

Roland de Vaux and G. Lankester Harding   25

F. Cyril James   35

Cave 4 Fragments Purchased for McGill – PAM 41.207   62

Cave 4 Fragments Purchased for McGill – PAM 41.208   63

Cave 4 Fragments Purchased for McGill – PAM 41.209   64

Cave 4 Fragments Purchased for McGill – PAM 41.210   65

Enlargement of McGill Marking "S" on Fragments from PAM   66

Scholars at work in the Jerusalem Scrollery – PAM 41.212   66

Stanley Frost   95

Papyrus Fragments in the Collection of McGill's Redpath Museum   136

Acknowledgments

This book is a collaborative, decade long effort shared between two colleagues who, for the past six years, have worked on different sides of the Atlantic. We contributed equally to the outcome and share the responsibility for any mistakes that may have been made. Nevertheless, as with any project that has been this many years in the making, we are indebted to numerous people and institutions. Hereby we gratefully acknowledge their invaluable contributions.

From the very beginning our work has received the support of B. Barry Levy, former dean of McGill University's Faculty of Religious Studies, and Eileen Schuller of McMaster University. Professor Schuller has been a stalwart supporter and graciously accepted our invitation to write a foreword to this book. To us it seems a fitting tribute, as Professor Schuller is also editor of one of the last of the official series of publications of the Dead Sea Scrolls, the *Discoveries in the Judaean Desert*. She has more than generously shared with us her time and experience and assisted throughout as conduit in establishing contact with Dead Sea Scrolls scholars around the world, who in turn kindly contributed their memories and knowledge. Among them we must first thank Frank Moore Cross who allowed us to interview him in May 2000 about his experiences as a member of the international editorial team in the 1950s. On that same day we were fortunate to spend the afternoon with a wonderful raconteur, the late John Strugnell, editor-in-chief of the editorial team until October 1990. Both men were tremendously kind, patient, and forthcoming in responding to our questions.

Stanley Frost, former director of the History of McGill Project and also former dean of the Faculty of Divinity,[1] shared his memories of the events here described that took place during his tenure at McGill in the 1950s and 1960s; as did Donna Runnals, also former dean of McGill's Faculty of Religious Studies. Professor Runnals helped arrange the acquisition of papyrus fragments from R.B.Y. Scott who bought them in Jerusalem in the summer of 1955. We would like to thank Ryan Byrne for his input on the matter of their publication in this volume. Our thanks also to Ellen Aitken, McGill's current dean of the Faculty of Religious Studies – her staunch support of the publication and launch of the book has been invaluable. Peter McNally, current director of the History of McGill Project, has also been a sounding board, mentor, and supporter of our book. Lawrence Schiffman of New York University and George Brooke of Manchester University were helpful in clarifying queries we had at various stages of the project. Emanuel Tov of Hebrew University and John Strugnell's successor as editor-in-chief of the international editorial team, in addition to kindly responding to our inquiries, helped to arrange invaluable access to the archives of the Israel Antiquities Authority. Our thanks also to Johann Cook of the University of Stellenbosch for his assistance in establishing contact with pertinent role players and for his careful and dedicated reading of a draft of this manuscript; Carla Sulzbach, McGill University, also read and commented on a draft of this manuscript – we are eternally thankful to both for their pointed remarks, innumerable references, and pertinent suggestions.

The staff of the McGill University Archives deserves to be singled out for their hospitality over a period of nine years and their never failing professionalism in managing our queries. The director, Theresa Rowat, the senior archivist, Gordon Burr, and the administrative coordinator, Mary Houde, made the McGill Archives an ideal working environment and this book is largely the result of their enthusiastic cooperation.

We especially thank the editors and staff of McGill-Queen's University Press, John Zucchi, Joan McGilvray, Joanne Pisano, and Lesley Andrassy. They have made the publication of this book a wonderful experience for both of us. The comments from the press's anonymous reviewers helped to greatly improve the manuscript.

As may be imagined given the scope of this project, we are highly indebted to archivists and researchers at various institutions around the world for their kind assistance in helping us to verify or track down information. In alphabetical order, we thank Edward Ball of the University of Nottingham, archivist of the British Society for Old Testament Study; Tobias Brinkmann, formerly of the Parkes Institute for the Study of Jewish/non-Jewish Relations at the University of Southampton and now of Pennsylvania State University; Robin Brunelle and Alex Thomson of the archives of the United Church of Canada; Giuseppina Carozza of the Birks Family Foundation; Catreena Hamarneh of the Archaeological Documentation Unit of the

Jordanian Department of Antiquities; Kevin Profitt, Lisa Frankel, and executive director, Gary Zola, of the Jacob Rader Marcus Center of the American Jewish Archives; James Rent, archivist for the Basilian Fathers in Toronto; Sandra Rosenstock, general and humanities reference librarian at Princeton University Library; Ayela Sussman and Arieh Rochman-Halperin of the Israel Antiquities Authority; and Helene Vallee of the archives of the Canadian Jewish Congress.

In October 2009 Weston Fields, executive director of the Dead Sea Scrolls Foundation, kindly shared the page proofs of his then forthcoming volume, *The Dead Sea Scrolls – A Full History: Volume One, 1947–1960*. Although our volume was already in copyediting at the time, his generosity allowed us to correct some errors and to make a few minor additions to the narrative.

For transcribing, scanning, and formatting documents we thank our graduate assistant, Shane Cass, and Laurel Wolfson, librarian of the Hebrew Union College Klau Library in Cincinnati. Stephen Kaufman of Hebrew Union College – Jewish Institute of Religion and Elena Pober assisted us with the translations from Arabic of some of the documentation. Annelize Venter and Nico Benson of the research office at the University of the Free State facilitated annual funding applications to the National Research Foundation (NRF). We would like to thank our student assistants in South Africa, Jean van Biljon and Francois Greeff; the university librarian, Ronet Vrey, and Estie Pretorius and Rothea Pelser at the interlibrary loan department of the University of the Free State, as well as Christo Lombaard at the University of South Africa, for their interest and unwavering assistance in expediting the acquisition of source material at crucial stages in the completion of this book. Carl Pace carefully and thoroughly indexed the book.

Financial support for this project has been generously provided by the office of the president of Hebrew Union College-Jewish Institute of Religion, David Ellenson, and by the office of the provost Norman Cohen; the former dean and vice dean of the Faculty of Humanities at the University of the Free State, Gerhard de Klerk and Engela Pretorius, the current dean, Lucius Botes, director of research, Frans Swanepoel; and, also, for a number of years, by the NRF of South Africa. Although this book is based on work supported by the NRF, any opinions, findings, and conclusions or recommendations expressed are those of the authors and the NRF does not accept any liability in regard thereto.

This book has been published with the help of a grant from the Canadian Federation for the Humanities and Social Sciences, through the Aid to Scholarly Publications Program, using funds provided by the Social Sciences and Humanities Research Council of Canada.

Permission to publish transcriptions of documents in the McGill University Archives has been granted by the director, Theresa Rowat. Permission to publish papyrus fragments purchased by R.B.Y. Scott has been granted by the Redpath Museum, Montreal. We are grateful to Barbara Lawson, curator of ethnology, for arranging the photography. Permission to publish correspondence from the late G. Lankester Harding and the Jordanian Department of Antiquities has been granted by Fawwaz Al-Khraysheh, director general of the Department of Antiquities, Jordan. Letters and documents from the archival collection of the Israel Antiquities Authority appear courtesy of the Israel Antiquities Authority – permission was granted by Baruch Brandl, archives and library director. Permission to publish transcriptions of the correspondence of Roland de Vaux has been granted by Jean-Michel Tarragon on behalf of the École Biblique et Archéologique Française de Jérusalem. Permission to publish the correspondence of R.B.Y. Scott has been granted by his children: Mary Poapst, John Scott, and the late Gavin Scott. We are grateful to them as well for sharing their memories of their late father and of his colleagues and friends, and for their support of this project. This volume is very much a tribute to the enterprise and academic rigour of their father.

We have made every effort to identify, credit appropriately, and obtain publication rights from copyright holders of illustrations in this book. Notice of any errors or omissions will be gratefully received and correction made in any subsequent editions.

In conclusion, we thank our families, friends and colleagues at McGill University, Hebrew Union College-Jewish Institute of Religion, and the University of the Free State for their continuous encouragement of a project that started out in response to a cursory mention of an obscure link between McGill University and the Dead Sea Scrolls. Our thanks to Jackie Naudé for first drawing our attention to this tidbit of information. And, as always, to Ryan Byrne and Vanessa Sasson, our scholarly companions and loyal friends: thank you.

Finally we thank our spouses. Neither of you were with us when this project began but you have supported us and it as if you had been. We could not be more grateful.

Jason Kalman
Hebrew Union College – Jewish
Institute of Religion (Cincinnati)
Department of Afroasiatic Studies
University of the Free State
South Africa

Jaqueline S. du Toit
Department of Afroasiatic Studies
University of the Free State
South Africa

Foreword

As I write this foreword in the last days of June 2009, the news media in southern Ontario is full of articles and sound bites about the opening of an exhibit of the Dead Sea Scrolls at the Royal Ontario Museum in Toronto. More than sixty years after they were first discovered, these ancient manuscripts are still able to excite, attract crowds, raise questions, and generate controversy.

Of the sixteen scrolls that are on display at the ROM, about one half were purchased originally by the Palestine Archaeological Museum in Jerusalem from the Bedouin with money that was given for this purpose by McGill University in Montreal, Canada. The $15,500 supplied by McGill in 1954 (and supplemented by $4,200 in 1955) was key to keeping together the thousands of small pieces of leather in a single collection so that they could be studied and published, rather than being sold at random in the markets and on the streets of the Old City in Jerusalem.

The full story of McGill's involvement in the 1950s and early 1960s and the significance of what the initiative of McGill professor R.B.Y. Scott meant for preservation and publication has remained largely unknown up until the present. Most standard textbooks and histories of scrolls scholarship devote a sentence or two to all the institutions that raised money to purchase scrolls in the early years (McGill University, Manchester, the Vatican, McCormick Theological Seminary, the University of Heidelberg, All Souls Church in New York). Jason Kalman and Jaqueline du Toit have now uncovered the full extent and significance of the story of how McGill University came to be involved and was the first foreign institution to react so quickly and incisively at a critical moment. Kalman and du Toit found rich primary data in the archives of McGill University, along with other significant letters and documents that are now held by the

Israel Antiquities Authority and other institutions, particularly the École Biblique et Archaéologique Française, Jerusalem.

In 1988, at the time of the fortieth anniversary of the discovery of the scrolls, for a presentation to the Canadian Society of Biblical Studies, I made a first attempt to search out what could be discovered about the involvement of Canadian scholars in the early years of scrolls research. I was able to find a few sources, including a very interesting short article (with an addendum by McGill Professor Donna Runnalls) that R.B.Y. Scott had written for ARC, the journal of the Faculty of Religious Studies at McGill in 1981. I had neither the time nor the resources to pursue the topic further, and so was delighted when I heard a decade later that two McGill graduate students were taking up the topic. Kalman and du Toit have produced a fascinating narrative of the decade between 1953 and 1963. They have supplemented the story itself by including in the book over one hundred primary documents, especially letters of R.B.Y. Scott, G. Lankester Harding, and Roland de Vaux, most of which are made accessible here for the first time. Also of prime importance are details supplied from their personal conversations with many of the key figures of these early years, a number of whom have now died.

Although in one sense the McGill purchase may be "only a footnote in the history" of the Dead Sea Scrolls saga, it is an important footnote. Kalman and du Toit have situated this specific series of events within the larger picture of the development of Canadian universities and scholarship in the postwar era. Through their intensive and careful research of this small piece, they have been able to shed light on broader issues, such as the composition and formation of the so-called "International Team" of scholars who played such a crucial role in the task of publishing this huge mass of fragments. Their careful treatment of the political complexities of the Near East in the 1950–1960s provides background to help understand some of the ongoing controversies and claims about the ownership of the scrolls.

In 1954 McGill was not able to follow up on Harding's invitation to send a scholar to be part of the International Team, nor was the university able to take up Archbishop Samuel's offer in early June 1954 to sell them his four intact scrolls from Cave 1; none of the scrolls of the "McGill purchase" ever left Jordan. But in the following decades, a number of Canadian scholars were invited to publish the *editio princeps* of specific manuscripts in the official *Discoveries in the Judaean Desert* series, and today there are professors and graduate students across Canada actively involved in scrolls research and publication (especially at Trinity Western University, University of Toronto, McMaster University, and the Université de Montréal). The

Dead Sea Scrolls eventually did make their way to Canada, though only for short-term exhibitions (in 1965, 2003–04, and 2009–10). At the current ROM exhibit, a few tiny fragments that R.B.Y. Scott had purchased on the streets of Jerusalem and subsequently donated to McGill University are on public display for the first time. A transcription of the small traces of lettering on these fragments is currently in publication by the editor of *Revue de Qumran*, Florentino García Martínez, in collaboration with Kalman and du Toit, and with the permission of the McGill Redpath Museum.

Everyone interested in the history of Canadian biblical scholarship and fascinated by the saga of Dead Sea Scrolls research owes a real debt of gratitude to Jason Kalman and Jaqueline du Toit for recovering for us the story of "Canada's Big Biblical Bargain."

Eileen Schuller
Professor, Department of Religious Studies
McMaster University, Hamilton, Ontario

Preface

The Dead Sea Scrolls, as you all know, are so called because they are not dead, they do not come from the sea, and not every one of the documents is a scroll. Otherwise the title is correct.

From the very day they came to light in 1947, the Scrolls have been the object of considerable scholarly opinion and controversy, and for over half that period they have fascinated the non-scholarly world also. Certainly no other archaeological or inscriptional find of the past century has evoked wider interest in relation to the Hebrew Bible, early Christianity, and Jewish sectarianism.

Harry Orlinsky[1]

The McGill University archives in Montreal, Quebec, are more than 8,000 kilometres from the caves overlooking the Dead Sea between Israel and Jordan. There 2,000-year-old fragments – primarily on parchment and related to early Judaism – were discovered in the middle of the twentieth century. A cache of documents found in Canada a half century later demonstrates that the distance is not quite as great as it might first appear. The university archives contain the records of a rarely discussed series of events that meant that for nearly a decade McGill University owned the largest collection of Dead Sea Scrolls material outside the collections of the Government of Jordan in Jerusalem. This book relates the story of that purchase.

The book is divided into two parts. Part I recounts and contextualizes the history of McGill University's purchase as presented in the R.B.Y. Scott Papers found in the McGill University archives. Chapter 1 acts as a general introduction, while chapters 2 and 3 are devoted to the reconstruction of the story of McGill's purchase of the scrolls. These two chapters contextualize the purchase within the broader historical and institutional environment. Chapter 4, which concludes the first part of the volume, explores the significance of the scrolls purchase for the current discourse on the ownership of national and cultural treasures.

All chapters refer amply to the correspondence in the Scott Papers and other archival sources consulted to complement the narrative. It should be noted that, to facilitate reading, foreign language correspondence is quoted in translation. We prepared these translations ourselves and helpful colleagues edited them. The original language text is transcribed in Part II.

The second part of this book consists of a collection of the transcriptions of more than a hundred documents from the archives of McGill University and the archives of the Israel Antiquities Authority (IAA). The material from the McGill University archives (primarily the hitherto unpublished R.B.Y. Scott Papers) was supplemented by archival records stored and accessed in the basement of the McGill Faculty of Religious Studies, kindly put at our disposal by then-dean, B. Barry Levy. Part II provides the reader with as much of the related primary documentation as necessary to reconstruct this history. Excluded from the published collection are letters from individuals whose literary heirs could not be located to grant permission for publication and letters from institutions where bureaucracy or other factors prevented the granting of permission.[2] Fewer than twenty documents were excluded and in most cases they are described in the body of the text or in the notes to the included documents. Following completion of this manuscript a handful of letters relating to McGill's purchase were discovered in the collection of the archives of the United Church of Canada. The contents of this correspondence have been incorporated into the narrative in the first part of this volume but transcriptions are not included in the second part because of difficulties related to acquiring copyright permission. The letters and other documentation included here are provided in chronological sequence and numbered individually..To facilitate access, the individual records, when cited in the first part of the book, are referred to in the notes by the surnames of the correspondents, the date, and the assigned number of the document. Thus, for example, Harding to Scott, 3 October 1953, Letter #3. Archival lot numbers are not indicated in the notes to Part I but are identified clearly with the text of the transcribed letters in Part II.

As mentioned, the documents transcribed have been heavily annotated to facilitate reading. The notes include biographical information on the correspondents and people identified in the texts, descriptions of locations mentioned, background information on events described, and bibliographic references for articles and books referred to. As a result the letters can be read in or out of sequence without great difficulty, but this has led to some unavoidable repetition between the notes to Part I and Part II.

Abbreviations are avoided as much as possible. The SBL *Handbook of Style* was our source of reference when the abbreviation of a term or name was deemed appropriate. Where the spelling of names of people and institutions in sources varied, we adopted the *Encyclopedia of the Dead Sea Scrolls*, as far as possible, as a guideline.

Abbreviations

Abbreviated by source

ASOR	American Schools of Oriental Research
BCE	Before the Common Era
Bib.	Biblica
BA	Biblical Archaeologist
BAR	Biblical Archaeology Review
BASOR	Bulletin of the American Schools of Oriental Research
BSOAS	Bulletin of the School of Oriental and African Studies
CBC	Canadian Broadcasting Corporation
CAD	Canadian Dollar
CJT	Canadian Journal of Theology
CNRS	Centre National de la Recherche Scientifique
CE	Common Era
DSD	Dead Sea Discoveries
DJD	Discoveries in the Judaean Desert
DSS	Dead Sea Scrolls
HUC	Hebrew Union College
HUC–JIR	Hebrew Union College – Jewish Institute of Religion
IOSOT	International Organisation for the Study of the Old Testament
IAA	Israel Antiquities Authority
IDAM	Israel Department of Antiquities and Museums
JQR	Jewish Quarterly Review
JD	Jordanian Dinar
JSP	Journal for the Study of the Pseudepigrapha, Supplement Series
JBR	Journal of Bible and Religion
JBL	Journal of Biblical Literature

Abbreviations

Alphabetized by source

ASOR	American Schools of Oriental Research
BCE	Before the Common Era
Bib	*Biblica*
BA	*Biblical Archaeologist*
BAR	*Biblical Archaeology Review*
BASOR	*Bulletin of the American Schools of Oriental Research*
BSOAS	*Bulletin of the School of Oriental and African Studies*
CBC	Canadian Broadcasting Corporation
CAD	Canadian Dollar
CJT	*Canadian Journal of Theology*
CNRS	Centre National de la Recherche Scientifique
CE	Common Era
DSD	*Dead Sea Discoveries*
DJD	*Discoveries in the Judaean Desert*
DSS	Dead Sea Scrolls
HUC	Hebrew Union College
HUC-JIR	Hebrew Union College – Jewish Institute of Religion
IOSOT	International Organization for the Study of the Old Testament
IAA	Israel Antiquities Authority
IDAM	Israel Department of Antiquities and Museums
JQR	*Jewish Quarterly Review*
JD	Jordanian Dinar
JSP*sup*	*Journal for the Study of the Pseudepigrapha: Supplement Series*
JBR	*Journal of Bible and Religion*
JBL	*Journal of Biblical Literature*

JRH	*Journal of Religious History*
NEA	*Near Eastern Archaeology*
NRF	National Research Foundation
PAM	Palestine Archaeological Museum
PEQ	*Palestine Exploration Quarterly*
RB	*Revue biblique*
REVQ	*Revue de Qumran*
ROM	Royal Ontario Museum
Sem	*Semitica*
SBL	Society of Biblical Literature
SR	*Studies in Religion*
USD	United States Dollar
UTC	United Theological College
VT	*Vetus Testamentum*
VTsup	*Vetus Testamentum Supplements*

PART ONE

If this collection is obtained for McGill it would probably be one of the largest, if not the largest, collection of Old Testament and other religious documents from the beginning of the Christian era and earlier, to be found outside of Palestine. Its importance in terms of prestige, and for graduate study and publication, is clear.

R.B.Y. Scott, 2 March 1954

I

Introduction: "I should perhaps recall to you ..."[1]

In July 1959 McGill University in Montreal, Quebec, patiently awaited the arrival of its allotment of fragments of Cave 4 manuscripts from the renowned Dead Sea Scrolls. Discussions about the housing of this valuable contribution to world heritage were in progress; the local newspapers were agog at the import this acquired collection might have for the profile of Canadian scholarship, and university authorities were taking the precautionary steps needed for the conservation of the ancient fragments and the concomitant influx of scholars who were expected to make annual pilgrimages to Montreal to work on these extant texts dating from before the time of Jesus until the destruction of Jerusalem in 70 CE.[2] The invaluable contribution to world scholarship of the materials included in the "McGill Collection" was hailed by early Dead Sea Scrolls scholars such as Father Roland de Vaux and Professor Frank Moore Cross in their correspondence with Professor R.B.Y. Scott, who had arranged McGill's purchase of the materials in 1954. This was indeed "Canada's Big Biblical Bargain," as one newspaper headline proclaimed.[3]

But the Cave 4 manuscripts never arrived in Montreal. McGill University, the first institution other than the Government of Jordan to purchase Dead Sea Scrolls legally, had its money (a payment of $15,363CAD in March and April 1954 and an additional purchase for $4,200 in December 1955) returned in mid-1963. The entire incident has become only a footnote in the history of a discovery hailed as one of the most important of the twentieth century. This book tells the story of the McGill purchase and at the same time endeavours to provide access to the hitherto unpublished papers of the late Professor R.B.Y. Scott through whose prolific correspondence we were able to assemble the intricate strands of this tale.

Robert Balgarnie Young Scott died on 1 November 1987 at the age of eighty-eight. His obituary in the *New York Times* recalled that he had been a professor affiliated with McGill University in Montreal from 1931 until 1955, when he joined the faculty of Princeton University until his retirement in 1968. It noted that he had written several books and added a cursory note to the late professor's distinguished academic career: "Dr. Scott helped recover fragments of the scrolls in 1951. They had found their way into the hands of private dealers in Bethlehem and Dr. Scott bought them on behalf of McGill."[4]

As is often the case in summary, the weaving together of several different stories into two sentences resulted in a statement that was almost entirely devoid of truth. It nevertheless contained an inkling of a historical nugget of information hitherto rarely recounted in public or acknowledged in the scholarly literature on the topic. Here we attempt to reconstruct the story behind these two sentences as a window on the history of the discovery and interpretation of the Dead Sea Scrolls, Cave 4 in particular, and the scholars involved in the study thereof in the "early years": the years between 1954 and 1963. The story is embedded in a brief consideration of the significance of a purchase of this kind for a Canadian institution of higher learning at this particular historical juncture; it also briefly considers the broader meaning of this historical event and its outcome for current reflections on movable cultural objects and their significance in the rise of nationalism in the twentieth century, as well as their integral contribution to identity formation.

CAVE 4

The events that resulted in McGill University's purchase started with the Bedouin discovery of the fourth of what were eventually eleven caves containing written material near the Dead Sea in the vicinity of an ancient settlement, Khirbet Qumran: "The first fragments from a new cave at Qumran arrived in Jerusalem on September 2, 1952 (or possibly as much as two weeks earlier ...) Within two days, over the weekend, de Vaux and Harding put together a team and excavated this fourth cave during the last week of the month ... It was immediately apparent to de Vaux and Harding that they had a serious problem. The amount of money necessary to rescue the vast collection of Cave 4 fragments threatened to overwhelm the financial resources of the privately endowed Palestine Archaeological Museum."[5]

In August 1953 Father Roland de Vaux[6] appealed to the international community of scholars to assist. In early 1954 McGill University became the first to act on de Vaux's request with an offer of funds. The university's lead was followed by the Vatican Library (October 1954 and December 1955), the University of Manchester (December 1954), the University of Heidelberg (1955), and McCormick Theological Seminary (1956), with others such as Oxford University and the All Souls Church in New York coming later. Beyond brief notice in the histories of the scrolls' discovery, the participation of these institutions in the preservation of the scrolls has been largely ignored. Various newspapers and academic journals recorded their purchases in the days and months that followed each, but the exact details, the people involved, accurate records of the financial transactions and the content of the contractual agreements, as well as the motivations of the participants, have remained largely obscure.

In the many volumes on the scrolls that started to appear in the 1950s describing the discovery of the scrolls and the state of research on them, McGill and the other purchasing institutions were mostly only noted; the extent and significance of their participation for the preservation of a largely intact corpus of the fragmentary remains was rarely recognized. First published in November 1955, Millar Burrows' *The Dead Sea Scrolls* states, for example, that, "On May 22, 1954, it was announced that a substantial part of the manuscript fragments from Cave 4 had been purchased by McGill University of Montreal for $15,000. A condition of the purchase is that they are to remain at the Palestine Museum for study and to be published in the same series with the other fragments. It is expected that this will take about two years. It is reported that other material has been purchased on the same basis by the University of Manchester in England."[7] The following year John Allegro[8] added that $15,000 was offered by McGill and supplied by a "widow lady" in memory of her husband, the Vatican had supplied somewhere between 700 and several thousand pounds, Manchester had offered £2,000 as two separate donations, and the German Governments of Bonn and Baden-Württemberg had contributed £4,500 for the purchase of fragments by the University of Heidelberg.[9] Józef Milik[10] captured the entire topic in one sentence, as is fairly typical: "In addition to the Jordanian Government which contributed £15,000, McGill University in Montreal, the Universities of Manchester and Heidelberg, McCormick Theological Seminary in Chicago, and the Vatican Library offered financial help in acquiring these fragments."[11] In his own work on the topic, published in 1956, even R.B.Y. Scott offered very little on the university's contribution to early Dead Sea Scrolls history: "When funds ran short," Scott recalled, "learned institutions abroad offered contributions so that the material could be bought up and saved from loss or destruction. In this way some of the scroll fragments from 'Cave Four' will come eventually to McGill University, to Manchester, Bonn and Heidelberg, and to the Vatican Library."[12]

It was to be expected that the matter of foreign institutions' purchase of Dead Sea Scroll fragments was, at the time, of negligible importance to a global public and scholarly audience entranced by the promise of the contents of the scrolls – what light they could shed on the ancient community that produced them and on early Judaism and Christianity – and, especially at first, on whether these fragments were indeed authentically ancient. In the late 1980s and early 1990s these concerns shifted. Forty years and longer after their discovery, access to the Cave 4 scrolls – the richest find – was still controlled by a small international team of editors first established in the 1950s by then-director of the Jordanian Department of Antiquities, Gerald Lankester Harding,[13] and Father Roland de Vaux, the director of the École Biblique et Archéologique Française in Jerusalem. The original editorial team and their successors, set up initially to manage the finds from Cave 4, maintained their right to publish the material, resulting in limited accessibility for global scholarship to a large percentage of the cache that remained unpublished and in the exclusive hands of the assigned editors. Access was limited at will by the presiding editors to anyone but their own students and close associates. Thus a *Washington Post* reporter noted in 1989: "more than four decades after discovery of the Hebrew and Aramaic documents, as many as half of them remain unpublished and unavailable to scholars except for a small coterie in possession of the documents."[14] This tight control over the manuscripts led to the perpetuation of conspiracy theories, the most pervasive stemming back to John Allegro, an early member of the original editorial team. Allegro and conspiracy theorists to follow contended that the Roman Catholic Church was actively involved in a concerted effort to prevent the entire contents of the scrolls from becoming available, as this would allegedly be detrimental to the foundations of Christianity.[15] Popular conspiracy theorists – of whose work that of Michael Baigent and Richard Leigh[16] is perhaps the best known example – took their cue from these early theories, and the successful perpetuation of this theme has led to such Dead Sea Scrolls myths finding their way into the twenty-first century via an intricate weaving of fiction and fact in works such as Dan Brown's *Da Vinci Code*.

In the early 1990s additional controversy resulted from two scholars' publication of a collection of hitherto unpublished Dead Sea Scrolls texts.[17] Robert Eisenman and Michael Wise were accused of "unethical appropriation" of previous work and of "borrowing heavily and without acknowledgement from the work of other scholars."[18] The matter was resolved fairly quickly, but the public's attention was redirected, if only temporarily, to those interpreting the scrolls rather than their interpretation.[19] This was not the only matter to grab headlines at the time. The publicity resulting from a lawsuit in which Hershel Shanks, the editor of *Biblical Archaeology Review*, was charged by Israeli scholar Elisha Qimron of infringing on his copyright by publishing part of a Dead Sea Scroll document the latter had reconstructed also captured the public and scholarly imagination.[20] As well, in September 1991 the Biblical Archaeology Society published the first of four volumes of Ben Zion Wacholder and Martin Abegg's *A Preliminary Edition of the Unpublished Dead Sea Scrolls: The Hebrew and Aramaic Texts from Cave Four*. Together the men had reconstructed a series of previously unpublished material, thus circumventing the official editorial team. The publication caused an outcry, but many scholars appreciated the accuracy of the texts and their easy availability.[21] This, along with the decision by Dr William A. Moffet of the Huntington Library (California) in September 1991 to allow access to duplicates of photographs of the scrolls in its possession,[22] contributed to ending the monopoly on the scrolls. In turn, the surge in scholarship after the scrolls became accessible with an announcement by the Israel Antiquities Authority in September 1991[23] resulted in a spate of new publications describing the scrolls, how they came to be discovered, and the history of the editorial team and its major players as seen through the lens of the bitter battle to establish access to the manuscripts. However, except for continued speculation on Vatican involvement in conspiracy theories and secret Vatican ownership of manuscripts with inflammatory contents, little interest has been paid to the seemingly mundane matter of the history of ownership of these important cultural objects.

The outcome of the purchases did receive some cursory attention in later publications. Thus, Hershel Shanks on the one hand, and James VanderKam and Peter Flint on the other, noted that in 1961 the Jordanians nationalized the scrolls and reimbursed the institutions involved.[24] That none of these institutions ever physically received their assigned allotments may help to explain why there has been little concern for the details of the purchases. Should one or more have taken physical possession before nationalization, the Dead Sea Scrolls would have become the subject of yet another legal battle, invoking the often toothless tiger that is the interpretative minefield of international law on movable cultural objects.

In truth, the cloak-and-dagger nature of the Cave 1 discovery and purchases resulting from it has always overshadowed the subsequent discovery and acquisition of the voluminous, but painfully fragmentary Cave 4 manuscripts. As far as can be established, the first Dead Sea Scrolls were discovered by Bedouin late in 1946 or early 1947 in a cave on the north-western shore of the Dead Sea in territory that was at the time under British Mandate. It became part of Jordan after 1948.[25] Eleven caves holding ancient manuscripts, associated shortly afterwards with the adjacent ruins of the settlement called Khirbet Qumran, were found over a period of nine years. This presented the world with what became known as the "greatest manuscript discovery" of the twentieth century.[26]

On 11 April 1948 Yale University announced that the American School of Oriental Research (ASOR) in Jerusalem, directed by Yale professor Millar Burrows, had examined three ancient scrolls from the area of the Dead Sea and that one more scroll remained to be unrolled for examination.[27] Very soon after, on 24 April 1948, Professor Eleazar Sukenik[28] revealed Hebrew University's purchase of scroll materials and his intention to publish them. The English-language *Palestine Post* carried the news of the discovery, which included ancient manuscripts of the Bible.[29] According to the article, Sukenik showed a fragment of a biblical scroll to an assembly of foreign and local journalists at a press conference and explained that the scrolls had been found by Bedouin in the caves near the Dead Sea and had been sold to antiquities dealers and the Bishop of the Syrian Convent in the Old City of Jerusalem. The day following the press conference, North American audiences had the discoveries brought to their attention by the *New York Times* in a news item entitled, "10 Ancient Scrolls Found in Palestine."[30] Canadian audiences read of the discovery a few days later.[31] As the Hebrew University and ASOR wanted to avoid a confrontation with the Jordanian Department of Antiquities, the discoveries had been kept quiet until the aforementioned news releases. Once informed of the discovery, the Jordanian official in charge, G. Lankester Harding, and the director of the École Biblique in Jerusalem, Roland de Vaux, planned a search for the cave where the material had been discovered.

Unfortunately, the administrative chaos that resulted from the withdrawal of British Mandatory supervision in Jordan delayed their plans, as well as the processing of the material retrieved. Harding, in his capacity as director of antiquities for Jordan, did not make his first public announcement on the scrolls until more than a year later.[32]

It was only by mid-May 1948 that a major academic journal officially announced the news of the discovery to the scholarly world. William F. Albright,[33] the president of ASOR, drew the attention of his readers to the recent popular press coverage of the discovery and summarized what was known from it.[34] In September a lengthy article by John Trever, who had examined and photographed the first scrolls at the American School, finally brought to light the details of how the scrolls had travelled from the caves into the hands of scholars.[35] Almost immediately the scholarly world began to debate the antiquity and authenticity of the scrolls. These debates were played out in both the popular press and in scholarly journals.[36] By the time the Cave 4 discoveries were announced in April 1953, and when McGill University purchased a large section of this discovery a year later, the public was ready to hear from the insiders who had access to study these ancient texts.[37]

Of immediate interest to scholars and non-scholars alike was the considerable number of ancient biblical[38] materials discovered in the large, albeit extremely fragmentary cache of manuscripts consisting mainly of so-called "sectarian" material. Although only twelve scrolls were discovered intact, the thousands of fragments found distributed among the eleven caves at Qumran represented approximately 900 manuscripts. Of these a large number (approximately 15,000 fragments or 550 manuscripts)[39] hailed from Cave 4, which is considered to have housed the most significant collection of manuscripts[40] recovered from the caves in the vicinity of a dry riverbed, the Wadi Qumran.[41] No wonder that this conglomeration of fragmentary manuscripts, in various states of decomposition, was later to be referred to as the "mother of all jigsaw puzzles."[42] One of the most renowned Dead Sea Scrolls scholars, Frank Moore Cross,[43] explained:

> Unlike the several scrolls of Caves I and XI which are preserved in good condition, with only minor lacunae, the manuscripts of Cave IV are in an advanced state of decay. Many fragments are so brittle or friable that they can scarcely be touched with a camel's-hair brush. Most are warped, crinkled, or shrunken, crusted with soil chemicals, blackened by moisture and age. The problems of cleaning, flattening, identifying, and piecing them together are formidable.
>
> The fragments when they are purchased from tribesmen generally come in boxes; cigarette boxes, film boxes, or shoe boxes, depending on the size of the fragments. The precious leather and papyrus is delicately handled by rough Bedouin hands, for the value of the material is all too keenly appreciated. Often cotton wool or tissue paper has been used by Bedouin to separate and protect the scraps of scrolls; and on occasion they have applied bits of gummed paper to pieces which threatened to crack apart or disintegrate.[44]

LEST WE FORGET

Fact and myth are intertwined as far as the details of the scrolls' discovery, recovery, early care, and study are concerned[45] and this chapter in its history cannot be accurately rendered without taking into account the social, geopolitical, and religious context of the time and of the players involved. Although McGill's purchase is only a small part of the Dead Sea Scrolls story, contextualizing it in this way demonstrates that its significance for understanding the whole far exceeds its size.

As is the case for the history of Dead Sea Scrolls discovery in general, much of the history of the discovery, purchase, and conservation of Cave 4 documents is shrouded in lore, supposition, mystery, and generalization. At a 1997 conference in honour of the fiftieth anniversary of the discovery of the scrolls, Frank Moore Cross, the first to be appointed to the international editorial team from outside Jerusalem to study the Cave 4 fragments,[46] addressed those assembled with an extensive narrative about his early experiences in Jerusalem: "I have been asked to report memories and tell tales of the early days when we were young and engaged in the most exciting project imaginable, the identification, piecing together, and editing of the scrolls of Cave 4."[47] John Strugnell, also a member of the team and later editor-in-chief,[48] similarly provided his version of "the early days" at a 1999 conference in Edinburgh.[49] Yet one can never dissociate these first person accounts from the acrimonious battle for access that separated the reminiscences from the events described. Cross's introductory comments refer to his recollections of the Cave 4 discovery, identification, and study as rather whimsical "memories" and "tales" denoting the ephemeral quality of an oral history.[50] Such recollections are often shaded by the fact that they build on previously published material to fill gaps and to "refresh" the memory of the raconteur. Part of the difficulty with these materials is the general problem with autobiography. "Autobiography," says Michael A. Meyer, "is a problematic genre of literature. One cannot expect it to be a balanced and wholly accurate representation. Remembering and forgetting are determined not only by temporal distance from the events described, but also by psychological factors that often unconsciously push certain recollections into the foreground and bury others. Autobiographers are explorers of the self, but they are also its fashioners. They configure the tale of their personal development and character in a manner that is most easily acceptable to themselves and that presents the self-image that they wish to convey to succeeding generations of their family or to a larger readership."[51] Simply put: a complete history and chronology of the period from 1952 when Cave 4 was discovered until the Six-Day War in 1967 when East Jerusalem and the scrolls came into the possession of Israel remains a desideratum, as much of the detail of what we know in print about the period comes from the narratives of participants recounted much later and often not without agendas.

The public and scholarly community at large remains dissatisfied with what is known of the early years. Early descriptions of the activities were penned by the participants at the time or soon after. As the history was unfolding, general updates were provided to the scholarly community in the pages of academic journals such as *Biblical Archaeologist*, *Bulletin of the American Schools of Oriental Research*, and *Revue biblique*. The *Revue de Qumrân* followed soon after. The first two became the early outlet for most of the members of the official editorial team, while the *Revue biblique* was used in these early years by Roland de Vaux primarily to describe the results of his archaeological excavations at Khirbet Qumran.[52] That this journal was published by the École Biblique where he was the director explains his preference.

In February 1953 Harding recounted the first excavations at Qumran and the discovery of new caves by the Bedouin.[53] And in February 1954 Frank Cross gave an account of the discovery of the new caves and described the race by de Vaux and Harding against the Bedouin to search for caves containing manuscripts and the arrangements made for the acquisition of the fragments and their study. He lauded Harding, whose quick work in securing funds meant that the collection could be studied fairly intact in one place and published without the risk of the innumerable individual parts being scattered on the looming black market. Furthermore, Cross included descriptions of the activities of the various scholars involved in the publication effort and their initial allotments; how the texts were humidified, cleaned, and prepared for study; and the use of non-acidic oil to bring out the faded script. The photographing, identification, and sorting of the fragments were likewise described.[54] Two years later, Cross provided an update on the activities in the scrollery, the room in the museum used for the study of the fragments. This time the report focused on the contents of the scrolls, noting that approximately 400 distinct manuscripts had been assembled of which more than three-quarters could be identified. Reporting on the acquisition of documents, he noted that funds had been supplied by the Palestine Archaeological Museum (PAM), the École Biblique in Jerusalem, McGill, Manchester, Heidelberg, and the Vatican Library, but that there were still fragments in the hands of the Bedouin. Finally he noted the efforts to publish some preliminary material elsewhere and emphasized that the primary focus was on the publication of the official editions.[55] Toward the end of 1956 Pierre Benoit, another member and future editor-in-chief of the editorial team,[56] provided the fullest description to date of the activities of the scholars involved. Benoit told of the discovery of the first ten caves, offering a chronology and a description of whether the cave was discovered by the Bedouin or by archaeologists. He described the roles of de Vaux and Harding, the École Biblique and the Jordanian Department of Antiquities, and the American School of Oriental Research in promoting the excavations, acquiring the fragments, and publishing the results. A description of the arrangements to publish the material in a series with Oxford University Press is offered, with a list of the collaborators and their contributions to the second volume. Most impressively, each of the scholars working in the scrollery provided several paragraphs on their work, including descriptions of the state of the fragments and their contents.[57]

In addition to these articles, three members of the team published books to share their first-hand view with the public. In 1956, John Allegro published *The Dead Sea Scrolls*. While most of the volume is devoted to the content of the scrolls and what they could teach us about ancient Judaism and early Christianity, the first fifty pages deal with the discovery of the first scrolls and their acquisition by Mar Athanasius Samuel[58] and Eleazar Sukenik in 1947 and 1948, as well as some of the later discoveries. In the brief section devoted to the activities of the scrollery, Allegro described some of the scholars and their projects, as well as how the scrolls were cleaned and identified. He also provided an outline of the future publication schedule.[59]

In 1957 Józef Milik published his French volume, *Dix ans de découvertes dans le désert de Juda*. This was followed in 1959 by an English translation thereof by fellow team member John Strugnell.[60] Similar to Allegro, although much more limited in detail, Milik described the early discoveries. He devoted no discussion to the activities in the PAM scrollery, instead choosing to explore the content of the scrolls, what could be said about their authors, and the relationship of the scrolls to the Qumran community.

The most detailed contemporary account remains that of Frank Cross in *The Ancient Library of Qumran* (now in a third revised edition). The book, first published in 1958, was based on Cross's 1956–57 Haskell Lectures delivered to the Graduate School of Theology, Oberlin College. While much of it is devoted to the scrolls' content, particularly the biblical manuscripts for which Cross was responsible, the first forty-six pages discuss the discovery, acquisition, and study of the scrolls. The footnotes demonstrate that Cross, in addition to his own hands-on work with the scrolls, also relied on the early publications of his colleagues, some of which are described above, to construct the state of the field.[61]

To summarize, this brief survey shows that almost everything we know of this period in the history of scrolls scholarship comes from the personal recollections of the people directly involved, mostly as a cursory by-product to the recounting of what was to them the more important aspect in the narrative: the content and origins of the discovery. Additionally, sections of the story have been disclosed by scholars serving secondary interests, such as defending a personal stance, proving a theory of origin, or contextualizing a collection of translated texts or an archaeological find.[62] Survey volumes by those not directly involved in the project in this period have likewise relied on these early articles and volumes or, as in the case of Neil Asher Silberman's *The Hidden Scrolls*, largely on re-interviewing some of the same people forty to fifty years after the fact.[63] Silberman nevertheless added an invaluable new methodological perspective. As part of his research he explored the archival holdings of several institutions, most importantly those of the IAA, where the records from the PAM are housed. He was therefore able to fill the gaps and corroborate the facts outlined in the interviews. His work was not the first to use these resources, but he was the first to attempt to fully synthesize them into the main narrative. Thus Silberman inaugurated a new era in the historiography of scrolls research.

Silberman's work was anticipated in 1993 by Stephan Pfann's published historical timeline for the history of the scrolls. This chronology appears in the companion volume to the *Dead Sea Scrolls on Microfiche* and here, too, much of the information was gathered from material in the IAA archives.[64]

Unfortunately, a volume devoted to describing the history of the scrolls as artefacts – Who found them? Who bought them? How were the arrangements made? How were the scrolls cared for and who cared for them? To whom did they or do they belong? – remains absent from our bookshelves. This has become an all the more pressing requirement since so many new sources of material have become available in recent years, such as Judith Brown's biography of her late father, John Allegro. Brown relied heavily on Allegro's personal archive for reconstructing the activities in the scrollery,[65] a source of information hitherto not widely available. In similar vein, a collection of letters from the personal collection of Anton Kiraz, a friend of Mar Athanasius Samuel, archbishop of the Syrian Orthodox Church at St Mark's Monastery in Jerusalem, was recently published.[66] Kiraz acted as go-between in the matter of finding an interested buyer for the scrolls from Cave 1, at the time in the hands of Mar Samuel. Kiraz claimed ownership of some of the early manuscript finds until his death in December 1993. These new, mostly documentary sources provide the historiographer with an alternative means of interpreting the thoughts, activities, and outcomes in Jerusalem at the height of the excitement over the scrolls discovery.

As for the glaring absence of an integrative study of the early years, equal blame probably rests on the fantastical nature of the history of the discovery, limited access to the manuscripts once discovered, scholarly obfuscation, the fragmentary and obscure nature of their content and the context of many of the documents, and the media.[67] Thus, while a comprehensive historiography of the early years of the scrolls' discovery has long been overdue, it would have been nearly impossible to write without the relative objectivity provided by temporal distance.

As mentioned, the purpose of this book is to shed light on only a small portion of the history of the discovery. Our focus is limited to a little known, underreported, and often misrepresented scrap of information on the Dead Sea Scrolls history of discovery: that between 1954 and 1956, McGill University in Montreal, Quebec, paid approximately $20,000 CAD for the purchase of Cave 4 Dead Sea Scrolls. This made McGill the owner of the largest collection of Dead Sea Scrolls (some 450 fragments) outside Jordan, which in turn spurred additional purchases by other North American and European institutions, including *inter alia*, the Vatican Library, the University of Manchester,[68] the University of Heidelberg, and McCormick Theological Seminary. The Jordanian Government subsequently nationalized the scrolls that had been purchased with the help of G. Lankester Harding and Roland de Vaux from the Bedouin who discovered them. McGill was in turn compensated for its loss by the eventual return of the university's investment in mid-1963.[69] Only recently has access to the primary documents related to the discovery and purchase of the Dead Sea Scrolls by McGill University through the agency of Professor R.B.Y. Scott made writing a history of these events possible. As such, McGill's purchase is used to showcase events in Jerusalem and its environs in the decade following the discovery of Cave 4, as seen through the correspondence of R.B.Y. Scott with major role players.

Apart from a brief autobiographical piece by R.B.Y. Scott that appeared in the McGill Faculty of Religious Studies journal, ARC, in 1981,[70] and a contribution by the authors to a recent volume of *Dead Sea Discoveries*,[71] no comprehensive rendering of the first outside purchase of Dead Sea Scrolls documents has ever been made. In addition, this book highlights the significant and hitherto undocumented role of R.B.Y. Scott, formerly a faculty member of McGill University and later of Princeton University, in the purchase of the Dead Sea Scrolls and the preservation of the integrity of the current collection.

THE SOURCES

This narrative is constructed by means of an in-depth study of related material preserved in the archival collections of McGill University, the United Church of Canada, and the IAA, which houses the records from the PAM (now the Rockefeller Museum),[72] beginning with the events leading up to McGill's purchase of the documents in the early 1950s and ending with McGill's reallocation of the donor's gift following reimbursement in 1963. Primarily, it relies on the letters of Professor R.B.Y. Scott and his correspondents.[73] Contemporary reports in the media, the minutes and reports of scholarly associations such as the American Schools of Oriental Research and the recorded recollections of participants have all been used to corroborate conclusions and to fill historical lacunae. Other sources include interviews with Professors Frank Moore Cross and the late John Strugnell, both of Harvard University, and Professors Stanley Frost, Donna Runnals, and B. Barry Levy, all former deans of the Faculty of Religious Studies at McGill University. All interviews were conducted by the authors during the spring and summer of 2000. In addition, consultation with Professor Eileen Schuller (McMaster University), Canada's foremost expert on the Dead Sea Scrolls, took place throughout the entire process of researching and documenting this history.

The primary sources in the McGill archives allow the story of the university's purchase to be reconstructed here and, for purposes of accessibility, the correspondence of R.B.Y. Scott is published for the first time here. Although we rely heavily on excerpts from his correspondence for our reconstruction of the purchase history in Part I of this book, we deemed it necessary for future research to include the bulk of the Scott Papers as is in Part II, rather than including just our interpretation of them. As mentioned in the preface, the letters and other documents appear in chronological sequence and are annotated to facilitate accessibility.

We also relied for elucidation and corroboration on the available correspondence between members of McGill's faculty and administration, G. Lankester Harding and Roland de Vaux, members of the editorial team, and Jordanian officials. These provide tremendous insight into the motivations and characters of the individuals destined to be responsible for the direction of future scrolls research over the next sixty years and more.

Against the backdrop of the current emphasis on the role of museums and private collectors and the often contested matter of ownership of antiquities,[74] we would have been negligent in not at least cursorily considering McGill's purchase in the light of current concerns. The historic purchase and subsequent events flowing from this are used to illustrate the difficulties in establishing national versus institutional "ownership" over movable cultural objects that are considered common to the international heritage of humankind. These letters and other documentation allow us the opportunity to explore the state of affairs that forced the Jordanian

Government to allow what it later considered national treasures to be sold to foreign institutions and the factors that shaped the eventual nationalization of the scrolls.

But first, to set the stage it is important not to divorce the story of the purchase of the Cave 4 Dead Sea Scrolls by a Montreal university from its connection to the fortunes of Canadian society at the time of purchase and the emerging trends in religion and higher education at North American academic institutions in the post World War II era.[75]

MCGILL AFTER THE WAR

The story to follow leaves little doubt that the opportunity presented to McGill University to acquire the Cave 4 material was the result of good timing: Professor R.B.Y. Scott fortuitously attended the August 1953 Copenhagen meeting of the International Organization for the Study of the Old Testament. Here he met Roland de Vaux and heard the cleric's plea for an institution to step forward to provide the funds to purchase the newly discovered Cave 4 scroll material from the Bedouin. Scott grabbed the opportunity presented by this offer and in turn was able not only to save the scroll fragments from possible loss or destruction but also to provide McGill University the opportunity of a prominent role on the stage of international scholarship. The potential benefits of the purchase for an emerging sense of Canadian identity does not seem from the correspondence to have been a predominant consideration for Scott in his decision to pursue de Vaux's request, but the benefits nevertheless helped convince the university principal and possible benefactors of the soundness of the project.

Scott's genius in convincing the institution and its principal to purchase the scrolls despite contemporary uncertainty as to their relative antiquity, his ability to secure private donors to fund the purchase, and his faithful communication of information on the topic to the public through the media were all intimately entwined with the state of public discourse on the role of universities in the transmission of Canadian culture and identity in the wake of the Second World War. While Scott the scholar was motivated to preserve and acquire valuable objects for study and public display, his motivations as a Canadian and as member and former dean of the Faculty of Divinity at a Canadian university at this particular historical juncture cannot be ignored.

At that time both Canadian society and its institutions of higher learning were in a period of transition. The war effort had, as in the United States, highlighted the importance of scientific development and universities responded by expanding the faculties of applied science, often at the expense of the humanities. As countermeasure, the Canadian intellectual elite by and large challenged this change of emphasis and encouraged the growth of the humanities. In no small way this counterbalance was seen as a means of combatting the dreaded Americanization of Canadian society and a feared loss of a separate identity. The study of religion, in particular, was perceived as a vehicle to offer Canadians answers to many of the tough societal questions raised by the war and the concomitant by-products of technological advancement, which did not come without a huge moral-ethical cost, such as the development of the means of mass destruction as illustrated by the detonation of the atomic bomb over Hiroshima and Nagasaki in 1945.

McGill's establishment of the Faculty of Divinity in 1948 is to be considered in this context. R.B.Y. Scott served as the first dean from 1948 to 1949.[76] The creation of the faculty did not go unchallenged. Most troublesome to the faculty was the assumption of its critics that it would function primarily as a place for the training of religious ministers, rather than as a unit of academic enterprise. R.B.Y. Scott clearly understood that the acquisition of the scrolls would remove any doubt as to the academic legitimacy of the newly constituted Faculty of Divinity. The corpus would also immediately establish an additional academic raison d'être for the faculty for years to come and attract graduate students and international scholars,[77] which in turn would demonstrate unequivocally that the faculty was a place for academic and not parochial concerns.

The purchase could also serve both the university and the country well from another perspective: the post-war influx of returning soldiers to Canadian universities created huge budgetary deficits[78] and logistical headaches, as Stanley Frost recounts in his biography of McGill's principal at the time, F. Cyril James:[79] "By January 1945, two thousand such students [disabled war veterans and surplus air-crew members] were registered [at Canadian universities]; by the end of the year, with the war successfully concluded, the number had risen to 14,500. Two years later it had reached 37,000. This was some two thousand more than the total student university population in the whole of Canada in 1939 ... Universities found themselves faced with doubled enrolments and immense problems ... shortages of classrooms, laboratories, books, equipment of all kinds, and especially teachers at all levels and in all disciplines."[80]

Frost makes it clear in his biography of James that the principal of McGill was immensely frustrated by the lack of vision and initiative displayed by all faculties in facing this challenge. R.B.Y. Scott's close relationship with the principal is evident from the Scott Papers, and as part of university leadership he could not have been unaware of the special challenges posed to

McGill. Quite possibly, therefore, Scott may have seen in this purchase the means not only for seizing the opportunity for McGill University to enter the international stage of scholarship but also for creating the kind of profile that could attract sorely needed funding. In the increasing bid to establish Canadian identity as separate from Great Britain and the United States, a purchase of ancient manuscripts ahead of the prestigious schools and museums in these countries must also have featured as important for the establishment of a growing sense of Canadian pride and independence.

In this light McGill's eagerness to purchase the scrolls could be considered a means of both advancing the study of religion as an academic discipline and supporting the university and the development of Canadian culture in general. The high profile of the scrolls could attract and draw the best and the brightest students and scholars, the very people who otherwise might be lured by the promise of the sciences and competing universities in the United States.

IDENTITY, OWNERSHIP OF OBJECTS, AND POSTCOLONIALISM

As to the broader matter of archaeological treasures and national identity, clearly the ethical question of ownership of movable cultural objects had not yet arisen as a serious consideration at the time of McGill's purchase. It certainly does not feature in the early years of the correspondence presented in this book. Possibly the mere expediency of preserving the discovery intact from the black market and the very real fear of dispersal into private hands overrode any other considerations at the time.[81] Recent events in Afghanistan and Iraq have sensitized the world to the fragile and tenuous nature of cultural objects left unprotected and at the mercy of political and religious agendas. Yet, the legal quagmire of ownership, especially of *movable* cultural objects, makes the protection of these fragile resources of serious, immediate, and international concern. The importance of such ownership for national identity formation can also not be overstated. Thus, in report after report in the period immediately following 12 April 2003, the denuding of Iraq's national heritage was bemoaned,[82] although little cognizance was given to the tenuous nature of the claims to ownership by even the State of Iraq, which is in itself a very recent colonial construct.[83] Yet Iraqis as a constituted societal entity, despite their early twentieth century colonial origin, were able to lay claim with ease to the preceding thousands of years of cultural heritage by means of an agreed common national identity and, most importantly, by means of territorial patrimony. Matthew Bogdanos, the military official who supervised the investigation of the looting of the Iraq Museum, highlighted the importance of this claim to cultural heritage (as preserved in the museum's holdings) in helping to rebuild the country: "Sharing pride in and mutual respect for each of the cultures that has flowed into the bloodstream of modern Iraq – Assyrian and Babylonian, Kurd and Shi'ite and Sunni – is the only hope for weaving these people, brought together by the British in a shotgun marriage eighty years ago, into a viable nation-state."[84]

In light of these events, the question of the importance of the Dead Sea Scrolls in the shaping of national identity in Jordan in the 1950s and early 1960s can also not be ignored. After the Six-Day War, that same notion was transferred to the State of Israel with a dissenting voice in the recent past emanating from the Palestinian community.[85] Thus the multiplicity of layers revealed in posing the question of ownership for the Dead Sea Scrolls far exceeds the boundaries of possession to encompass history, conservation and custodial considerations, linguistic and cultural interests, religious attachment, physical ownership, and national identity claims. Cindy Carson has summarized the situation thus: "The Dead Sea Scrolls themselves are [currently] the property of the state of Israel. Some of the Scrolls were found in Israeli-controlled areas, others were ultimately sold to the government of Israel, and some came to Israel as the spoils of war. Few today seriously dispute Israel's property right in the Scrolls themselves. And yet, an argument can be made that the Scrolls have other, or additional, owners; specifically, that those with a cultural interest in the Scrolls are entitled to a property interest in them as well. In a politically turbulent, multicultural area like the Middle East, however, many groups may have some degree of cultural interest in the Scrolls."[86]

There can be little doubt that the Scrolls, their ownership, and their stewardship played an important role in national identity formation. This is historically true for Jordan and Israel, but also for Canada and the other countries whose educational institutions bought material from this discovery. Although Carson is correct in her observation that few may dispute Israel's current claim to the bulk of the manuscript material, the question cannot be ignored as to how a country that did not exist when the first scrolls were discovered came to have *de facto* and apparent *de jure* ownership of them and of subsequent finds. Because of the tumultuousness of Middle-Eastern politics during the period between 1947 and 1967, the answer to this particular question is an intricate one that has not received much attention to date. What follows is certainly no attempt to answer this burning question, but only a contribution to the complexity of the matter of ownership and the Dead Sea Scrolls.

Finally, this book is an attempt to reconstruct a little known part of the history of the discovery and purchase of Dead Sea Scrolls from individual papers and records of the parties involved in their acquisition and study. In many ways the materials help corroborate what is already known. In other instances it contradicts lore that has been taken for history after countless repetitions over a period of sixty years from the discovery of the Dead Sea Scrolls. It tells the story of a Canadian scholar who did significantly more than "recover fragments of the scrolls in 1951." In taking the risk to get involved in the purchase of Cave 4 fragments R.B.Y. Scott helped ensure that the discovery remained largely intact, hence greatly facilitating the study and reconstruction of the immensely fragmentary and invaluable Cave 4 Dead Sea Scrolls manuscripts for generations to come.

2

"Telling tales of the early days"[1]: McGill Buys the Dead Sea Scrolls

In the winter of 1946–47 Bedouin of the Ta'amireh tribe discovered a cave containing ancient scrolls in the cliffs that rise above the western shore of the Dead Sea.[2] Four of the scrolls were sold by the Bedouin to a Bethlehem antiquities dealer, Khalil Iskandar Shahin (Kando),[3] who in turn sold them to Mar Athanasius Yeshue Samuel, the Metropolitan of the Syrian Orthodox Church in Jerusalem. Three others were sold to Eleazar Sukenik, the Hebrew University archaeologist, who purchased them through another Bethlehem antiquities dealer, Feidi al-Alami.[4] Even though British Mandate and then Jordanian law required that the Jordanian Government's antiquities authorities be informed of archaeological discoveries in Jordanian territory, the unearthing of these scrolls did not come to the attention of G. Lankester Harding, the director of antiquities, until late 1948.[5] Harding immediately initiated a search for the source of the first scrolls, and the cave later labelled as Cave 1 was found by excavators in January 1949. Meanwhile, the Bedouin, having found that the caves could yield objects of monetary value, went likewise in search of possible sources of new material to sell. Despite the efforts of Harding and others to cut off the Bedouin's supply by beating them to the discovery of new caves, the most significant cache was found by the Bedouin in February 1952 in what came to be known as Cave 4.[6] Although the story is less well known than the legendary discovery of Cave 1 by Mohammed edh-Dhib, who reportedly tossed a stone into a cave while searching for a lost member of his herd, breaking a ceramic jar, Cave 4 likewise carries with it a magical story of its accidental discovery by the Bedouin.[7] Cave 4's story is recounted best by Józef Milik, a member of the editorial team assigned to publishing the finds:

One evening in one of their tents, a group of Ta'amireh were discussing the recent finds which were winning them world-wide fame ... and a substantial income. A remark roused a venerable grey-beard from his somnolence, calling his mind back to something which might be of interest to keen cave-hunters. It happened long ago, during his youth, he explained, when he was hunting in the region of Qumrân. He was following a wounded partridge, when, suddenly, it disappeared into a hole not far from the ruins. With great difficulty he reached his prey, which had fallen into a cave, and there he collected an old terra-cotta lamp and a few potsherds. The younger tribesmen noted carefully the topographical details that the old man gave, equipped themselves with a bag of flour, ropes and primitive lamps, and went down to Qumrân. Using their ropes, they finally climbed into the right cave ... and set to sifting its earth. They had already turned over several cubic meters of earth when, suddenly, their hands came upon a compact layer of thousands of manuscript fragments. Their courage and perseverance had its reward.[8]

By September of 1952, fragments from Cave 4 started to appear on the antiquities market.[9] As quickly as the material appeared, it was purchased by the PAM. And, as funds began to dwindle in the same month, the Hashemite Kingdom of Jordan provided the museum with 15,000 Jordanian dinar (JD) to help purchase more of the Cave 4 fragments that the Bedouin had brought to the attention of the scholarly community.[10] Simultaneously, Harding approached American and European museums and libraries with the hope of soliciting donations to aid the PAM in making further purchases to be maintained as part of the Jordanian cultural heritage. Yet, by August 1953 no funds had been forthcoming from academic institutions or museums and the 15,000 JD provided by the government was all but depleted. The situation remained desperate well into the early part of 1954. John Allegro, at that time an editorial team member nominated by the British School and working at the PAM on Cave 4 texts,[11] described the situation in a letter to his wife:

> [Milik] came in this morning with the gloomy news that there's no more money in the chest to buy fragments with. There is probably one third as much again in the hands of the Bedu [sic], and it seems Harding and de Vaux are losing hopes of ever being able to get them ... Probably something like £10–£15,000 is required – this is not an impossible figure. The trouble probably is that neither Harding nor de

Vaux can spare time for a publicity tour, but I feel that this is just what is needed.[12]

Unbeknownst to Allegro, Father Roland de Vaux, the director of the École Biblique and also director of excavations at Qumran from 1949 until 1958, had already made an impromptu plea for financial help at a conference of his peers in Copenhagen. The plea preceded Allegro's letter by more than six months yet the latter's author was seemingly unaware of the fruitful negotiations that de Vaux's public appeal had inspired.

R.B.Y. SCOTT AND THE DEAD SEA SCROLLS

Professor R.B.Y. Scott of McGill University had attended the first conference of the newly established International Organization for the Study of the Old Testament held in Copenhagen in August 1953.[13] His attendance was fateful, since he went despite his inability to participate as a presenter.[14] The son of a minister, Scott (1899–1987) was ordained by the United Church of Canada in 1926 and earned a PhD at the University of Toronto two years later.[15] Immediately thereafter, he began his teaching career at Union College in Vancouver. In 1931 Scott moved to the United Theological College (UTC) of Montreal and until 1948 served as professor of Old Testament language and literature.[16] With the establishment of the Faculty of Divinity at McGill, constituted with the cooperation of the associated theological colleges, including UTC, Scott was appointed to the university's staff and became the faculty's first dean and professor of Old Testament literature and language. A man of varied interests, he published on biblical prophecy and wisdom literature, ancient weights and measures, seals, cosmology, and climatology.[17] From the time of the first announcement of the discovery of the scrolls, Scott paid close attention to the news arriving from the Middle East and the reports of scholarly research that followed it. His papers indicate that he avidly scanned the print media and collected a series of newspaper clippings covering the events dating from 1949 well into the 1960s.[18]

McGill's course catalogues indicate that throughout his entire career as member of McGill's faculty Scott remained responsible for teaching "Old Testament 1a – An Introduction to Old Testament Studies."[19] The course curriculum included significant discussion of the composition of the Pentateuch and textual criticism. Scott's interest in these matters persisted throughout his career and, at least in part, made the discovery and

R. B. Y. Scott at Montreal's Windsor Station, returning from travel abroad, 6 July 1951. Photo courtesy of John Scott.

interpretation of the Dead Sea Scrolls so exciting to him. Scott also was already offering a graduate level course in the Dead Sea Scrolls in the academic years 1953–54 and 1954–55. This was a first in Canada. The course description reads:

> THE DEAD SEA SCROLLS OF ISAIAH. (1) Reading of the Scrolls from facsimile plates and comparison with the Massoretic text, as a study in Hebrew palaeology and textual criticism; and (2) Examination of the scientific periodical literature relating to the discovery and dating of the Dead Sea Scrolls, as a study in Biblical archaeology and historical criticism.[20]

G. Lankester Harding (left) and Roland de Vaux (right) explore Dead Sea cave, 12 December 1958. Photographed by David Boyer. Published with the permission of National Geographic Image Collection/Getty Images.

Scott's visit to Copenhagen was well repaid when, on the third day of the meeting, Father Roland de Vaux announced during an informal and, by all accounts unrehearsed, presentation that was later recounted by Scott: "This announcement was to the effect that funds had run out before it had been possible to recover from the Bedouin by purchase all the manuscripts [from Cave 4] which they have found; and that, if any institution would provide the additional funds required, the right of export and possession would be guaranteed, on certain conditions. The conditions [were] that the material thus obtained would be kept in Palestine until it could be studied, compared and matched with the other finds, and published – in the interest of scientific control of the total discovery. This, said Père de Vaux, might take two or three years."[21]

Professor H.H. Rowley of the University of Manchester later referred less than enthusiastically to the same presentation by Father de Vaux in his report on the first IOSOT Congress.[22] This was partly because Rowley was not present at de Vaux's talk. It should also be remembered that the imminent Professor Godfrey R. Driver of Oxford University, who at the time had serious doubts about the antiquity of the scrolls, had the honour of presenting the very first paper at IOSOT.[23] IOSOT was therefore by no means a unanimously receptive audience to de Vaux's plea. Furthermore, as Rowley commented, de Vaux's talk was not a prepared fundraising speech:

> Professor I. Engnell, of Uppsala, who was expected to read a paper on this day, was prevented by illness from attending, and as his paper had not been sent it could not be read or printed in the Conference volume, to which reference is made below. Professor A. Parrot, of Paris, was not able to be present at the Congress, as he had to go to Mesopotamia for excavations. Hence his paper was not read, but will be found in the Conference volume. Father de Vaux was therefore asked to give an informal talk on the latest news of the discoveries in the Judaean Desert and the excavations in Qumran in 1953. He told of the successive rich finds of 1952, including fragments of almost every book of the Old Testament, and a large number of apocryphal works. It is clear that both Old Testament scholars and New Testament scholars will have materials to keep them occupied for many years, when all the texts have been published.[24]

The availability of Cave 4 material for purchase by foreign educational institutions resulted primarily from de Vaux's plan to safeguard the integrity of the collection. The plan, it was hoped, might prevent the continual stream of discovered manuscript fragments from being scattered over the globe by the powers of the black market and the not insignificant demands of private collectors. To preserve the manuscripts as a collection, some form of remuneration scheme had to be implemented. In fact, it required two schemes. The first was what Weston Fields refers to as the "Harding-de Vaux Plan": the Jordanian Department of Antiquities and the PAM entered into an agreement with Kando stipulating that if he, as sole intermediary, offered the scrolls material brought to him by the Bedouin first to the PAM, it committed to purchase it from him at a fair price and neither he nor his sources would face prosecution for looting antiquities.[25]

The plan dated to 1949, and while this arrangement secured fragments for the Museum from Cave 1, what neither Harding nor de Vaux could foresee was the huge discovery to be made in the two adjacent caves, referred to together as Cave 4.[26] Although the Jordanian Government was persuaded to provide handsomely, money ran out after the first purchases and the unforeseen happened: even more fragments from Cave 4 kept streaming in. This state of affairs continued until the last batch of Cave 4 documents was bought from Kando in 1958.[27]

This set of circumstances inspired the second part of the scheme, essentially the "De Vaux Plan": the public appeal for the purchase of materials by foreign institutions, with certain caveats. Hence, on 23 November 1953, and after responding to Father de Vaux's impromptu appeal at IOSOT the previous August in Copenhagen, Professor R.B.Y. Scott received a cable message from Harding: "Government have agreed to scheme please send your contribution earliest possible."[28] This put the official stamp of approval on the purchase agreement that had been several months in the making and was announced six months later in May 1954.[29] Frank Moore Cross describes the exact details of, and rationale for, this arrangement in *The Ancient Library of Qumran*:

> After the Department of Antiquities, the Palestine Museum, and other institutions in Jordan had expended their financial resources for the purchase of antiquities, the Council of Ministers of Jordan passed legislation permitting reputable foreign institutions to purchase additional lots of manuscripts of Cave IV remaining in Bedouin hands. Such purchases were arranged by the Director of Antiquities, on the condition that scrolls so purchased remain in the Palestine Archaeological Museum for editing, after which they are to be distributed to their owners. Such an arrangement had several advantages. First of all, it prevented loss by destruction or smuggling at the hands of Bedouin; it permitted the fragments to be bought through established official channels at standard prices (about $2.80 per square centimetre of inscribed surface); and more important, it kept the great mass of fragments in one center for editing. Had they been scattered, much of their usefulness would have been destroyed, since obviously much of the joining of fragments into large complexes can be done only with the original leather. Finally donors were to receive in this plan, not the unsorted fragments belonging to the actual lot which their money happened to purchase, but *all* fragments belonging to a group of manuscripts equivalent in size to the amount contributed for purchase.[30]

From the correspondence dated between the IOSOT meeting and the telegram addressed to R.B.Y. Scott in November of 1953, it seems that de Vaux may have spoken out of turn in offering the scrolls to prospective institutional donors. At the time of the plea, neither Harding nor the Jordanian Government had agreed that institutions could purchase scrolls of their own for export from Jordan. That Harding preferred to approach the government for permission only after an offer had been secured is apparent. However, this approach to solving their financial troubles had been under discussion in Jerusalem since the previous year.

In late fall 1952 Harding was beginning to come to terms with the idea of allowing foreign institutions the opportunity to buy Dead Sea Scrolls material. He still preferred to find a donor to purchase the fragments on behalf of the museum, but no individuals or institutions had come forward. On 8 November 1952, Carl Kraeling, then president of ASOR,[31] wrote to Harding reminding him of the content of a previous communication: "As I indicated in my last letter, it will probably not be easy to raise money to help the Palestine museum buy materials now on the market but it might be possible to get money for the purchase of the scrolls and scroll fragments through you or Père de Vaux on the understanding that they could be acquired with your permission by reputable American museums."[32] The earlier letter confirmed that, while not opposed to seeking funds to purchase the fragments, Kraeling preferred that the funds be used to continue archaeological expeditions to find the source of the materials, in order to, "take the wind out of the bedu [sic] sails by seeing that the area with the caves is so overhauled archaeologically that the prospects of further discoveries become minimal."[33] Although the expeditions took place as foreseen, ironically the Bedouin still cleared the vast majority of the ancient materials from Cave 4 before the archaeologists arrived on the scene. They continued to make other cave finds ahead of official professional expeditions.[34] As to the purchase of fragments, Harding approached a number of institutions with direct offers, but these proved fruitless. De Vaux was therefore forced to act despite the far-reaching implications of his public offer should it result in a positive response. It opened up the very real possibility that the intact collection – a crucial matter underpinning the entire purchasing activity at the time – could and would be compromised after publication by allowing the scrolls to leave Jordanian territory permanently. The possibility of more than one institution with title to the documents further implied that the unity of the collection, which was already compromised by the Bedouin, would in effect be destroyed forever. The quandary this created is best expressed by John Allegro, who noted that one of the Cambridge colleges had decided against donating funds or purchasing fragments, "since they thought it undesirable that the collection should be split up. Overlooking the patent fact that unless they're bought by somebody soon they'll go to the tourists!"[35]

The ambiguity surrounding the official status of de Vaux's offer is evident in the telegrams traded between Scott and Harding. On 25 September 1953, Scott sent word that McGill wished to send funds to procure the remaining scroll fragments.[36] Harding's response clearly indicates that he was unclear as to the university's intentions. He asks: "Does University wish to acquire fragments or would funds be offered as donations. If latter to whom offered."[37] On the same day, Scott replies: "Desire follow suggestion Devaux [sic] raise funds acquire fragments for University following study publication Jerusalem."[38] The following month Harding informed Scott that similar offers had been made by other (unnamed) institutions and that the entire matter was put before the Government of Jordan to make, "a firm decision on the principle of allowing some of the material to be sent abroad after study here [in Jerusalem]."[39]

SCOTT'S CANADIAN COLLEAGUES AND THE DEAD SEA SCROLLS

As further qualification it should be noted that Scott's active involvement in the acquisition of the scrolls on behalf of McGill University was not inspired solely by the doubtful oratory skills of Father de Vaux or the coverage that the discovery received in the popular and academic press. Scott's interest was significantly stimulated by the close ties he maintained with two Canadian scholars who had served as annual directors of ASOR in Jerusalem.[40] Professor Fred V. Winnett of the University of Toronto served as annual director in 1950–51 as the discovery of the scrolls was unfolding.[41] Scott, on sabbatical from McGill, spent this crucial time in the history of the discovery of the scrolls in Jerusalem at ASOR. He could not but be exposed to and aware of the hive of activity surrounding the continued discovery of caves and fragments. In fact, Scott's first public comments on the scrolls preceded his attendance at IOSOT by a month. In a publication of the United Church of Canada,[42] Scott summarized the content of the contemporary *New York Times* articles he had collected and an article by de Vaux in the *Revue biblique*.[43] Clearly, even at this point, Scott saw himself as a mediator between the academy and the laity in matters of interest to both.

The other Canadian scholar, Professor A. Douglas Tushingham of Queen's Theological College (Kingston, Ontario) and later of the Royal Ontario Museum,[44] helped to sustain Canadian awareness of the ongoing events in Jerusalem as he served as director of ASOR in 1952–53, the crucial year in which Cave 4 was discovered.[45]

In *The Dead Sea Scrolls*, Millar Burrows refers to the reported discovery of Cave 4 in August/September 1952, just as Tushingham assumed the directorship. He recounts that Tushingham and two other ASOR fellows engaged in a fruitless expedition to search for additional caves with Józef Milik and Yusif Sa'ad,[46] secretary of the PAM.[47] Tushingham himself commented only briefly on the excursion: "The School year was formally opened on October 4th with the annual tea and reception to which all the notables of Jerusalem and friends of the School are invited. At this tea Père de Vaux informed me that work had to be begun immediately in a new manuscript cave area. The Department of Antiquities and the Ecole Biblique [sic] could not assume the responsibility at the moment. Would the American School take it on? With the assistance of Mr. Joseph Sa'ad and experienced personnel from the staff of the Museum, we did. But the results were not what we had hoped. The Bedu [sic] had been there before us."[48]

Although both Winnett and Tushingham thus had firsthand experience and were actively involved and acutely aware of the *status quo* of matters as to the discovery and collection of the Dead Sea Scrolls in Jerusalem, it was Scott who committed to the appeal made by de Vaux. Winnett attempted to find donors for the University of Toronto but met with little success. In March 1954 he wrote to Scott: "I wonder if you could send me *tout de suite, s'il vous plaît*, a few bits of information which I might use in pressing my case. Do you know if the remainder of the find is still for sale, that is, is anything left to purchase?[49] Can you give me any information as to the amount and character of the 'stuff' you have acquired for $15,000?[50] And what is the nature of your agreement with Harding? Have you the right to publish? And do you know how much it would take to purchase what is left? I have one lead here which has not said no and so I would like to arm myself with a few specific bits of information before coming back at them."[51]

Tushingham, likewise, attempted to find donors but was not successful.[52] However, having seen Qumran material first-hand, he later proved a useful resource to Scott and provided him with extremely pertinent guidance in the process of negotiating the terms of purchase, professing to be "tickled absolutely rosy" at the news of Scott's successful quest for a donor.[53] Concerning McGill's potential purchase he wrote:[54]

> I don't think that you need have any doubts about the genuineness of the material. I think both De Vaux and Harding[55] are not going to be taken in by ~~alien~~ fake[56] material. There have been several attempts but they have always been caught and I know of only one faked fragment that was purchased before its spuriousness was discovered. I don't think you need to worry about fakes.[57] Lateness is another matter, though. If you are buying a block of mss. the date may be anything. But you

should not get a *mixture* of late and early.[58] If you wish, why don't you wire Harding and ask him the approximate date of the new material;[59] then you will know what you are getting into. If it is too late for you,[60] you can then wait for more finds, or perhaps put up the money for the outright purchase of some of the materials now at the Museum which are held only on a down-payment. I imagine that the Museum and the Jordan Government would permit. [sic] this. You think that Harding might be tempted to keep some interesting pieces from the lot purchased by McGill.[61] I think that is likely, but you must remember that the antiquities law of Jordan says that *all* unique pieces must remain there.[62] Now in the matter of thousands of MSS, this clause is going to need some interpretation. But I doubt, for instance that Jordan would part with the Bar Chochba letter.[63] That is unique so far, though fragments of others have been found and they might dispose of them. But, if Harding were to act to keep some particular piece from your collection, I think he would give you a good piece to take its place.[64]

Despite their best efforts, neither Tushingham nor Winnett was able to secure adequate donations to arrange a purchase. Yet they both appreciated Scott's success and Winnett in particular hoped that McGill's announcement of its purchase might possibly encourage additional donors to come forward. Undoubtedly all three men were struck by the importance of obtaining "a sizable chunk of this material for Canada."[65] It is important to note that all of the correspondence between Scott and these two Canadian scholars preceded the actual purchase of the scrolls by McGill and therefore indicates Scott's trust in his colleagues' ability to advise him. It also seems to indicate a friendly collegial collaboration rather than a rivalry. McGill's success in acquiring the scrolls reinforced a Canadian sense of pride and, in no small way, encouraged the men's future cooperation.

Following the Second World War, Canada was involved in discussion about what it meant to be Canadian. Having fought alongside Great Britain and the United States, Canada had in many ways come into its own as a result of the war. Its previous relationship with England was now counterbalanced by the growing power of the United States with its pervasive media and emphasis on popular culture. Caught between the two, or pulled from both directions, Canadians in the 1950s experienced a period of self-reflection on how to distinguish themselves and forge their own separate identity. By and large in the postwar period, "Canadians believed that they had finally emerged from the shadow of Great Britain."[66] But this did not mean that Canada made a complete break from Britain. As a member of the British Commonwealth, Canada's politicians maintained their political relationship with other commonwealth countries even while they tried to create an independent and distinct international identity for themselves.[67] If colonial history tied Canada to Great Britain, then geography proved the driving force for its love/hate relationship with its neighbour to the south. Canada was situated north of a much more populous nation. A nation that produced huge quantities of cultural goods they were prepared to share. Canadians, or at least their cultural elite, were extremely concerned about the risk "Americanization" posed to the emerging Canadian identity.[68] Of great concern was the fact that Canada, in many respects, had traded the colonial ties of Great Britain for the cultural and economic domination of the United States. The American political scientist, H. McDowall Clokie, noted in a contemporary article: "If colonialism has any economic aspect for Canada, as a correlative of economic imperialism, it might be more appropriately used regarding relations with the United States than regarding those with Britain."[69]

The pride Tushingham, Winnett and others expressed in the acquisition of the Dead Sea Scrolls for Canada must also be understood in this context.[70] The ability of McGill, as a Canadian university, to buy the largest collection of ancient fragments and play host to this collection outside the Middle East ahead of both British and American institutions had the potential to gain international notice not only for McGill but for the whole country. Hence, the Canadian aspect of the purchase was trumpeted by the popular press to rally Canadians' pride in its educational institutions.

The press interest in Scott as a *Canadian* scholar on the world stage preceded the purchase and his pride in his nationality is likewise evident in the press reports and his own writings. In 1951 as Scott returned from a period of study at ASOR Jerusalem, the *Montreal Star* asked him about the importance of his identification as a Canadian: "The fact that he was a Canadian was of considerable advantage to Professor Scott. 'Canadians,' he said, 'are held in high regard in the Middle East. There were six [scholars] from Canada [including Tushingham and Winnett] engaged in research under the auspices of the school. We were frequently thankful we could show Canadian passports which invariably produced friendly reaction in the countries we visited.'"[71]

The Canadian perspective was again highlighted when McGill announced its purchase in May 1954. The *Gazette* (Montreal) reported that the announcement described the "romantic details of how an august university in Canada did business through a government department of another country with wandering tribesmen of another land."[72] In 1956 the *Toronto Daily Star* noted that McGill's efforts were going to bring the scrolls to Canada and that they were considered by scholars, "as more precious for Old Testament knowledge even than the famous Codex Sinaiticus of the British Museum and the Codex Vaticanus of the Vatican Museum." This statement is followed by a subsection of the article titled in bold "Canadians Interested." The subsection continues to give a description of all Canadians involved in the study of the scrolls:

> From the first, Canadians have been involved with the Dead Sea Scrolls. Prof. F. V. Winnett of University college [sic], University of Toronto, was serving as director of the American School of Oriental research [sic] in Jerusalem when Dr. Millar Burrows of the Yale graduate school announced the findings to the world.
>
> Dr. Scott has worked in Palestine as have other Canadians representing Protestant elements among the scholars. At present Dr. Forrestal [sic] of the Basilian Fathers and the Pontifical Institute of Medieval Studies, in Toronto, is in Jerusalem studying the scrolls.[73] Dr. Harry Orlinsky, professor of Bible at the Hebrew Union college [sic] in New York, is a Toronto man.[74] He was the first to translate completely the book of Isaiah found in the cave in 1947[75] and he was the authority engaged by the Israeli government to work on the authenticity of the scrolls.[76]

The named individuals were all proud Canadians who saw their scholarly efforts as fitting tribute to their country and their countrymen. In this vein, Scott commented to McGill's principal on his continuing efforts to secure the scrolls: "I will not pretend that my feeling that I should continue work on this project is dictated solely by a sense of duty. I am proud to have been instrumental in obtaining the Scroll fragments for Canada and for McGill, and I have a deep interest in carrying the project to a successful conclusion."[77] Scott's efforts were about setting McGill apart and distinguishing Canadian institutions of higher learning. The purchase of these cultural objects for Canada allowed the nation to join the intellectual world stage. It was at this time and within this mindset that, during a board meeting to discuss McGill's funding, the phrase describing McGill as "the Princeton of the North" was coined.[78] In purchasing the scrolls, McGill University would acquire something that Princeton, and others, could only aspire to.[79] Next to the great institutions of higher learning of Great Britain and the United States, Canada could hereby demonstrate a legitimate claim to be the best, the only, or the greatest.

SECURING MCGILL'S PURCHASE

Following his return to McGill University after the IOSOT Copenhagen conference in August 1953, Scott immediately initiated a correspondence with Harding. While de Vaux functioned as mouthpiece on the matter of the purchase of the fragments, only Harding, as Jordanian director of antiquities, had the authority to act on behalf of the government to arrange an institution's purchase of national movable cultural property. By the end of September 1953, Scott and the McGill University principal, F. Cyril James, started to actively canvass for funding of between $12,000 and $15,000 in Canadian funds, which was considered sufficient to acquire the available manuscript material.[80] This was no small commitment on the university's part. A few months later, for example, John Allegro related the response received by Harding from Professor H.H. Rowley of the University of Manchester. Writing to his wife in late March 1954, Allegro recounted: "HHR [Rowley], characteristically, went hot-foot to the authorities of the University, and asked for £250. The Committee thought this was too little and are supplying £1,000 ... a wonderful example of Manchester's liveliness, and HHR's in particular. He hopes I will keep an eye on their interests out here and see they get something valuable for their money."[81] Although Manchester's reaction was somewhat slower than that of McGill, it suggests that Rowley's rather unimpressed tone in describing de Vaux's presentation in Copenhagen the previous year had changed, although it is still not clear as to whether he truly grasped the extent of the find and therefore the extensive funding required.

Scott seemed to have a far firmer grip on this reality. His encouragement of McGill's participation in the acquisition of scroll fragments clearly showed that he foresaw the benefits of the Cave 4 purchase for the university. But it is also clear from the correspondence that quite early on he also foresaw the major pitfall that later came to haunt the eventual purchase: the length of time it would take before the collection would reach Montreal. Nonetheless, Scott emphasized to James the rare prospect for McGill University provided by the purchase to stake a claim and make a contribution to international scholarship:

> This seems to me a remarkable opportunity for McGill to obtain a collection of documents of the utmost value for Biblical research and for the history of Judaism ... The documents, though fragmentary, are priceless. It is only the fact that the archaeological authorities can deal directly with the finders, and must do so urgently before the material

F. Cyril James (right), returning from travel abroad, 1946. Published with the permission of Graetz Bros./McGill University Archives, PR027113.

gets into the hands of dealers, that makes it possible to obtain such precious material for such a sum. When one considers that a few years ago the British Museum paid the Soviet Government £100,000. [sic] for the fourth century Codex Sinaiticus of the Greek Bible,[82] the sum now needed seems small indeed ... With such a wealth of material available all at once, the exhaustion of funds calls for help from outside, and provides an opportunity which may not recur.[83]

Scott had little difficulty convincing James to support the university's acquisition of the scrolls. At the institutional level the scrolls would certainly attract international attention and aid in promoting the university. On a personal level, James had been deeply religious from his early teens in the wake of the First World War. At one time he considered becoming a parson. Appreciating the young James's enthusiasm, the rector of St Mary's Church in the London borough of Hackney opened the parish archives for him to explore. James traced its history back to the early fourteenth century. This, along with frequent Bible classes, inspired James's lifelong interest in the history of the church and in Christianity.[84] Such commitment led James to push for the establishment of the Faculty of Divinity at McGill in 1948 and most likely inspired his fervent support of Scott's endeavour to acquire the ancient fragments which, as Scott often repeated, shed light on early Judaism and Christianity in the land of the Bible and the birthplace of Jesus.

James relied on Scott for assurance as to the authenticity and value of the fragments. Scott, in turn, relied just as heavily on de Vaux and Harding. He was convinced that de Vaux (who, at the time of McGill's purchase, was undertaking the third season of excavation at Khirbet Qumran) and Harding were trustworthy and competent, both in negotiating a fair price and in guaranteeing the authenticity of the finds purchased. Harding's reliability was reasserted in Tushingham's correspondence with Scott.[85] But this was nevertheless a brave new world in which an ability to know who to trust proved of the utmost importance.

Trust was also at stake in another institution's decision not to provide funds for the purchase of scroll fragments. In October 1952, nearly a year before de Vaux's public appeal, Harding had approached the British Museum with an offer to buy fragments for exhibit in London. In a letter dated 23 October 1952, Harding offered that, "The only conditions would be that the whole of the material would have to be worked over (sorted, pieced together, etc.) here [in the PAM], and prepared for publication."[86] By the time of Scott's appeal to James, the British Museum had already declined the offer to buy Cave 4 fragments because the institution did not want to purchase antiquities sight unseen. "We are all three sorry we cannot offer more practical help," wrote Thomas Downing Kendrick, director of the British Museum (1950–59) to Harding on 8 November 1952, "but we must make it clear that the Museum would not be able to help you financially by buying a part of the manuscripts until we had the originals here that Fulton[87] would like to recommend the Trustees to buy. For that reason we think sending Photostats [sic] might be a good beginning."[88] The patent reluctance of the British Museum to show any particular enthusiasm for the project or active interest in the purchase, collection, and ultimate preservation of the scrolls baffled and angered many in Jerusalem. The most colourful depiction of the sense of frustration is yet again encapsulated by John Allegro: "The biggest museum in the world ought to be able to put money into the project of presenting these priceless things to the world without expecting to see bits and pieces like a bargain basement. If they financed research they wouldn't expect to see material things for their money."[89]

CANADIAN HIGHER EDUCATION AND THE FACULTY OF DIVINITY

How much Scott knew of the British Museum's decision when he approached Principal James is unclear but his justification for the expenditure by the university was particularly well prepared. He argued for the scholarly opportunities that owning scroll material would create: "The possession of a collection of documents, even in fragmentary condition, from the epoch of the beginnings of normative Judaism and the rise of Christianity, would attract research scholars for many years, and put the name of McGill into many scholarly publications."[90] Given the financial challenges faced by the university at the time, there can be little doubt that the publicity from the purchase of the scrolls would have been quite welcome, along with the resultant greater international exposure, to encourage donations to the university. Moreover, the acquisition of the scrolls also made an important statement as to the state of affairs with regard to the teaching of religion and the humanities in general at Canadian institutions. As such, the motivation for purchasing the scrolls was intimately tied to the forces that encouraged the creation of McGill's Faculty of Divinity almost six years earlier.

Following the Second World War, Canadian institutions of higher learning were subject to a period of extreme flux. As Canadian historian, Philip Massolin, notes, "[in the] process of academic modernization, universities went from being isolated, elitist colleges with liberal arts faculties at their centres to modern research facilities, reliant on government funding and responsive to the expansionist mood of the 1950s and 1960s. By the late 1960s, higher learning became firmly enmeshed in the public ambit. The practical, utilitarian orientation of the universities reflected a world that was preoccupied with expansion, technological advancement and material well-being. In such a world, the humanities and liberal arts – once pre-eminent foci of the academy – lost that pre-eminence."[91]

The traditional raison d'être of universities changed virtually overnight, in large measure as a result of their contribution to the war effort. As is to be expected, these changes also reflected a general shift in Canadian society. The same technological advances that had allowed for success in war now brought with them a proliferation of consumer products that irrevocably changed the lifestyle of the average Canadian.[92] Many Canadians, as indeed many people all over the world, came to view technology as a panacea. As a result, university education changed forever. The universities were now expected to continue their educational emphasis on the practical and functional as training grounds for scientists and others who could make use of their learning for the advancement of society through technology.[93] Furthermore, Canadians' growing consumer needs acted as incentive for universities to train even more graduates to invent the technology necessary for product manufacture and distribution. This promoted a view of education as almost entirely utilitarian. Postwar educational institutions had little choice but to adapt accordingly.

The success of Canadian troops in the war and the growth of Canadian industry thus offered Canada in the postwar years hitherto undreamt of opportunities for prosperity, wealth, and security. Advancement in the material and political realm, however, also brought with it concern from intellectuals that the development of the cultural resources of the young nation had not kept pace. For the pessimists among them, Canada as a cultural entity, "threatened to regress, reflecting the wider cultural decadence of the western world."[94]

Concerned with this utilitarian approach to the university, William Everett McNeill, the outgoing vice-principal of Queen's University in Ontario, singled out in his 1947 convocation address three matters that universities were obligated to consider. The first was "the balance between sharing knowledge and teaching skills," followed by "cultural heritage" and "character":

> The cultural heritage – Skills are not enough. Though they make great and happy men, they do not make the greatest or happiest ... It is not enough merely to be wise in one's own work. The view is too short. The individual must see beyond his immediate task; he must gain a sense of life as a whole; he must make his own richer in thought and feeling and beauty by drawing on the cultural heritage for ampler vision, ampler values.
>
> Character – In the final reckoning what one is counts more than what one knows or does. The Hitlers of this world are transient. The abiding powers of the human race are moral ... almost any system will serve if worked by good men; any system will fail if worked by self-seekers.[95]

In addition to the changing attitude to education and resultant de-emphasis of the humanities in the curriculum, defenders of the humanities and religion saw themselves pushed out of the public discourse. From their perspective, the poster child for technological advancement, the atomic bomb, although undoubtedly a scientific marvel, raised a number of serious moral and ethical issues. While many Canadians believed that science continued to progress and had the potential to help solve the social problems of the day, religion's defenders responded that religion was needed more than ever.[96] Religion, they argued, had over centuries developed the ability to respond to matters within the human domain that science could not. Religion offered a response to the moral and ethical issues raised by scientific development and universities served as a logical platform to provide a meeting place for these ideas. Social critics argued that the humanistic academy could serve the Canadian public in a way that the new university could not. The latter could help ameliorate the material conditions of society but the former held the potential to enable, "humanity to remain tied to its traditions while helping moderns to cope with contemporary societal malaise."[97]

The establishment of the McGill Faculty of Divinity in 1948 was thus envisioned as a means of providing students with the tools necessary to confront the increasingly complex society of the latter half of the twentieth century. Although an economist by training, Principal James was not prepared to see religion removed from public discourse and therefore became a stalwart supporter for the establishment of a Faculty of Divinity at McGill.

The creation of such a faculty was first proposed in 1865 when, beginning in the 1860s, four independent theological colleges affiliated themselves with McGill.[98] It seems that lack of cooperation between the colleges, in part, prevented its establishment. Nevertheless, by 1912 the once independent colleges agreed on a program of cooperative education and it was assumed that this would eventually lead to the formation of a faculty. However, rifts within the Presbyterian community undermined these efforts, as did opposition from within the university, on academic grounds. It was argued by some that McGill "teaches pure science. It could not teach any 'ology' or 'ism' and be true to its high ideal."[99] Because of the efforts of F. Cyril James and board member William Massey Birks,[100] whose son Henry[101] arranged the funds for the purchase of the scrolls, McGill's Faculty of Divinity was nevertheless established by vote of the university Senate in February 1948. Thus, the process of establishing a Faculty of Divinity had been ongoing for more than eighty years when Scott became its first dean in 1949. In his inaugural address, Scott established in great detail his vision for what the faculty, as the home of biblical studies, had to offer McGill and Canadians in general:

> I suggest to you, then, in the first place, that the Old Testament as a corpus of literary and historical documents, is of immense human

interest and cultural value. It is a living literature, accessible to, and in the main understandable by the average man – if he will give it more than casual attention. Moreover, it is of unusual historical interest, both for the understanding of religious origins, and as a doorway into that ancient world of the Near East where mankind's earliest major civilizations emerged.

Second – as something of a footnote to the first – I would point out that for the serious student the field of Old Testament and related studies, far from being one where all questions have long been settled, is instead a vast and expanding area of philological, literary, historical and theological research, where he may profitably concentrate the scholarly investigations of a lifetime.

Third, I am going to suggest that the experience of human conflict as recorded in this volume, its thoughts concerning the nature and destiny of man, and concerning the relation of God to man and to human history, are of peculiar and timely importance in the Twentieth century.

And finally, I affirm that the Old Testament which, as has been said already, was the first Bible of Christianity, has still its indispensable place in the life, worship, and thought of the Church, – a place whose importance now needs re-thinking and re-affirmation.[102]

Scott's articulate description of the value of religion resonated with Principal James, who later commented in a 1955 lecture, "It was easier to walk with God, and work with Him, in simpler Eastern lands on Mediterranean skies [in the time of Paul] than it is in a crowded bus on Sherbrooke Street [in downtown Montreal] in a world that is arguing about the atom bomb."[103] But Scott's rhetoric could not assuage all critics. During the many years of debate leading up to the creation of the faculty, much concern had been raised that it would be, like the affiliated theological colleges, primarily a place for the training of ministers. In this context the establishment of the graduate program helped to reinforce the faculty's academic identity. In the first year of the program, 1950–51, only one student enrolled.[104] By the following year, the number had increased to eight (two of these were specifically working in Islamic studies).

Scott therefore likely understood the purchase of the scrolls as helping the institution in three ways. First, it could aid in the expansion of graduate studies and would help in securing the faculty's reputation, and the study of religion as a legitimate academic enterprise. He reported as much to the board in March 1954.[105] Second, among the concerns raised by McGill's governors and staff at the time of the establishment of the Faculty of Divinity was the possibility that it would remain an essentially Christian confessional institution. In opposing the creation of the Faculty of Divinity, a group of dissenting professors voiced the concern that, "a largely denominational Faculty would be viewed unfavourably by 'many of our English Catholic, French-Canadian, and Jewish Students and their parents and coreligionists.'"[106] The scrolls' purchase would afford the faculty the opportunity to reach out and find common ground with non-Christian communities, particularly Montreal's well-established Jewish community.

In this respect it is also important to note that Scott and James first turned to the Montreal Jewish community to help raise funds for purchasing the scrolls. Although nothing appears to have come of this initial contact, the scrolls did succeed in bringing the communities closer together.[107] In November 1955 Scott was invited to give a lecture by the Adult Education Committee of the Eastern Region of the Canadian Jewish Congress and he spoke to a capacity crowd at Moyse Hall at McGill University. Scott's address was entitled: "The Discovery and Importance of the Dead Sea Scrolls." In all of the Congress's publicity related to the event, as on the invitation, Scott was presented as the person responsible for arranging the purchase of scrolls for McGill.[108] And, yet again, McGill was the beneficiary of the resultant positive publicity in the Montreal newspaper the *Gazette* in the week leading up to the lecture: "In 1951, Prof. Scott visited the first cave in which the scrolls were discovered and has since played an important part in acquiring for McGill University a collection of these scrolls which he considers to be the largest outside Jerusalem."[109] The *Gazette*'s reference to the lecture on 22 November 1955 opened with an essentially ecumenical statement by Scott, who asserted: "Far from undermining the foundations of Judaism and Christianity, the discovery of the Dead Sea Scrolls will help Christians and Jews to see better where these foundations stand in the soil of history."[110]

In 1956 Temple Emanu-El, a Reform Jewish congregation, invited Samuel Sandmel of Hebrew Union College to speak on the scrolls and yet again turned to Scott, this time for a response.[111]

The communities came together, again, to discuss the scrolls on 6 February 1961, when Norman Golb, then professor at Hebrew Union College and later of the University of Chicago, addressed an audience at Temple Emanu-El in Montreal on the "Religious Significance of the Dead Sea Scrolls." Two guests were in attendance that evening: Professors Wilfred Cantwell Smith, by then the director of McGill's Institute of Islamic Studies, and Stanley Frost, dean of the Faculty of Divinity. Golb's talk was the keynote lecture of the Temple's "Institute on Judaism for religious educators of various denominations." Frost suggested that Golb's lecture before Jews, Christians, and Muslims was the result of processes that had unfolded over the previous five years, leading to increased tolerance and understanding. The scrolls contributed to these processes as public discussion of them became a new trend: "Dr. Frost said the solitudes [of the religious groups] are being invaded and the isolations breaking down in Montreal. Leaders of the Protestant, Catholic and Jewish faiths today find themselves speaking to groups of other faiths on matters of information."[112]

Scott's actions and the support they received within McGill's Faculty of Divinity must be understood within this broader context and particularly with respect to the inter-faith activities in which the faculty so actively participated. While the purchase of the scrolls did not open the door immediately to adding a Jewish scholar to the faculty, or to the expansion of Jewish studies course offerings, it did successfully initiate a closer relationship between the university and the Jewish community.[113]

Finally, Scott believed the purchase of the scrolls would also assist the institution to fulfill its obligation to inspire discourse on religion in the public sphere. Scott understood that the public fascination with the scrolls could be used to attract students and the public to the study of religion. As for students, the actual fragments could serve a dual function. As well as being religious artefacts, they offered an interest for the scientifically minded. McGill historian Stanley Frost notes:

> It is a fact, in some ways regrettable, in some ways compensatory, that great wars stimulate technologies to swift advances. It was particularly true of World War II, but in this case the technologies made possible, or acted as catalysts for, new dimensions of comprehension ... The most noticeable of these advances began with rocketry ... [But i]t was not only space that expanded ... Carbon 14 and other dating technologies gave man a tool for interpreting archaeological data, and for gaining additional insights into previously gathered material. Dramatic finds such as those in the Dead Sea desert, at Mohenjo-Daro in India, at Ebla in Syria, made archaeology an exciting science again ... The horizon of the past was pushed back, and again the consequence was that man entered upon a new understanding of himself.[114]

In addition to carbon-14 dating and similar scientific testing, the need to conserve and protect McGill's fragments likewise required the expertise of scientists and the application of new technology. But, for Scott, more important than this outcome was the fact that the public was already inspired by the scrolls. Interest in the scrolls could be turned into interest in the critical study of the Bible:

> Now that the tremendous public interest in the Dead Sea Scrolls has subsided somewhat – an interest sparked by the unlikely spectacle of a pioneering essay on the subject by Edmund Wilson ... in the *New Yorker*[115] – it should be easier to view that discovery in perspective in the broad field of Biblical research. Scholars did, indeed, share something of the excitement in such a totally unexpected find, as in any field they do when important new evidence comes to light. To them, however, it was only one of many such discoveries through which our knowledge of the world in which Christianity arose and of the documents which have come down to us from it is being constantly added to.[116]

In turn, Scott reasoned, critical study of the Bible could lead to theological inquiry of a very personal kind: "The record [of the experiences of religion, that is, the Bible,] can and must be examined objectively as a literary, historical and religious datum which has come down to us from the past. But it also is a fact of objective observation that the meaning and power of the Bible is not confined to the past. In it the God who spoke through Moses and the prophets, through Jesus Christ and his disciples, still speaks to those who will listen."[117]

FUNDING THE PURCHASE

Despite James's sympathy for Scott's project, there remained a significant hurdle to overcome. The university budget could not have sustained an expenditure of this nature and a private donor had to be found. Scott had a keen appreciation for the media as intermediary between himself, a lay audience, and, most importantly, such prospective donors.[118] In January 1954 Scott penned a brief article for the *Montreal Star*.[119] It outlined the discovery of the first scrolls, the additional discovery of Cave 4 by the Bedouin and the potential importance thereof for the study of the Bible, early Judaism, and the study of Christianity. The article closed with a plea: "UNFORTUNATELY [sic] not all the manuscript finds, by any means, have yet been recovered from the hands of the Bedouin who have discovered them. The Palestine Museum and the Department of Antiquities have expended all funds at present available, and it is estimated that $15,000 to $20,000 more is needed. If a reputable education institution in this country – or its friends – will provide this urgently needed money, the Jordan Department of Antiquities will permit the acquisition and export of what is purchased, after a stated period for study of it in Jerusalem. The urgent thing is to salvage this precious material before it is too late."

The plea did not go unnoticed. Scott took a copy of the article when he went to see a potential donor, a fellow elder at the Erskine Church and an influential businessman in the Montreal community, Henry Birks. Birks was impressed by the article and agreed to approach other donors on Scott's behalf. By 1 February 1954 Birks phoned with the news that his aunt, Mrs J. Henry (Elizabeth) Birks, had offered $15,000 CAD for the purchase.[120]

While in the end Scott was responsible for finding the donor, clearly he was not working alone. Principal James was an enthusiastic supporter of the project and actively participated in the search for donors. Scott could demonstrate the importance of the scrolls for study but James could confirm their value to the status of McGill University. This team effort is evidenced from an appeal for funds to Lazarus Phillips, an important Montreal lawyer, graduate of McGill, and future Canadian senator. James established the contact but Scott was responsible for providing Phillips with the details. Scott knew his audience well. In appealing to Phillips, a prominent member of the Jewish community, he noted the importance of obtaining, "these priceless documents from a Palestinian Jewish community of the beginning of the present era."[121] Yet, when negotiating with the broader, predominantly Christian, Montreal community, Scott emphasized that the scrolls' importance is incalculable: "for they will throw the light of contemporary evidence on the century which saw the crucifixion of Jesus Christ and the burning of the Jerusalem Temple by the Romans."[122] Scott's and James's positions in finding a donor and arranging the purchase is reinforced in a letter from Ralph R. Johnson, a representative of the Birks family. In the letter James, as principal, was granted the right of final approval by the donor: "Many demands are made on the Foundation's funds, hence the reason for my telephone call to you this morning. Dr. Scott has indicated that the value of such an acquisition to McGill would be great, both as study material and in terms of prestige. If you concur in the judgement of Dr. Scott, I am authorized to contribute to the University for the purchase of these documents an amount of from $15,000.00 to $20,000.00, leaving the final decision with regard to the sum to your discretion. Our hope would be that they could be procured for the minimum amount suggested."[123]

In communicating his appreciation to the donor, Mrs Birks, James responded: "Professor Scott has undoubtedly told you of the unique quality of these fragments but I should like you to know that I share his happiness and pride in the fact that McGill will be able to acquire them through your generosity."[124]

The editor's note at the end of the *Montreal Star* article previously mentioned clearly indicates that Scott and James were negotiating a fine line in soliciting funding from a limited group of donors who might otherwise have contributed to McGill for different purposes: "Most of these rare finds will eventually reach the libraries of national museums or the large universities. It occurs to us that some of them, at least, should be obtained by McGill University. We hope that means will be found to accomplish this without disturbing the regular university budget."[125]

James's enthusiasm for the project at a time when the nature of funding for Canadian universities was in transition is all the more to be appreciated. The enormous influx of returning soldiers created a particularly acute problem for McGill. As a private institution through much of this period, McGill addressed any shortfall between student fees and operating costs by means of endowment funds and donations. But the increased number of students after the war meant that the gap between the collective student fees and the collective operational costs grew exponentially.[126] McGill, as a private institution, did not have access to the top-up funds required to address the needs of all the students and faculty. In this McGill was not alone – the same difficulties plagued other Canadian institutions. Thus, the National Council of Canadian Universities, with McGill's Principal James as its chair, began petitioning the government for statutory funds, and in 1951 the federal government of Canada agreed that the universities were to share an approximately $7 million grant payment.[127] While this was perceived as good news, McGill was left in a difficult position. Maurice Duplessis, the ultra-nationalist premier of Quebec,[128] refused the grants because he considered it an incursion of the federal government on education, which was deemed a provincial jurisdiction. The difficulty for McGill was that while James had successfully campaigned for the funds, his own institution could only benefit for a year. In 1952 Duplessis refused the grants but McGill's governors made up the shortfall. In 1954 Duplessis offered grants to Quebec institutions renewable in the subsequent years. This included McGill as beneficiary but the funding amounted to less than half of what had been promised by the federal government.[129]

At this particularly painful juncture, in 1953, while McGill was still in the grips of managing this dire lack of public funds, the opportunity presented itself to purchase the Cave 4 fragments. The university's financial hardships were evident to Scott and certainly delayed the purchase, as he noted in mid-December of that year to Harding: "I at once communicated with Principal James of McGill University, and he in turn got in touchwith [sic] a gentleman who had earlier indicated his confidence that funds could be secured for this purpose from private donors whom he had in mind.

So far there has been no tangible result, but I do not draw pessimistic conclusions from this. The people concerned are extremely busy, and just now there is a major financial campaign on for support of the general University budget. It might have been easier to secure more immediate action if I had been able to follow up at once the proposal originally submitted to Principal James in September."[130]

Nevertheless, even before finding a definite donor, Scott continued to negotiate the terms of the purchase with Harding. In early December 1953 he requested details concerning the process by which fragments purchased with funds from McGill would be identified as belonging to the university; who was caring for them and how they were being cared for, and when the fragments might be ready for export. Arrangements for the payments were also discussed. Scott was concerned as to whether the funds should be directed to the Department of Antiquities of Jordan or to the PAM.[131] This question was particularly pertinent as the current arrangements for purchase were being made in negotiation with Harding, as representative of the Jordanian Government, but the original offer had been presented by Roland de Vaux, associated with the PAM. On 30 December 1953 Harding confirmed the Jordanian Government's agreement to allow McGill to purchase materials with the proviso that they remain in Jerusalem until their study was completed.[132] Because of this letter, Scott was finally able to confirm the negotiated deal with the Government of Jordan. For the first time, long after he had promised a donation to Harding, Scott had tangible proof as leverage to raise funds from prospective donors.[133] The tacit agreement to fund the project, once received from the Birks family, allowed Scott to continue negotiations with Harding and to secure the approval of the principal and the Board of Governors of McGill. With regard to Harding, a series of cables between Scott and Harding, on 15, 16, and 17 February 1954, show that Scott sought assurance of the provenance and antiquity of the scroll fragments before the purchase was finalized. Only once Harding confirmed that all the fragments were indeed from Cave 4 did Scott indicate to him that funding was assured.[134] Thus the negotiations between Scott, Harding, the Birks family, and Principal James were only completed by March 1954, when the first payment was made.

SECURING AUTHENTICITY AND ANTIQUITY

Concern for the nature of the content, provenance, and antiquity of the fragments to be blindly acquired by McGill was not inappropriate. G.R. Driver in 1951 famously observed, as Frank Moore Cross pointed out: "what is the date of these [scroll] copies? This is an exceedingly difficult question to answer ... Professor Albright answered this question in an hour, Mr. Trever somewhat modestly spent two days over it!"[135] As indicated by the implied sarcasm as to the determination of date, doubts were rife.[136] The risk that Scott and Principal James took on behalf of McGill should not be underestimated. No other institution would commit as much to the purchase of Cave 4 fragments as McGill.

Despite Scott's explicit confidence in Harding and de Vaux with regard to the authenticity of the materials they were purchasing sight unseen, by this time Solomon Zeitlin[137] had commandeered the *Jewish Quarterly Review* (*JQR*) for the purpose of challenging the antiquity of the scrolls. Between 1949 and 1964 Zeitlin wrote some two dozen articles questioning their age and authenticity.[138] In the period in which the McGill purchase took place, he published four articles.[139] Perhaps most important in this regard is his "The Fiction of the Recent Discoveries Near the Dead Sea," in which he explicitly challenged the material claimed to be from Cave 4: "Possibly the Bedouin who discovered the Hebrew mss. in caves near the Dead Sea placed them there in advance, as a great financial value had been set upon the previously supposedly discovered Hebrew scrolls. The mss. may have come from the Geniza,[140] or from the libraries and synagogues which were sacked and looted first in 1929, and later during the war between the Jews and the Arab countries."[141] The debate in *JQR* was fuelled in part by Tovia Wechsler's[142] recollection that he was shown two scrolls (derived from Cave 1) at St Mark's Monastery in the summer of 1947, one the Isaiah Scroll and the other he supposedly recognized as a haftarot scroll.[143] He believed the latter was relatively late and concluded that both scrolls were not especially old. In 1949 Zeitlin published, "Where Is the Scroll of the Haftarot?"[144] The article is significant for the debate regarding the authenticity of the scrolls, as it was the "lateness" of the marginal notes that aided detractors in arguing that both it and the Isaiah Scroll were forgeries. Wechsler and Zeitlin used this account to argue that the story of the discovery of the scrolls could not be trusted and that the fragments had likely come from a genizah located near or in Israel.[145] This debate continued for years and during Scott's 1951 tenure at ASOR in Jerusalem the *JQR* published a number of articles by Zeitlin and Wechsler that raised the matter of the whereabouts of the haftarot scroll once again.[146] Winnett and Scott, both at ASOR in Jerusalem in 1951, even went in search of the missing scroll. Millar Burrows recorded their visit in his recollections of the events, published in the *JQR*: "On March 21, 1951, Professor Winnett wrote to me as follows: 'This afternoon Prof. R.B.Y. Scott and I called on Father Boulos Gelph to inquire about the Hebrew scroll concerning which you wrote to Dr. Pritchard. Father Boulos had only yesterday received a letter from the Archbishop asking him to make the scroll available. He, and also his interpreter Bar Som, assured us that the only Hebrew manuscript which they had in 1947 was a comparatively modern scroll of the Torah which had been presented to the late Archbishop by a Jew named Phinehas in 1929.'"[147]

Apparently Scott's participation in these activities inspired his commitment to preserving what he firmly believed were indeed authentic antiquities. Although his impression of this outing is not preserved in his papers, it seems that the inability to find the mystery haftarot scroll at St Mark's allowed him to conclude, like Burrows, that the scrolls were authentic and that Wechsler had erroneously identified what he had seen.[148] In the words of Eileen Schuller, "And so, with the testimony of two Canadian scholars, the matter was put to rest."[149]

Concern about the authenticity and antiquity of the scrolls also disturbed potential British sources of funding. As to the British Museum's reluctance to provide funds for the Dead Sea Scrolls, John Allegro commented to his wife, "It's being left to the Yanks and the French to get in on them. I suppose it springs from the scepticism with which they were received in Oxford circles, and the country has followed suit."[150] The debates concerning the dating of the material were wide-ranging and Oxford professor G.R. Driver, who, unlike Zeitlin, in 1950 and beyond was more open to the scrolls' possible antiquity, continued to be concerned about their potentially late date based on archaeological and palaeographic grounds.[151]

Nevertheless, Scott, and therefore also McGill, were not particularly distracted by these concerns. William F. Albright, the father of Biblical archaeology in the United States, had made his feelings about the scrolls' authenticity clear from the time of their discovery. In responding to the challenges of Zeitlin and those who sided with him, Albright had already commented in 1951, before the discovery of Cave 4 and the additional evidence that it provided, that:

> It is true that there are a few recent writers who have denied the authenticity and antiquity of the Scrolls, but their arguments are without merit and have been rejected by all competent students who have come to the subject with sufficient background and who have kept themselves fully informed of the progress of discovery and research. After the excavation of the cave and the study of the finds by the leading specialists in this country, England, the Continent, and Palestine, we may rest assured that the Cave Scroll of Isaiah dates from the neighborhood of 100 B.C. ...

and that not a single piece found in the cave is later than the early years of the Herodian Age at latest.¹⁵²

A communication from Albright directly to Scott as the McGill negotiations were concluding suggests that Scott may have been even more convinced of the scrolls' antiquity and importance for Old Testament scholarship than Albright: "Though I have been rapped on the knuckles from all directions for rashness in proclaiming the importance of the Dead Sea Scrolls, I have not ventured to go as far as you suggest going. However, I think that you are right — certainly in principle ... In any case, I'll back you up."¹⁵³

THE JOHN HENRY BIRKS COLLECTION OF ANCIENT PALESTINIAN MANUSCRIPTS

Therefore, with full confidence in the scrolls' antiquity and authenticity, on 4 March 1954 McGill University established an account in the name of the J.H. Birks Manuscript Collection with a donation of $20,000 CAD from the John Henry Birks Foundation under the supervision of R.B.Y. Scott.¹⁵⁴ A first cheque from the account made out to Harding for $5,000 USD was issued by the university on 4 March 1954.¹⁵⁵ A consequent sum of $10,363.52 USD was issued on 8 April 1954.¹⁵⁶ The communications between Scott and Harding make clear that neither man had been provided with any additional details as to the identification of the manuscript fragments. Scott knew nothing more than that McGill University was to receive fragments from the collection of material retrieved from the caves of the Dead Sea. At that time there was no indication of quantity or specific identification. For this information, the first institutional purchaser outside the Government of Jordan had to wait at least another year.

In the light of events to follow, it is important to emphasize the exact nature of the purchase agreement reached between R.B.Y. Scott on behalf of McGill University on the one hand and Lankester Harding on behalf of the Jordanian Government on the other. No contract between the two parties was found in any of the existing documentation.¹⁵⁷ This situation eventually caused problems for McGill but led to more formal arrangements with institutions who became involved in the acquisition of material from Cave 11. Scott nevertheless provided a summary of the nature of the purchase agreement put forth as three "conditions" in his 1981 personal recollection. According to this account, the agreement stipulated:

1. The scrolls had to remain in Jerusalem, "with the committee until ready for publication."
2. Furthermore, that, "when the distribution was made to contributors, pieces of the same manuscripts would be kept together; any exchanges would be for pieces of equal value."
3. The third condition was, "unmentioned but ... taken for granted," namely that, "government policy would be the same when the Scrolls were ready for shipment as it had been when the bargain was struck and the payments were paid." [158]

The final condition was indeed a rather naive assumption on the part of Scott and his negotiating partners, given the volatile politics of the Middle East past and present, which in the end proved the final undoing of the transaction.

When McGill made its first payments in March and April 1954, the university bought its share of Cave 4 documents with implicit trust in the *bona fides* of de Vaux and Harding. Harding's response to Scott after the first purchase indicated that he was particularly worried about possible disappointment as a result of misplaced expectations. "Again, I must emphasize," wrote Harding to Scott on 11 March 1954, "that I can give no idea of the contents of what I propose to buy for you, for as you can imagine it takes some time to identify the book to which a fragment belongs, but I think I can safely say that it will be a representative collection."[159] On 17 April 1954, a week after the second payment dated 8 April 1954, Professor Wilfred Cantwell Smith,[160] then director of the renowned McGill Institute of Islamic Studies, became the first university representative to see the fragments in the scrollery in Jerusalem. Smith met with Harding in person. His visit should not be taken as implied mistrust in Harding as mediator. Rather, it indicated an understandable need for confirmation of the purchase by a representative of the institution itself. Scott wanted a McGill envoy to have face-to-face contact with Harding. He was convinced that only in this way could the university gain an understanding of what was really happening in the museum in Jerusalem, something that could not be conveyed in writing alone.[161] Smith visited the scrollery for less than a day on his way back from attending a conference of the Egyptian Society for Historical Studies in Cairo. He met with Harding, who elaborated on the importance of McGill's involvement. Harding also stressed that McGill's collection of scroll fragments would be the largest outside Jerusalem. Furthermore, Harding seemed particularly perturbed by the British Museum and other universities who refused to act on any requests for funding or involvement. This, of course, only increased his appreciation of McGill's efforts.[162] During his visit, Smith toured the Jordanian Government's collection of Qumran fragmentary material and confirmed that it was pressed and arranged between approximately sixty plates of glass. McGill's fragments were stamped with the identifying letter "S" (for Scott) and were arranged under an additional twenty-four glass plates. The work undertaken by Frank Cross, Roland de Vaux, and Józef Milik (the three team members that Smith was informed were to work on the McGill collection) was, according to Smith, particularly impressive given that they had received the material assigned to McGill but a week before his arrival.[163]

Following Smith's return, he submitted a written report on his Jerusalem visit to Scott, received on 21 May 1954.[164] Immediately afterwards, Scott prepared notes for a press release for James to finally announce the purchase to the public:

> Notes for Press Release re
> "John Henry Birks Collection of Ancient Palestinian Manuscripts"
> (May, 1954)
>
> Principal F. Cyril James announces the acquisition for the Faculty of Divinity, McGill University, through the munificence of the John Henry Birks Foundation, of a collection of manuscript fragments of the Old Testament and related works dating from the beginning of the Christian era and earlier. These will be of the utmost importance for the study of Judaism in the time of Christ, and for the study of the Old Testament text. They are part of a find made in a cave in the Judaean Desert near the Dead Sea in September 1952, the remainder of which is in the hands of the Jordan Government and the Palestine Museum. The Faculty of Divinity collection will be unique outside of Palestine. It was obtained for McGill by purchase from the Beduin [sic] who made the find, as a result of prolonged negotiations conducted by Professor R.B.Y. Scott of the Faculty of Divinity with the Department of Antiquities of the Jordan Government. The Director of the Dept. of Antiquities, G. Lankester Harding, F.S.A., has declared that the genuineness of the documents is beyond question, and has written to "congratulate the University on having acquired what is certainly the finest collection of these unique manuscript fragments outside the original Government collection".
>
> Since the accidental discovery in 1947 of the famous "Dead Sea Scrolls", including a complete copy of the Book of Isaiah, five other

caves containing parts of the library of the Jewish sect of the Essenes have been found in the same vicinity, about ten miles south of Jericho. The ruins of the sect's community centre at Khirbet Qumran have been excavated by British, French and American archaeologists. The most extensive and important finds were made in what is now known as "Cave Four", and of these about one quarter have been obtained for McGill. They will remain at the Palestine Museum in Jerusalem (Jordan) for about two years for classification and study, before being shipped to this country.

The excavation of the community centre of the Essenes at Khirbet Qumran by Father R. de Vaux of l'École Biblique in Jerusalem has demonstrated conclusively that it was occupied by the sect from the second century B.C. to the First Jewish Revolt, as a result of which Jerusalem was destroyed by the Romans in 70 A.D. Evidently on the approach of Roman armies the Essenes were dispersed, after concealing their library in surrounding caves so well hidden that some were not discovered until the twentieth century. Ancient authors record similar discoveries in the same vicinity in the third and in the eighth centuries A.D. In the community centre have been found the remains of a "scriptorium", with a table, inkpots and a basin apparently for ritual washings; here evidently some at least of the newly found manuscripts were copied by the scribes from older examples.

The fragments of the John Henry Birks Collection are still in process of being cleaned and identified, so that it is not yet known what it comprises, except that there are included both Biblical and non-Biblical manuscripts. The material previously acquired by the Jordan Government from the same cave includes parts of every book of the Old Testament except Chronicles, and also commentaries, paraphrases, apocryphal works (some previously unknown), together with ritual documents of the Essene sect.

These finds, of which McGill has been so fortunate as to acquire a significant portion, will throw a flood of light on the history of Judaism in the post-Maccabaean period, and on the crucial epoch of the rise of primitive Christianity. In addition, they give glimpses of the form of the Old Testament text a thousand years before the copying of the Hebrew scrolls from which our English Bibles and other translations have been made. The study of them will keep scholars busy for fifty years or more, and the results of such studies must be of far-reaching importance for the Christian and Jewish faiths.

James's press release on 22 May 1954, although technically written by Scott, had not been completely motivated by Smith's confirmation of the quality of McGill's purchase, although the press did respond positively to the fact that Smith had seen the scrolls in person.[165] Scott and James had discussed the idea of a press release at a 24 March 1954 meeting and had agreed to wait until McGill's fragments were identified and photographs were made available for publication along with the press release. They assumed this would happen by September 1954.[166] Their announcement was moved up in no small part because the announcement of the gift from the Birks family was published in McGill's 1953–54 annual report, listed among gifts received for restricted purposes as, "Birks, John Henry, Foundation, for Ancient Palestinian Manuscripts .... $15,000." The report also contained a review of the Faculty of Divinity by Dean Thomson,[167] who noted: "By the generosity of the Birks Trust, the University has been able to acquire important Mss. and Scrolls that have recently been discovered in Palestine. These Scrolls are of great antiquity, belonging to the first and second centuries of the Christian era and are likely to have important bearings on the text of the Old Testament and are related to the life and times of the apostolic age. When these Scrolls are brought to the University, they will be a unique collection of great value and will provide important material for research."[168] Given the public nature of these documents, it was anticipated that news of the purchase would be forthcoming without any official control over the manner and details of the report. James and Scott therefore had little choice but to pre-empt this by an earlier announcement in the press.

Despite the announcement's tendency towards Canadian pride in the purchase, the irony is that the May 1954 press release was carried only by the two local papers in Montreal, the *Gazette* and the *Montreal Star* (the French language press does not appear to have covered the story), as well as the *New York Times* and the London *Times*.[169] No notice was apparently sent to newspapers in Ottawa or Toronto, and it was only in August 1955, more than a year after the event became public, that Scott appeared for the first time in a radio address on the matter for the Canadian Broadcasting Corporation (CBC).[170] ASOR's mouthpiece, the *Bulletin of the American Schools of Oriental Research* (BASOR), carried the scholarly version of the announcement entitled "Acquisition of Dead Sea Scroll Fragments by McGill University" in October 1954: "McGill University has announced the acquisition of the 'John Henry Birks Collection of Ancient Palestinian Manuscripts.' The material is all from Qumran IV and apparently comprises the balance of the fragments from this cave which the Government had not already acquired ... The material is to remain at the Palestine Museum for about two years for study and will be published along with the rest by Oxford University Press."[171] Preparing the announcement for publication gave *BASOR*'s editor, William Albright, the opportunity to congratulate Scott personally on the purchase and to inform him that the news he was hearing about the contents of the Cave 4 fragments from Frank Cross and others was "very exciting."[172]

McGill students did not receive a full account of the purchase until the autumn of 1954 when Scott's journalist son, John, wrote a multi-page article for the *McGill News*.[173] Parenthetically, news of the purchase was shared with Canada's Jewish community most explicitly when the Canadian Jewish Congress received permission to reprint John Scott's *McGill News* article in its October-November 1954 *Congress Bulletin*.[174]

The announcements in the press were successful in helping Scott keep his promise to James that the purchase would garner McGill international recognition. By August 1954 Scott was already able to report to James that:

> Several well-known Biblical scholars have expressed great interest in, and envy of, the McGill acquisition. Prof. Frank Cross of Chicago,[175] who examined the fragments in Jerusalem, says that the 'farsighted action' of McGill undoubtedly saved much precious material from dispersion and loss.[176] Prof. Millar Burrows of Yale is noting the acquisition in a book he is writing this summer.[177] Prof. W.D. Davies of Duke[178] told me that he feels New Testament studies will have to wait on the fuller identification and valuation of these 'very important' finds. I heard from the Secretary of the British Society for Old Testament Study[179] that the McGill acquisition had been announced at the Jubilee meeting in Edinburgh in July.[180]

In later histories of these events McGill's acquisition is dated to the time of the press release at the end of May or early June of 1954, but the R.B.Y. Scott Papers indicate that a number of discrepancies exist in the sequence of events as outlined.[181] Although McGill is correctly acknowledged as the "first foreign institution to purchase scroll fragments," this was, first of all, not "a one-time purchase for $15,000."[182] A second and quite substantial additional purchase of $4,200 USD was made on 29 December 1955,[183] to bring the total to nearly $20,000 spent on the scrolls by McGill.[184] Second, the archived documents indicate that the first purchase took place as two distinct events on 4 March and 8 April 1954.[185] This discrepancy is significant in that by moving the events from June back to March, Scott's actions at a time when many in the scholarly community were still volubly expressing their uncertainty as to the worth, age, extent, and nature of the finds seem all the more remarkable. Corroboration for the antiquity of the scrolls was hard to find as the editorial team had only just started its work and fragments originating from Cave 4 continued to be purchased in a constant stream until 1958.

This confirmed earlier purchase date in March 1954 and the Scott Papers' indication that Harding had been given the go-ahead even earlier, at the end of January of that year, confirming the purchase amount and possible date of final payment,[186] means that McGill's negotiations of purchase coincided with the constitution of the editorial committee.[187] The arrangements included an invitation by Harding to McGill to appoint a scholar to the team as early as October of 1953 in a letter from Harding to Scott: "I am very glad that you agree to the conditions of the fragments remaining here until completion of study: this is a most important point. Perhaps you have some one [sic] you would like to send to assist in this work? I am trying to bring together an international group of scholars for the purpose."[188] This invitation was thus issued at the time (October 1953) when József Milik started work on the Cave 4 fragments in the scrollery in Jerusalem. Frank Moore Cross, the first of the Cave 4 team to arrive, began work in May of the same year, months before McGill demonstrated interest in purchasing the documents. Ultimately, no scholar from McGill joined the team as a full-fledged member, although Willard Oxtoby, who had worked on the concordance of Cave 4 non-biblical texts in the late 1950s,[189] did eventually join the McGill faculty from 1960 until 1964.[190] Note, however, that the scholars who worked on the concordance were not appointed officially to the editorial team.

Although McGill never responded to the offer to appoint a scholar to the Cave 4 editorial team, a letter from Scott to Harding indicates that Scott planned to spend a significant portion of 1955 studying McGill's material at the scrollery in Jerusalem. "I am beginning to hope," wrote Scott in March 1954, "that I may be able to come out to Jordan myself about a year from now, to work for two or three months under the experts who are examining all this material, and thus to be in a better position to continue co-operation with them after the material has come to McGill. We wish to collaborate in the most effective way in scholarly studies of our part of this material, and not merely to hoard it as a curiosity."[191] On 23 April 1954 de Vaux wrote to R.B.Y. Scott in response to this wish. It appears from de Vaux's response that Scott understood his actions as an acceptance of Harding's offer to join the editorial team. "We will naturally be very happy to welcome you to Jerusalem as part of the team preparing the edition of the manuscripts," wrote a diplomatic de Vaux, "but I doubt that a stay of two or three months will be sufficient for effective work: you'll have just the time to learn how we manipulate the fragments and to begin to assemble them and to read them. Guided by experience, we ask of our collaborators at least a year of work in Jerusalem."[192] Eventually Scott's visit was further reduced to just a month as he prepared to take up a position at Princeton University in the fall of 1955. Thus it came about that McGill never appointed a representative to the exclusive Cave 4 editorial team.[193]

Harding's invitation to designate a McGill scholar to the editorial team had come as part of the negotiations for the purchase in October 1953. The PAM archives reveal that Harding made a similar offer to the British Museum in 1952, noting that if the museum purchased fragments they had to wait until they were sorted and studied before export: "But this task would need several Scholars to work on it, and it would be most desirable if the British Museum, both on its own behalf and as a Member of the Board of the Palestine Museum, could send someone to participate in the work."[194] Although the purchase of documents was considered, the British Museum could not accept a position on the editorial team: "There is no question about the British Museum being ready to consider the purchase of part of the find, but we could not help you by sending a member of the staff to assist in the long business of the survey and publication of the material. Indeed, as the member of the staff concerned would obviously be Leveen, I suppose for political and religious reasons, even a short visit of inspection would be impracticable."[195]

Whether Harding had the authority to offer membership may be debated, but it is worth noting that Scott presumed open access to the scrollery in 1954 and intended to assert this in 1955. In April 1954, Scott raised the possibility with James for McGill to apply for an institutional membership to ASOR. Again, McGill's presumed open invitation to appoint a scholar to the Cave 4 editorial team is never part of his argument to James in favour of institutional membership. It may therefore safely be assumed that Harding at no time indicated to Scott that ASOR membership, as ASOR was a trustee of the PAM, was needed to guarantee McGill participation on the editorial team. This is very important, as it runs counter to the generally expounded version of events as relayed by Weston Fields: "In his capacity as Curator of the Museum Harding took charge of the appointment of the Cave 4 Team. The team was to be composed of two representatives from each of the four prominent schools of archaeology represented on the Museum's Board: French, American, British and German. The political situation made it impossible to include representation from Israel."[196] Frank Moore Cross appears to contradict Fields's version of the centrality of Harding's role, but Harding's singular role is nevertheless confirmed in the Scott correspondence of the McGill archives.[197] Cross, however, states: "I have discussed the story of the origin of the international team in some detail owing to the distorted accounts which have appeared in print, notably the claim that de Vaux appointed the team and drew its members from among his cronies, mostly Catholics, and an alternative, equally tendentious claim that Gerald Harding, the Director of Antiquities of Jordan, made the appointments ... the ratification by Harding was *pro forma* since he was *ex officio* secretary of the Board as curator of the Museum, in addition to being Director of Antiquities of Jordan."[198]

COMPLETE SCROLLS FOR MCGILL?

Despite the limited attention it received from the broader Canadian media, the press release concerning McGill's purchase did have international ramifications and stimulated the interest of another hitherto unknown party: on 3 June 1954 McGill was offered four Dead Sea Scrolls. On 5 August 1947 Mar Athanasius Yeshue Samuel, the Syrian Archbishop in Jerusalem, had purchased from Kando four Dead Sea Scrolls from Cave 1. He paid 60 JD. The scrolls consisted of 1QIsaiah^a (1QIsa^a), the Genesis Apocryphon (1QapGen), Pesher Habbakuk (1QpHab), and the Rule of the Community (1QS). In 1949 the archbishop left for the United States, where in 1957 he became the metropolitan of the Syrian Orthodox Church of Antioch in the United States and Canada. He took the four scrolls with him in the hope of finding an American educational institution willing to purchase them to fund the church. The archbishop held onto the scrolls for close to seven years, as he had great difficulty in attracting a buyer.

The availability of the four scrolls for purchase was first announced in the *New York Times* in April 1949[199] but they were only sold in 1954. According to Edmund Wilson, the archbishop was unable to sell the scrolls in the United States because their publication by ASOR[200] meant that libraries and scholars no longer required the originals to have access to the content of the scrolls. While it had been hoped that their publication and study might increase their value, this seemed to have had the opposite effect.[201] By contrast, Hershel Shanks has argued convincingly that the archbishop's inability to dispose profitably of the scrolls resulted from the lack of demonstrable title to the material: "As a self-proclaimed sovereign, Jordan claimed title to the scrolls. From Jordan's viewpoint, Mar Samuel had smuggled the scrolls out of East Jerusalem (and the Old City), which was also in Jordanian hands at the time. Since Jordan's claim to the scrolls had appeared in the press, Mar Samuel surely knew of it. In short, he could not give good title. Any purchaser would have to worry about a suit by the Hashemite Kingdom of Jordan, seeking return of the scrolls – any purchaser, that is, except Israel; Israel and Jordan were technically at war. For Jordan to sue Israel would imply recognition of the Jewish state, a step that Jordan would be unwilling to take."[202]

To complicate matters, Israel had taken the bold step of openly claiming ownership to the archbishop's scrolls. An article in the *Palestine Post* on 21 April 1949 reported that the Hebrew University (via Eleazar Sukenik) had negotiated an agreement with the archbishop to purchase the scrolls from him but the outbreak of war had interrupted the sale.[203] The Hebrew University made a public appeal, since the scrolls were offered for sale in the United States, that foreign institutions should, "if approached with an offer of any of the manuscripts ... reject the offer so as to make it possible for them to be returned. The appeal declared that this country [Israel] was the proper place for the manuscripts as they belonged to the spiritual heritage of all its communities."[204]

Solomon Zeitlin continued to raise the matter of the ownership of these scrolls well into 1957, insisting that the archbishop had smuggled the scrolls out of Jerusalem despite Jordanian claims to ownership,[205] an issue he had raised first in 1950.[206] Zeitlin's interest in the ownership of the scrolls served his argument that they were medieval or later, and perhaps even forgeries. From his perspective, the story of their discovery was so mired in contradictions that it simply could not be true.

The archbishop's scrolls were also offered to McGill. In a letter dated 3 June 1954, Charles Manoog,[207] acting on behalf of Mar Samuel, offered the scrolls to McGill, inspired by the news of the university's earlier purchases made public at the end of May. He wrote to Principal James: "As a trustee of the 'Four Dead Sea[208] Scrolls' which you no doubt are acquainted with, I would like to inform you that these scrolls are now offered for sale, I am enclosing a leaflet describing these scrolls."[209] Eventually Yigael Yadin[210] would purchase them, by means of an intermediary, on behalf of Israel.

The archbishop later noted the importance of McGill's announcement as impetus for him to try once again to sell the scrolls. In the final pages of his autobiography he notes that by 1953 caring for the North American church had become his priority. The scrolls weighed on him as he felt they were robbing him of funds and energy. He nonetheless believed that he had little choice but to patiently wait for the day when God called upon him to reveal the scrolls one more time:

McGill Buys the Dead Sea Scrolls

The call came early in May of 1954.[211] It was long distance – Montreal. I could not guess who the caller could be.
"Good afternoon, Your Excellency," my friend said as he identified himself. "Have you seen the papers?"
Busy with correspondence that morning and planning an immediate trip to the Jacksonville congregation, I had only glanced at them. I told him this slowly, taking the moment to prepare myself for whatever new charges, suspicions, vilifications, I might now learn of.
"A school here – McGill University – has just purchased some of the Dead Sea Scrolls."
"Has – what?" It seemed impossible. Certainly, Israel would not sell hers, and if the story referred to the scrolls now held in trust, it was a brazen fabrication.
"No, Your Excellency," he explained. "Not the Scrolls. As a matter of fact, it was only a group of fragments. They purchased them from the Jordan Government."
"Did they reveal the price paid?" I asked.
"Yes, Your Excellency. Fifteen thousand dollars."
Fifteen thousand dollars – *for only a group of fragments!*
Certainly the time was ripe now for a more direct approach. I had considered advertising, but the trustee, Mr. Charles Manoog, did not encourage me. I paced the floor of my study. "Is this the time?" I asked myself. "Is this the way? Dear God, help me to know the right course, I prayed."[212]

Therefore, as a direct result of McGill's announcement of purchase, the archbishop placed the now famous advertisement offering the four scrolls for sale in the classifieds of the *Wall Street Journal* on 1 June 1954. Before discussions with McGill could commence, clandestine representatives of Israel responded and opened negotiations for the purchase of the advertised scrolls. As it was, McGill did not receive Manoog's letter until 7 June 1954,[213] after negotiations between Yigael Yadin's representative and the archbishop were well underway. According to Yadin, his representative wrote to the address provided in the *Wall Street Journal* on 2 June 1954 indicating interest in purchasing the scrolls. A reply from Charles Manoog, dated 4 June 1954, was received two days later.[214] By 18 June 1954 the archbishop had agreed to the sale and by 1 July 1954 it was formally concluded. It was not announced to the public until early 1955.[215]

In the end, because of a lack of additional funds and of clear title, McGill would certainly have declined the offer, although the university never had the opportunity to do so because of Yadin's swift response. Scott replied to Manoog on behalf of James that McGill appreciated having been informed of the availability of the scrolls but was in no position to make additional purchases. At a personal level, Scott inquired as to the price and whether, in light of Jordanian antiquities laws, clear title of ownership could be provided.[216] Scott's letter is remarkable in that it demonstrates that he had no similar concern as to whether his purchase of the Birks fragments broke Jordanian law.

McGill's involvement in these events, although hitherto not mentioned in any official history of the Dead Sea Scrolls, did garner some local press interest. In February 1955, when Israel's purchase of the four scrolls was finally made public by Israeli Prime Minister Moshe Sharett, a Montreal *Gazette* headline declared: "Price: $250,000. Israel Buys 4 Scrolls Once Offered McGill."[217]

IDENTIFYING MCGILL'S FRAGMENTS

In contrast to the offer from Manoog, where the scrolls presented were made available to be examined and identified before purchase, Scott and McGill still remained in the dark as to the exact nature of the collection of fragments they had purchased from the Government of Jordan. Although Wilfred Cantwell Smith saw McGill's collection of fragments in April 1954, he could do very little in an afternoon to identify any of it. But he did confirm that the John Henry Birks Collection contained both biblical and extra-biblical fragments: "The most interesting so far noted was a fairly large fragment of Daniel (I did not make a note of this at the time, and somehow my memory is uncertain: I do believe that it was Daniel, but somehow 'Numbers' also plays in my mind), which was of a version quite unlike anything so far identified."[218] Given that the fragments had only been in the museum for a week, it was perfectly understandable that they had not yet been identified. However, by early June 1954 Scott was growing impatient with the lack of information coming from Jerusalem. In early June Scott reminded Harding that he had promised him photographs and expressed his disappointment that he had not received any in time for the first press release and McGill's convocation.[219] A letter to Frank Cross, dated 22 June 1954,[220] apparently addressed the same issue. Cross received Scott's missive only in August of that year after he had returned to the United States from Jerusalem and the best Cross, at the time on vacation in Wisconsin, could do was to let Scott know that McGill now owned the largest piece of Daniel (presumably the same piece recalled with great uncertainty by Wilfred Cantwell Smith):

> I cannot tell you anything specific as to content. I could have had I heard from you in Jerusalem. The reason is simply that the lots from Cave Four each interlock like the confused pieces of a jig-saw puzzle. I do remember the lot was unusually well preserved (though like the others extremely fragmentary). Some exquisite pieces of the LXX-type Samuel were in it, of course. As Harding intimated to you, it contains pieces of the same mss with which we have been working. They were stamped on the reverse for McGill, and then identified, and placed in position with their counterparts from other lots. Two other lots were bought and treated similarly this spring, so that they are mixed in my head – as you can imagine, with some 200 mss in the entire lot, and each separate lot giving a fairly full representation of the whole. My memory only applies to the biblical mss but I think the largest piece of a Dan. MS belongs to McGill. I think it is of no help to you, however, for me to guess.[221]

Finally, on 31 August 1954, Scott received infra-red photographs of some of the McGill fragments, along with the classic picture of scholars at work in the scrollery.[222] The pictures had only been taken in late July.[223] Harding permitted the publication of two of the pictures in the aforementioned *McGill News* article by John Scott: a picture of the men at work and one plate of fragments marked, "Sample Plate S."[224] From these pictures Scott was able, with a bit of labour, to deduce some of what was in the collection. Along with a number of sectarian documents, he identified portions of five chapters of the Book of Daniel,[225] chapter 2 of Jonah,[226] and chapter 32 of Deuteronomy.[227] He was particularly interested in the Deuteronomy text because it shared a number of similarities with the Septuagint version – the Greek translation of the Old Testament.[228] Scott did not receive a full accounting of the McGill collection until he produced the list himself on his visit to the scrollery in the summer of 1955.[229]

PRINCETON UNIVERSITY CALLS

Beginning in December 1954 Scott's hitherto straightforward professional existence became complicated. It began with his request for a leave of absence from April to August 1955, along with appropriate funding for travel to Jerusalem to participate in the study of McGill's fragments.[230]

Photograph of plate of scroll fragments purchased for the McGill collection, PAM 41.207, 1954. Courtesy of the Israel Antiquities Authority.

The leave was granted on 9 March 1955. Funding was secured from Dean J. Thomson of the Faculty of Divinity, with an additional grant from the J.H. Birks Foundation in support of the study of the "Collection of Ancient Manuscripts." In November of the previous year Scott had been approached to assume the principalship of the United Theological College in Montreal. But in March 1955 he withdrew his name from consideration as he was of the opinion that his future role in academia was differently inclined: "it is in Biblical studies that I feel that I can make my widest and most lasting contribution."[231] Scott's withdrawal foreshadowed a letter dated 30 March 1955 in which he announced that he was leaving McGill University for a position at Princeton University.[232] Princeton initiated a Graduate Studies Program in Religion in 1955, although Religious Studies was instituted there as a discipline in 1940 (the department was established in 1944). The appointment of

Photograph of plate of scroll fragments purchased for the McGill collection, PAM 41.208, 1954. Courtesy of the Israel Antiquities Authority.

a senior scholar in Old Testament was part of an initiative to firmly entrench this project at Princeton. Scott accepted the newly established named professorship, the William H. Danforth Professorship of Religion, which he retained until his retirement in 1968.[233] Despite his decision to leave McGill University, Scott remained committed to the John Henry Birks Collection of Judaean Desert Scroll Fragments, as the purchase was now formally known. Scott wrote to Principal James indicating his desire to continue participating in the process of securing McGill's materials and shared this with the Birks Foundation: "My one serious hesitation in accepting the Princeton invitation is the responsibility I feel to the donor[234] and to McGill for completing the setting up of the J.H. Birks Collection ... I have a deep interest in carrying the project to a successful conclusion."[235] Scott was hopeful that the short overnight train journey between Princeton and Montreal meant that he could continue to participate in related activities. He wanted the scrolls to remain an important part of his academic pursuits.[236] Sadly it transpired

Photograph of plate of scroll fragments purchased for the McGill collection, PAM 41.209, 1954. Courtesy of the Israel Antiquities Authority.

that although he did write a number of popular pieces about the scrolls, they never became a central part of his work and he eventually turned his attention to other interests.

How might the history of McGill's scrolls have differed had Scott opted to stay in Montreal? This is impossible to determine. But the effect of Scott's departure had a clear impact, as the story of the purchase changed course considerably after Scott left McGill in the fall of 1955. This was exacerbated in 1956, when Harding was removed from his position as director of antiquities. Thus, in a single year two of the primary players in the initial purchase were lost.[237] It took more than a year before McGill found a replacement for Scott.

Scott's intended, but declared all-too-short, three-month trip to Jerusalem, was thus further truncated by his move to Princeton, and no McGill scholar was ever appointed to the international editorial team. Yet, despite his resignation from McGill, the Birks Foundation and McGill still funded Scott's

Photograph of plate of scroll fragments purchased for the McGill collection, PAM 41.210, 1954. This photograph was used to illustrate John Scott's 1954 article in the *McGill News* which first brought the purchase to the attention of the university's faculty, students, and alumni ("The Dead Sea Scrolls," p. 24). Courtesy of the Israel Antiquities Authority.

month-long trip to Jerusalem because it was perceived as part of the ongoing process of negotiating the study and transfer of McGill's collection.[238]

SCOTT IN JERUSALEM

Scott left Montreal for Jerusalem on 27 April 1955 and returned on 28 May 1955. During this period he toured the excavation site at Qumran with Roland de Vaux, who had directed that season's excavation until just a few weeks before.[239] This gave Scott the opportunity to discuss the history of the excavations with him. De Vaux told Scott that neither he nor Harding had originally planned to excavate the settlement. They had hoped

Three of the photographs from the PAM which Scott received were marked in the lower left with "Sample Plate S" where "S" indicated that the purchase was for "Scott". Courtesy of the Israel Antiquities Authority.

Scholars at work in the Jerusalem Scrollery – PAM 41.212, 1954. This photograph was used to illustrate John Scott's 1954 article in the *McGill News* which first brought the purchase to the attention of the university's faculty, students, and alumni ("The Dead Sea Scrolls," p. 24). Courtesy of the Israel Antiquities Authority.

to explore some of the caves to confirm the provenance of the scrolls on the market, but no more. Harding and de Vaux had wandered through the minimal surface remains in 1949 and, as a result, de Vaux changed his mind about digging: "'What led you to reconsider, and undertake the excavation?' I [Scott] asked de Vaux, as we stood amid the maze of buildings he has since uncovered. 'We were not satisfied,' he said. 'Something in here,' he added tapping the back of his head, 'told me to go back and have another look.' Twenty-two years of archaeological experience in Palestine had given him a sixth sense. So at the end of 1951 they went back. In a few weeks they uncovered the remains of a kind of monastery."[240]

The excursion also provided Scott with some insight into de Vaux's need to return to the area season after season. Travelling from Jerusalem to Qumran, de Vaux driving the station wagon, they passed border patrols and check points. Finally, de Vaux announced, "We have passed the last Arab outpost ... This is No Man's Land. The Israelis are 14 miles away. Here I am King."[241] For de Vaux, working at Qumran presented a haven away from the politics and constant consultation with the powers that be in the Jordanian Government and the continual struggle for funds. At Qumran he was away from the political conflict between Jordan and Israel that constantly needed to be negotiated while working in and around the scrollery in Jerusalem.

The insights gained were appreciated, and so was the tour of the site as a means of giving Scott first-hand knowledge of the community where de Vaux believed many of the scrolls had been produced. But the primary importance of Scott's trip for the history of McGill's purchase was that for the first time McGill's fragments were catalogued. This allowed for the production of documentation that most closely resembled an official purchase agreement.

The latter consists of a letter to Harding from Scott dated 4 May 1955 and Harding's response on behalf of the Jordanian Government on 10 May 1955.[242] Scott's letter outlined his understanding of the agreement as interpreted in meetings with de Vaux and Harding in early May 1955, soon after his arrival in Jerusalem.

The stipulations were as follows: First, all manuscript fragments purchased on McGill's behalf were to be stamped with the letter "S" for "Scott."[243] Second, after identification and matching of the Cave 4 fragments, McGill was to be provided a proportionate share of composite documents with some substitution of "S" stamped pieces to maintain the integrity of manuscripts in other collections. Third, with the expectation that the biblical text fragments were to be identified and studied by the summer of 1956, this portion of the McGill collection could be prepared for shipment first. Some part of the collection might therefore reach Montreal earlier, with the rest to follow. Fourth, in the official publication of the Cave 4 material, the "J.H. Birks Collection at McGill University" was to be acknowledged. Finally, a list of stamped pieces purchased for McGill was to be compiled with the recognition that the final allotment might disagree with the list, due to necessary future substitution. Some sample photographs were likewise to be provided by the PAM. McGill in turn agreed that the list, the photographs, and any other documents would remain confidential and would not be shared in any public forum until after official publication of the allotted fragments.[244] In response Harding confirmed that all the stipulations were acceptable to the Department of Antiquities of Jordan.[245]

By mid-May 1955, Scott had listed 414 fragments from fifteen books of the Hebrew Bible, along with apocryphal and sectarian works. As if to reinforce Harding and de Vaux's commitment to deliver the first part of McGill's collection in 1956, he wrote to James informing him that the men had already begun to discuss the shipment and transportation of the fragments to Montreal. Harding had recommended that it should be shipped via diplomatic channels through the embassy in Amman.[246]

Shortly after his return to Montreal, Scott provided James with a report on his trip.[247] To honour McGill's agreement to confidentiality, one copy of Scott's compiled preliminary list of McGill's fragments was provided to the bursar of McGill University for safekeeping and one was sent to the Birks Foundation; Scott kept two: one for himself and one for his as yet unnamed replacement at McGill University. A further copy of the list was sent to Harding with a letter informing him of this arrangement.[248] The list Scott compiled ran over twenty-one typed pages and included 436 items, each marked with a measurement and a tentative identification.[249]

Despite the heavy emphasis on confidentiality and later assertions of a conspiracy to keep the scrolls from the general scholarly community, it is quite clear that conditions were not particularly restrictive in 1955. In all fairness, the free access granted Scott resulted in large part from the fact that he had, quite literally, bought into the project. In the report on his visit to Jerusalem, Scott commented, "I arrived in Jerusalem ... [and] was cordially received by Père R. de Vaux ... and Mr. Lankester Harding ... and given the freedom of the manuscript room where six scholars are working on the scroll fragments."[250] He devoted most of his time to locating, measuring, and examining McGill's manuscript fragments.[251] Since the McGill fragments had been interspersed with the government and museum's collections along with those purchased by other institutions in order to assemble "complete" manuscripts, it can only be assumed that the work of locating McGill's collection meant examining each glass frame individually. In describing to

Harding the process he followed to compile the list of McGill fragments, Scott revealed his freedom of movement in the museum when he acknowledged that the list was not, "quite complete, as some pieces were away for photographing; one plate was backed with paper and the stamps could not be seen (I did not feel justified in disturbing the plate in Mr. Allegro's absence)."[252] It is evident that Scott's hesitancy to disturb the private work space of an editorial team member rather than any official prohibition prevented him from open access to everything.

Just prior to leaving Jerusalem to return to Montreal and then on to Princeton, Scott managed to purchase an additional number of fragments for the McGill collection. On a visit to the Old City, Scott encountered an antiquities dealer, Mahmud the Silwani,[253] who informed him that he knew some Bedouin with a matchbox of fragments from ancient manuscripts found near Qumran. Scott returned to the museum to secure permission from Harding to purchase the material if it proved to be authentic. The purchase raised a number of concerns as Harding had an existing arrangement to purchase all material through Kando to limit price differentiation and the prospect of Bedouin selling their finds to the highest bidder on the black market. Harding granted permission to Scott to buy the fragments in the hope that the direct contact with the new seller, "might open a new channel of communication with the tribesmen who are holding back what they have."[254] Opinions among the scholars working in Jerusalem differed, yet some suspected as much as £5,000 worth of manuscript fragments remained in the hands of the Ta'amireh tribesmen.[255]

As it transpired, two Bedouin came to the museum to meet Scott, who had arranged for Claus-Hunno Hunzinger[256] and Patrick Skehan[257] to help him evaluate the material, since they had been working directly with the manuscripts.[258] The three men did their best to authenticate the seventeen fragments. Skehan thought he recognized some of the script from manuscripts with which he had been working.[259] Together they "agreed that all but one of the tiny pieces of leather and papyrus – seventeen in all – were probably authentic, and some of them certainly so."[260] The fragments were purchased for £17 ($45.33 CAD). The price was consistent with what had been paid for the fragments forthcoming from Kando, which meant that they could not be held responsible for upsetting the delicate balance in negotiations by pushing up the market price and encouraging the Bedouin to bypass Kando. In addition, a collection of coins was purchased and the entire assemblage was turned over to Harding for inclusion with McGill's previous acquisitions. The material was only studied and evaluated after Scott's departure, with Hunzinger reporting to Scott upon completion:

> Concerning your exciting last-minute-purchase I can now write you the good news that Mr. Harding does not want to keep the coins here but told me that I may send you the whole hoard including the two silver coins of Tyre. The Hammonds[261] are ready to take the collection with them, since this is the easiest way, indeed, and they hope to deliver the coins to you personally in the early fall.[262] I am the longer the more convinced that the hoard is actually coming from Qumran and no I cannot but congratulate you for this wonderful acquisition.
>
> The little fragments were, of course, not of too great an importance, but in any case it is shure [sic] that they are – at least partly – coming from cave four, since there are several pieces that could be identified as belonging to certain manuscripts of this cave. And the piece of leather that – together with the two other tiny fragments in the collection – contains the English name Rowntree provided us with one of the best jokes in the Qumran story, though until now nobody was actually able to find a plausible explanation for the puzzling phenomenon. But I think, people like Zeitlin should never hear of this, for they could make too bad a use of it.[263]

Although the purchase of these fragments by Scott created great excitement and a feeling of participation, the nature of Scott's role was to change as he left Montreal for Princeton, despite Principal James's wish to the contrary, as included in his response to Scott's report: "In light of what I have already said to you in previous conversations I need scarcely add that I am very glad indeed at the further testimony of your continuing interest and responsibility ... Your own knowledge and help will be invaluable at all times in the future and, in a more personal vein, I am happy that the Birks Collection will give us a continuing contact with you in spite of your translation to Princeton."[264] Just how committed Scott was to the collection became apparent with the unfolding of a second purchase of Qumran fragments by McGill in late 1955 during Scott's first semester at Princeton University.

MCGILL'S SECOND BIG PURCHASE

In the first week of December 1955 Harding informed Scott of the availability of additional fragments from Cave 4.[265] De Vaux sent the details describing the need to make this purchase to Scott in a letter dated 18 December 1955.[266] Scott did not receive the letter until after he returned to Princeton from spending Christmas in Montreal. Even without the details from de Vaux's later communiqué at his disposal, Harding's letter inspired him to begin negotiations with the Birks family to provide additional funds. When Scott arrived in Montreal, he quickly went to visit Henry Birks and by 20 December had received a commitment for an additional $4,200 CAD (£1,500).[267] He immediately cabled Harding, "1500 pounds agreed writing – Scott."[268] Scott's eagerness to arrange the funds was initially the product of the general excitement but he soon came to recognize the absolute necessity of expediting the purchase. De Vaux's letter, received between Scott's telegram to Harding and the actual transfer of funds, was sent with the hope of hastening the process. His letter informed Scott that a new group of intermediaries held approximately $5,000 worth of Cave 4 fragments. The price had jumped from previous purchases as new middlemen meant the addition of new commissions. The difficulty for the editorial team was that their desire to publish official and definitive editions fuelled the need to have all the pieces from Cave 4 available before the volumes could be prepared to go to press. As de Vaux wrote: "There will yet be a great interest in seeing them purchased as early as possible, first because the price can only rise higher and above all because we will have here in our hands all of the material from Cave 4 and so the editorial work can be completed: it is actually blocked, for we cannot publish anything while we know that other pieces are on the market to fill in certain lacunae in our texts. And this delays so much the distribution of the pieces already purchased by different owners."[269]

De Vaux further indicated that although negotiations were in progress with the Dutch Government to provide some funding, an additional contribution from McGill would prove helpful in alleviating the immediate crisis.[270] A second purchase by McGill would also mean that the Cave 4 material would not be subject to even further subdivision among an even larger pool of institutional donors, thus allowing for at least a certain amount of integrity to each "collection." The matter was even more urgent because the $5,000 of available material was the remaining half of an assemblage for which the PAM had already depleted funds provided by the Vatican.

According to de Vaux's letter, more than a year after McGill's first purchase, the Vatican sent 3,000 JD to purchase Cave 4 material. The purchase, although made in December 1955,[271] was only officially announced in May 1956. Ernst Vogt, rector of the Pontifical Biblical Institute in Rome, was quoted in the *New York Times*: "I think details of these contributions disclosed by me have not been published before."[272] In January of that year Scott had made the Vatican's purchase public in an interview with the *Toronto Daily Star*.[273] According to the interview, Scott, once again setting Canada apart from its southern neighbour and the Commonwealth, suggested that because McGill and the Vatican "were willing tentatively to accept the scrolls' authenticity on trust," they were to "receive treasures which the richest universities in the United States and the British Museum itself will not have."[274]

As for the Vatican purchase, Vogt stated that the Church had made a previous purchase when the material first became available in 1952. This early date seems unlikely, especially in light of the restrictions laid down by the Jordanian Government, which were only lifted in late 1953 after McGill indicated its interest.[275] In a November 1954 BBC broadcast, H.H. Rowley of the University of Manchester offered that, "To prevent [the sale of fragments on the black market] the Jordan Government has consented to allow collections of the fragments to be bought by suitable institutions, provided they are bought through official channels and carefully examined before leaving the country. McGill University promptly sent $15,000 to be used for this purpose, and Manchester University, helped by a private gift from a public-spirited citizen, sent £2,000.[276] The Vatican Library in Rome has also made a purchase."[277] According to Stephen Pfann, the first of two Vatican purchases of Cave 4 materials was made in October 1954, well after the date suggested by Vogt.[278]

Nevertheless, Scott took the urgency of the appeal for additional funding to heart. When, by the end of 1955 he had still not received confirmation that the Birks' funds had been forwarded to Harding, he urged the university bursar to send the funds by the more expedient wire-transfer rather than by a bank draft.[279] A draft was sent on 29 December 1955 and was received by Harding on the fifth day of the new year, 1956.[280] The import of the procurement of funds for the cash-strapped project is evident from the speed at which de Vaux acted thereafter. In communicating his appreciation to Scott for arranging the funds, he noted: "As soon as your telegram was received I advanced the necessary sum from the funds of the École [Biblique] and the purchase was made."[281] This additional purchase, according to de Vaux, though more expensive, was well worth it. Although the collection contained, "Almost no new documents ... they complete very happily the fragments of already known manuscripts."[282]

The opportunity for McGill to acquire more ancient manuscript material could not have come at a more opportune time and in his letters Scott repeatedly points to James's enthusiasm for the additional purchase. Between 26 November and 2 December 1955, James had been in Israel to lecture on the economic and political development of Canada. During the visit he toured the country with the Hebrew University president, archaeologist Benjamin Mazar, the chair of the Department of Archaeology, Nahman Avigad, and the military general, archaeologist, and man responsible for bringing the archbishop's scrolls to Israel, Yigael Yadin. In addition to visiting the sites excavated by these men, including Bet Shearim where Mazar began excavating in 1936 and Avigad continued to explore, as well as Hazor where Yadin had ended his first season of excavation just three weeks earlier, James had the opportunity to discuss the scrolls. Concluding his report on his visit, James ties the most recent developments in Israel in with the past, noting: "The dynamic economy of the new State of Israel so dominates one's impressions that it is only in retrospect that other conclusions emerge. Of these impressions from the past, the most interesting is that provided coincidentally by the discovery of the Dead Sea Scrolls ... The Dead Sea Scrolls give us a new picture of Palestine as it was at the birth of Christ, revealing a wide latitude of doctrine and religious practice and suggesting, in the Manual of Discipline, the existence of Jewish sects who held to ideals and beliefs closely similar to those of the early Christian Church."[283]

James did not attempt to visit the scrollery in East Jerusalem to see McGill's collection during his visit. In part this resulted from the poor security situation in Jerusalem at the time. On this, he comments: "From the windows of the King David Hotel where I was staying one could look out and see the barbed wire of the Israeli frontier with its sentries, and 300 to 400 yards away across the no man's land which is the valley, see the walls of the old city of Jerusalem with the Arab sentries patrolling them. Contact between the two parts of the city is along a single road that leads through what is known as the MANDELBAUM gate, and no individual can conveniently go through this gate if he is either Jew or Arab."[284] Since he was neither "Jew or Arab" James might have been able to visit the PAM. However, the short duration of his trip meant that he could not take up an invitation he received from the Jordanians. He laments his inability to travel to the Old City: "The old city of JERUSALEM, remembered from the Bible, the Garden of GETHSEMENE, the MOUNT OF OLIVES, and the city of BETHLEHEM, are all on the Arab side of the barbed wire, and although I was invited to visit Jordan, the time available was obviously too short for me to take advantage of the invitation."[285] Given what he had seen and heard during his brief time in Israel, the importance of the scrolls had certainly been reinforced. Within two weeks of his return he found Scott in his office asking for aid in securing more material for McGill. It seems unlikely that he could have refused Scott's request. Furthermore, the Birks family had committed to providing up to $20,000 and only three-quarters of the funds had been spent by that time.

With the material secured, Scott arranged the necessary details so McGill could prepare a press release on this second purchase. This he sent to James on 18 January 1956. In his reply on 24 January 1956, James requested that Scott himself prepare the press release. No copy of it, if it was ever composed, is found in the McGill archives. But Scott had already provided an interview on the topic to the *Toronto Daily Star*, which announced the purchase on 16 January 1956.[286] The Montreal papers announced the purchase only on 15 February 1956, when Principal James made the news public. The delay resulted from James's absence from McGill beginning on 24 January 1956 due to meetings of the International Association of Universities.[287]

SCOTT, THE MEDIA, AND THE LAITY[288]

The importance of the fact that Scott was responsible for all of McGill's public announcements on the scrolls should not be overlooked. Clearly Scott, even before he became interested in the scrolls, saw himself as translator of the academic study of the biblical world for a lay audience. Note also that Scott appreciated the role of press coverage in achieving this purpose. In 1951 Scott's visit to Jerusalem on official leave from McGill University to study under the auspices of ASOR was announced in the local press. His trip received coverage in the Montreal newspapers in December 1950 and they also reported on his return in July 1951.[289] These articles already provide evidence that Scott had a sincere interest in making his audience understand the relationship between the scientific and academic study of the Bible. He also seemed to appreciate the biblical interests of the lay reader of the text in a manner not often the case for the average academic.

A typical section from these articles reads: "Dr. Scott said his research on weather and climate was an important phase in the work of the Bible scholar. 'The Bible is simply full of references to the weather and the study of meteorological records and other material can be of great value in many aspects of Bible research,' he said. For instance, he explained meteorological records and ancient references to climatic and weather conditions could cast a great deal of light on the Bible story of how Joshua bade the sun stand still during his battle with the Canaanites."[290]

The same sense of responsibility to the public was demonstrated in Scott's dealings with the press as regards the scrolls. Even before the first purchase by McGill University, Scott published an article on the discoveries in the *United Church Observer*, entitled "More Treasure Trove Dead Sea Region Discoveries,"[291] and another in the *Montreal Star*, "More Astonishing Discoveries Have Been Made in Palestine."[292] Scott's presence in the media became all the more apparent after Edmund Wilson's popular article, "A Reporter at Large: The Scrolls from the Dead Sea," appeared in *The New Yorker*.²⁹³ Although Scott was in Jerusalem when the article appeared, it was eventually brought to his attention by Principal James, who noted that, "the best summary given that I have seen in print regarding the Dead Sea Scrolls and the Essene Monastery was in *The New Yorker* a couple of weeks ago where Edmund Wilson took up nearly twenty pages with a complete account of the history of the discoveries and some rather interesting comments on the content of the documents themselves. If you have not seen this you might like to look at it as an interesting presentation from the layman's viewpoint."²⁹⁴

Wilson's work inspired significant public interest and following his return in 1955 from Jerusalem, Scott gave a series of three reports on CBC Radio on the Dead Sea Scrolls.²⁹⁵ While the first two discussed the history of the discovery of the scrolls and the importance of the site at Qumran, the final one dealt with the implications of the finds for those who held the Bible sacred. In a newspaper article in 1955, Scott addressed a very real concern in the public imagination:²⁹⁶ he affirmed that the scrolls did not undermine the foundations of Judaism and/or Christianity.²⁹⁷ The talks on the CBC were expanded and published in 1955 as *Treasure from Judæan Caves: The Story of the Dead Sea Scrolls*, providing an introduction to the Dead Sea Scrolls for a lay audience.²⁹⁸

Scott's commitment to communicate academic discourse to the general public was best represented by the foreword to this volume: "Though there is in fact a large and growing literature, the scholarly restraint of those directly concerned with the discoveries has left the general public to learn of them mainly through short spasmodic accounts in the press. Yet when the story is told consecutively, many with little or no previous knowledge of it find it fascinating, and those who value the Bible realize its importance."²⁹⁹ Scott remained a presence in the media at a time when controversy grew following John Allegro's earliest pronouncements, with the concomitant rift this created with the rest of the Cave 4 editorial team, as well as with de Vaux and Harding.³⁰⁰ In January 1956 Allegro made three consecutive broadcast appearances with the scrolls as topic for BBC Radio. In the 16 January broadcast he discussed the early discoveries. The second, on 23 January, concerned the contents of the scrolls, the archaeological site at Qumran, and the nature of the sect that had lived there. On 30 January 1956, during the third broadcast, he made some of the first controversial comments about the relationship between the scrolls and the early church, arguing that, like Jesus, the sect's Teacher of Righteousness had likely been crucified when turned over by the Wicked Priest to gentile troops. The similarities he found between the Dead Sea Scrolls and the story of Jesus in the New Testament led Allegro to conclude that it was not impossible "that the Church was able to take over such collections compiled long before its time by a similar religious community."[301] Allegro's comments were repeated in the press with embellishment, thereby leading the way in establishing the belief among the general public that the scrolls contained material that undermined early Christianity.

The editorial team was understandably unimpressed by Allegro's interpretations of the material he was editing and was additionally troubled by his decision to make his conclusions public in a less than scholarly environment. On 16 March 1956 de Vaux, Milik, Skehan, Starcky,[302] and Strugnell published an open letter in the London *Times* in which they challenged his conclusions and publicly distanced themselves from his views. After examining the same fragments on which Allegro based his conclusions, the team reported: "We find no crucifixion of the 'teacher', no deposition from the cross, and no 'broken body of their Master' to be stood guard over until Judgment Day.[303] Therefore there is no 'well-defined Essenic pattern into which Jesus of Nazareth fits', as Mr Allegro is alleged in one report to have said. It is our conviction that either he has misread the texts or he has built up a chain of conjectures which the materials do not support."[304] Allegro's views concerned Scott enough to respond in the press. It also provided him an additional opportunity to align himself with the editorial team. Scott took up Allegro's views and other similarly disquieting ones in a number of publications and his scholarship and continual media presence placed him among the recognizable public authorities on the Dead Sea Scrolls in North America at the time. When the *New Republic* ran a series on the significance of the scrolls for religious thought, Scott's response was included alongside those of William Albright, Frank Moore Cross, Millar Burrows, and others.[305] This volume was framed as a response to Edmund Wilson. It opened: "Before and since Edmund Wilson's fascinating story of the discovery of ancient scrolls in Palestine caves, biblical scholars and laymen have been debating how, and if, the findings might alter religious faiths. In this symposium, ten outstanding authorities give their personal views."[306] Scott took the opportunity to attack two key problems raised by Wilson's book, the expansion of his *New Yorker* article.[307] The book, Scott believed, was instrumental in producing a terribly skewed response from the public to the scrolls. First, Scott challenged the implication that similarities between the Teacher of Righteousness and Jesus undermined Christian faith: "For the lay public to imagine that the discoveries are all together [sic] *new in kind*, or that the foundations of Christianity are shaken by the disclosure that a pre-Christian Jewish sect had many similarities of belief and practice is a mistake. No one seriously imagines that Christianity was born in a vacuum and many parallels and influences from its environment have been pointed out in the past. The Church has, in fact, resisted attempts to divorce the faith radically from its Jewish heritage."[308]

Scott also challenged Wilson and those like him who produced as fact what could be no more than supposition. Here he warned the public, "A second fallacy is to mistake the announcement of *tentative views* put forward by individual scholars for the considered judgement of scholarship ... Hypotheses have been proposed which have yet to be substantiated, particularly some of the more sensational claims made about anticipations of the Gospel story. We must be sure that obscurities in the texts are not being manipulated in the interests of a theory."[309]

In addition to correcting what he suggested were misrepresentations of the contents of the scrolls, Scott devoted himself to reinforcing the importance of their discovery. His defence derived both from his absolute commitment to their importance and from the fact that McGill had spent a large sum of money on them. As mentioned earlier, on 6 February 1956 Samuel Sandmel, professor of Bible and Hellenistic Literature at Hebrew Union College–Jewish Institute of Religion in Cincinnati, gave a lecture at Temple Emanu-El in Montreal: "The Dead Sea Scrolls and the New Testament." As to the importance of the scrolls, Sandmel unequivocally declared that they, "change nothing, clarify nothing, and add relatively little to our knowledge of Christianity and Judaism."[310] Although his comments were intended to challenge Edmund Wilson's claims about the scrolls and Christianity,[311] they caused a flurry of interest and, along with numerous responses, were carried in newspapers throughout the United States and Canada.[312] McGill's second purchase of scroll fragments was officially announced the following week[313] and as such it was important that, despite Scott's move to Princeton, in the Canadian press he remained the voice to be heard.[314] In contrast to Sandmel, Scott therefore emphasized that the scrolls, "represented every book of the Old Testament, Esther alone excluded, that they added a hitherto unknown wealth of Essene writing, and that we now have [biblical] manuscripts 1,000 years older than anything we had before ... [The scrolls] were of 'immense importance.'"[315] Lending weight to his comments, according to the article, was the fact that Scott had himself visited Qumran and the Jerusalem museum where the scrolls were housed.

Ultimately, by arranging the purchase of the scrolls, Scott functioned as guardian of the physical artefact, while in the press he became a guardian of their public interpretation. Following the second purchase of Birks Foundation manuscripts, Scott fulfilled his role as guardian in a twofold manner: he continued to canvass prospective donors for sorely needed funds to purchase additional fragments; and he made the arrangement of appropriate transportation to Montreal and the long-term conservation of McGill's purchase in Montreal a priority.

3

"We must ride out the crisis"[1]: The Efforts to Bring the Dead Sea Scrolls to Montreal

In April 1956 Scott informed de Vaux that he had become aware of further discoveries of manuscript material in the area of Qumran (Cave 11 had been discovered in February 1956 by the Bedouin).[2] In the same letter he indicated that he had been in discussion with the Princeton University librarian and believed that as much as $20,000 USD could be raised to support additional purchases with terms similar to those arranged for McGill University.[3] Scott clearly did not see purchasing material for Princeton as a conflict of interest with his continued commitment to the purchase and preservation of the McGill collection, presumably as the funds made available from the Birks family had by this time been almost entirely depleted.

But any further communication between Scott and de Vaux on a possible donation by Princeton University was essentially put to rest with de Vaux's assertion that a similar arrangement was out of the question: "We are actually looking for donors who would permit the Palestinian Museum to purchase the documents and to keep them in Jerusalem."[4] For obvious reasons de Vaux and Harding preferred that Cave 4 materials stay together as much as possible, but these new finds were from another cave. Bringing scrolls to Princeton would certainly have been a windfall to a new professor in a prestigious faculty chair. Although in a subsequent letter Scott thought that finding a donor might still be possible, the matter was closed by a request from Scott to be informed should manuscripts become available for outright purchase.[5] Meanwhile, funding for the said purchases in the manner envisaged by de Vaux and Harding was made available by Elizabeth Hay Bechtel[6] and the Royal Academy of Sciences of the Netherlands. The donations made it possible for the PAM to pay almost $84,000 USD for multiple boxes of fragments, including 11QNew Jerusalem and 11QTargum of Job.[7]

Despite the unavailability of manuscript material for Princeton, the archives clearly indicate that Scott kept himself occupied with making arrangements for the safe export of McGill's scrolls from Jordan. The correspondence indicates that, at least initially, it was understood that the biblical manuscripts from Cave 4 were expected to be ready for physical transfer to McGill in 1956. While the acquisition of further fragments and more discoveries certainly delayed the delivery, there was the belief both in Montreal and in Jerusalem that the material would become available for export in the not-too-distant future. As a result of this belief, by early 1956 Scott began to ask questions about the procedures related to their transportation and care. Of these, the most pertinent and detailed was the following communiqué with de Vaux: "The authorities at McGill have begun to ask questions about how the fragments are to be properly cared for when they finally arrive, so that they can be kept in safety and preserved from deterioration. Have you any suggestions to make? Will it be necessary to have them kept in a safe with automatic temperature and humidity controls as has been suggested? My own feeling is that they should be hermetically sealed between glass plates, and kept in a safe, with trays that could be drawn out for examination. Mr. Harding said he thought they should be shipped in plastic, rather than glass, to avoid damage from possible breakage of glass."[8]

In response to this first inquiry on conservation from Scott, de Vaux suggested that it was perhaps too early to raise these concerns, thereby seeming to suggest that the anticipated delivery would be delayed. He did offer some advice: "The experience that we have of a few years when the documents were kept at the Palestine Museum indicates that it suffices that they are between two plates of hermetically sealed glass. We can envision as well a mounting under plastic, which renders the transport and handling much easier. But we do not have the necessary materials yet."[9] In the meantime, despite the delay, Harding was carrying out a provisional division of the Cave 4 materials. Although the materials were not yet ready to be released, preparations were underway to facilitate the process. The first official list of McGill University's allotment offered by Harding on behalf of the Jordanian Government was received in June 1956. The list included eighty-six 10" by 12" plates, plus an additional collection of unidentified smaller pieces. Twenty-eight of the plates represented biblical material and fifty-eight were non-biblical.[10] Abbreviated codes indicated the scholar on the editorial team responsible for each plate.[11] (see figure 1)

Figure 1 First Official List of McGill University's allotment

Biblical Books
Plate no.

C	3	Genesis, manuscript	c	M 15–17	Jubilees, ms.	a
	5	" "	e	20	" "	d
	7	Exodus, "	b	29–30	Enoch "	c,d
	10	" "	e	36	" astronomical	d
	16–18	Numbers, "	a	41	Testament of Levi, Aramaic	b
	29	Deuteronomy "	h	43	" Naphtali	
	31	" "	g	46	Pseudo-Daniel, ms.	b
	32	" "	l	55	Rule of the Community	f.
	34	Joshua, "	b	58	Damascus Document	a
	46	Samuel "	c	67–68	" "	c
	49	Jeremiah, "	b	86	Barakoth (Blessings)	b
	59	Minor Prophets "	d	88–89	Mishmaroth (Priestly courses)	a
	62	Ruth "	a	115	Unidentified in Cryptic B	
	67–68	Daniel "	a	122–23	Sapiental work	b
				124	" "	e
Sn	1–3	Exodus in Paleo Hebrew	b	130	List of names	
	19	Deuteronomy				
	23–24	Isaiah, manuscript	c	Sl 10	Joseph cycle	
	36–37	Psalms "	b	20–21	Psalms of the fathers	c
	47–48	Leviticus lxx version		27–28	Pseudo-Jeremiah	d
	50	Greek, non-Biblical		31–32	Proto-Mishnah	a) Purity
				35	" "	e) regulations

Non-Biblical Works

				42	Liturgical work ms.	4
				45	" "	8 (tongues of fire)
Sy	3–4	Pseudo-Enoch, b, Aramaic		50–51	Sapiental work	Ic.
	10	Visions of Amram, b, Aramaic		60	" "	3
	20	Visions of the 4 kingdoms b		66	Hodayot (Hymns)	c.
	22–24	New Jerusalem, Aramaic		73	Hymnic work, ms. 1	
	29	Visions, ms. c. Aramaic		76	" " ms. 5	
	32	Halachic work		80	" " ms. 10	
	35	Liturgical prayers b	A 90	Commentary on Hosea	
	37	Apocalyptic work		18	Astronomical work	
	48	Unidentified Hebrew		24	Sapiental work	e
	50, 51, 54d	Unidentified Aramaic	H 3a	Milhamah (War rules)	

HARDING GETS "GLUBBED"

Much of the impetus for the sudden acceleration in preparatory work for export may have come from stirrings of political upheaval in Jordan. The changing political climate raised concerns about the foreign ownership of scroll material.[12] As a result of the increasing popularity of Egypt's Gamal Nasser's push for Arab nationalism, Jordan's King Hussein began the process of removing British officials from positions of influence in the kingdom. The most notorious of these was the firing of John Baggot Glubb (1897–1986) in March 1956. Glubb had served as commanding general of the Arab Legion from 1939 until his removal in 1956.[13] The axe fell on Harding as well. The Jordanian authorities announced Harding's dismissal on 28 June 1956.[14] The move to get rid of Harding does not, however, appear to have been solely a result of the rise in nationalism. In reporting the events to James, Scott commented: "As you probably know, Lankester Harding has been dismissed as Director of Antiquities of Jordan – 'Glubbed', they say – from Sept. 30th. This was due partly to the wave of Arab nationalism and partly to intrigue by a former subordinate."[15] Intrigue, unfortunately, would follow Harding until he departed from Jordan in September.

Preceding the announcement of Harding's dismissal, William Foxwell Albright had, according to the press, claimed that two scrolls had been stolen: "Two – possibly more – newly discovered Dead Sea Scrolls have been stolen by Arabs and are being held for ransom, a leading authority on the documents said yesterday ... The recently found sheepskin scrolls were stealthily removed from under the noses of their guards by Bedouin – nomadic desert Arabs – Albright said."[16] Because of what looked like incompetence on the part of his department, Harding was forced to respond publicly that no scrolls were missing or had ever been. Furthermore, he noted, the newly discovered scrolls were in the possession of the PAM where they were being studied.[17] In responding to a representative from the BBC, Harding explained that Albright claimed "that he never mentioned the words 'theft' or 'ransom'; that this was an invention of the Press."[18] The non-event unfortunately did little for Harding's reputation in Jordan and likely made his ability to act on behalf of his donors that much more difficult. In early August 1956 Jordanian newspapers had published an article attacking Harding's management of the scrolls. At the end of the first week of August, Harding wrote to the minister of education: "I would refer to the article published in various papers on Thursday last, the 2nd. Aug. [sic], making serious allegations against my personal integrity in connection with the Dead Sea Scrolls. I must in this connection lodge a formal protest with the Government against such malicious misrepresentation, and to ask that as they are not true the Government should issue an official denial."[19] Among the most problematic charges made by the press was that Harding and the board of the museum were acting together to facilitate sending the manuscripts out of the country. To this Harding responded that not only were manuscripts not being sent out of the country, but that he had secured a loan for the PAM to allow it to purchase new discoveries and keep them in Jordan.[20] However, despite Harding's protests, foreign ownership of the newly discovered scrolls was a topic of significant concern to the Jordanian public and shaped the future of the previously purchased Cave 4 materials as well.

Scott heard of Harding's dismissal as director of antiquities from several sources beginning in July 1956. First, Harding wrote to Scott on 9 July from Amman to inform him of the dismissal and assured him that he would "leave everything in order" in Jerusalem before he left; his plan was to go there for another month or two.[21] William Bentley, McGill's bursar, brought the news to Scott's attention in a short note dated 26 July 1956.[22] In the note Bentley thanks Scott for sending a copy of Harding's distribution list and draws his attention to the dismissal of Harding, which Bentley had noticed reported in the press.[23] A letter from Tushingham to Harding makes clear that by the middle of July of that year Scott was already much concerned by the dismissal:

> Dear Gerald: Although the news of your leaving was in the local paper, I missed it. However, Bob Scott wrote me in some haste to inform me. He was afraid for his scroll fragments. At that time apparently there was nothing said of your staying on until the late summer ... I remember that you talked of retiring several times, and – at least since Glubb's dismissal – you cannot have been without some suspicions that the same thing would happen to you. On the other hand, I know how much you love Jordan and the work there and how strongly you felt against leaving at this time – in medias res, as it were – especially with the scrolls still 'unfinished business'. Well, all I can say is: Take congratulations or commiserations from me as you wish.[24]

Despite Tushingham's assumption that the dismissal could not have been unexpected, Harding told Scott that the Jordanian government's "action has rather taken us by surprise."[25]

MEETING WITH DE VAUX IN STRASBOURG

Scott planned to meet with a number of colleagues at the Strasbourg IOSOT meeting in August 1956 to discuss the current uncertain situation.[26]

The second international meeting of IOSOT was hosted by Strasbourg University's Centre de Recherches d'Histoire des Religions from 27 August to 1 September 1956. Roland de Vaux was president of the congress.[27] In light of the possibility that the uncertainty might necessitate expediting the export of McGill fragments, Scott planned to use the conference as an opportunity to learn more about the transportation and preservation of the scroll materials from de Vaux and his other colleagues.[28] Harding's dismissal by the Jordanians would become effective on 30 September 1956 – this left little time to act. In his meeting with Scott, de Vaux reported that an emergency meeting had been held at the museum in Jerusalem to consider the shipment of McGill's fragments before Harding's dismissal became official. This plan of action was discarded because editing would not be completed in time; it was expected to take another year.[29] Furthermore, it was assumed that any petition for an export permit by Harding at that point would be summarily rejected by the government and might even prejudice later applications. De Vaux encouraged Scott not to give up hope, since he had official documentation, including the distribution list from Harding, which confirmed McGill's ownership of the fragments.[30] What Scott heard from de Vaux at the meeting was hardly new. De Vaux had written to him in late July assuring him that while Harding's dismissal was a significant difficulty, the official documentation would help to secure McGill's purchase when things settled.[31] Even before this, though, Harding had written Scott in early July telling him of the meeting at the PAM and of the fact that the government could not, at the time, be petitioned to release the scrolls fragments: "It would be fatal if they started to raise objections now, as I should not have the time to counter them."[32] Additionally, Harding provided Scott with a list of three letters between himself and the Jordanian prime minister that confirmed McGill's purchase and the government's approval of the sale.

De Vaux's suggestion that the scrolls should be exported before the end of Harding's tenure makes clear that he too recognized that Harding's departure would create difficulties for later attempts to export the scrolls. Concerning this period and its effects Weston Fields concludes, "Virtually every British employee of the government was dismissed. In one of the most unfortunate incidents in the whole story of the scrolls, Harding was forcibly removed from his position as director-general of the Department of Antiquities of Jordan. Although he retained his position with the still private Palestine Archaeological Museum, he took up residence in Harissa, near Beirut, Lebanon. This was a blow to the acquisition and publication of the scrolls from which the project never fully recovered."[33] In late August Scott wrote to Harding in Harissa to confirm the reference numbers for the

Jordanian documents that recorded McGill's purchase. Harding explained his move to Lebanon as follows: "It proved in the end inadvisable for me to remain on in Jerusalem, so I came straight on here as soon as I found somewhere to live. Conditions are not too happy in Jordan at present, and I was very glad to get away."[34]

In Harding's stead Scott came to rely heavily on Roland de Vaux. But the fact that Harding had managed all of the paperwork and arrangements related to the sales gave the government an excuse it would attempt to take advantage of at a later stage. The government further benefited from the new director of the Department of Antiquities' lack of any past history with the foreign purchasing institutions, while de Vaux, who would step into the breach to represent them, had no official status in Jordan.

Returning to the events in Strasbourg, Scott took the opportunity to meet numerous scholars at work on the scrolls, including Henri del Medico,[35] Claus-Hunno Hunzinger of the editorial team, André Dupont-Sommer,[36] and Godfrey Rolles Driver.[37] Many of Scott's colleagues at IOSOT had institutional investments in the scrolls and were therefore concerned about the potential impact of the political upheaval in the Middle East. In attendance at the meeting were both Rowley of Manchester and Karl Georg Kuhn of Heidelberg and they discussed their particular take on the problematics of the situation with Scott.[38] Heidelberg had provided £4,500 for the purchase of Cave 4 fragments in the spring of 1955.[39] In July 1956 Kuhn had written to Harding that he intended to be in Strasbourg to meet with de Vaux and the other Jerusalem colleagues. He requested that Harding attend and join them to discuss the implications of his dismissal and the political situation in Jordan.[40] Harding did not attend and his removal from the Department of Antiquities had an inevitable impact on the matter at hand. In the meantime Scott was left to prepare for whatever eventuality might follow. The inclusion of Heidelberg and the Vatican among the investors in Cave 4 material was, as far as de Vaux and Scott were concerned, quite beneficial. In both cases the funds proferred originated from state funds rather than individual institutions, which meant that government pressure could be applied on Jordan should they decide to renege on the initial agreements. In addition, the British and American ambassadors to Jordan both acted as trustees of the PAM, thereby strengthening the political pressure that might be put on Jordan in the event of trouble.[41]

The congress in Strasbourg proved especially helpful in tightening the bond among the scholars who risked losing their scroll allotments. Collectively the group had some bargaining power, and in the wake of the looming Suez Crisis they would need it.

THE SUEZ CRISIS AND THE SCROLLS' TEMPORARY MOVE TO AMMAN

During the Suez Crisis in late 1956, work on Cave 4 manuscripts came to a complete halt when the material was moved from the scrollery at the PAM to the Ottoman Bank in Amman for safekeeping. In reporting on this period to the members of the Society of Biblical Literature (SBL), G. Ernest Wright, the ASOR representative to SBL, described the situation in dire terms:

> Because of the charges of malfeasance in relation to the scrolls levelled against Mr. Harding, it was feared that the MSS would be transported to Amman where they could no longer be studied. While the team is a long way from completing its sorting and fitting of the gigantic puzzle, nevertheless the major part is finished and work on the publications can continue with the aid of photographs. This is fortunate, because during the first week of September when Dr. Strugnell[42] alone was left of the team and when all British citizens were being hurried out of the Middle East in evident preparation for what was ultimately to come, all ± 450 plates of fragments were packed away by Dr. Strugnell and Mr. Yusuf Saad, Secretary of the Palestine Museum, in the special boxes made for them. The job took the whole of one long Sunday afternoon, and as a witness to part of it I can say that it will take even longer to unpack them than it did to pack them. When hostilities broke out against Egypt, the boxes were transported to Amman for safekeeping. At present the possibility of further work upon them is very much in doubt ... Meanwhile, how much publication of the previously discovered material will be delayed by the events of this fall, and what will happen to new discoveries now that the chain of confidence between Bedouin and Mr. Harding has been broken – these are very large questions indeed.[43]

The plates of fragments were only returned six months later in March 1957. The deposit of the scroll material in Amman was a disaster, not only because of the delays it caused to the work of the editorial team at this crucial time but also because of the hostile climatic conditions in the bank vault where the scrolls were deposited for safekeeping. Concerning the fragments' condition as a result of this move, Joseph Fitzmyer, who was in Jerusalem to work on the concordance of the manuscripts in 1957 and 1958,[44] commented: "[T]he fragments between plates of glass were boxed up and carried to the Ottoman Bank in Amman, where they lay in a basement for several months and suffered no little damage from dampness and mildew."[45]

Nevertheless, the eventual return of the fragments to the PAM early in 1957 gave some cause for hope.

In the meantime, Scott concluded, based on discussion with de Vaux, that the crisis created amidst the wave of rising Arab nationalism could be waited out.[46] But, as Harding had been dismissed, the situation still remained of grave concern. De Vaux's limited optimism in Strasbourg nevertheless encouraged Scott to focus his attention on his continued investigation of the proper care for the scrolls in transit and upon arrival in Montreal.

PRESERVING THE MCGILL COLLECTION

During this period two questions concerned officials at McGill University as to the consequences of their purchase of ancient scrolls: first, where the materials should be housed on campus, and, second, how they should be cared for. With regard to the former, it had been Scott's desire that the scrolls be housed in Divinity Hall (now the Birks Building). The university librarian, Richard Pennington, eventually came to believe that they should be accommodated in the Redpath Library, where a temperature controlled vault could also accommodate rare but significantly less ancient manuscripts related to Canadian history.[47]

The discussion on accommodation included one of the very few contributions on the scrolls by the dean of the Faculty of Divinity at the time. James S. Thomson became dean following Scott's resignation from the post in 1949. Yet all communications related to the acquisition of the scrolls took place directly between Scott and Principal James, with Thomson only occasionally involved to provide the proverbial rubber stamp of approval. Dean Thomson's October 1956 letter on the topic of where the scroll collection should be located on campus highlights his general lack of participation on the matter. In response to an inquiry by the university librarian, Thomson admitted his distance from the project and its contents: "Frankly, I know very little about the actual scrolls; what material is to come to us or its nature, and I am not quite sure that even this has been entirely settled."[48] Although it appears as if Scott was acting as a free agent as regards the scrolls during his time at McGill, the administrative support he received from Principal James in effect negated the need for Dean Thomson's participation.[49] Furthermore, the encouragement he received from the faculty, especially Wilfred Cantwell Smith, demonstrated that he was not acting alone.

Scott made a number of inquiries with regard to preservation and care of the manuscripts.[50] Of significance was a communication with Harold

James Plenderleith, who was keeper in the research laboratory at the British Museum.[51] During the summer, Scott had paid a visit to Plenderleith in London.[52] Scott followed up with a letter in October 1956. Plenderleith was able to offer little more than a description of how humidity could be controlled, having not had the opportunity to examine McGill's scroll fragments: "Control of temperature is unnecessary, but humidity must be kept within reasonable bounds. This is most easily achieved by building a cupboard with containers of silica gel[53] kept in the bottom and a fan at the top to ensure a gentle circulation of air. The fan is kept working until equilibrium is established and the air in the cupboard dried. Every time the cupboard is opened admitting air from the outside, the fan is set working to circulate the air and dry it. In this way the humidity inside the cupboard (which should, of course, have tight fitting doors), is kept more or less under control."[54]

Plenderleith first became acquainted with the scrolls and the people involved at a meeting of the Palestine Exploration Fund in London on 14 July 1949.[55] Harding brought fragments retrieved from the first expedition with de Vaux to London for consultation on preservation at the British Museum. Plenderleith, at the time an archaeological chemist on the staff of the British Museum, announced the results of his examination of the material and displayed it for the media in early August 1949. He concluded that all the fragments he was able to investigate were of parchment and dated from approximately 150 BCE.[56] He also offered a number of suggestions for cleaning and preservation of the fragments.[57] In 1955 Plenderleith was sent three boxes of fragments by the PAM for his examination in London. His research on these concerned the investigation of the initial treatment and separation of the fragments received from the Bedouin and excavations and did not concern their long-term preservation.[58] Despite his limited access to the fragments at that time, Plenderleith later wrote a series of reports for the PAM when he became director of the International Centre for the Study of the Preservation and the Restoration of Cultural Property created by UNESCO and housed in Rome. In 1962, at de Vaux's request, Plenderleith closely examined numerous scroll fragments and made a number of important recommendations on their care and preservation.[59]

In January 1957 Scott still remained confident that the scrolls would eventually come to McGill. In a letter to James he commented with certainty on the outcome: "I imagine that when the McGill scroll fragments finally arrive there will be a good deal of public as well as scholarly interest."[60] A letter from the prefect of the Bibliotheca Apostolica Vaticana[61] indicates that the Vatican likewise believed they would receive their allotment. In writing to Scott the prefect offered the following concerning the care and preservation of the fragments: "As till yet none of the scroll fragments did come in our possession, it is rather difficult to tell what arrangements will be taken in order to provide properly for them. We ought first to see and examine them and only then we will be able to inform you what will be, according to our opinion, the best way to preserve them safely from any kind of deterioration."[62]

FLEETING OPTIMISM

Some short-lived encouragement for the status quo of the purchase agreements came in November 1956 when an additional purchase of material was made. On 30 November 1956, the *New York Times* reported on the first purchase of Cave 4 material by an American institution, McCormick Theological Seminary in Chicago. The article confirms that the conditions of purchase were consistent with those laid down in the McGill arrangement. It notes that the fragments, "will remain in the Palestine Archaeology Museum for study, editing and publication. Then they are to be released to the seminary here."[63] During the summer of 1956 and before Harding's departure, Frank Cross had arranged for the purchase of materials by McCormick, where he was at the time a faculty member. The seminary purchased 2,100 cm^2 of fragmentary material for $6,000 USD.[64] The amount was not made known at the time of the purchase. The inflated headline in the *Chicago Tribune* the same day declared that McCormick would receive nine Dead Sea Scrolls at an estimated cost of up to $75,000.00.

The funds were donated by the founder of the Nutrilite Foundation, Carl F. Rehnborg, a vitamin manufacturer, and his wife. According to the article in the *Tribune*, Cross described the collection as including extremely fragmentary texts of a hymn, the book of Jeremiah, two manuscripts of Daniel, Ecclesiastes, a portion of an apocalyptic text on papyrus, a wisdom text, a paraphrase of Genesis, and a liturgy.[65] Although the purchase was not quite as large as McGill's, Cross was in much the same position as Scott, with the exception that he participated in studying the Cave 4 material in Jerusalem and thus had greater first-hand knowledge of the situation. Cross, writing to Scott in March 1957, was rather pessimistic, but still held out some hope that the matter might be resolved in favour of the institutions that had purchased scroll fragments:

> Kraeling has just been in Jordan attempting negotiations. The scene is depressing, both as to the future of "our" manuscripts, and as to the

role of the department of Ghureibah in interfering in our affairs.[66] I do think we will be able to continue work and publication. But work will be differently administered ... Whether we will be reimbursed or not (or even given our allotments) remains for the future. I suspect that pressure just now may do more harm than good, at least in regard to the staff's freedom. However, I can be more objective since I warned the Seminary here and our donor that I suspected the Government would renege; they proceeded with open eyes. This was last summer after the trouble had started. So I personally prefer your counsel of patience, at least until Kraeling reports in full.[67]

The difference in administration Cross referred to was the new committee established by the order of 25 February 1957 from the minister of education and discussed by de Vaux in his letter to Scott on 9 March 1957.[68] The minutes of the first meeting of the new committee do not preserve any discussion of matters related to ownership but they hint at an important factor in the vicissitudes of the nationalization discussion.[69] According to the minutes, the Lebanese ambassador had approached the Jordanians with a request to supply manuscript fragments for short-term exhibit at the Beirut Museum the following week, beginning on 1 April 1957. The committee agreed to share the fragments with the Lebanese at the request of the royal family.[70] Considering the matter, they adopted three principles: that unstudied fragments could not leave the country under any circumstance; that short-term loans of studied and preserved fragments were permitted; and that future policy would prevent exhibit of the material outside of Jordan because allowing them to travel meant that their value as a tourist attraction would be diminished and they might risk damage during shipment.

While the Jordanians did not hold to the third principle, eventually lending the material to be exhibited by the British and others, the foregrounding in this context and at this time of their value as a means of contributing to tourist revenue rather than their worth as national treasures with intrinsic historical value should not be overlooked.

JORDAN ATTEMPTS TO NATIONALIZE THE SCROLLS

Although January 1957 was a time for optimism, February brought with it another challenge for the purchasing institutions. At the end of that month Scott received a letter from Professor Rowley at the University of Manchester informing him that the Jordanians had decided to prevent the export of the scrolls to McGill, the Vatican, Manchester, McCormick, and

Heidelberg.[71] The communication between Rowley and Scott resulted from the establishment of a new Jordanian policy with regard to the ownership of the scrolls. In January 1957 the minister of education provided the Department of Antiquities with the details. Of primary importance are the first three stipulations of the order presented by the minister of education:

1) I acquire,[72] in the name of the Government, all ancient Manuscripts which were discovered in the area of the Dead Sea, as well as those which will be discovered in that site or any other site in Jordan. This will include the Manuscripts in Hebrew, Aramaic, Arabic, Greek and Phoenician languages and also in any other language. It also includes all kinds of Manuscripts such as the Biblical Scrolls and what was written on paper, parchment, papyri, bronze or any other material.
2) No export abroad of these Manuscripts shall be permitted: nor shall be permitted to export neither Photographs nor anything else of these Manuscripts.
3) All rights for printing, publishing, translating and studying of these Manuscripts are reserved to the Jordan Government.[73]

The news prompted Scott to immediately write to both Rowley and de Vaux. In Scott's letter to the latter, he requested more pertinent guidance in the matter of the ownership of the scrolls.[74]

The altered position of McGill from passive to active claimant to the scrolls was primarily a response to a section of a letter dated 3 February 1957, from de Vaux to Rowley, which Rowley had forwarded. At Scott's request, Rowley provided a transcription of the original French:

I actually have grave concerns for the Dead Sea manuscripts. The Government has the intention of appropriating all of the fragments found or yet to be found, including those that were acquired by foreign institutions. All export will be prohibited, and the Government reserves all rights to study and to publication. We promise without doubt to indemnify the institutions but I do not know when or how this will be done. It is a crazy story and, unfortunately, I have no way of opposing this enterprise; no reason can act against that which appears to them as a national duty, the only recourse is a diplomatic action which I put in place here but which will need to be pressed from the outside. I thought it necessary to put you on guard against the serious danger which threatens these documents and the rights that Manchester acquired to them. You might judge it opportune to keep your government informed and to ask for its intervention. It must then furnish it with the documents that you have and which your ambassador in Amman does not possess: your correspondence with Mr. Harding, establishing the amount of your contribution, the legal validity of the purchase made with the agreement of the Jordanian Government and by the intervention of the Director of Antiquities, the official list of the lot which came to you with the promise that it would be left for you after study. Do not forget the reference to the number of the letter of the Minister of Education authorizing these purchases and establishing the conditions. I do not know if an intervention will be effective, but it must at least be attempted. We will do then all that we can.[75]

De Vaux's 9 March 1957 response to Scott was more optimistic than Rowley's rendering. His optimism resulted at the very least from the fact that the manuscripts had been returned to the museum from the bank vaults where they had been stored during the Suez Crisis: "The work is under the control of an official committee named by the minister of education and which comprises five members, three Jordanians, the director of the American School and myself.[76] The committee must aid and survey the preservation of the manuscripts, their study and their publication. In the order naming the committee nothing is said of the ownership of the manuscripts. If there had been anything in this regard, I would have refused to participate in the committee. The legal questions as to the ownership and export remain in suspense and we may yet protect the rights of the institutions by continuing to work with gentleness and patience."[77]

De Vaux encouraged Scott and James to use diplomatic channels to remind the government that it had taken McGill's funds, offered in good faith, and that a contract was in place: "To help us, and to defend your rights, I recommend that you make the same approach as Manchester. McGill University can send, by an intermediary official of the government of Canada or by the representative of Jordan in Canada ... a letter to the director of antiquities in Amman saying that they [McGill] have 'learnt' that the Jordanian government has proposed to acquire the manuscripts for itself and demanding official information on the subject."[78]

De Vaux further actively encouraged Scott to leave his name out of any correspondence. Any work he attempted to do to protect the institution's rights, which was a major concern on his part, would be undermined if his interference became known. In forwarding the material excerpted from de Vaux's letter, Rowley indicated that a protest via the British ambassador to Jordan, Charles Hepburn Johnston, had already been made but had received no reply.[79] However, so concerned was Scott with de Vaux's request, that in informing James of the need to act quickly he included a model letter to the director of antiquities in Jordan that he had drafted.[80] James forwarded the letter via the Jordanian ambassador in Washington, D.C. to the director of antiquities, informing both men of his concern over the recent rumours. The letter outlined the history of the agreements with Harding and demanded assurance that Jordan planned to deliver the plates owned by McGill.[81] At the time, Jordan had no diplomatic representation in Canada. The letters were therefore transmitted to the Jordanians in Washington via the Canadian ambassador to the United States of America, in accordance with de Vaux's advice.[82]

In early April 1957 both James and Scott were given a small reason for optimism in the form of a report in the journal of the American Schools of Oriental Research.[83] The report of the president of ASOR, A. Henry Detweiler,[84] in the April 1957 issue of *BASOR*, suggested a positive (and improving) relationship with the new Jordanian administration: "I am sure that all of you have been avidly reading the accounts of the political upheavals in the Near East ... The affairs of the School have gone on with scarcely any interruption ... One of the big moments in recent weeks in Jerusalem was a visit by Dr. and Mrs. Kraeling[85] who, as usual, were most cooperative in their various negotiations with the local authorities in regard to the affairs of the School and, particularly, in regard to the Scroll project."[86]

JAMES'S INTEREST IN ARCHAEOLOGY

By this time Principal James had acquired an avid personal interest in archaeology and not only in the scrolls. While, as a religious man of his times, his interest in them and Middle Eastern archaeological sites was inspired by his commitment to the Bible, his interest in archaeology expanded to other places and times. In 1955 James travelled to Greece to tour archaeological sites of interest. Of his visit to Crete, he commented:

> I am fascinated by the place. To describe the treasures would be impossible – and too many people have done it – but all the things I expected, and more, are here. It must be 35 years since I first read about the Minoan civilisation and here it is ... This evening I walked down to the sea – across which the Minoan ships sailed to garner wealth – and felt that Atlantis never disappeared. It was men who forgot what [this island] had produced in that short four centuries from about 1900 to 1500 B.C. – when there was nothing on the Acropolis [in Athens]

but mud huts ... But much more important than any of the individual ruins is the deepening impression of the whole island as a great center of civilisation 3000 years ago ... Not only Zeus but the whole Greek civilisation was born on this island: I am sure of it![87]

James provides a hint of his similar interest in ancient Israel in a letter to Scott, dated 10 December 1957, where he notes Yigael Yadin as a close acquaintance, "since I stayed with him at his dig at Hazor when I was in Israel."[88] As noted above, during that particular trip to Israel he visited numerous sites with Mazar, Yadin, and Avigad.[89] Because of Scott's encouragement, in April 1954 James had enlisted McGill as institutional member of ASOR. When Scott left for Princeton, communications about membership and publication subscriptions were sent directly to Principal James and not to the dean of the appropriate faculty as might have been expected.[90] In May 1956 James was informed that he personally would be receiving ASOR publications that had been disseminated since Scott had left for Princeton. In response he commented, "I am delighted to hear that I shall receive the newsletters of the American Schools of Oriental Research and thus keep up my reading which was so greatly stimulated in these subjects by Professor R.B.Y. Scott's enthusiasm."[91] James's letter of 3 April 1957 to Scott, about Detweiler's BASOR report mentioned above, suggests that even after a replacement was found for Scott on the faculty and as representative of the university to ASOR, James continued to stay abreast with ASOR's publications.[92] The correspondence also makes it clear that James kept up his reading on the Dead Sea Scrolls. James alerted Scott to the earlier mentioned article by Edmund Wilson in *The New Yorker*, as well as to the work of Millar Burrows: "Incidentally I have just been reading Barrows' [sic] long volume on the Dead Sea Scrolls[93] with a great deal of interest and notice, in passing, that you and McGill University are about the only names that are mentioned outside of his long and involved record of the various controversies."[94]

A REPLACEMENT FOR SCOTT

For all the disruption and concern that 1956 and 1957 brought for McGill and Scott in particular, by December 1957 the issue of the nationalization of the scrolls had faded into the background and again the matter of preservation and care predominates the correspondence. In this period a new player entered the stage: Stanley Frost was hired in 1956 to replace Scott as professor of Old Testament Literature and Language at McGill University. He came to McGill from the University of Bristol and, arriving in Montreal at

Stanley Frost holding an ancient jug he acquired during a visit to Jordan, 1960. Photograph by Paul Lagace for the *Montreal Star*. Published with the permission of the *Gazette* (Montreal).

the age of forty-three, was already a relatively senior scholar. By 1958 Frost was appointed dean of the Faculty of Divinity when his predecessor became moderator of the United Church of Canada. Frost remained dean until his 1963 appointment as dean of Graduate Studies at McGill.[95] Stanley Frost's sudden appointment and his swift advancement through the ranks were indicative of Principal James's faith in his administrative capabilities. By 1959 Frost became McGill's primary representative to Jordan with regard to the Dead Sea Scrolls. Frost was brought into discussions on the scrolls in May 1958 in correspondence with Scott. The situation in Jerusalem remained quiet and for the most part no news appeared to be good news, as Scott noted to Frost: "This week I wrote to de Vaux for some information about the status and prospects of the McGill Birks D.S.Scoll [*sic*] fragments, as it is high time we had a further report. Have you heard anything from him? Last year the situation with the Dept. of Antiquities was still a delicate one, but by now things seem to have settled down."[96]

In responding to Scott's letter, de Vaux had provided surprisingly good news. Although it would take two more years, McGill would receive its allotment. De Vaux described the activities that had taken place during this lull in correspondence: "A director of antiquities of Jordan, who was unbearable, had attempted to confiscate all of the fragments of the manuscripts for the benefit of the government. He obtained for this [purpose] a letter signed by his minister. This director was finally replaced last July [1957] and I immediately fought a great deal to obtain a retraction of that letter. The letter is annulled and the commitments made by the government with regard to the institutions that purchased the lots of fragments from cave 4 remain valid. The rights of ownership of McGill for its lot are therefore safeguarded."[97]

It appears, in part, that the government's decision to reverse the January 1957 ruling resulted from the ongoing negotiations over the material from Cave 11. As a result of a shortage of Jordanian funds to arrange the purchase of the new scrolls discovered by the Bedouin, the Department of Antiquities was in the difficult position of having to find foreign institutions to supply the funds in exchange for publication rights and other similar stipulations. A record of reneging on previous agreements with foreign institutions would have understandably made any current negotiations extremely difficult. A change in position was therefore a logical conclusion. This is reflected in the minutes of the board meeting of the PAM in December 1957. According to the minutes, "The President considered it desirable to record that the decision of the Jordan Government was an inspiration and encouragement to the Trustees who would now be in a position to accept donations offered towards the purchase of those highly valuable Manuscripts, and thus save them from being smuggled out of the Country."[98] Furthermore, the annulment of the letter may have resulted from the Jordanian government's considered inability at the time to refund the monies provided for the earlier purchases by foreign institutions.

With this positive news, discussions of transportation and conservation continued and Scott, understandably given his distance from McGill, handed primary responsibility to Frost to arrange the completion of McGill's project. This was done with James's approval.[99]

By mid-1958 it looked as if some of the material might be available for shipment by the end of 1959 and therefore, in May, de Vaux informed Scott to expect a two-year delay.[100] The communications preserved from June 1958 make it clear that the further delay of McGill's receipt of the scrolls, now held back since 1956, and particularly, the two-year delay still to be anticipated, was as much about the scientific recording of data by the editorial team as about the unstable political situation.[101] The primary importance of one or the other of these two factors as reason for the postponement constantly fluctuated.

SCOTT RETURNS TO JERUSALEM

In June 1958 Scott wrote to de Vaux of his intention to be in Jerusalem in the summer of 1959. He expressed the hope that some of the material might be ready for transport by that time.[102] De Vaux's reply did not include any promises but did leave the possibility open that some of the material might indeed be ready: "As I had previously written, I am making all possible efforts so that the work on the original fragments from cave 4 will be finished by the end of 1960, and I shall reckon myself very happy if I can obtain this from my collaborators under the circumstances. I can therefore promise nothing for the summer of 1959. From a scientific perspective, there is the certain possibility that the study of the biblical fragments will then be finished, but it remains to be seen if, from a political perspective, it is necessary to ask then for their distribution to the institutions or if it will be better to wait until it all has been completed."[103]

Thus in July 1959 Scott spent the summer in Jerusalem and excavated at Gibeon.[104] During this time he met with de Vaux and Cross. The meetings resulted in eight points of agreement set out in a memorandum marked as "Private & Confidential."[105] Work on the Cave 4 scrolls was expected to be completed by 30 June 1960.[106] In the months preceding the intended completion date de Vaux contacted the purchasing institutions with the recommendation that they apply for export permits to the director of antiquities in Amman. In the event that no reply from the government was forthcoming, the institutions should collectively approach the Jordanians through diplomatic channels. At the time of export and shipment, the boxes used to transport the fragments to the Ottoman Bank in Amman during the 1956 Suez Canal Crisis could again be used. It was hoped and advised that each institution should provide a representative to be present in Jerusalem to manage the final arrangements. In exchange for the government's cooperation in the export of the material the institutions had to agree not to publish or exhibit any of the allotments that had not yet been officially published. In this way the members of the team could continue to maintain their rights to publication. A right to publication of the fragmentary material, that, according to John Strugnell, the editors had been granted exclusively by Jordan, "as an incentive they used in recruiting the scholarly manpower they wanted – they had no other lure to use to secure the services of mainly unpaid editors other than guaranteeing their rights to bring to a suitable end the work in which they were to invest so much time and effort."[107]

The insistence that the institutions could not publish or exhibit unpublished materials was necessary to maintain this agreement with the editors. While Scott frequently indicated in the press that the scrolls would occupy the minds of scholars for fifty years, neither he nor the editors could have predicted that it would take that length of time to publish the material.[108]

While this restrictive policy would raise significant concern in the scholarly world into the 1990s when the editorial team's monopoly was finally broken, none of the participants from McGill ever raised this point as a matter of concern. They seemed satisfied that they would receive the scroll fragments, followed eventually by a complete set of infra-red photographs of the materials once official publication was completed. Furthermore, providing McGill agreed, volume 4 of the official DJD publication was to be issued under a joint imprint of McGill University, the PAM, and the Jordan Department of Antiquities.[109]

In writing about his meeting in Jerusalem to McGill's donor, Scott reported that the key issue in all of this was that: "It is <u>very important</u> to have things handled without publicity until the stuff actually reaches Montreal."[110] This point is strengthened by a brief examination of the turmoil created by the purchase of the last known pieces of Cave 4 from the Bedouin a year earlier, in July 1958.

BUYING THE LAST PIECES FROM CAVE 4

The final pieces known to come from Cave 4 were purchased with funds from a second donation by McCormick and from the Unitarian Church of All Souls in Manhattan. McCormick's purchase amounted to $4,500 USD, again donated by the Nutrilite Foundation.[111] On 20 July 1958 the PAM purchased an "Incomplete miniscule scroll of Deuteronomy containing 5.5 columns,"[112] with funds received from All Souls. Their donor, who at the time chose to remain anonymous, was mining executive Thayer Linsley (1882–1976) who provided $5,000 USD after he was inspired by a series of lectures given by Frank Cross at the church the previous spring.[113] In contrast to the McCormick purchase, which was kept quiet, the All Souls' purchase generated a tremendous amount of unwanted publicity, at least from the perspective of parties in Jerusalem. Following the turmoil resulting from the rise of Arab nationalism in 1956, the PAM had made efforts to avoid publicity when foreign donors became involved with the scrolls.[114]

Unfortunately, when All Souls made their acquisition known to the public, the papers did not accurately report the conditions of the purchase. The Jordanian daily newspaper, *Ad-Difaa*, carried a Reuters report on 21 September 1958 which stated: "A Member of the Unitarian Church has bought these Scrolls, which, it was said, are in good condition. But these scrolls are still in the Palestine Archaeological Museum due to the regulations in force in Jordan."[115] The news of another foreign institution purchasing Jordanian treasures must have stirred protest in Jordan as Yusif Sa'ad, the museum curator, wrote to *Ad-Difaa*'s editor to correct the story and explain that the monies were received as a gift: "The Unitarian Church in America donated the money to the Palestine Archaeological Museum for the purchase of the Dead Sea scrolls. The Scrolls purchased are of course, the permanent property of the Museum, an enrichment of the historical treasures in our Country, like many other Scrolls we have been able to acquire through the generosity of different Donars [sic] from all over the world."[116] On the day this letter was written, Sa'ad also wrote to Cross asking him to speak to the church in the hope that it could get the American newspapers to correct the story.[117] A more accurate rendering of the story, for which Cross was interviewed, was published by *Time Magazine*. The report noted that, "All Souls Unitarians will have to travel to Jerusalem to see their acquisition as Jordanian law prohibits any cave finds from being taken out of the country. But the church will have its share of scholarly glory; the new scroll will henceforth be known in bibliographies as the 'All Souls Deuteronomy'."[118] Here, in contrast to *Ad-Difaa*'s rendering, it is clear that the material would not leave Jordan. The contributions from both institutions were gifts in keeping with a January 1958 agreement between the Department of Antiquities and the Jordanian prime minister. The ruling, 26/10/548 of 23 January 1958, states: "I agree to the delegation of Father de Vaux, Director of the Dominican School and Member of the Board of Trustees of the Palestine Archaeological Museum, to collect donations from abroad for the purpose of buying the ancient Manuscripts still remaining with Dealers on the markets, which Manuscripts to be kept in the Palestine Archaeological Museum."[119] But, although McCormick's second contribution was a gift to the PAM, it nevertheless maintained ownership to the fragments purchased during the summer of 1956.

FURTHER EDITING DELAYS

With the continued acquisition of new material, the prediction of only an additional year of work to complete study of the scrolls also proved wildly optimistic.[120] However, it continued to be assumed by a number of parties that the project could be completed by 1960.[121] De Vaux, in a March 1959 letter to John Allegro, already laid out the accelerated schedule and the reasons for it, warning: "I should tell you that this study will not be able to carry on in Jerusalem after the end of June 1960: this is in fact the last date set for the distribution of fragments among the Government, the Museum and the institutions that have bought them. Also, it is the date when the aid that Rockefeller gave for photographing the manuscripts will come to an end, and the Museum's own resources will not allow it to continue this service. Therefore the editors must gather before this date all the documents they need."[122] Although by 1960 much of the material had been photographed, catalogued, and roughly identified, most of the fragments were still decades away from thorough transliteration, translation, study, and publication.[123] But, as de Vaux did manage to ready all plates for shipment, after 1960 "identifying additional fragments" could no longer be blamed as "the main scholarly challenge," according to Neil Asher Silberman.[124] Of this same period, Frank Moore Cross recalls:

> De Vaux pressed the team to finish our jigsaw puzzles, our search for new manuscripts, and especially our attempts to identify the remaining unidentified fragments. We were not happy, feeling that this was an administrative decision rather than a scholarly decision. It is recorded that at this juncture 511 manuscripts had been identified, consisting of 620 glass plates. There were twenty-five plates of unidentified fragments left over. Such enumeration grossly distorted reality as we saw it. Most of the small fragments on the so-called identified plates were half-identified. That is, leather, lineation, and script suggested that they belonged with an identified manuscript but the fragments were not placed.[125]

Nevertheless, it is not entirely clear from the archival sources that either Scott or Frost was made aware of the broad nature and extensive scope of the developing crisis. Frost visited the PAM in May 1960. The purpose of his trip was to see the collection firsthand to be able to fully comprehend the preparations that needed to be made for its accommodation at McGill. Even before the trip Frost was concerned about the implications of housing the Dead Sea Scrolls at McGill. These he categorized according to two main categories. The first was the matter of preservation of the material – the types of glass and exhibit space that would be necessary. The second was that McGill did not have the manpower to accommodate scholars who wished to visit the collection to examine and study the fragments. McGill needed a scholar who was familiar with the scrolls and "could be Curator of the Scrolls and Research Assistant in Old Testament textual matters."[126] Frost also hoped to make personal contact with the appropriate Jordanian authorities to aid the eventual application for export permits.[127]

During the visit Frost and Sa'ad travelled to Amman, where they met with the acting director of the Department of Antiquities, Dja Bey Rifa'i, and with the minister of education, Sheikh Shingiti.[128] Frost provided both men with copies of all the necessary correspondence and they assured him that, at the appropriate time, the application for an export permit would be approved.[129] Frost was much relieved by the results of his meetings and the assurances that the agreements would be honoured.

The government's cooperation was that much more appreciated because at the same time a third party, apparently working on behalf of Jordan, was working to acquire not only McGill's fragments but all the Qumran material. John Allegro had created a scheme to raise £1 million to buy all the scrolls housed in the PAM, reconstruct the ruins at the site of Qumran, and create an exhibit space for all the scrolls there. By that time he had already raised £20,000.[130] Allegro's plan was not simply to centralize ownership of the scrolls but to wrest control of their publication from the hands of editors with particular religious commitments, with de Vaux an obvious target.[131] As early as January 1959 Allegro had approached the Jordanian director of antiquities, pressing the idea that the editorial team needed to be replaced by a larger group of scholars. This, Allegro suggested, could be achieved by finding a millionaire to supply the funds for the purchase of all the scrolls: "I am sure that some millionaire in the [United] States or elsewhere will put up the million dollars if we offer to call the collection by his name ... Then the scrolls can stay in *Jordan* – and I think this is terribly important. I do not want to see that stuff scattered all over the world, and it would be worth considering whether, with the money, we might be able to pay back those who have given some already, like Manchester, in order to keep what they bought of Cave Four in Jordan."[132]

Allegro continued to press the director on this matter. The influence Allegro wielded should not be underestimated: in December 1961, to reward his commitment to Jordan's cultural heritage, he would be appointed honorary adviser on the scrolls to the Government of Jordan by King Hussein and the Jordanian royal family.[133] While the plan did not come to fruition, Allegro's persistent pressure on the matter of the nationalization of the scrolls was felt by both the director and King Hussein.

Nevertheless, during his May 1960 visit to Jerusalem, de Vaux assured Frost that he expected McGill's fragments to be ready for export by the first of July of that year. Additionally, the director of antiquities promised him the cooperation of the department in acquiring the necessary export permit. The minister of education, responsible for overseeing the Department of Antiquities, also assured Frost that he foresaw no difficulties in granting the required permit.[134] Frost's optimism upon his return is most evident in his report to the local press: "It is hoped, Dean Frost said, that a selection of [McGill's fragments] will be put on public display at the university this fall."[135]

But all was not good news. Frost's public statements went against de Vaux's express desire to avoid publicity. It seems that among the reasons for de Vaux's insistence on minimizing publicity at this point was that he knew that it would have been impossible to meet the original agreement to the government's satisfaction and hence to export the material. The agreement between McGill and Harding required that the material be published before it left Jordan. But, while the fragments had for the most part been identified, the editorial team was still a long way from publication. Nevertheless, since the middle of 1959 de Vaux had been adhering to a somewhat different schedule, combined with an altered interpretation of the original agreement as set out in the original memorandum.

EVEN MORE EDITORIAL DELAYS

The publication and eventual export schedule became all the more complicated when, in 1960, the difficulties in the PAM and with the editorial team were exacerbated. Between 1942 and 1949, Carl Kraeling had served as the chairman of the grants committee of the American Council of Learned Societies, which was largely supported by the Rockefeller Foundation.[136] During this period he became a confidant of John D. Rockefeller, Jr. Thus it transpired that in 1953, while serving as president of ASOR, Kraeling convinced Rockefeller to support a team of scholars to study the scrolls at the PAM in Jerusalem. Rockefeller supplied an initial $30,000 USD and by 1960 had contributed close to $100,000 USD. Although some have argued that with the death of John D. Rockefeller, Jr in May 1960, funding for the project was cut, it seems more likely that due to the slow pace of work and the political turmoil surrounding the nationalization of the scrolls, the foundation administering the funds chose not to renew the three-year grant provided in 1957. Therefore, as hope faded as far as the editorial team's ability to honour their latest deadline for publication was concerned, it became apparent that the scholarly study of the materials would have to be completed by the team away from the scrollery at the PAM.[137]

The funding crisis had a twofold effect: not only did the scholars studying the scrolls no longer have access to this source of funding but ready funds for the purchase of any remaining manuscript material from the Bedouin were depleted.[138] In this light, an active attempt to get the material from Jordan to the purchasing institutions as agreed became essential for de Vaux to insure continued work on the scroll fragments for purposes of publication and easy access. As late as November 1960 de Vaux also tried to convince more institutions to buy material the PAM could no longer afford. As institutions interested in providing funds for Cave 11 material would be hesitant if the Jordanian government reneged on earlier agreements, de Vaux must have been able to present a firm belief in the government's assurance to stand by its earlier commitments. De Vaux's persistent search for donors, and his hope that Montreal and McGill would continue to be supportive, is evident in an interview with Montreal reporter Peter Mellors in Jerusalem, published in November 1960:

> "The Bedouin do not know how to look after the scrolls," [de Vaux] explained. "They maltreat them. They bury them in the ground. Every day that we do not buy them" – He sawed the air with his white-robed arms – "the scrolls deteriorate a little bit more."[139]
>
> "Then," he went on, "the Bedouin might grow impatient with us and sell fragments to unauthorized buyers. *Quelle catastrophe!* How can scholars study scattered scrolls? They are worthless then!" The white sleeves swept the air in a gesture of despair.
>
> "We are looking for universities to buy these scrolls," de Vaux said, pointing his pipe at me. "The university's own scholars would be able to come here and study the scrolls, and prepare them for publication – by the university itself."
>
> "McGill University bought some scrolls," he added as I was leaving. "Wouldn't others in Canada like some too?"[140]

The changed nature of the agreements that might be concluded with a new set of donors is evident from de Vaux's above plea: now the material remained the property of Jordan and the "purchasing" institutions acquired only the rights to publish the material, keeping in line with the January 1958 agreement between the Jordanian prime minister and the Department of Antiquities.

EDITORIAL WORK COMPLETED

On 4 June 1960 de Vaux wrote to representatives of each of the purchasing institutions to inform them that the work at the PAM had been completed. He provided details for the transfer of the fragments and their envisioned final shipment:[141]

> The Palestine Archaeological Museum asks you to nominate a representative who will come personally to Jerusalem to take delivery of your lot, supervise its packing, and see to its dispatching. The fragments will be handed over to him in the same condition in which the Museum preserves them, in other words, flattened, grouped together according to the Manuscripts to which they belong, and kept between plates of glass. This arrangement has guaranteed their preservation in good condition in the dry climate of Jerusalem, and it will suffice for their transport abroad. It has, however, a provisional character and each Institution in consultation with its technical advisers must take those measures of conservation which will suit its different climate and conditions. As for packing, the Museum has designed a type of box which would protect the Manuscripts during transport, and it can have such boxes made at the expense of any Institution which so desires.[142]

All the purchasing institutions and the Jordanian government received near identical letters. McGill acknowledged receipt of the letter with a petition directly to the Jordanian government for the necessary export permit.[143] A letter from the vice-chancellor of Manchester confirms that it too received de Vaux's recommendation to apply for an export permit. The letter, from W. Mansfield Cooper, dated 23 June 1960, indicates that they understood that the permits had to be secured and that they were obligated to "arrange to pick up the manuscripts personally."[144] In accepting their respective collections, each institution was asked to commit to three conditions: only texts already published could be displayed in public exhibitions; the institutions could not authorize a scholar to publish any of their respective texts until after the *editio princeps* had appeared; and no photographs of unpublished texts could be given to other scholars until the *editio princeps* appeared.[145]

On 4 June 1960, the same day as his letter to the various funding institutions, de Vaux further wrote a letter to the director of antiquities to inform him as well of the near completion of the project. He took elaborate care to remind him of the purchases made by foreign institutions and the need to honour them:

> On the proposal of the director of antiquities, the Jordan government allotted JD.15,000 for [the purchase of fragments], but this sum was not sufficient to acquire all the fragments. As, at that time, the government was not in a position to make a new grant, the council of ministers took in 1953 a decision to the effect that bona fide foreign institutions would be authorised to buy the remaining fragments under the following conditions: –
> 1) the purchases would be negotiated by the director of antiquities himself, using the money sent by the aforesaid institutions;
> 2) all the fragments would be kept at the Palestine Archaeological Museum for so long as the work of preparing them for publication should last, the editing work being entrusted to an international and interconfessional team of scholars acceptable to the department of antiquities;
> 3) at the end of this work of reassembling and deciphering the fragments, each institution would receive as its property not the mixed lot actually bought with their financial contribution but a group of manuscripts which would correspond, both in quality and quantity, to the amount of their contribution ...
> The total amount of their contributions was larger than the sum first allotted by the government ...
> In Spring 1956, the task of classifying and identifying the fragments was advanced enough to enable the director of antiquities to draw up a provisional division list of the fragments, and each institution concerned received at that time an official letter from the department of antiquities, indicating the composition of its share. The McCormick Theological Seminary was not yet included in this first list, as its financial contribution was received and spent only a little later, at the beginning of July 1956. This list had a provisional character, but subsequent study seems really to necessitate very few changes in it; they are the result of either a better understanding of the texts or of new purchases of fragments, they are mostly additions and they merely increase the value of each lot. I should like very much, Sir, to study with you these changes, in order to establish a final division list, which will meet with your approval.[146]
> The work on the fragments themselves, indeed, is now drawing to an end in the Palestine Archaeological Museum and, in July 1960,

the manuscripts from Cave Four will be at the disposal of the government and the institutions which contributed to their purchase. Notice has been given to these institutions that, as far as the Palestine Archaeological Museum is concerned, work on the lots finishes at the end of the current month, June 1960; but they were also warned that the fragments could not leave the Palestine Archaeological Museum until each institution should have obtained an export permit from the department of antiquities; they were instructed to apply directly to you for that purpose.[147]

De Vaux's final distribution lists are preserved in the archives of the IAA.[148] No copy was found in the archives of McGill University and none of the correspondence suggests that the lists were ever distributed to the institutions or even discussed with the director of antiquities. According to the final division, McGill was to receive the following:

Final 4[149]
CAVE IV. DISTRIBUTION LIST
MCGILL UNIVERSITY I

Label		Content	Number of plates	Remarks
C[150]	3	Gen. c	1	
	5, 5a	Gen. e,k	1	5a on one plate with McGill C3
	7a, 7b	Ex. b	2	1 plate added
	10	Ex. e	1	
	16–18	Num. a	4	1 plate added
	29	Deut. h	1	
	31b	Deut. g	1	
	32a	Deut. k	1	
	34	Josh. b	1	
	46a,b	Sam. c	2	1 plate added
	(49)			(transferred to McCormick)
	59	Minor Prophets d	1	on one plate with McGill C 62a
	62a	Ruth a		on one plate with preceding
	67–68	Dan. a	2	
	======			
Sn	1b–3	Ex. paleo-hebr. a	4	1 plate added
	19	Deut. square script	1	Published[151]
	23–24'	Is. c	3	1 plate added
	36–37'	Ps. b	3	1 plate added

	47–48'	Lev. In Greek	3	1 plate added. Part of pl.47 publishd [sic]¹⁵²
	50,50'		2	1 plate added
	======			
M	15–17	Jub. a	2	
	20	Jub. d	1	
	30', 30''			
	29–30	Eno. c,d	4¹⁵³	one fragm. published¹⁵⁴
	36'	Eno. astron. d	1	
	42	Test. Levi b	1	Formerly: M 41b
	43, 43'	Test. Nepht.	2	43' formerly: McGill A 24,28
	47a	Pseudo-historical	1	
	55	S. f	1	
	58	D. a	1	
	67–68	D. c	2	
	86	Berakot b	1	
	88–89	Mishmarot a	2	
	115a	Cryptic B ms. b	2	
	122–123	Sapiential	2	
	124a	Sapiential	1	
	130a	List of names	1	
	======			
A	9,9'a	Pesh. Hos. a	2	One plate added
	18	Astron. Cryptic	1	
	(24)			(Became a part of McGill M 43')
	(28)			(Became a part of McGill M 43')
	======			
H	3a	Milhama b	1	
	======			
Sl	10,10'	Joseph	2	1 plate added
	20–21'	Ps. of the Fathers c	4	2 plates added
	27	Psalms Jer.	1	
	28	Noachic	1	
	31–32	Proto-Mishna a	2	
	(35b)			(Transferred to McCormick with addition of provisory M 132, no suppressed)
	42b	Liturgical 4	1	on one plate with McGill Sl 45
	45	Liturgical 8		on one plate with preceding
	50–51	Sapiential	3	1 plate added: 50' from PAM acquisition
	(60)			(Transferred to PAM Sl 60,60' on exchange for Sl 50')

[End page 1]

Final 5
CAVE IV. DISTRIBUTION LIST
MCGILL UNIVERSITY 2

Label		Content	Number of plates	Remarks
Sl	66	Hodayot c	1	
	73a,b	Hymnic	1	on one plate with McGill Sl 76
	76	Hymnic 5		on one plate with preceding
	80a	Hymnic 10	1	
	======			
Sy	3–4	Ps. Eno. B	2	
	4bis	Noach	1	1 plate added
	10–10 bis	Vision Amram a	2	1 plate added
	20	Four Kingdoms b	1	
	22–24	New Jerusalem	2	
	29a	Vision (Aram.Q)	1	
	(32)			(Became: Bt 1)
	(35)			(Became: Bt 6)
	37	Apocalyptic	1	
	48	Unidentified (Hebr.A)	1	
	50–51	Unident;		
	(Elect of God)		1	50–51 on same plate
	54b	Unidentified (Aram.D)	1	
	======			
Bt	1	Halachic Work	2	Formerly: Sy 32
	6	Liturgical prayers	1	Formerly: Sy 35

Total plates in the final distribution list: 94[155]
(Total plates in the provisional distribution list: 84)

According to the final distribution lists, compared to McGill's 94 plates, the Jordanian Government was to receive 314 plates, the Vatican Library 62, the University of Manchester 41, the University of Heidelberg 48, and McCormick Theological Seminary 10. The École Biblique was to retain 16 plates of material that had been acquired primarily from the formal excavations carried out by de Vaux rather than by purchase from the Bedouin. The PAM expected to receive 19 plates it had purchased with its own funds and 11 it had purchased with financial gifts from McCormick, All Souls Church, and Oxford University.

The rush to complete the preliminary study of the material and the impetus to export the plates clearly resulted from the pressure placed on de Vaux and the team by the loss of the Rockefeller funding. The scholars had little choice but to complete as much of the hands-on work with the intact collection of fragments as soon possible before the fragments left the scrollery and were distributed among the donors. De Vaux clearly grasped that the funding crisis could create a situation in which the government could claim that the work could not be adequately completed and thus prevent the material from leaving Jordan until it considered the work completed.

THE SECOND ATTEMPT TO NATIONALIZE THE SCROLLS

By September 1960 Frost still had not received any response from the Jordanian government on his June 1960 request for an export permit. Concerned, he cabled de Vaux: "Have received no reply to my two letters to department seeking export permit stop Have you any information."[156] He received a telegram from Yusif Saʿad indicating that de Vaux was away but promising that he would write as soon as possible.[157] In September and October 1960 de Vaux was leading the archaeological excavation at Tell el-Farʿah (North).[158] On 2 October 1960, during a short weekend stop in Jerusalem, he responded to Frost: despite his best efforts to complete the work and arrange for export, the Jordanians planned to keep the material in Jordan. De Vaux suggested that the decision might be reversed, as had happened before, if diplomatic pressure was applied.[159]

In the earlier July letter informing the institutions that their material would soon be available, de Vaux had stated clearly that in the event that the export permits were denied he could do very little, as the PAM was not a government agency. Ironically, this position proved to be helpful in the present situation. In mid-August, the director of antiquities had written to de Vaux requiring that he communicate the details of the government's decision to nationalize the scrolls to the funding institutions. De Vaux was able to buy more time for the institutions with his reply:

> I very much regret to inform you that the Palestine Archaeological Museum is not in the position to communicate this government decision to the institutions involved in the purchase of fragments from Qumran Cave IV. All transactions concerning these purchases were negotiated directly between the institutions themselves and the director of

antiquities. It was the director of antiquities who notified the Institutions of their share of fragments which was allotted to each of them. In conformity with the Jordan Antiquities Law the institutions applied to the director of antiquities for an export permit; the government decision is the answer to these applications. It is, therefore, up to the department of antiquities and not the Palestine Archaeological Museum to communicate the government decision to the institutions concerned.[160]

De Vaux's uncooperative reply and his letter to Frost informing him of what was happening provided an opportunity for action to be taken before the government could communicate their final decision to the institutions directly.

At this stage the Jordanians may have considered it safe to once again claim the scrolls for the nation, as they had reason to believe their actions would go unchallenged. Frost, perhaps unknowingly, foreshadowed this issue in his report of his meeting with de Vaux in Jerusalem: "During my visit, Père de Vaux several times expressed his satisfaction that the University had evidenced its interest in this matter by sending a personal representative at so opportune a time, that is, just prior to the announcement that the manuscripts were ready for release. He said that my visit reminded the Jordanian Government that the earlier agreements concluded by them were by no means regarded by the University as a dead letter. McGill was the only institution which had done this, and he really appreciated our continued interest."[161] Although the Frost visit had highlighted McGill's serious commitment, his visit also suggested a lesser commitment on the part of the other institutions.

De Vaux's 2 October 1960 letter to Frost nevertheless allowed room for hope: while the Council of Ministers of Jordan had once again asserted national ownership of all scroll material, as a result of diplomatic pressure applied by the ambassadors of Britain and the United States, the council was reviewing its decision.[162] The two ambassadors were first approached to become involved because they were both trustees of the PAM. On this, the American correspondence has been preserved. On 22 August 1960, Sheldon T. Mills, the American ambassador to Jordan, wrote to the prime minister, Hazza al-Majali, requesting clarification of the Jordanian position. According to his letter, the Jordanians' desire to nationalize the scrolls, thereby preventing their export to the foreign institutions, had appeared in the 29 July 1960 edition of *Falastin*.[163] Of the Jordanian decision he wrote: "I have full confidence the Government of Jordan was and remains grateful to those eminent foreign institutions which provided the funds so that the remaining fragments from Qumran Cave Four could be acquired from the Bedouins rather than being sold to tourists or smuggled abroad. I also am confident that the Royal Government would take every means to avoid any action which might throw doubt on its good faith and its relations with the learned institutions of the world, particularly since archaeological activities by such institutions provide Jordan with one of the first means of making Jordan known favourably abroad and interesting tourists in visiting Jordan."[164]

Mills likely knew, as did the Jordanians, that the issue of reputation was a non-starter. Tourists would visit Jordan to see the scrolls. A good reputation would not attract tourists to Jordan when they could examine the original scrolls in the United States, Canada, or Europe. On 24 August 1960, the prime minister sent the director of antiquities to speak to Mills and to confirm the accuracy of the press article. The following day, Mills again wrote to the prime minister informing him repeatedly of the adverse effect the decision was likely to have on Jordan's reputation.[165] He then personally visited the minister of education, responsible for the Department of Antiquities. The minister concluded that "the scrolls and fragments should remain in Jordan, that the 1952 Cabinet decision on the basis of which the arrangements had been made with the four institutions was obscure, and therefore he recommended that their money be returned."[166]

To increase the pressure on the Jordanian Government, Frost used multiple diplomatic channels. He began with a letter dated 11 October 1960 to Paul Beaulieu, the ambassador at the Canadian embassy in Beirut, as well as to the British ambassador in Amman.[167] By good fortune the Canadian ambassador had a member of his mission, Donald Munro,[168] on a visit to Jordan the following week and replied that he would look into the matter for McGill: "I should perhaps tell you that Jordanian newspapers have lately carried reports that the Council of Ministers of the Jordanian Government recently decided to place a ban on the export of the Scrolls. Whether any such ban is intended to extend to all fragments, or to certain ones only, is a matter which Mr. Munro will be able to inquire into more fully. In any event, he will make a particular point of trying to get an official confirmation of these reports."[169] During Munro's visit, meetings were held with Dr Awni Dajani, the director of antiquities in Jordan, the *chargés d'affaires* of both the American and British embassies, with the Apostolic delegate in Jerusalem, and with Father de Vaux.[170] The meetings were not particularly fruitful and served little more than to clarify that none of the institutions had yet succeeded in obtaining an export permit and that no copies of the official documents related to the purchase and receipt of funds were recorded with the Jordanian Department of Finance. As a result, not only would the institutions not receive their allotments, but the reimbursement of the funds to the institutions – as an alternative – was also on hold. Beaulieu reported as much to Frost:

> Dr. Dajani, the present Director of Antiquities, said to Mr. Munro [the Canadian representative] that he was planning within the next day or so to be writing to each of the institutions asking if he could be informed of the manner in which the funds were first transmitted to his predecessor. According to the Director, there are no records in the Jordanian Ministry of Finance of the receipt of the funds, nor of their conversion into Jordanian dinars. Judging from a letter, No. 18/3/637, from Mr. Lankester Harding to Dr. Scott at McGill, receipts for at least some of the funds must have been made out and sent to the purchasers. Dr. Dajani, however, claimed that he was in the difficult position of being unable to provide the Jordanian Department of Finance with a detailed statement of the funds paid over, and in what currencies payments were made. From Dr. Dajani's point of view such information was required to prepare the ground so that the Jordanian Ministry of Finance could reimburse the various institutions, in accordance with the most recent Cabinet decision, in the currencies originally used in the transactions.
>
> As I mentioned in my previous letter, the Jordanian Council of Ministers has decided that the fragments should remain in Jordan and that the institutions should be reimbursed. Dr. Dajani is now toying with the idea of suggesting to the five institutions that, following the Cabinet decision, two courses were open to them:
> (a) that they be reimbursed in full for the payments, or,
> (b) that they might like to have established in Jordon [sic], foundations in their respective names, where the Scroll fragments assigned to them will be displayed.[171]

Discussions among the dignitaries and with de Vaux, but excluding Dajani, nevertheless encouraged the institutions to try once more to have the Jordanians revisit their decision. Most significantly, the Canadian ambassador concluded that fear of Israel was driving the Jordanian decision: "I may add that Père Devaux [sic] is of the opinion that one of the reasons the Jordanian authorities are unwilling to let the fragments leave the country is that they are haunted by the fear that they will be repurchased and show up in an archaeological institution in Israel."[172] Soon after, this view was presented in the national press:

Because King Hussein of Jordan could not take any more needling from Egypt's Gamal Abdel Nasser's propaganda machine, Montreal's McGill University, the Vatican Library, Manchester University and a half dozen museums, which five years ago paid a small fortune for fragments (not complete manuscripts) from the Dead Sea Caves, will now be happy if they can get their money back.

After prolonged stalling, Jordan finally reneged on the delivery, even though the international team of scholars had prepared for publication the last of the sold fragments. The reason is simple. Egyptian propaganda has for years blamed Jordan for allowing most of the manuscripts to be sold to Israel via the United States.

The Jordanians had once believed that such a thing could not happen, but 250,000 U.S. greenbacks and an unidentified buyer did the trick. King Hussein knows only too well that his shaky throne could tumble under renewed accusations of dealing with Israel.[173]

Any negative Egyptian propaganda on Jordan's management of the Dead Sea Scrolls matter must be understood in the context of the centrality of Egyptian antiquities to the establishment of its own national identity. In 1922 the British had granted Egypt semi-autonomous status. Despite this, the antiquities service and the major museums remained in the hands of European scholars. Thus the French scholar Pierre Lacau (1873–1963) served as director of the Egyptian Antiquities Service from 1914 until 1936. He was replaced in 1936 by another Frenchman, Étienne Drioton (1889–1961), who served as director of the Egyptian Museum of Cairo as well. In 1926 Gaston Wiet (1887–1971), a fellow of the French Institute of Archaeology, was appointed director of the Cairo Museum of Arab Art. Only in the early 1950s did this situation change. In the spring of 1951, Wiet was forced from his position by pressure from the nationalist Wafdist government. As a result of the Free Officers' Coup in July 1952, Drioton eventually returned to France.[174] The removal of foreign figures from seats of cultural power and influence, along with British officers in the military and government bureaucracy, was essential to the Egyptian nationalist movement. For the first time in a century Egypt alone controlled its antiquities and national treasures.[175] Nasser was among the leaders of the 1952 coup and took control of the government in 1954. It had been up to Nasser to win, "both political independence and full national control of museums, archaeology, and educational institutions."[176]

In 1959, when the Aswan Dam threatened to flood Nubia, potentially destroying sensitive archaeological sites, Egypt was forced to turn to UNESCO and Western governments for help in exchange for a share in the discoveries and the export thereof.[177] This created ongoing tension and left the Egyptians sensitive to the very limited power they had over their own cultural heritage. By comparison, in 1957, at the time of the setting up of the purchase agreements here discussed for the Dead Sea Scrolls fragments, it was also rumoured that Nasser's Egypt was willing to sell treasures from the Tutankhamen collection because of a dire need for Western currency. The response in the press to the rumour appears to accurately reflect both the Egyptian self-perception and Egypt's concern over Jordan's willingness to sell the scrolls: "It would certainly be a catastrophic confession of weakness if the present government entertained a notion of selling anything so acutely concerned in the nation's *amour propre* as the Tutankhamen treasures."[178]

Despite the not-inconsiderable pressure from other Arab states, Jordan's determination to retain the scrolls was not only the result of the influence asserted by Egypt. In addition to increasing Jordanian national pride, the scrolls also held the possibility of increasing the Kingdom's limited fortunes in terms of tourist revenue. Therefore the Jordanians had as many good reasons to void their agreements with the foreign institutions as the institutions had to counter the Jordanian efforts.

THE TREASURE OF THE DEAD SEA SCROLLS

McGill's apparent loss of the scrolls did not deter Frost. In his own presentations to the media he continued to favour the position that McGill would persevere and eventually receive the material allotted to the university in the purchase agreement. On 26 November 1960 he was quoted in the press as confirming that after thirteen years [from the date of the original discoveries] some of the scrolls were now coming to Canada and to McGill.[179] Frost, inspired by de Vaux's thoughts on the Israel connection, would later suggest to the Jordanian minister of education that if McGill were allowed to have its fragments, "the University is ready to give a solemn undertaking never to dispose of these fragments to any other party whatsoever."[180]

Despite Frost's assurances, Jordan's disappointing loss of the entire collection of relatively intact scrolls from Cave 1 remained an open wound. And, as has already been suggested, the great emotive power[181] created by Jordan's loss of ownership of these cultural objects was also informed by other practical considerations in making the final decision to nationalize the scroll fragments. Although the Jordanians claimed that these materials were a part of the "spiritual legacy of all mankind,"[182] national identity and monetary value at times trumped that view.

The earlier stutter-steps toward nationalization of the scrolls had been reversed because of the government's recognition that it could not afford to reimburse the institutions that had purchased Cave 4 materials. This could not be done either in terms of their present value or original purchase price.[183] According to Scott, de Vaux told him that, "the letter of the former Minister of Education declaring that all the Scrolls would be retained in Jordan was definitely countermanded by the Council of Ministers, after strong (and risky!) representations by himself and the Museum. The Government will stand by its bargain because it cannot afford to refund the money given."[184] By 1960 this situation appears to have changed. Earlier, the Jordanians had expressed concern about the loan of the material for display outside the country, as it was a tourist attraction that could potentially increase the number of visitors to Jordan. They recognized the global public's willingness to pay to see the material for themselves but it was only by 1960 that they truly came to understand the financial potential inherent to the ownership of the scrolls. A November 1960 news article in the London *Times* records an announcement by the Jordanian director of antiquities, Awni Dajani. Accordingly, the board of trustees of the PAM had "agreed in principle to exhibit the Scroll of 'Psalms' at the Washington National Gallery in exchange for £21,000, while another scroll would be shown at a Dutch Museum for £20,000. Others would be loaned to the British Museum for £25,000."[185] A similar report appeared in the Montreal *Gazette*.[186] It seems that the Jordanian authorities came to understand that, apart from the principle of non-estrangement of cultural property, keeping the scrolls in Jordan would prove more lucrative than allowing them to be sent abroad to the institutions that purchased them relatively "cheaply" in 1954 and 1955.[187] Such a step would have certainly undermined the economic benefit to the kingdom. Although none of the planned exhibits took place, the scrolls were eventually exhibited in London in December 1965.[188] The *Times* article includes one more interesting fact: "An American archaeologist, Dr. Brownley [sic], is to be allowed to study certain scrolls in return for a payment of £3,000." While the exact arrangement remains unclear – presumably Dajani was speaking of William H. Brownlee who was affiliated with ASOR – it is quite clear that the negotiations over publication rights to the Cave 11 Psalms Scroll demonstrated to the Jordanians that scholars and scholarly institutions were prepared to pay significant sums of money in exchange for rights to study or publish the scrolls without endangering

Jordan's custodial rights to the scrolls.[189] It came to be understood that national treasures could fill national treasuries.[190]

This is no small conclusion. Even though the monetary significance of the scrolls to Jordan may have been underplayed in the undeniably legitimate nationalistic fervour that claims to the scroll fragments evoked, the centrality of the matter of "value" – monetary or otherwise – to national interests in cultural heritage in general cannot be ignored.[191] Frank Fechner's explanation of the aims of cultural property law illustrates this best in terms of instances of estrangement of movable cultural objects and the claims thereto by source nations: "The law of cultural property is primarily based on the interests of the states concerned. If a cultural object is of high monetary or identificatory value, states will contest the ownership, and many of these cases are resolved by compromise. If a cultural object is of less monetary or identificatory value, states often neglect its preservation."[192]

REQUEST FOR PROOF OF PURCHASE

On 22 October 1960 the inevitable had happened. Frost, along with the representatives of the other institutions concerned (the Vatican Library, the University of Manchester, the University of Heidelberg, and McCormick Theological Seminary) received a request from the Jordanian minister of education to submit all official documents related to their purchase: "We have found it difficult to gather this information because neither the registers of the Ministry of Finance, nor of the Comptroller of the Department of Antiquities, nor of our accounts with the Ottoman Bank show any record of any payments made by you for the above mentioned purpose."[193]

The lack of confirmatory documentation on the part of the Ministry as far as McGill's purchase is concerned may be easily explained. In part, the difficulty stemmed from the fact that the payments Harding had received from McGill were made out in his name and were paid in cash to the Bedouin, seemingly bypassing the bank. But the Jordanian claim to have no documents relating to the purchase also functioned as a stalling tactic on the part of the government. By claiming they had no record of the purchases, the Jordanians forced the institutions to prove their right to ownership. In principle, the Jordanians could argue that the agreements were the result of a free agent, Harding, who acted without government approval.[194] If his activities had been legitimate, it could be argued, certainly appropriate records of it would have been kept by the applicable government agencies. In requesting the forwarding of copies of the pertinent documents, Jordan transferred the responsibility from the government to the institutions themselves to prove their right to ownership. If the purchasers could not prove that an agreement was in place, the government had no liability for reimbursement and there was no good reason to allow the fragments to leave Jordan.

But McGill's purchase was well documented[195] and McGill's evidence for the purchases was submitted by Frost on 23 November 1960 with a polite argument against reimbursement and a repeated request for an export permit:[196] "I trust that Your Excellency will find here all the information which he needs in order that the requisite export permit may be issued. Your Excellency will recall that I wrote to the Department of Antiquities on June 10, 1960 requesting the issue of such a permit, and that I wrote again on August 5, 1960 saying that I have received no reply to my previous letter. Your letter of the 22nd of October makes no reference to my previous letters nor to the issuance of a permit, but I trust that you now have full and sufficient information in order that such a permit may be issued forthwith."[197]

Along with the letter to the minister of education, Shingiti, Frost continued his approach by diplomatic means by sending a letter describing the situation to the Canadian secretary of state for external affairs, Howard Green. Green's response was not particularly helpful: "I think that concentration by all the various interested parties on 'quiet diplomacy' offers the best hope for a successful outcome in this matter."[198] In conclusion, he sympathetically assured Frost that Canadian representatives in the Middle East would continue to help however possible.[199] The Canadian government, however, clearly did not wish to create an international incident over the purchase of fragments of ancient scrolls. Thus in August 1961 Frost received a follow-up letter in which the Canadian government suggests that reimbursement was the best solution for all: "It is our understanding that by the terms of this decision ownership of all the Scrolls found in the Dead Sea area since 1953 must remain the property of the Hashemite Kingdom of Jordan and be retained within that country. The decision also involves the repayment to the educational institutions of funds paid for the export from Jordan of the Scrolls. I presume that the Government of Jordan has already written you and informed you of this decision, and I would trust that the matter is now in process of settlement."[200] But Frost was not yet prepared to relinquish McGill's claim to ownership of the Cave 4 fragments, a right that was not solely the result of the transfer of thousands of dollars:

> The University has a full legal claim to the allocation made to it in 1954 and does not intend to forgo its right to these fragments. They are of considerable interest to Biblical scholars throughout the world and to have this collection in Canada would greatly increase the quality

of the work done here, besides attracting scholars and visitors from
far afield. McGill's contribution was prompt and timely when it was
greatly needed, and was I believe the largest made. Without this help,
the Museum authorities would not have been able to recover the scrolls
from the Bedouin. We have therefore not only a legal but also a strong
moral right to our allocation of fragments.[201]

In June 1961 Frost, again along with the representatives of Manchester,
the Vatican, Heidelberg, and McCormick, received a single response to their
petitions from Shingiti, the minister of education of Jordan. The response
was a brief note asking how they wanted to be reimbursed and where the
money should be directed along with a copy of the 8 May 1961 cabinet
resolution declaring the scrolls the property of Jordan:[202]

> The Cabinet has reviewed all the resolutions passed by them since 1953
> on the subject of the Dead Sea scrolls. After study, the Cabinet arrived at
> the following conclusions:
> 1. Because of their antiquity-importance as well as their scientific, historical and religious value, it is necessary to keep these scrolls in the Kingdom.
> 2. The funds, which have been previously paid by educational establishments for the purpose of exporting the scrolls, shall be returned.
> 3. Financial assistance for the collection of the scrolls in the Kingdom shall henceforth be accepted as free offer in exchange for such facilitation as the Government may grant to the giver for the study of the scrolls, their photography or their publication in general service to history and knowledge. The Jordanian Government shall, however, be entitled to prevent, in such time and circumstances as it sees fit, the exposition of these scrolls outside the Hashemite Kingdom of Jordan, in agreement with the offering institutions.
>
> The reason for this is that these scrolls constitute an indivisible part of the history of Jordan in particular and of the spiritual legacy of all mankind. This being the case, neither the antique treasure as a whole nor any part thereof shall be allowed to be lost through transfer of property rights to any party.[203]

After several unsuccessful early attempts by the Jordanians to nationalize the scrolls, Frost recognized with this resolution that the likelihood of McGill taking possession of its collection was dwindling. Frost nevertheless made a counter offer based on the wording of the third section of the cabinet resolution: "I note in particular the wording of the last sentence of the first paragraph of section 3: 'the Jordanian Government shall, however, be entitled to prevent, in such time and circumstance as it sees fit, the exposition of these scrolls outside the Hashemite Kingdom of Jordan, in agreement with the offering institutions'. I wish to enquire whether the interpretation is correct that the Jordanian Government, while retaining full legal possession of the fragments originally allotted to this University, would be prepared in lieu of returning the money paid by us in 1954–55 to allow the collection to come to McGill on long loan, in order that it may be displayed to the public and further studied at this University."[204] The proposal received no written reply. Had there been one, it most certainly would have been negative.

Meanwhile, the British ambassador received confirmation that the Jordanians had agreed to allow exhibition of loaned material outside Jordan: "It is understood that the Jordan Government will give permission for Scrolls to be exhibited abroad on suitable conditions to be agreed at Government level, and that priority will be given in this matter to countries from which contributions have been received."[205] However, the Jordanians were offering short-term loans of scroll material to the British and others for £25,000. In light of this, the suggested long-term loan of ninety-four plates in exchange for McGill's earlier contribution of approximately $20,000 CAD would have damaged Jordan's ability to benefit financially from controlling the vast majority of this collection of scrolls material.

When, by October 1961, McGill had still received no response, Frost again turned to the Department of External Affairs of Canada, which agreed to communicate on McGill's behalf with the Jordanians.[206] External Affairs Canada was not convinced of the acceptability of McGill's proposal to the Jordanians: "It occurs to us that your request for a 'permanent' or 'long-term' loan of the fragments may perhaps go farther than the Government intended. Nevertheless, we will communicate with our Embassy in Beirut to see if an official enquiry can advance your request in any way."[207] When by March 1962 still no Jordanian response was forthcoming, Frost wrote again to Shingiti: "I have not received any reply ... and therefore I have no alternative but to request the return of the monies paid by this University."[208] This extensive delay was not solely the result of stalling on the part of the Jordanians. The parliamentary elections of October 1961 almost certainly played a part.

Nonetheless, on 20 June 1962 Frost informed Scott of what appeared to be the final outcome of their collective effort: "I know that you will be disappointed to know that the fragments will not come to McGill but there does not now seem to be any possibility of obtaining them, and we can put the money to good use in other ways."[209] Scott responded that he hoped at the very least to have the material exhibited in Jordan as the McGill collection. But the university had decided that reimbursement was more beneficial.[210]

From March to June 1962 no response came with regard to the return of McGill's funds. Additional letters were carried through diplomatic channels by the under-secretary of state for External Affairs of Canada, but met with no success.[211] And again R.B.Y. Scott returned to the scene. Scott spent the academic year of 1962–63 at ASOR in Jerusalem. Frost sent copies of the correspondence ahead of Scott to Jerusalem by means of government officials. He hoped that Scott in person might be able to help arrange reimbursement. Scott arrived in Jerusalem in June 1962. On 27 June 1962 Frost was informed by Dr Awni Dajani that the monies were ready for settlement.[212] The Jordanian government, however, wanted the PAM to turn over trusteeship of the manuscripts to the Department of Antiquities before the funds could be released. Since this had not yet taken place, the monies could not be paid. On the day Dajani wrote to Frost, he also wrote to Yusif Sa'ad, then curator of the PAM, requesting that all the scrolls be handed over to the government: "I request you to take the necessary steps for handing over, to the Directorate of Antiquities, along with complete detailed lists, all the Dead Sea Scrolls which have been bought with the funds given by the five foreign educational Institutes mentioned below, including the Scrolls bought by the Department of Antiquities."[213]

The delay in the transfer resulted from the inability of the curator to act without a resolution from the museum board of trustees. Sa'ad met with Dajani and explained the situation. Dajani in turn asked that a translation of his original Arabic letter be circulated to the trustees of the museum, but by 10 July 1962 Sa'ad had still received no response from them.[214] In mid-August 1962 Dajani again requested the transfer of the manuscripts because, "the foreign Institutes, who have contributed towards the salvage of the Dead Sea Scrolls, are now pressing hard for the refund of money paid by them."[215] By December 1962, aggravated, Scott complained to Dajani on McGill's behalf that nearly six months had passed since the letter indicating that the monies were ready to be reimbursed. Furthermore, he had recently heard that guardianship of the scrolls had been removed from the museum by the government: "there is no longer any obstacle to the prompt repayment to McGill which you promised in your letter of June 27th. I hope that you will give this matter your attention at the earliest possible time in view of the long delay since that date."[216] As early as September, the government had stated publicly that they were taking the scrolls from Jerusalem for display in Amman: "Jordan's Antiquities Department announced Saturday [29 September 1962] it will take over all the Dead Sea Scrolls in the Palestine Archaeological Museum in the Jordanian sector of Jerusalem in October ... The department said it will refund the money given by foreign organizations and institutions to buy the scrolls from shepherds and Bedouins who found them."[217]

A PERSONAL DISAPPOINTMENT

The monies payable to McGill University finally arrived in April 1963.[218] The University received its original $19,563.52 and used a quarter of the funds to create a collection of materials and books related to the Dead Sea Scrolls for the university. Nevertheless, all involved experienced a tremendous sense of loss. On 8 April 1963, reporting the final receipt of McGill's money from the Jordanian government to Scott, Frost wrote: "Thank you very much indeed for all the care and trouble you have taken about this. We know in some ways it represents a personal disappointment that the fragments never came to McGill but the initiative you took ... meant a very great deal for the Scrolls' project at that time."[219]

McGill's loss of the Cave 4 collection of fragments and the subsequent reimbursement received little more than cursory reference among other scrolls discussions in the national and local press. The most extensive coverage appeared in the *Montreal Star* in March 1962: "The Jordanian government ... in claiming sole proprietorship, is going no further than other Middle East governments. Its action, not startling in itself, disappoints those foreign institutions – including Manchester, Heidelberg and McGill universities and the Vatican Library – which together had raised £21,000 to help the museum to buy scrolls from the nimble Bedouin who f[ou]nd them. The scroll fragments promised in return they will not now have. Instead it seems, they will be reimbursed for their payments and will have to be content with loan exhibitions. At the same time the museum has agreed with the Jordan government that while the government is owner, the museum [the PAM] shall be the keeper – and possession is, after all, nine points of the law."[220]

As far as the media was concerned, the story was over. The press remained silent on the topic after this. Scott would address the matter once more years later in 1981 when he was asked to recollect the events in a personal account to the McGill Religious Studies newsletter, ARC: "Even though McGill and the other learned institutions failed in the end to gain possession of their promised Scrolls, the effort was more than worthwhile. These priceless relics of antiquity were saved for the use of Biblical and historical scholarship. All – or almost all – have been carefully examined and photographed. Otherwise they might have been damaged further by unskilled handling or sold to tourists as souvenirs."[221] Scott took the opportunity to salute Roland de Vaux for his efforts on McGill's behalf: "The chief credit in any case belongs to the late Père de Vaux. When we met afterwards he said to me – 'I risked my life to get the money back!' I do not think he was exaggerating; for such a man this was an affair of honour."[222]

In truth, the story is one of heroic action on the part of many. The Jordanian government supplied funds early on when their budget could ill afford it in times of economic hardship after the war. Harding and de Vaux staked their reputation and relentlessly sought donors to save the newly discovered material from dispersal on the black market.[223] Scott, James, the Birks family, and McGill took a chance when no other institution was willing to do so. And so all the role players in this story contributed to safeguard the Dead Sea Scrolls collection from dispersal and ensured the preservation of an ancient treasure for all who identify with it because of religious, linguistic, geographical, national, or cultural affiliation.

4

The Real Question:[1] The Nation, the Object, and Owning the Past[2]

Cultural heritage – one's own or a nation's heritage – is central to a sense of purpose and place in the world. Artworks, religious icons, monuments, literary manuscripts, traditional myths, and rituals, hold the power to create a profound sense of belonging ... Sustaining identity is not only a matter of valuing heritage but also requires the framing of one's own past against that of others through appropriation and possession. The collecting of antiquities has been essentially a practice of representation as well as ownership. Struggles to come to grips with the question of who owns the past have, consequently, been perennial ones.

Claire Lyons[3]

On 1 November 1966 the Jordanian government nationalized the Palestine Archaeological Museum, a private institution, and also its holdings, of which the most important were the scroll fragments from the Dead Sea.[4] Although Jordan had reasserted ownership of the Dead Sea Scroll fragments in May 1961,[5] now also the PAM, as the physical custodian of the scrolls since purchase from the Bedouin, had been nationalized. The purpose was clearly to keep the Dead Sea Scrolls collection – the most important of the holdings of the museum – intact and firmly in Jordanian custody and preserved in a national museum under direct government control.

John Allegro's correspondence in the latter part of 1966 provides insight into what he, as honorary adviser on the scrolls for Jordan, considered as the priorities to be set for the museum after nationalization. But his correspondence can also be interpreted as his rationalization of the decision to nationalize. The deteriorating state of the fragments and the excruciatingly slow publication rate are repeatedly emphasized by Allegro as motivation for action.[6] In a September 1966 memorandum to the Jordanian prime minister, indicating Allegro's foreknowledge of the decision to nationalize, he would impatiently write: "Already far too much time has been lost in tackling the very difficult situation posed by the finding and custody of the Dead Sea Scrolls. The grave responsibility for the care and publication of these documents will shortly fall upon Jordan."[7]

Days earlier, in a letter to Dajani on 13 September 1966, John Allegro had described the circumstances at the PAM to emphasize the responsibility the government was taking on, but undoubtedly also to influence government policy vis-à-vis the scrolls after nationalization:

> The situation at the Museum in Jerusalem is far less happy where the Scrolls are concerned and must give cause for grave concern ... Very clearly something urgent has to be done to ensure that adequate steps are taken to safeguard the fragments, and to stir up those responsible for the long overdue publication of the Cave Eleven material ... These delays must not be allowed to continue, and after the end of the year, responsibility for seeing they do not will rest entirely on the heads of your Department and the Government. The Trustees having failed in their duties, the onus will fall upon your people, and the finger of accusation of the world will point unjustly at Jordan unless something is done soon ... Also involved is a world appeal for money to prepare the published fragments for preservation ... to enable them to be properly housed where all may see them and scholars may study them, and to enable further searches to be made under the direction of the Department of Antiquities for more.[8]

Allegro would offer the appointment of an "overall Director of Scrolls"[9] as a solution to address the challenges outlined above and to raise the much needed money for conservation of the collection. This was not an unbiased approach, especially as far as the proposed replacement of de Vaux was concerned. Allegro's agenda as expressed by his daughter, Judith Brown, was that, "He believed that since they [the scrolls] were found in Jordan they belonged to Jordan, and the Jordanian government should look after them. Because he saw them mishandled and access blocked by de Vaux and the Trustees, he wished to have them removed from their control."[10]

But Allegro's vision for the scrolls after nationalization would never come to pass. Less than a year later East Jerusalem and the museum, as a nationalized institution, became part of Israel after the Six-Day War. War broke out on 5 June 1967. The museum had been used as a firing position by the Arab Legion and was captured by Israeli troops but not before suffering extensive damage on the outside.[11] William G. Dever was in Jerusalem during the war and provided a first-person account of its aftermath in a report dated 8 August 1967 to the readers of the *Biblical Archaeologist*. He reported the following about his first glimpse of the museum after the war:

> The Palestine Archaeological Museum we found sealed off. An inspection tour a few days later revealed that the exterior of this beautiful building was pock-marked by small-arms fire, particularly around the inner courtyard, and that the tower, which had been used as a gun position by the Jordanians, was rather badly damaged. Precious objects which had survived in the soil thousands of years lay broken by ricocheting bullets ... The Dead Sea Scrolls Gallery was empty. Readers of the BA may not know that the Museum ... had been nationalized late last year by Jordan. The government of Israel considers her agencies the legitimate successors to those of the Jordanian government, and has placed the Museum under the supervision of the Department of Antiquities of the Ministry of Education and Culture. The Department ... has asked the Israel Museum to repair and reopen the exhibits under a temporary curator. The galleries reopened about July 1, and a recent visit to the Museum showed very little evidence of what had happened ... The Scroll Gallery is still empty, but reports about the 'mysterious disappearance' of the Scrolls are dismissed by Dr. Magen Broshi, Curator of the Shrine of the Book at the Israel Museum, and Dr. Joseph Naveh of the Department of Antiquities, who are charged with making a catalogue of the Scrolls in the storerooms. Although the lack of a complete inventory of what was formerly in the possession of the Museum makes it difficult to be certain, they feel that nearly all of the thousands of fragments will eventually be accounted for.[12]

Broshi and Naveh's assessment proved true. Despite having contingency plans in place, this time the fragments had not been moved as had happened during the Suez Crisis. Weston Fields relates: "Dr. Awni Dajani ... Director of Antiquities of Jordan, had set out from Amman, having taken upon himself the responsibility of transporting the scrolls from Jerusalem, but was forced to turn back because the Amman-Jerusalem road had been severely cratered by bombing. When Israeli troops captured the Palestine Archaeological Museum after a fierce gun battle, they found all the Dead Sea Scrolls, packed in wooden crates in the basement, ready for transfer to Jordan, but still in Jerusalem."[13] By order of Yigael Yadin,[14] Professor Nahman Avigad of the Hebrew University and Dr Avraham Biran as the Israeli director of antiquities gained access to the museum shortly after its capture, on 6 June 1967.[15] Avigad and Biran were the first Israeli scholars to see the fragments.[16] Thus, in June 1967 possession of the collection was transferred from Jordan to Israel with the capture of East Jerusalem and the 1966 decision by the Jordanian government to nationalize would allow Israel to gain possession of the main respository of the scrolls. The primary collection of discovered material from the Dead Sea was now in Israel's custody and reunited with the scrolls from Cave 1 that Israel already owned. There were some exceptions: the Copper Scroll (3Q15) was not in Jerusalem at the time of the war. It is currently located in the Archaeological Museum of Amman, Jordan, along with approximately twenty other scroll fragments. These were on loan for purposes of exhibition at the time and were not returned to the museum after the Israeli takeover.[17]

Sadly, the nationalization of the collection by Jordan and later transfer of custody to Israel did not better the position of the scholarly community as far as accelerated publication and open access were concerned.[18] In a 26 July 1967 meeting with de Vaux, the Israelis set two conditions for de Vaux and his team: "One was that they were to proceed quickly with the publication of the thousands of fragments they had had at their disposal for so many years ... Our [the government of Israel's] second condition called for a change in the title of the official series of publications of what little *had* been allowed to see the light of scientific day. They had been called 'Discoveries in the Judean Wilderness of Jordan'.[19] We wanted some reference to the fact that the studies were now continuing under Israeli auspices."[20] Hence, the status quo prevailed. On 27 July 1967 the *Jerusalem Post* reported: "Scholars who worked on the Rockefeller Museum's Dead Sea Scrolls before Israel took over the museum last month are assured first publication rights for their researches. This was decided yesterday at a meeting between Pere [sic] de Vaux, chief scrolls editor, Prof. Yigael Yadin representing the Shrine of the Book and Dr. Avraham Biran, director of the Antiquities Department."[21]

The push to transfer ownership to the foreign purchasing institutions and the unstable political situation in the late 1950s and early 1960s had added a sense of urgency to the editorial team's activities[22] and encouraged the speedy publication of the material. But the momentum was quickly lost. The loss of funding for the editorial team and their activities in the scrollery in June 1960 had a distinct impact on the consequent lag in publication and matters were further complicated after the nationalization of the scrolls in 1961. The editorial team never again had the luxury of working together in one place. "Had publication ensued quickly, the international team would have emerged as heroes for their expert and speedy work. But the various delays that took place after they left Jerusalem, coupled with the denial of access to other scholars, eventually led to the controversy," comments Lawrence Schiffman of this lost opportunity in the history of scrolls research.[23] Cross, Skehan, and Strugnell left Jerusalem for academic positions in the United States. Cross went to Harvard;[24] Skehan to Catholic University in Washington, D.C.,[25] and Strugnell to Duke University in North Carolina and later also to Harvard.[26] Allegro returned to the University of Manchester[27] and Milik went to Rome and later returned to Paris.[28] The scholars worked primarily from photographs of the material. Not only did the distance impede scholarly interchange of ideas, their absence from Jerusalem also meant that they were away from the watchful eye of the editor-in-chief. The first volume of Cave 4 materials appeared only in 1968. (De Vaux had delayed the publication in the hope that more editors would have material ready for publication.)[29] As well, de Vaux's attention had turned to encouraging the acquisition of further documents from Cave 11 and the acquisition of the Samaria Papyri discovered in February 1962 in a cave in Wadi ed-Daliyeh.

PRESERVATION OF THE FRAGMENTS, 1962–1966

In the period following the nationalization of the scrolls, as John Allegro and others pushed the Jordanians to exhibit abroad, in March 1962 de Vaux had Harold Plenderleith examine the fragments with the goal of improving the conditions of their preservation.[30] According to Pnina Shor and Lena Libman, Plenderleith's primary task was to examine the Ezekiel scroll, which was later published by William H. Brownlee (11QEzekiel).[31] A review of de Vaux's reports shows that Plenderleith also examined a number of fragments containing texts from the Minor Prophets.[32] Plenderleith understood from press reports and from discussion with de Vaux that some of the material was destined for exhibition in Great Britain. His subsequent concern about the condition of the scrolls (including the Copper Scroll) led him to write to the director of the British Museum, Sir Frank Francis, as he considered the parties to the exhibit were, "blundering ahead with the best of intentions without thinking to take expert advice on the condition of the material which [was] the very first aspect that should [have] come up for consideration."[33] Mostly, Plenderleith was concerned by the possible involvement of the British Museum in planning the exhibit and he refused to "take the responsibility of being a party to the scheme for foreign exhibit." He warned de Vaux that the fragments should not be moved: "One thing I feel I ought to urge most strongly and that is the necessity of preventing the mounted scrolls from being moved unnecessarily. The membranes are often more brittle than the glass mounts and the result of accident could be imagined! They should on no account be allowed to leave the building at least until they have been suitably prepared ... and indeed I would go further and tend to be rather strict in emphasizing the matter to scholars that there is really a serious responsibility in subjecting the fragments to unnecessary movement."[34]

Plenderleith's written communications indicate that he was aggravated by John Allegro's push for the Jordanian authorities to exhibit the scrolls abroad and had him in mind when informing de Vaux that his concerns be emphasized to scholars. Despite these concerns, or perhaps because of them, Plenderleith wrote to de Vaux with recommendations on how plastic sheets could be custom-cut to better protect the fragments if they were to be transported for exhibition.[35] Plenderleith's report led de Vaux to approach Sir Frank Francis at the British Museum for help, since there was no one appropriate available in Jerusalem to prepare the material for mounting as Plenderleith had suggested. Furthermore, the financial strains on the museum did not support the appointment of an expert conservator.[36] In September 1962 Francis contacted Dajani, the director of the Jordanian Department of Antiquities, and offered to train a technician at the British Museum laboratory who could, after a month or six weeks, return to Jerusalem to work in the scrollery. It was hoped that UNESCO might supply some funds to support the effort.[37] By October 1963 it had been decided that Valerie Foulkes of the British Museum would visit the scrollery to train an assistant who could continue the work of conservation after her return to London.[38] Foulkes arrived eventually in the last quarter of 1963 to examine the materials and to begin the effort to mount some of the fragments between new custom-cut sheets of plastic.[39] As a result of her efforts approximately forty-five plates of fragments were remounted.[40] Unfortunately, the efforts of Plenderleith and Foulkes accounted for only one-twelfth of the material in need of care. And, despite de Vaux's best efforts, the museum's funds could not accommodate all the fragments requiring conservation. De Vaux's request to foreign museums for financial help in exchange for exhibition provided only limited resources. By 1966 the materials remained in poor condition, as noted by Allegro after his aforementioned visit to the scrollery: "I discovered that virtually nothing had been done about preserving the parchments. Indeed, I saw glass plates containing our texts lying on top of one another, thus subjecting the fragile skins to unacceptable pressures. There is, of course, no temperature or humidity control possible in the Museum, and still the vast majority of the texts are unpublished. Some are still unstudied even."[41]

The period between 1960 and 1966 saw further publication delays and continued deterioration of the fragments until the 1 November 1966 nationalization of the PAM.⁴² As the museum was now nationalized in its entirety, the scrolls were never moved to Amman, as initially planned. When East Jerusalem fell to the Israelis in 1967, the museum and its contents were turned over to the custody of the Israel Department of Antiquities and Museums (IDAM), predecessor of the IAA.⁴³

THE "NATION AND THE OBJECT"

It would be remiss to close this account without contextualizing this historical event within the broader scope of the discourse on movable cultural objects. In the context of the Dead Sea Scrolls, specifically, the related matter of intellectual copyright and ancient documents has received greater prominence since the much publicized lawsuit concerning the reconstructed fragments of 4QMMT in the 1990s.⁴⁴

It should first be emphasized that the purchase of Cave 4 fragments by McGill falls outside the parameters of the pressure by source nations for the repatriation of "stolen" or "estranged" movable cultural objects from market nations, for which the Elgin Marbles have become the poster child. The fragments never left Jordanian territory⁴⁵ consequent to the purchase and therefore no claim can be made that McGill's purchase – although preceding the 1970 UNESCO *Convention on the Means of Prohibiting and Preventing the Illicit Import, Export and Transfer of Ownership of Cultural Property* – in spirit violated this convention which is, according to Fitz Gibbon, "still the most important international instrument dealing with cultural property."⁴⁶ This position holds true despite John Henry Merryman's concerns as to its "ideological basis" for "export control legislation in source nations," which has foregrounded a nation-oriented approach to cultural property.⁴⁷ To the contrary, as this account attests, McGill's Cave 4 fragments were legitimately purchased from the Jordanian director of antiquities, with Harding as representative and with full government sanction.⁴⁸

The Scott Papers also clearly indicate that the purpose of the McGill purchase was first and foremost an attempt to preserve the integrity of the find for the sake of scholarship and to prevent the dispersal of such a collection before authoritative publication could take place: "The long delay [before shipment to Montreal] results from the right and proper decision to assemble and publish the material before letting it be scattered," Scott wrote to Henry Birks on 1 July 1959 from Jerusalem, after an inspection of McGill's allotment in the scrollery. Scott continued: "When one realizes that the 'team' engaged on this is made up largely of people who come from abroad for part of the year and from local scholars who have other work on hand – and who must work extremely carefully when they can give the time – it is remarkable that so much has been finished."[49]

Although national interests such as the prestige the scrolls would bring to Canada may have played a role, the archival documentation clearly shows that this was not the driving force behind the purchase. It may therefore be argued that McGill's purchase occurred in the spirit of an object-oriented approach to encourage what John Merryman, in the context of legal policy, calls the interdependent considerations of preservation, truth, and access: "The most basic is preservation: protecting the object and its context from impairment. Next comes the quest for knowledge, for valid information about the human past, for the historical, scientific, cultural and aesthetic truth that the object and its context can provide. Finally, we want the object to be optimally accessible to scholars (for study) and to the public (for education and enjoyment)."[50]

Although not resulting from a legitimate excavation, McGill's purchase did not represent an "illegitimate acquisition"[51] as the provenance of the fragments was established by the principals involved in the sale. Harding, in his official capacity as director of antiquities for Jordan, substantiated this to Scott on 19 April 1954 at confirmation of receipt of funds: "But meantime I must congratulate the University on having acquired what is certainly the finest collection of these unique manuscript fragments outside the original Government collection. That they originate from Qumran Cave IV is affirmed already by finding some pieces which fit to others in the first lot."[52] The exact fragments allocated to McGill were also confirmed in an enclosure to a letter from Harding to Scott dated 6 June 1956.[53]

Despite the above, it should be noted that McGill University, as a corporate member of ASOR, would quite probably have been prevented from any similar purchase had the Dead Sea Scrolls been discovered under the same circumstances after the 1970 UNESCO Convention. The Statement of ASOR Policy on Preservation and Protection of Archaeological Resources passed by the board of trustees on 18 November 1995 and revised on 22 November 2003 explicitly states that: "ASOR members should not participate, directly or indirectly, in the buying and selling of artifacts illegally excavated or exported from the country of origin after 1970."[54] Illegal discovery by the Bedouin and purchase via the middleman, Kando, would technically have constituted a breach of this prohibition.

Furthermore, although the purchase coincided with the 1954 *Hague Convention for the Protection of Cultural Property in the Event of Armed Conflict*,[55] and the circumstances of their discovery were indeed volatile, as it happened shortly after the birth of the State of Israel, the fragments were not purchased or moved under conditions of armed conflict. And, although Cindy Carson makes a strong argument for "ownership" of the Dead Sea Scrolls by the State of Israel as "spoils of war," any claim to patrimony by Israel, based on the principle of succession, would have postdated the McGill purchase of Cave 4 fragments.[56]

Therefore, what makes this purchase significant in this context is not its flouting of convention but the example it sets of the fluctuating contested territorial patrimony of the region in which the fragments were discovered. This, in turn, indicates the nation-oriented approach that seemed to have dominated the subsequent history of McGill University's purchase of Cave 4 fragments from Jordan.

In recent political discussions the scrolls have yet again featured in this context: in the post-Oslo discussion of the formation of a Palestinian state, Palestinian officials have called for repatriation of the scrolls. The following excerpt from a CNN report illustrates their position: "[The] ruins of Qumran, the Essene center where the scrolls were discovered, is [sic] in the West Bank, and there are some Palestinians who believe they have a better claim to this archeological treasure than the Israelis. 'They have been found in Palestine, and they should be also studied by Palestinians,' said Hamdan Taha of the Palestinian Archaeology Department. Israelis, as might be expected, vigorously contest arguments that the scrolls are like other ancient artifacts seized by former imperial powers. 'These things, I think, belong to the people of this region,' says Joe Zias, an Israeli researcher. 'You have to realize these things were written by Jews for Jews.'"[57]

Israeli scholars consider their connection to the Dead Sea Scrolls material as dictated by more than territorial links. It is part of their historical and cultural patrimony. It is unclear that Jordan ever made an extensive case for similar ties to the material. That is not to say that the territorial link should be overlooked or ignored. In matters of law, "the dominant element in deciding the status of movable cultural property is the principle of the territorial link. The criterion of a given country's closeness to *patrimoine intellectuel* comes second."[58]

Without doubt the scrolls have played an important role in the nationalist propaganda of the countries involved. Sukenik's purchase of the first scrolls on the eve of the United Nation's establishment of Israel was hailed as more than mere coincidence.[59] The replacement of Harding with a Jordanian director of antiquities and the first stirrings in the move to nationalize the scrolls were most certainly intertwined with a growing Jordanian national consciousness. Essentially, the Jordanian move to nationalize the scrolls was an act of "repatriation" after they sold the scroll fragments but before the fragments could leave the country. In this case the act of repatriation served to reinforce Jordan's national independence in a way that seems to be part and parcel of repatriation claims in general, as Prott and O'Keefe have noted: "Attempts to retrieve cultural properties of importance from other States may be seen as an attempt to assert the authority and independence of their own State. Assertions of such claims may be an attempt to overcome feelings of powerlessness and economic dependence engendered by colonialism and its aftermath."[60] The sale of the scroll fragments therefore represented Jordan's ceding of its rights to material perceived as its own. In the Jordanian prime minister's May 1961 letter, the Jordanian government's attitude towards this kind of funding arrangement indicated a change. Article 3 of the letter states: "Financial assistance for the collection of the Scrolls in the Kingdom shall henceforth be accepted as free offer in exchange for such facilitation as the Government may grant to the giver for the study of the scrolls, their photography or their publication in general service to history and knowledge."[61] Henceforth the government could comfortably accept funds without ceding power or authority to the donors.

The change in Jordan's claims with regard first to territory, and later to cultural heritage, seems to have reflected the changing nature of the international discourse on these matters. According to Merryman and others, the Hague Convention of 1954, which protected cultural property during wartime, focused primarily on this material as part of the common heritage of mankind but reinforced matters related to the territorial link of the material. By contrast, the 1970 UNESCO Convention shifted focus and was much more interested in the individual country's patrimonial link to the cultural property in question.[62] Thus, Jordan's changing claims appear to follow the changing nature of the international discourse on cultural property. On 11 December 1959 Stanley Frost provided Henry Birks with a comprehensive update, in the form of a memorandum, on the status of the McGill purchase of Dead Sea Scrolls. As the possibility of nationalization again reared its head, Frost wrote:

> I have had several conversations with Professor R.B.Y. Scott who was out in the Hashemite Kingdom of the [sic] Jordan last summer, and he informs me that the work on the Scrolls should be completed by about May and that the Scrolls should be available to be sent to this country about June [1960]. But the political situation is a little difficult. There is widespread feeling against the further dispersal of the treasures of the East to the wealthier countires [sic] of the West and this links in with Arab nationalist feelings. You may remember that there has been at least one

attempt to go back on the original contract but the King and Council of Ministers have clearly indicated their intention to abide by the original agreement, but no politician in Jordan wishes to be in any way associated with the granting of permission for the Scrolls to leave the country.[63]

Thus it was only to have been expected that the emerging Jordanian nation viewed with suspicion any claims on its patrimonial heritage that may have been considered a return to the bonds of its colonial past. The nationoriented approach to cultural heritage and the Dead Sea Scrolls in particular therefore governed the Jordanian government's impetus for nationalization and henceforth altered the fortunes of scrolls history. In this co-mingling of the import of time and space, the purchase occurred in a post World War II environment where source nations such as Jordan came to favour the "cultural nationalism" approach to cultural objects: "objects *belong* within the physical boundaries of the nations within which they are found or with which they are historically associated."[64] Without referring to the old adage of hindsight, the Jordanian emphasis on national heritage did serve to recognize the importance of contextualization as part of a larger "complex object," namely, the intact maintenance of the "collection" of Dead Sea Scrolls from Cave 4 in one place, no matter how fragmentary. Although the initial purchase agreement, by allowing for the substitution of fragments to keep reconstructed manuscripts together, did recognize contextualization to a certain extent, the preservation of the collection from Cave 4 as a unit was still preferred. The preservation of context is the further elaboration on Merryman's notion of preservation: "True physical and contextual integrity ... affect meaning and beauty, and their loss produces consequences analogous to those that follow from destruction. We care about context for the same reasons that we care about the objects themselves. The significant difference is that mere decontextualization may be reversible; destruction seldom is."[65]

In attempting to offer yet another perspective on the initial history of the discovery and purchase of Dead Sea Scrolls, we have aimed to highlight the constitutive contribution made by McGill and other institutions in the preservation of the Dead Sea Scrolls as a common cultural heritage of humankind. In the subsequent history the subordinate emphases on *truth* and *access* came to dominate, but it was the *preservation* of these invaluable fragments as a contextual unit, to the best of the ability of the government of Jordan, the PAM, and all parties involved, that allowed us to proceed to this debate. Because, as Colin Renfrew has observed: "It is only through the proper study of the context of archaeological finds that it is possible to begin the task of their interpretation ... Very little of this interpretation can be achieved from the study of single objects taken out of context. They do not contribute to our knowledge of the past; indeed they are parasitic upon that knowledge, for they themselves can only be dated, authenticated and given any kind of interpretation by comparison with similar artefacts that have indeed been found within a coherent context."[66]

"GREAT SCOTT"[67]

Professor Robert Balgarnie Young Scott died on 1 November 1987. He was eighty-eight years old and it had been forty years since the discovery of Cave 1 at the Dead Sea and twenty since the Six-Day War and the transfer of control over the scrolls to Israel. De Vaux had died in 1971 and had been succeeded by Father Benoit as editor-in-chief. Upon his retirement in 1984, Benoit was succeeded by John Strugnell, who was later replaced because of deteriorating health and the anti-Semitic comments he had made in 1990 to an Israeli journalist, Avi Katzman.[68]

Four years after Scott's death, in September 1991, the Israel Antiquities Authority finally announced free access to the scrolls. Lawrence Schiffman would look back at this momentous event and declare: "Now with the opening of the entire corpus to scholars, the speed of publication ... progressed ... The greatest benefit of open access is that it is now possible to gain an accurate sense of the nature and significance of the entire collection. A new era of intense, in-depth research is just beginning."[69]

The official publication of the Cave 4 fragments, so earnestly awaited by Scott and others, was completed in 2009. The final volume of the series, *Discoveries in the Judaean Desert*, is expected in 2010.

POSTSCRIPT

"The harvest of this patient waiting"[1]

For all their efforts, neither Scott nor McGill University were left entirely empty-handed. Included here, for the first time, are high-resolution and infrared photographs of five fragments from the collection of McGill's Redpath Museum.[2] The catalogue record for the fragments reads: "Five Hebrew manuscript fragments on papyrus – four of which have writing on them. The collection was bought from Dr. R.B.Y. Scott by the Faculty of Religious Studies in October 1978."[3]

The fragments were purchased by the Faculty of Religious Studies from Scott, who in 1978 was retired from Princeton University and living in Toronto, Ontario. In preparing to move into a retirement home, Scott sold the university his collection of some 300 ancient coins and a small matchbox including the fragments and an unused matchstick.[4] According to Scott, following his purchase of seventeen fragments for McGill from a Jerusalem antiquities dealer in 1955[5] (recounted in chapter 2), he sent them, along with some coins, to Harding to include with McGill's other fragments in the PAM. Harding returned the coins along with a fragmentary piece which showed no indication of writing.[6] It was this fragment that Scott preserved in the matchbox. When Runnals examined the fragment in 1978, she saw that it was in fact a few fragments adhered together by time and separated them with a pair of tweezers. According to Runnals, she tentatively identified the fragments, based on the cursive script, as related to the material from Wadi Murabba'at.[7] The five fragments measure: (a) 1.3 x 1.95cm, (b) 1.6 x 1.95cm, (c) 4.6 x 4.15cm, (d) 1.45 x 2.1cm, and (e) 0.9 x 1.2cm.

Postscript

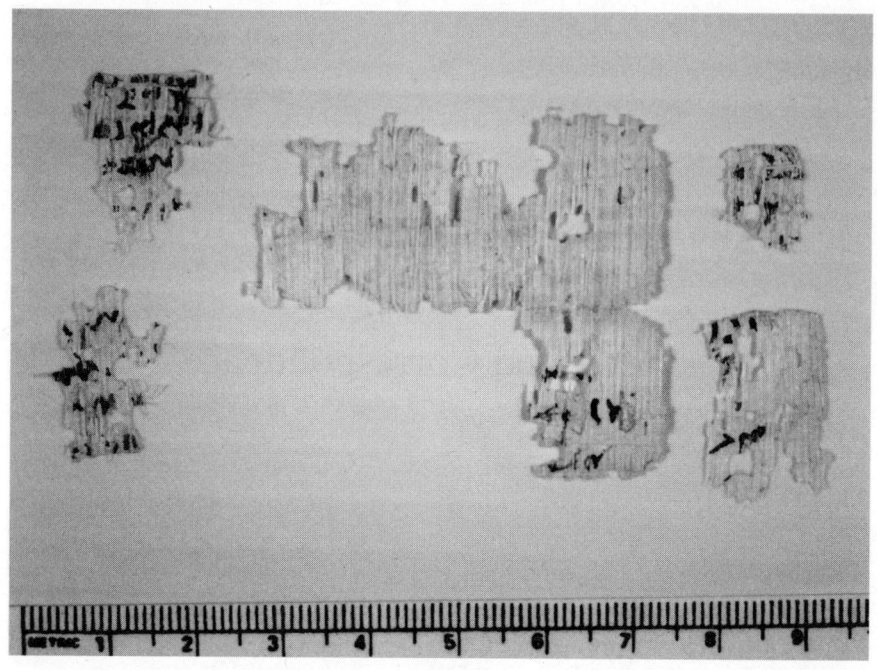

Papyrus fragments acquired by R. B. Y. Scott in the Old City of Jerusalem, 1955, and now in the collection of McGill's Redpath Museum. Published with the permission of the Redpath Museum and the Canadian Conservation Institute.

PART TWO

Annotated Correspondence

Introductory Remarks

Letters with McGill archival sources appear courtesy of the McGill University archives, while letters with IAA archival numbers appear courtesy of the IAA. Permission for reproduction of all letters has been granted by the family of R.B.Y. Scott, the Jordanian Department of Antiquities, the IAA; L'École Biblique in Jerusalem, and McGill University.

Although our purpose is to publish the letters in the McGill collection, a number of letters related to the McGill purchase were found in the archives of the IAA. They added significantly to the understanding of McGill's participation in the purchase of Cave 4 material and have therefore been included here.

In the two instances where copyright law prevented the reproduction of letters written in response to correspondence originating at McGill, descriptions of the responses are included in gray textboxes.

The letters and other documentation appear without any adjustments to spelling, punctuation, spacing, or grammar. The letters are annotated to allow for contextualization, avoiding the need to constantly refer to Part I. This occasionally leads to some unavoidable repetition in the footnotes.

LETTER #1

Archive: McGill, RG34, Container: 0001, File 6: Dead Sea Scrolls.

Cable[1] sent Sept. 25th, 1953:
Harding[2] Director Antiquities Amman -
University considering offering funds procure remainder scroll fragments. Please cable amount and conditions –
Robert Scott
McGill University.

Reply cable received Sept. 28th, 1953:
Robert Scott, McGill University.
Thanks your encouraging cable. Does University wish to acquire fragments or would funds be offered as donations. If latter to whom offered -
Harding.

Cable sent Sept. 28th, 1953:
Harding Director Antiquities Amman -
Desire follow suggestion Devaux raise funds acquire fragments for University following study publication Jerusalem.
Robert Scott
McGill University

Cable received Oct. 2rd, 1953:
Cable and letter received stop matter now being studied. Writing -
Harding.

---

1 This document is a single-paged typed transcript of telegram communications between Scott and Harding. None of the original telegram forms or receipts of communication are preserved in the files.

2 Gerald Lankester Harding (1901–1979) was director of the Department of Antiquities of Jordan from 1936 until 1956.

Annotated Correspondence 141

LETTER #2

Archive: McGill, RG34, Container: 0001, File 6: Dead Sea Scrolls.
McGill, RG2, Container: 0179, File 6243: Divinity: DSS & Birks Donation.

28 September 1953[3]   Montreal

Dear Dr. James,[4]

When attending the International Congress of Old Testament Scholars at Copenhagen in August,[5] I heard a lecture by Pere R. de Vaux of l'Ecole Archeologique Francaise in Jerusalem[6] on the recent astonishing finds of ancient manuscript fragments in the Judaean desert. Afterwards at dinner I had the opportunity of discussing with him an announcement made during the lecture which struck me as most important, and of possible interest to McGill.

This announcement was to the effect that funds had run out before it had been possible to recover from the Bedouin[7] by purchase all the manuscripts which they had found;[8] and that, if any institution would provide the additional funds required, the right of export and possession would be guaranteed, on certain conditions.[9] The conditions are that the material thus obtained would be kept in Palestine until it could be studied, compared and matched with the other

---

3 At the top of this letter, it is marked "copy."

4 Frank Cyril James (1903–1973) was principal and vice-chancellor from 1939 to 1962. For a biography and evaluation of this period, see Frost, *The Man in the Ivory Tower*.

5 The first conference of the Society met on 23 to 25 August 1953. Approximately 150 people were in attendance, including the spouses of the participants. See Rowley, "The International Old Testament Conference in Copenhagen," 423–8.

6 Roland de Vaux (1903–1971) was director of the French-Dominican École Biblique in Jerusalem. From 1954 until 1970, he served as the editor-in-chief for the publication of the Cave 4 manuscripts.

7 Of the Ta'amireh tribe.

8 Cave 4 was discovered by the Bedouin in August 1952 and it was only by 1958 that all the material from the cave could be acquired. See de Vaux, "Découverte, Fouille et Achats," 3–5.

9 See the previous telegram to Harding, 28 September 1953, Letter #1.

finds, and published, – in the interest of scientific control of the total discovery. This, said Pere de Vaux, might take two or three years.¹⁰

About $20,000. has already been expended for this purpose by the Department of Antiquities and the Palestine Museum, and no more is available at present.¹¹ It is estimated that a further $12, 000 – $15,000. is required (revised in light of Harding's letter of 3 October 1953).¹² This seems to me a remarkable opportunity for McGill to obtain a collection of documents of the utmost value for Biblical research and for the history of Judaism from the Maccabean period to the Second Revolt against the Romans. The documents, though fragmentary, are priceless. It is only the fact that the archaeological authorities can deal directly with the finders, and must do so urgently before the material gets into the hands of dealers, that makes it possible to obtain such precious material for such a sum.¹³ When one considers that a few years ago¹⁴ the British Museum

---

10 Although the vast majority of the matching and identification would be completed by mid-1960, the last volumes of this material were not in press until 2009, more than fifty years after their discovery.

11 By early 1953 some $42,000 USD had been spent purchasing the first 15,000 fragments. The funding situation created multiple collections and multiple owners. The Jordanian government owned the most significant portion. The PAM owned its own materials, in large part a result of the excavations directed by de Vaux. Both these collections would grow with private donations from abroad. McGill and other foreign institutions would purchase their own collections. At least initially, the museum purchased the material by its own means. It was only afterwards that the Jordanian government would step in to purchase the material as, at least in principle, what the Bedouin was doing was illegal because all antiquities discovered should have been turned over to the government for examination. See Fields, "Discovery and Purchase," 211.

12 Letter #3. Either this copy of Scott's letter to James was dated incorrectly, or this is an indication that the "copy" was revised after receipt of the mentioned letter from Harding.

At the time Harding had no inkling of how much material was in the hands of the Bedouin. This number continued to grow as the quantity of fragments available expanded. It rose again as the price of individual pieces inflated when the demand for the final scraps of the discovery increased.

13 A deal was struck between the PAM and the Bedouin. This required the Bedouin to sell all the material to the museum at an agreed upon price in order to avoid prosecution for selling looted antiquities.

14 In the last week of December 1933. The price was reduced from the £250,000 asking price offered to the Americans a few years earlier. See "Codex Sinaiticus: Purchase Price to be Spent in England," *Times* (London), 23 December 1933, 7.

paid the Soviet Government £100,000. for the fourth century Codex Sinaiticus of the Greek Bible, the sum now needed seems small indeed.

I should perhaps recall to you that the first find of ancient scrolls near the Dead Sea was made in 1947, and has aroused world-wide interest.[15] These were Biblical and non-Biblical works in Hebrew, apparently coming from the library of the first century Jewish sect of the Essenes.[16] The new finds are both more abundant and more fragmentary. They came to light between November 1951 and September 1952, in four different localities in the Judaean desert.[17] At Qumran, where the buildings of the sect were excavated in 1951,[18] and in that vicinity, about forty caves and rock crevices have been explored[19] and in five of them manuscript fragments have been found, together with a unique bronze scroll with Hebrew lettering (still to be unrolled).[20] One of the caves was found by Bedouin in the absence of the archaeologists, and large quantities of manuscript fragments were removed before [end page 1] the archaeologists returned.[21] This appears to be the richest and most diversified collection of material so far discovered since the original 1947 find, and the authorities have made strenuous efforts to recover by purchase what the Bedouin had taken. What has been recovered, together with what was still in the cave when the archaeologists arrived, appears to represent a wide selection of Biblical, apocryphal, sectarian and secular documents from the period between the Maccabees and the First Revolt, 66 A.D.

---

15 By this time, some of the complete scrolls from Cave 1 had been purchased by Eleazar Sukenik of the Hebrew University. The remainder were in the hands of Archbishop Athanasius Yeshue Samuel, head of the Syrian Jacobite Monastery of St Mark in Jerusalem. These scrolls would eventually be offered to McGill University in June 1954, but were sold by Mar Samuel to the State of Israel. On this sale, see Yadin, *The Message of the Scrolls*, 46–52.

16 This standard hypothesis for the origins of the scrolls, as it came to be known, continues to be debated, although the majority view still maintains an Essene connection for the Qumran community.

17 Cave 2 was discovered in February 1952, Cave 3 in mid-March, and Cave 4 in August of the same year. Cave 5 was discovered in September 1952, contemporaneous with this letter.

18 In November and December 1951, Harding and de Vaux did soundings at the site. See de Vaux, "Fouille au Khirbet Qumrân: Rapport préliminaire," 83–106.

19 See de Vaux, *L'Archéologie et les Manuscrits de la Mer Morte*, 40–6.

20 The Copper Scroll (3Q15) was discovered in Cave 3.

21 Between 22 and 29 September 1952, de Vaux's team excavated Cave 4 but were not nearly as successful in finding manuscripts as the Bedouin, who had discovered the cave and cleared the better part of the hoard.

At two other sites some distance away a wealth of material chiefly from the period of the Second Revolt has come to light.²² Again the Bedouin were first on the scene, and still retain part of the contents of the caves. The fourth site has produced New Testament material in Greek and Syriac from the fifth to eighth centuries.²³

Any doubt as to the genuineness of the finds of 1947 has been overwhelmed by the events of the last two years. Two of the caves were discovered by archaeologists themselves, untouched by clandestine explorers; and the major discoveries in Cave 4 at Qumran and in Cave 2 at Murabba'at²⁴ had only been partially exploited when the official party arrived. There are dated documents of the second century from Murabba'at, and the numismatic evidence at both places is decisive.²⁵ Finally, the extraordinary efforts of the authorities to produce large sums out of their meager resources is evidence as to the judgments of those best qualified to judge.

With such a wealth of material available all at once, the exhaustion of funds calls for help from outside, and provides an opportunity which may not recur. Negotiations with the Bedouin would be carried on by foremost experts like Pere de Vaux and Lankester Harding, Director of Antiquities, who, moreover, have been intimately connected with the discoveries from the first and have already had much experience in these particular negotiations. No one else could be as competent, both with respect to the prices paid²⁶ and to the genuineness of what is purchased.

---

22 Inscribed papyri at Khirbet Mird were found by the Bedouin in July 1952. The Bedouin brought manuscripts in all probability originating from the caves at Nahal Hever to the PAM in August 1952 and July 1953. See Patrich, "Mird, Khirbet," 563–6, and Eshel, "Hever, Nahal," 357–9.

23 Khirbet Mird is about 8 kilometres from Qumran. In addition to Greek and Syriac materials, the site also yielded Arabic manuscripts.

24 After earlier discovery by the Bedouin, four caves at Murabba'at were explored by Harding, De Vaux, and Barthélemy in 1952. The manuscript finds at Wadi Murabba'at were published in 1961 as two volumes of *DJD*, volume 2. Cf. Benoit, Milik, and de Vaux, *Les Grottes de Murabba'ât*.

25 De Vaux, who excavated Qumran, was committed to the idea of a relationship between the inhabitants of the site and the owners of the manuscripts. He used numismatic evidence to date the habitation level. See de Vaux, *L'Archéologie et les Manuscrits de la Mer Morte*. De Vaux's conclusions have been the subject of debate. On this, see for example, Magness, "Two Notes on the Archaeology of Qumran," 37–44, and Magness, *The Archaeology of Qumran and the Dead Sea Scrolls*.

26 The initially negotiated rate was 1 Jordanian Dinar/1 British Pound per inscribed centimetre. This arrangement prevented the discoverers from destroying manuscripts

In spite of the fact that there would be some delay in obtaining possession of the purchases (should this proposal be implemented) the value of such an acquisition to McGill would be very great, both as study material and in terms of prestige. The possession of a collection of documents, even in fragmentary condition, from the epoch of the beginnings of normative Judaism and the rise of Christianity, would attract research scholars for many years, and put the name of McGill into many scholarly publications. Should we succeed in obtaining all or most of this material, especially that from Qumran Cave 4, the collection would be unique outside Palestine. Even if later finds were still to be made such a collection would remain outstanding.

If there is any further information I can supply, I shall be most happy to do so.

I remain, Sir,
Yours faithfully,
R.B.Y. Scott.

LETTER #3

Archive: McGill, RG34, Container: 0001, File 6: Dead Sea Scrolls.

3 October 1953
The Hashemite Kingdom of Jordan, Department of Antiquities.

Ref: 18/2/G6G

Dear Dr. Scott,

Many thanks for your cables and now your letter,[27] which makes the position quite clear.[28] I have received similar offers from other institutions,[29] and I have

---

even further, as they were paid by the size of the parchments rather than by the quantity of individual fragments.

27 Letter not preserved.

28 As indicated in the cables, Harding was unclear as to whether McGill University wished to donate funds to the PAM for the purchase of fragments or was purchasing fragments for itself.

29 The "institutions" Harding is referring to remains uncertain. He had offered a similar deal to the British Museum and the Library of Congress as early as late 1952, but neither could accept the inevitable condition that they could not examine the materials before purchase.

put the whole matter to the Government and asked for a firm decision on the principle of allowing some of the material to be sent abroad after study here.[30] As soon as I receive their decision I will cable you; meantime I have looked over some of the fragments which are still in the hands of others, and it is much more than I had guessed. The sum involved, I think, would be between £10,000. and £12,000.,[31] and any part of this that you contributed would, of course, receive proportionate allocation. I imagine Pere de Vaux made it quite clear that the material is all fragmentary: I should not like generous contributors to feel afterwards that they had not had their money's worth!

I am very glad that you agree to the conditions of the fragments remaining here until completion of study: this is a most important point. Perhaps you have some one you would like to send to assist in this work? I am trying to bring together an international group of scholars for the purpose.[32]

It is most encouraging that so much interest is being taken in the fragments, and I hope to be able to give you a satisfactory answer soon.

Yours sincerely,
G. Lankester Harding
Director of Antiquities.

---

30 This confirms what we know from the correspondence: that Harding also made the offer to other institutions before he had government approval.

31 This is triple the amount reported by Scott to James after his meeting with de Vaux in Copenhagen.

32 A similar offer appears in Harding's letters to the British Museum and the Library of Congress. This detail changes the usual understanding that Harding wished to form the team from members of the archaeological schools working in Jerusalem. See Kendrick to Harding, 8 November 1952, IAA Archives, Box 73, PAM 1117: Dead Sea Scrolls (cave no. 4), jacket 1; and letter to John D. Jernegan of the U.S. Department of State, 20 October 1952, IAA Archives, Box 73, PAM 1117: Dead Sea Scrolls (cave no. 4), jacket 1.

LETTER #4

Archive: McGill, RG34, Container: 0001, File 6: Dead Sea Scrolls.

Cable received Nov. 27th, 1953:[33]
Scott, McGill University.
Government have agreed to scheme please send your contribution earliest possible.[34]
 Writing.

Harding.

LETTER #5

Archive: McGill, RG34, Container: 0001, File 6: Dead Sea Scrolls.

25 November 1953   Montreal

Dear Mr. Phillips:[35]

Principal James has suggested that I inform you of receipt of the following cable from Lankester Harding, Director of Antiquities for Jordan –

---

33 Scott's transcription of the cable is misdated. It should read 23 November 1953. Cf. James to director of antiquities, 30 March 1957, Letter #79 and Scott to Phillips, 25 November 1953, Letter #5.

34 Unfortunately, no letters related to the Jordanian Government's agreement have been preserved. According to the draft letter enclosed with Scott to James, 19 March 1957, Letter #76, the government's agreement was provided in three documents: a letter from the prime minister to the minister of education agreeing to allow foreign institutions to acquire scroll fragments: Ref. No. 26/1/1/8723 of 21 November 1953; a letter from the director of antiquities to the minister of education asking for clearer interpretation: Ref. No. 18/3/14 of 30 November 1953; and, a reply from the minister of education stating that the export of scroll fragments would be permitted: Ref. No. 39/2/12463 of 23 December 1953.

35 Lazarus Phillips (1895–1986) was a 1928 graduate of McGill Law School. An attorney of note in Montreal, he later ran a failed campaign for a seat in parliament (1943) and was in subsequent years appointed a Canadian senator (1968–70). As a major benefactor of Montreal's Jewish community, this letter demonstrates that McGill University did attempt to involve the Jewish community in the purchase.

Government have agreed to scheme please send your contribution earliest possible writing – Harding "[36]

This means that Mr. Harding can guarantee the right of possession and export of the manuscript fragments which he is able to buy with funds supplied on behalf of McGill University, following an agreed period for their identification, study and possible publication at the Palestine Archaeological Museum.

In view of the fact that other institutions also are interested in obtaining some of these priceless documents from a Palestinian Jewish community of the beginning of the present era, the sooner we can act the better. As soon as Mr. Harding's letter arrives I will send a copy to you.

With deep appreciation of your interest,
I am,
Yours sincerely,
R. B. Y. Scott
(Professor of Old Testament Literature)

LETTER #6

Archive: McGill, RG34, Container: 0001, File 6: Dead Sea Scrolls.

8 December 1953   Montreal

Dear Mr. Harding:

Two weeks ago I received your welcome cable saying that the Govt. had agreed to the scheme we had discussed, concerning purchase of the Judean Desert[37] scroll fragments.

The cable indicated that you were writing me at the same time, but no further word has been received.

I at once communicated with Principal James of McGill University, and he in turn got into touch with a gentleman who had earlier indicated his confidence that funds could be secured for this purpose from private donors whom he had in mind.[38] So far there has been no tangible result, but I do not draw pessimistic conclusions from this. The people concerned are extremely busy, and just now

---

36 Harding to Scott, 27 November 1953, Letter #4.
37 Word inserted below line.
38 Lazarus Phillips.

there is a major financial campaign on for support of the general University budget.[39] It might have been easier to secure more immediate action if I had been able to follow up at once the proposal originally submitted to Principal James in September.[40] However, I fully realize the desirability from your standpoint of action as soon as is feasible, and will do my utmost to bring this about without overplaying my hand.

When your letter comes I expect it will indicate what you have in mind about such matters as the way in which fragments purchased with ~~for~~ McGill funds would be set aside and designated as ultimately to come to the University: who would have charge of them meanwhile, and under what conditions; the time which will probably be required for study of them before they could be exported; whether part could be sent before all would be available; etc. And to whom would payments be made ? To the Dept, of Antiquities, or to the Museum?[41]

I will keep you informed of progress, and will be glad to hear from you at your convenience.

Yours sincerely,
R. B. Y. Scott

---

39 As a result of the need to educate the influx of returning veterans of World War II, McGill and other Canadian universities ran into financial trouble. For McGill, the funding problems were not resolved until 1960 when federal funds became available to the university. See Frost, *The Man in the Ivory Tower*, 230.

40 The delay was a result of slow action on the part of the Jordanian Government to approve the arrangement.

41 The money was eventually directed to Harding at the Department of Antiquities. For example, a copy of a bank draft dated 8 April 1954, and made out in Harding's name for $10,363.52 USD, is preserved in the McGill University Archives, RG4 Container: 239, File: Birks, John Henry – Collection, Judean Manuscripts – Dead Sea Scrolls.

LETTER #7

Archive: McGill, RG34, Container: 0001, File 6: Dead Sea Scrolls.

27 January 1954   Montreal

Dear Mr. Harding,

Your letter of 30th December[42] reached me early this month, and with this definite information about your Government's decision I have been able to proceed to raise the necessary funds. I have been hoping to find some individual who would be interested enough to give a substantial sum so that what would be purchased would be a significant collection. By great good fortune a gentleman to whom I went for counsel has been able to interest such a person, and he telephoned me to-day that he is pretty sure that a contribution of $15,000. (Canadian)[43] will be available about the middle of February.

The arrangement cannot be final until some one else has been consulted who is not available until then. However, my friend because of his relationship with the prospective donor is in a position to feel confident that the money will be forthcoming, and has authorized me to advise you to that effect. I, therefore, cabled you to-day – SUBSTANTIAL AMOUNT FEBRUARY WRITING – in order that you may be able to make any necessary plans. I did not mention the sum of money in the cable so as to avoid any possibility of leakage of information putting up prices. This may have been an unnecessary precaution, but I thought it best to be on the safe side.

I presume the money will be paid to you by McGill University by bank draft, but if it is possible to have it sent by cable I will try to arrange that.

The conditions laid down by the Jordan Government as stated in your letter of Dec. 30th are of course accepted. With your long experience in such negotiations I know that you will expend the money to the best advantage, and it may be that you will not think it advisable to appear to have too much to spend, and will not make all your purchases at once. Will this money be kept in a special account against which specific purchases will be charged?

You will hear from me again as soon as I have further information to pass on.

Yours sincerely,
R.B.Y. Scott.

---

42 Letter not preserved.

43 Approximately £5,000. For conversion rates, see PACIFIC Exchange Rate Service, "Foreign Currency Units per 1 British Pound, 1948–2006." http://fx.sauder.ubc.ca (accessed: 18 July 2007).

LETTER #8

Archive: McGill, RG34, Container: 0001, File 6: Dead Sea Scrolls.

1 February 1954   Montreal

Dear Dr. James:

I am pleased to be able to report the prospect of success in my efforts to raise funds for the purchase of the Judean Desert Scrolls.

As suggested in my conversation with you before you went away, I wrote a short popular article (copy enclosed) for the Saturday "Design for Living" page in the STAR,[44] and indirectly this opened the way. Having had no further word from Mr. Lazarus Phillips about his prospects, I went to see Mr. Henry Birks[45] who is one of my fellow elders at Erskine Church[46] as well as Chairman of the U.T.C. Board.[47] I did not know until he told me that he is to become a member of the University Board of Governors.

In any case, I made it clear that I was not asking him for money, but for suggestions, mentioning my hope that there might be a lady of means in the city or someone else who was not now involved in the campaign for general University funds. Mr. Birks was genuinely interested in the STAR article and other material I showed him, and said he would approach two people whose names occurred to him. A few days later he phoned and said: "I think I have $15,000 for you".

---

44 R.B.Y. Scott, "More Astonishing Discoveries Have Been Made in Palestine," *Montreal Star,* 23 January 1954, 21.

45 Henry Guifford Birks (1892–1985). Nephew of John Henry Metcalf (J.H.) Birks (1870–1949) and Elizabeth Birks (1884–1982), who would supply the necessary funds, and the son of William Massey Birks (1868–1950), who was responsible, in large part, for the establishment of McGill's Faculty of Divinity. The Montreal Birks family made their fortune expanding a jewelry business established by Henry Guifford Birks's grandfather, Henry Birks (1840–1928).

46 The Erskine and American Church was formed by a merger in 1934 of the Erskine and American Churches. It stands at the corner of Sherbrooke and du Musée Street in downtown Montreal. The Montreal Museum of Fine Arts now owns the building.

47 United Theological College Board. Scott joined the faculty in 1931 and was responsible for overseeing the establishment of the Faculty of Divinity at McGill, of which the college was an affiliate.

The prospective donor is Mrs. J. Harry Birks.[48] The contribution will not be definite until she and Mr. Birks have had the opportunity to consult the lawyer for the J.H. Birks estate, who is away ill, but is expected back early in February. Mr. Henry Birks is quite confident the money will be forthcoming, and authorized me to advise Mr. Harding of the Jordan Dept. of Antiquities to this effect, since other institutions also appear to be negotiating with him. If we at McGill get the full amount of scroll fragments which this money will buy (i.e., if some of it has not already been bought for other institutions), it will be a collection of important and perhaps sensational significance. I have just read a study of fragments of I and II Samuel from the Qumran Cave 4[49] (from which most of the material we hope to get has come);[50] it is dated by the palaeographer in the first century B.C., and makes it probable that the traditional text of the Hebrew Bible must be radically revised in the light of the new discoveries. These scrolls are far more than curiosities from antiquity; they are epoch-making in the literal sense, so far as Biblical studies are concerned.

Yours sincerely,
Scott

LETTER #9

Archive: McGill, RG2, Container: 0179, File 6243: Divinity: DSS & Birks Donation.

2 February 1954   Montreal

Dear Professor Scott,

Thank you very much indeed for your letter of February 1st which reached my desk this morning with the very happy news that Mr. Henry Birks has become so

---

48 That is Mrs John Henry Metcalf (J.H.) Birks. Mrs Birks was J.H.'s second wife, Elizabeth Leggo McConnel Birks. J.H. Birks died in 1950, leaving a trust for charitable purposes.

49 Cross, "A New Qumran Biblical Fragment Related to the Original Hebrew Underlying the Septuagint," 15–26. Frank Moore Cross would become the insider Scott turned to for first-hand reports on McGill's collection. See for example, Cross to Scott, 12 Aug. 1954, McGill University Archives, RG34, Container: 0001, File 6: Dead Sea Scrolls.

50 All the material allotted to McGill University would come from Cave 4.

interested in the Judean Desert Scroll that there is a good prospect of $15,000 becoming available for the purposes that you and I had discussed.

This is indeed good news and I am delighted to have it at this time because I shall be seeing Mr. Birks on Friday to talk over various University problems and can put this one in its proper focus.

Congratulations and renewed good wishes, I remain,
Cordially yours,
F. Cyril James

LETTER #10

Archive: McGill, RG34, Container: 0001, File 6: Dead Sea Scrolls.

Cable sent Feb. 15, 1954
Harding Director Antiquities Amman –
  Need assurance fragments from Qumran or similar date significance – Scott[51]

Cable received Feb. 16, 1954
Scott McGill University Montreal
All fragments from Qumran Cave Four
– Harding

Cable sent Feb. 17, 1954
Harding Director Antiquities Amman –
Contribution assured arranging details
– Scott

---

51 In sending this cable, Scott was following advice given to him by A. Douglas Tushingham a few days earlier (Tushingham to Scott, 12 February 1954, McGill University Archives, RG34, Container: 0001, File 6: Dead Sea Scrolls).

LETTER #11

Archive: McGill, RG2, Container: 0179, File 6243: Divinity: DSS & Birks Donation.

2 March 1954   Montreal

Dear Dr. James:

Enclosed is the memorandum for which you asked. I have made it as concise as possible. From the file I have selected copies of the following supporting documents:

i) Letter from Mr. Harding dated 3rd Oct. [52]
ii) Letter from Mr. Harding dated 30th Dec. [53]
iii) My letter to you dated 28th Sept., which sets out in more detail what I have summarized in the memorandum. [54]

Yours sincerely,
R.B.Y. Scott

LETTER #12

Archive: McGill, RG34, Container: 0001, File 6: Dead Sea Scrolls.
McGill, RG2, Container: 0179, File 6243: Divinity: DSS & Birks Donation.

2 March 1954   Montreal

<u>Memorandum</u> on

the offer by the J.H.Birks Foundation of $ 15,000 – 20,000 for the purchase of a collection of "Judaean Desert Scroll Fragments" through the Department of Antiquities of the Hashemite Kingdom of Jordan.

---

[52] Letter #3.
[53] Letter not preserved.
[54] Letter #2.

1. The "Judaean Desert Scroll Fragments" are part of an immensely important find of Biblical, apocryphal and sectarian manuscripts dating from before the fall of Jerusalem in 70 A.D., located in a cave near the Dead Sea in March 1952. The Bedouin had found the deposit and cleared most of the cave before representatives of the Department of Antiquities arrived. A large part of what they had taken has been purchased by the Department, until available funds were exhausted. This has been studied by an international group of scholars at the Rockefeller Palestine Museum at Jerusalem, and already it is clear that it includes the oldest (fragmentary) manuscripts of the Old Testament yet discovered, as well as other works illustrating the life of Judaism in the 1st century A.D. and earlier.
2. Last August I learned from Pere R. de Vaux of l'Ecole Biblique in Jerusalem that the Department of Antiquities, having exhausted its funds, would welcome an arrangement with an institution of learning which would enable the Department to recover from the Bedouin the remainder of the manuscripts. The right of possession and export would be granted, subject to the proviso that the material bought would remain in Jerusalem for about two years for examination in the interests of scientific control of the whole deposit. In subsequent correspondence with Lankester Harding, Director of Antiquities this proposal has been confirmed officially on behalf of the Jordan Government (see attached letter dated 30th December 1953).[55]
3. The authenticity of the manuscripts is beyond question. Part of the deposit remained in the cave when the official party arrived, and the fact that the meagre resources of the Department of Antiquities have been strained to obtain as much as possible of the balance is evidence of the value placed on the find by those best qualified to judge. I know personally both Pere de Vaux and Mr. Harding, and Professor Tushingham of Queen's confirms my judgment that these experienced archaeologists and other palaeographers at Jerusalem would be quick to detect any attempt to include forgeries.
4. If this collection is obtained for McGill it would probably be one of the largest, if not the largest, collection of Old Testament and other religious documents from the beginning of the Christian era and earlier, to be found outside of Palestine. Its importance in terms of prestige, and for graduate study and publication, is clear.

---

55 Letter not preserved.

LETTER #13

Archive: McGill, RG34, Container: 0001, File 6: Dead Sea Scrolls.

11 March 1954   Amman

Dear Dr. Scott,-

Thank you for your cable and letter of Feb. 27th,[56] and apologies for being late in answering but I am out in the field very much in these days.[57] I hope by now the initial $5,000. is on its way, as the material is only waiting the arrival of the cash for us to take it over.[58] I had seen and priced it some time ago, so there is no further bargaining to be done, and I think your $15,000. will cover all that is with my regular agent in Bethlehem.[59] It looks an interesting lot of stuff, but I cannot say what it comprises until we start to study it. As regards what remains, this I have not seen and shall not see until I am actually in the market for it, as it is in the hands of people who are a little afraid of showing themselves to me. But my agent will use what I give him from your funds, not merely to recoup his outlay but to try and tempt the rest into his hands. So it is rather a vicious circle; I cannot say how much remains with any certainty until I see it, and I cannot see it until I have bought and paid for the present lot! Piecing together the not too reliable information I have been given by various people who claim to have seen or heard of pieces with different people, I got the impression that almost as much again remains, but in fact I find that hard to believe. So you see I cannot really help you regarding your proposed extra sum, but of course the more cash, the more pieces. Again, I must emphasize that I can give no idea of the contents of what I propose to buy for you, for as you can imagine it takes some time to identify the book to which a fragment belongs, but I think I can safely say that

---

  56 Letter not preserved.

  57 The third excavation campaign by the Department of Antiquities, the École Biblique, and the PAM at Qumran, directed by de Vaux, took place between 15 February and 15 April 1954. See de Vaux, "*Chronique Archéologique: Khirbet Qûmran,*" 567–8.

  58 The first $5,000 USD was sent by U.S. cheque payable to G. Lankester Harding with the letter dated, 4 March 1954. The letter is not preserved, nor is a copy of the cheque. Both are described in Frost to minister of education, 23 November 1960, Letter #106. A copy of the McGill debit voucher dated 4 March 1954, and listing the cheque as USA 5029, is preserved in McGill University Archives, RG4, Container: 239, File: Birks, John Henry – Collection, Judean Manuscripts – Dead Sea Scrolls.

  59 Khalil Iskandar Shahin, otherwise known as Kando (1910–1993).

it will be a representative collection. The sum of £15,000[60] sterling was spent on acquiring the fragments we have at present, which will give you an idea of proportion. It is a good idea to buy American dollars, though the exchange here varies only a very little. I shall be glad to receive the whole of your sum as soon as possible.

I shall be very pleased to see Prof. Cantwell Smith[61] when he is here, and it will be a pleasure to discuss the whole affair with him. He will be able to see at first hand the sort of difficulties we are up against.

With best wishes,
Yours sincerely,
G. Lankester Harding

LETTER #14

Archive: McGill, RG34, Container: 0001, File 6: Dead Sea Scrolls.
McGill, RG4, Container: 239, File: Birks, John Henry – Collection, Judean Manuscripts – Dead Sea Scrolls.

15 March 1954   Montreal

Dear Mrs. Birks,[62]

This is a tardy letter because last week was more than usually busy but I do want to express to you, both personally and officially on behalf of the Board of Governors, warm appreciation of the gift from the John Henry Birks Foundation of $15,000 to $20,000 in order to enable us to acquire the Judean Desert Scroll Fragments which will be preserved in the Faculty of Divinity as the "John Henry Birks Collection".

---

60 Provided by the Jordanian Government.
61 Wilfred Cantwell Smith (1916–2000) at the time served as director of McGill's Institute of Islamic Studies. During the last week of March 1954 he attended the Conference of the Egyptian Society for Historical Studies in Cairo and visited Amman and Jerusalem on his return trip.
62 A near identical acknowledgement was sent to Birks's representative, Ralph R. Johnson, as well (James to Johnson, 15 March 1954, McGill University Archives, RG34, Container: 0001, File 6: Dead Sea Scrolls).

Professor Scott has undoubtedly told you of the unique quality of these fragments but I should like you to know that I share his happiness and pride in the fact that McGill will be able to acquire them through your generosity.

With renewed thanks and best personal wishes, I remain,

Cordially yours,
F. Cyril James

LETTER #15

Archive: McGill, RG4, Container: 239, File: Birks, John Henry – Collection, Judean Manuscripts – Dead Sea Scrolls.

16 March 1954   Amman

Dear Dr. Scott,

Many thanks for yours of the 4th[63] together with the first cheque for $5,000. On the basis of this I hope to get the available material into my hands and complete payment when the rest of your contribution arrives. Meantime my letter of 11th March has probably reached you, which I think answers most of your queries. There are certainly no forgeries. I shall look forward to seeing Prof. Wilfred Cantwell Smith and discussing the whole matter with him, including the question of publication which you raise. As soon as I have more information on the material I will write you again.

Your Sincerely,
G. Lankester Harding
Director of Antiquities.

---

63 Letter not preserved.

LETTER #16

Archive: McGill, RG34, Container: 0001, File 6: Dead Sea Scrolls.
McGill, RG2, Container: 0179, File 6243: Divinity: DSS & Birks Donation.

27 March 1954   Montreal

Dear Mr. Harding:

Thank you for your two letters of the 11th and 16th of March, which answer my questions and bring the good news that the $15,000 will cover all that is with your agent at Bethlehem. There has been some delay in sending the balance because of the busy-ness and later the illness of the University Principal, so that I had to wait nearly four weeks for an interview. But this week I have been able to clarify the situation with him and also with the representative of the donor,[64] and the balance is to be sent to you by cheque on or about March 31st. It will be, in U.S. funds, several hundred dollars more than $10,000, as the exchange is about 3% in favor of the Canadian dollar. I am keeping in mind your saying – "the more cash, the more pieces",[65] if you have a small balance in hand on our account, you may be glad of it if some smaller lot turns up that you want to get into your hands.

My colleague Professor Cantwell Smith is to be in Cairo this week for a conference of the Egyptian Society for Historical Studies, and it will probably be about April 20th before he comes to Amman. It is possible that he will find it impossible to go there at all, but he hoped when he left here this month to be able to do so. We should find it of interest and value to have someone make direct personal contact with you and then return here with an understanding of the situation which is more than can be conveyed by correspondence. I am beginning to hope that I may be able to come out to Jordan myself about a year from now, to work for two or three months under the experts who are examining all this material, and thus to be in a better position to continue co-operation with them after the material has come to McGill.[66] We wish to collaborate in

---

64 Ralph R. Johnson.
65 Quoted from Harding to Scott, 11 March 1954, Letter #13.
66 Scott met with James on 24 March 1954 and it appears from Scott's notes that he had received general support for his eventual trip to Jerusalem and the principal's encouragement to approach the Birks family to help fund the trip. Scott seemed to believe that in travelling to Jerusalem he was taking a place on the editorial team. From

the most effective way in scholarly studies of our part of this material, and not merely to hoard it as a curiosity. I gather from Professor Tushingham that it will be published, along with the other finds, in an Oxford University Press series of volumes, and am delighted to learn this.[67]

You will hear from me again shortly.

With best wishes,
Yours sincerely,
R.B.Y.Scott

LETTER #17

Archive: McGill, RG34, Container: 0001, File 6: Dead Sea Scrolls.
McGill, RG2, Container: 0179, File 6243: Divinity: DSS & Birks Donation.

8 April 1954   Montreal

Dear Mr. Harding

Enclosed is a bank draft on New York for the balance of the money to be sent you to purchase on behalf of McGill University the available Scroll Fragments from Qumran. The amount is $10,363.52, of which $ 363.52 is the exchange premium gained by converting the sum given into U.S. dollars.[68] This brings the total amount sent you to $ 15,363.52.

When you acknowledge receipt of this second amount, would you kindly enclose for the University Bursar a note of the total amount received from McGill University "for the purchase on behalf of McGill University of a collection of ancient scroll fragments from the Judaean desert ". The Bursar needs this for

---

a later response by de Vaux it appears clear that Scott had little inkling of the enormity of the task ahead for the editorial team (De Vaux to Scott, 23 April 1954, Letter #21).

67 Tushingham visited Montreal on 16 March 1954, and the matter may have been discussed then (Tushingham to Scott, 12 February 1954. McGill University Archives, RG34, Container: 0001, File 6: Dead Sea Scrolls).

Volume 1 appeared in 1955 (Barthélemy and Milik, *Qumran Cave 1*, DJD, vol. 1).

68 A copy of the bank draft made out in Harding's name for $10,363.52 USD is preserved in the McGill University Archives, RG4, Container: 239, File: Birks, John Henry – Collection, Judean Manuscripts – Dead Sea Scrolls.

accounting purposes. Later, when the material has been identified and classified, we would like to have a list of it to complete the record of purchase.[69]

We shall await with much interest word from you as to the completion of the transaction, and any further information you can give us from time to time as to the nature and extent of the material.

Yours sincerely,
R. B. Y. Scott

LETTER #18

Archive: McGill, RG34, Container: 0001, File 6: Dead Sea Scrolls.
McGill, RG2, Container: 0179, File 6243: Divinity: DSS & Birks Donation.
McGill, RG4, Container: 239, File: Birks, John Henry – Collection, Judean Manuscripts – Dead Sea Scrolls.

19 April 1954   Amman

Dear Dr. Scott,[70]

Thank you for yours of the 8th with cheque for $10,363. I enclose a receipt for the total amount in the form you ask for.[71]

Yesterday I had the pleasure of meeting Prof. Cantwell Smith and showing him the fragments which I have acquired for you, so he will be able to give you a first hand account of everything. It is indeed a very fine lot and includes some good large pieces. I actually got it into my hands a week ago, so there has not been time to do more than sort it and identify a few of the more obvious works. As soon as I can give you more definite news, perhaps in a couple of weeks, I will write you again.

---

69 Scott would eventually assemble the first list during his visit to Jerusalem in the summer of 1955. For the list, see chapter three.

70 This letter is Scott's transcription of Harding's original. The original has not been preserved.

71 The receipt is preserved in McGill University Archives, RG4, Container: 239, File: Birks, John Henry – Collection, Judean Manuscripts – Dead Sea Scrolls, and reads in part: "Received from the McGill University, Montreal, Canada, the sum of U.S.$.15,363.52 for the purchase on behalf of the said University a collection of ancient fragments from the Judean desert."

But meantime I must congratulate the University on having acquired what is certainly the finest collection of these unique manuscript fragments outside the original Government collection. That they originate from Qumran Cave IV is affirmed already by finding some pieces which fit to others in the first lot. I do hope you will be able to come out and see everything for yourself.

With best wishes,
Yours sincerely,
G. Lankester Harding
Director of Antiquities.

LETTER #19

Archive: McGill, RG2, Container: 0179, File 6243: Divinity: DSS & Birks Donation.

21 April 1954   Montreal

Dear Dr. James:

You may remember that at our recent interview I raised with you the question of McGill University's becoming a Corporate Member of the American Schools of Oriental Research. I have long felt that McGill, like Toronto and Queen's, should belong to this institution, which for over fifty years has carried on archaeological work of outstanding importance in Palestine and Mesopotamia.

Membership not only means association with eighty-six other institutions in support of fundamental research in this field, but opens the way for professors and advanced students to participate, as lecturers or fellows at the Schools in Jerusalem and Baghdad. There are two endowed fellowships awarded by competition, I believe, annually. While we do not at present have candidates in a position to apply, there is reason to hope that, with the further development of graduate studies in the Faculty of Divinity and in the Institute of Islamic Studies, there will be such candidates before long. I know that Professor Wilfred Smith agrees with me that it would be to the advantage of McGill to belong to the A.S.O.R. The cost of Corporate Membership is $100. per annum. A faculty member is designated to represent the Corporate Member.

Much of the original and continuing work on the Judaean Desert Scrolls is being done by representatives of the A.S.O.R. who are at the Jerusalem

School,[72] and the Bulletin carries a good deal of published work on this subject.[73] With the acquisition of the John Henry Birks Memorial Collection, it seems to me all the more important that McGill University should belong to the A.S.O.R.

I enclose for your information a copy of the latest issue of the Bulletin, and would draw your attention to the report of the Trustees' Meeting, and to the list of Institutional Corporation Members.[74]

Yours sincerely,
R. B. Y. Scott

LETTER #20

Archive: McGill, RG2, Container: 0179, File 6243: Divinity: DSS & Birks Donation.

22 April 1954   Montreal

Dear Professor Scott,

Thank you very much for your letter of April 21st with its suggestion that McGill University should become a corporate member of the American Schools of Oriental Research.

I notice that you have sent a copy of your letter to Dean Thomson[75] and if he supports the proposal, I shall be very glad indeed to make an appropriate recommendation to the Executive and Finance Committee of the Board of

---

72 Frank Moore Cross and Patrick Skehan were the ASOR members working in the scrollery in Jerusalem at the time. They were primarily responsible for fragments of biblical texts. As mentioned, Cross was one of the first members to join the editorial team in 1953. Monsignor Patrick Skehan (1909–1980), of the Catholic University of America, was appointed to the team in 1954, during his tenure as annual professor at the Jerusalem School.

73 On ASOR's involvement with the Dead Sea Scrolls, see King, *American Archaeology in the Mideast*, 111–24.

74 Cadbury, "December Meeting of the Board of Trustees," 2–3; "Annual Meeting of the Corporation," 4; and "Members and Contributors," 4–5.

75 James S. Thomson (1892–1972), succeeded Scott as dean of the Faculty of Divinity in 1949.

Governors at its May meeting,[76] although I suspect that the decision of that Committee will depend somewhat on the action (or lack of action) by Mr. Duplessis[77] during the next few weeks.[78]

With best personal wishes, I remain,
Cordially yours,
F. Cyril James

LETTER #21

Archive: McGill, RG34, Container: 0001, File 6: Dead Sea Scrolls.

23 April 1954   Jerusalem

Cher Professeur Scott,

Je m'excuse de répondre aver un peu de retard à votre lettre du 19 mars:[79] je suis rentré de notre fouille de Qumrân depuis quelques jours seulement.[80]

---

76 The application for membership proceeded and the trustees of ASOR elected McGill to institutional corporate membership on 27 December 1954. See Reed, "Annual Meeting of the Corporation," 4–5.

77 Maurice Duplessis was the conservative premier of Quebec from 1936 to 1939 and from 1944 to 1959. During this period the federal government had offered funds to support Canada's universities. Because education fell under provincial jurisdiction, Duplessis forced McGill and the other Quebec academic institutions to reject the needed funds to avoid federal incursion in provincial business. This left universities such as McGill in dire straits. See Frost, *The Man in the Ivory Tower*, 185–90.

78 James became so interested in ASOR's published material that even after Scott left for Princeton, he continued to manage communications with ASOR for McGill himself. In May 1957, ASOR offered to send copies of *BASOR* and other material to him directly. He responded: "I am delighted to hear that I shall receive the newsletters of the American Schools of Oriental Research, and thus keep up my reading which was so greatly stimulated in these subjects by Professor R.B.Y. Scott's enthusiasm." See Walton to James, 15 May 1954, and James to Walton, 17 May 1954, McGill University Archives, RG2, Container: 0179, File 6243: Divinity: DSS & Birks Donation.

79 Letter not preserved.

80 The excavation took place between 1 February and 1 April 1954.

J'ai été très heureux que notre conversation de Copenhague[81] ait porté des fruits aussi magnifiques et que l'Université McGill consacre une somme importante à l'achat de fragments manuscrits de la Mer Morte. Dès que Mr Harding a reçu votre premier envoi, il a fait l'achat. Le lot est maintenant au Musée et comprend de très beaux fragments de livres bibliques et non bibliques. Tout cela provient de la Grotte 4, trouvée par les Bédouins en fin 1952 et achevée de fouiller par nous. F. Cross et l'abbé Milik[82] en ont commencé l'étude.

Nous serons naturellement très heureux de vous accueillir à Jérusalem dans l'équipe qui prépare l'édition des manuscrits, mais je doute qu'un séjour de deux ou trois mois soit suffisant pour un travail efficase: vous aurez juste le temps d'apprendre comment on manipule les fragments et de commencer à les assembler et à les lire. Guidés par l'expérience, nous demandons à nos collaborateurs au moins un an de travail à Jérusalem.[83]

Je viens de recevoir de bonnes nouvelles de Doug Tushingham, qui revenait de donner une conference sur les manuscrits à McGill University.

Je vous redis le plaisir que j'ai eu à vous revoir cet été à Copenhague et vous prie de croire, cher Professeur Scott, à l'assurance de mes sentiments les meilleurs,

R. de Vaux

LETTER #22

Archive: McGill, RG2, Container: 0179, File 6243: Divinity: DSS & Birks Donation.

20 May 1954   Montreal

Memorandum for Dr. R. B. Y. Scott
re McGill fragments in the Jerusalem Museum

Visit of Prof. Wilfred Smith, April 17, 1954

I had lunch with Dr. Lancaster Harding in Jerusalem, and he then took me to the Museum. He showed me first a room full of Dead Sea Scroll fragments,

---

81 At the 23–25 August 1953 meeting of IOSOT.

82 Józef T. Milik (1922–2006), together with Cross, was one of the first members of the editorial team.

83 This comment corroborates Harding's offer of a position on the editorial team to McGill and confirms de Vaux's knowledge of it.

belonging to the Jordan Government. These were mostly arranged in groups pressed between glass plates or plastic plates (perhaps 12" by 18" each) – I should guess maybe sixty in all. Considerable work had been done on them, fitting various pieces together, deciphering, translating and so on; a great deal remains still to be done. There was, of course, much of quite fascinating interest.

He then took me into an adjoining room, where the McGill material was housed. It too was being sorted and placed between plates – about twenty-four[84] so far, with many smaller pieces still to be sorted. Each fragment of the McGill collection had been stamped with a tiny S ("for 'Scott'"), to identify it – as the Government collection had been stamped with a tiny G ("M would be ambiguous, for 'McGill' or 'Museum'"). The most interesting piece so far noted was a fairly large fragment, of Daniel (I did not make a note of this at the time, and somehow my memory is uncertain: I do believe that it was Daniel but somehow "Numbers" also plays in my mind),[85] which was of a version quite unlike anything so far identified. Some of the material in both groups presented a Hebrew original for the Septuagint version – a crucial discovery.[86] The McGill collection contained both Biblical fragments and extra-Biblical items – the latter opening up the whole fascinating field of the cultural Near Eastern history in the Hellenistic period.

At present working on the McGill material, according to Dr. Harding, are: Frank Cross, Père de Vaux, and a Dominican called Melik.[87] Dr. Harding pointed out that manifestly considerable work would have to be done on all the fragments, both the Jordan Government's and McGill's, before any of them could leave Jerusalem, since obviously if two fragments fitted together they should be kept together. He assured me that if any piece was lost to the McGill collection on this principle, another piece of comparable value and interest would be substituted – this seemed to me clear and [end page 1] cogent, and

---

84 "Four" is added in pen above the line. The copy of the letter preserved in McGill's archives is that forwarded by Scott to Principal James. It is unclear whether Smith made this addition for Scott, or Scott for James, after discussion with Smith.

85 This is the first indication to Scott of any of the contents of McGill's purchase. Based on later discussions, it was most likely a piece of Daniel that he viewed.

86 Scott was already aware of the crucial nature of this matter, having read Frank Cross's 1953 BASOR article ("A New Qumran Biblical Fragment Related to the Original Hebrew Underlying the Septuagint," 15–26); see Letter #8. Nevertheless, information about the recognition thereof and about McGill's acquisition of some of these fragments was quite important, given how little time had been devoted to their examination since their purchase only a few weeks earlier.

87 Józef T. Milik.

his own integrity seemed quite adequate guarantee.[88] He further stated that arrangements had already been made, and apparently McGill had been so advised, that all publication of the material itself should be in a standard format, by the Oxford University Press.[89]

Dr. Harding made the fairly obvious point that it would be extremely desirable if Dr. Scott could himself visit Jerusalem to see the whole collection and work on the material in situ.

Dr. Harding was very enthusiastic indeed about the whole matter, and obviously greatly impressed with the initiative and wisdom of McGill in acquiring these finds. He stated quite flatly that McGill's collection would be, as at present standing, the finest in the world next to that of the Jordan Government which would remain in the Jerusalem Museum. He spoke of the lack of willingness of the British Museum and of other universities, who might have been expected to jump at such an opportunity, to break from their traditional rules by putting up the money for something which could be examined only after it was bought, not before.[90] By sticking to this formula, he said, they have missed a rare and striking opportunity to acquire priceless material which constitutes the most significant development in Biblical studies for many generations. He certainly felt strongly that McGill was to be complimented on its enterprise and judgement.

Dr. Harding also explained to me the general context of the caves and the finds, showed me other material in the Museum from the same sites, including the work benches on which apparently the Scrolls had been copied; and the like.[91] I must say that to me the whole matter was little short of exciting.

Wilfred Cantwell Smith

---

88 This agrees with Tushingham's observations to Scott in the earliest communications about the McGill purchase.

89 On the history of the Oxford publication series, *Discoveries in the Judaean Desert*, see Tov, "Discoveries in the Judaean Desert," 205–8.

90 Discussed above, Letter #3. See Kendrick to Harding, 8 November 1952, IAA Archives, Box 73, PAM 1117: Dead Sea Scrolls (cave no. 4), jacket 1, for the negative response of the British Museum to Harding's offer of material to this institution for purchase.

91 The "benches" were discovered in excavations by de Vaux. For discussion thereof, see de Vaux, *L'Archéologie et les Manuscrits de la Mer Morte*, 23–6. The discovery of these items was essential to describing the room in which they were found as Qumran's "scriptorium." The identification of the items has been challenged. See for example, Clark, "The Posture of the Ancient Scribe," 63–72.

LETTER #23

Archive: McGill, RG2, Container: 0179, File 6243: Divinity: DSS & Birks Donation.

21 May 1954[92]

Dear Mrs. McMurray:

I have prepared the enclosed material in case Dr. James should wish to use some or all of it in making a press release on the Birks collection of Judaean Desert Scrolls, since I understand that the Birks Foundation gift has been listed among those received by the Board of Governors.[93] Four copies are enclosed: in addition to the 'Star' & the 'Gazette', Prof. Wilfred Smith suggests the 'N.Y. Times' should get it.[94]

A subsequent story could give details and photographs, when these have been received.

Yours sincerely,
R.B.Y. Scott

---

92 Handwritten cover letter to Principal James's secretary, Dorothy McMurray, who began at McGill in James's predecessor's office in 1929. On McMurray and James, see Frost, *The Man in the Ivory Tower*, 68–70.

93 Scott and James discussed the idea of a press release at their 24 March 1954 meeting. They assumed they would make the news available in September of that year, when they expected to have photographs of the fragments purchased. See Scott's notes on his interview with James, 24 March 1954, McGill University Archives, RG34, Container: 0001 File 6: Dead Sea Scrolls. As the announcement of the gift was published in the annual report (McGill University, *Annual Report, 1953–1954*, 201) they decided to move forward with a press release.

94 The three papers named, as well as the London *Times*, would eventually cover the announcement. See "McGill Buys Priceless Scraps of Old Testament Manuscripts," *Gazette* (Montreal), 22 May 1954, 19; "McGill Gets Part of Rare Bible Find," *Montreal Star*, 22 May 1954, 3–4; "McGill University Buys Ancient Bible Scrolls," *New York Times*, 24 May 1954, 21; and, "Biblical Manuscripts $15,000 purchase by McGill University," *Times* (London), 24 May 1954, 6(G).

Scott sent a near identical announcement to the *Canadian Journal of Theology* where it was published verbatim: "The John Henry Birks Collection of Ancient Palestinian Manuscripts," 51–2.

Enclosure:

Notes for Press "release re
"John Henry Birks Collection of Ancient Palestinian Manuscripts"[95]
(May, 1954)

Principal F. Cyril James announces the acquisition for the Faculty of Divinity, McGill University, through the munificence of the John Henry Birks Foundation, of a ~~unique~~ collection of manuscript fragments of the Old Testament and related works dating from the beginning of the Christian era and earlier. These will be of the utmost importance for the study of Judaism in the time of Christ, and for the study of the Old Testament text. They are part of a find made in a cave in the Judaean Desert near the Dead Sea in September 1952, the remainder of which is in the hands of the Jordan Government and the Palestine Museum. The Faculty of Divinity collection will be unique outside of Palestine. It was obtained for McGill by purchase from the Beduin who made the find, as a result of prolonged negotiations conducted by Professor R.B.Y.Scott of the Faculty of Divinity with the Department of Antiquities of the Jordan Government. The Director of the Dept. of Antiquities, G. Lankester Harding, F.S.A.,[96] has declared that the genuineness of the documents is beyond question, and has written to "congratulate the University on having acquired what is certainly the finest collection of these unique manuscript fragments outside the original Governement collection".[97]

Since ~~1947~~ the accidental discovery in 1947 of the famous "Dead Sea Scrolls", including a complete copy of the Book of Isaiah, five other caves containing parts of the library of the Jewish sect of the Essenes have been found in the same

---

95 Scott relied heavily on Frank M. Cross ("The Manuscripts of the Dead Sea Caves," 2–21) for the background information on previous discoveries, excavations, and the description of the contents of the scrolls. However, he also followed the published reports in academic journals and the newspapers quite closely, as the collection of clippings in his files demonstrates (McGill University Archives, RG34, Container: 0001, File: 7 Dead Sea Scrolls: Clippings and Correspondence). In his first published piece on the scrolls, which preceded the press release by almost a year, and the Copenhagen meeting and the fortuitous lecture by De Vaux by a month, Scott refers to articles in the *New York Times* and to de Vaux's articles in *Revue biblique*. See R.B.Y. Scott, "More Treasure Trove: Dead Sea Region Discoveries," *United Church Observer*, 15 July 1953, 5, 28.

96 Name inserted above text.

97 Harding to Scott, 19 April 1954, Letter #18.

vicinity, about ten miles south of Jericho. The ruins of the sect's community centre at Khirbet Qumran have been excavated by British, French and American archaeologists. The most extensive and important finds were made in what is now known as "Cave Four", and of these about one quarter have been obtained for McGill. They will remain at the Palestine Museum in Jerusalem (Jordan) for about two years for classification and study before being shipped to this country. [end page 1]

The excavation of the community centre of the Essenes at Khirbet Qumran by Father R. de Vaux of l'Ecole Biblique in Jerusalem has demonstrated conclusively that it was occupied by the sect from the second century B.C. to the First Jewish Revolt, as a result of which Jerusalem was destroyed by the Romans in 70 A.D. Evidently on the approach of Roman armies the Essenes were dispersed, after concealing their library in surrounding caves so well hidden that some were not discovered until the twentieth century. Ancient authors record similar discoveries in the same vicinity in the third and the eighth centuries A.D.[98] In the community centre have been found the remains of a "scriptorium", with a table, inkpots and a basin apparently for ritual washings; here evidently some at least of the newly found manuscripts were ~~copied~~ copied by the scribes from ~~earlier~~ older examples.

The fragments of the John Henry Birks Collection are still in the process of being[99] cleaned and identified, so that it is not yet known what it comprises, except that there are included both Biblical and non-Biblical manuscripts. The material previously acquired by the Jordan Government from the same cave includes parts of every book of the Old Testament except Chronicles, and also[100] commentaries; paraphrases, apocryphal works (some previously unknown), together with ritual documents of the Essene sect.

These finds of which McGill has been so fortunate as to acquire a significant portion, will throw a flood of light on the history of Judaism in the post-Maccabaean period, and on the crucial epoch of the rise of primitive Christianity. In addition, they give glimpses of the Old Testament text a thousand years before the copying of the Hebrew scrolls from which our English Bibles and other translations have been made. The study of them will keep scholars busy for fifty years or more, and the results of such studies must be of far-reaching importance for Christian and Jewish faiths.

---

98 A summary of these stories of earlier discoveries is found in Filson, "Some Recent Study of the Dead Sea Scrolls," 96–9; and it may have been Scott's source for this information.

99 Word inserted above the line in pen.

100 Words inserted above the line in type.

LETTER #24

Archive: McGill, RG34, Container: 0001, File 6: Dead Sea Scrolls.

8 June 1954 Montreal

Dear Mr. Harding:

Thank you for your letter of May 31st,[101] in which you say that you are having some pictures taken of some of the Scroll Fragments of the McGill Birks Collection. This is good of you, and I appreciate it. Perhaps some of the $363. surplus above the $15,000[102] could be applied to the cost of the infra-red photograph[y?][103]

In your previous letter of April 19th you spoke of sending me, "perhaps in a couple of weeks", some indication of the contents of the collection. We have no indication of this, except that it contains some fine pieces and that both Biblical and non-Biblica[l] works are represented. I know that the preliminary sorting of the material will take some time, but as soo[n] as you can give me any information at all I shall be most eager to receive it. Professor Cantwell Smith was most impressed with what he saw, but his inspection was necessarily brief, and he did not take notes of what he saw.

When I cabled you asking you for a photograph for a press announcement I was anxious to have somethin[g] before McGill Convocation. Realizing that your work often takes you away from Amman, I went ahead with a statement in general terms, as there was some possibili[ty] of the newspapers breaking the news inaccurately.[104] I have also notified Professor Millar Burrows of Yale, and Professor Albright. The latter will put a brief prelimi[nary] note in the October issue of B.A.S.O.R.[105]

---

[101] Letter not preserved.

[102] As a result of the conversion from Canadian to U.S. funds. See Scott to Harding, 8 April 1954, Letter #17.

[103] The letter runs off the edge of the page. Reconstructed words are placed in square brackets.

[104] As a result of the information in the university's Annual Report (McGill University, *Annual Report, 1953–1954*, 48, 201).

[105] Albright served as the editor of *BASOR* for almost forty years, beginning with the February 1931 issue and ending in April 1969. Scott's note on McGill's purchase was included in the October 1954 issue, cf. Scott, "Acquisition of Dead Sea Scroll Fragments by McGill University," 8.

When photographs arrive, they probably w[ill] be exhibited in the small Museum of Biblical Antiquitie[s] at Divinity Hall in McGill. Will you please tell me explicitly what may or may not be done in the matter of publishing these as illustrations in connection with press articles or other such printed references to the McGill Birks collection? I do not wish to transgresss any way the agreement with the Oxford University Press, but naturally it may be years before these particular fragments appear in that series. Would it be possible f[or] Frank Cross to send a short article on the McGill frag[ments] to Albright for the B.A.S.O.R. ?[106]

[Conclusion of letter cut off. Undoubtedly the correspondent is R.B.Y. Scott].

LETTER #25

Archive: McGill, RG2, Container: 0179, File 6243: Divinity: DSS & Birks Donation.

9 June 1954   Montreal

Dear Mr. Manoog:[107]

Principal F. Cyril James has asked me to reply to your letter of June 3rd about the Dead Sea Scrolls.[108]

Naturally we are interested to hear that the four Dead Sea Scrolls found in 1947 are being offered for sale. Although there is little likelihood that McGill University would be in the market for further purchases of this material so soon after the acquisition of the J.H.Birks Collection, I personally would be interested to know what price is being asked, and whether a clear title of ownership could

---

106 Apparently, Frank Moore Cross never wrote an official notice, although he did make note of McGill's purchase in "A Report on the Biblical Fragments of Cave Four in Wâdī Qumrân," 9–13.

107 Charles Manoog (1903–1989) was a Worcester, Mass., businessman who befriended Mar Athanasius Samuel when he became the head of the Archdiocese in the U.S. and Canada. See Samuel, *Treasure of Qumran*, 185–201.

108 On 7 June 1954, James forwarded a copy of Manoog's letter of 3 June to Scott. Manoog wrote that the announcement of McGill's purchase appearing in the *Gazette* (Montreal) had inspired him to offer for sale four additional complete scrolls (James to Scott, 7 June 1954 and Manoog to James, 3 June 1954, McGill University Archives, RG34, Container: 0001, File 6: Dead Sea Scrolls).

be given in view of the requirements of the Antiquities laws of the Jordan Government.[109]

Yours sincerely,
R. B. Y. Scott
Professor, Old Testament Literature

LETTER #26

Archive: McGill, RG2, Container: 0179, File 6243: Divinity: DSS & Birks Donation.
McGill, RG4, Container: 239, File: Birks, John Henry – Collection, Judean Manuscripts – Dead Sea Scrolls.

31 August 1954   Montreal

Dear Dr. James,

Since I last spoke to you on the subject of the Qumran Scroll Fragments acquired for McGill as the "John Henry Birks Memorial Collection" there have been some interesting developments which I have pleasure in reporting.

Mr. Lankester Harding, Director of Antiquities, has sent me infra-red photographs of four "frames" of the fragments, in addition to a picture of the large room in the Palestine Archaeological Museum where these and many others are in the process of being studied. Two of these photographs, with Mr. Harding's permission, will be used to illustrate an article in the forthcoming issue of the McGill News.[110]

---

109 The archbishop outlines his own difficulties with demonstrating ownership and title in *Treasure of Qumran*, 172–201.

110 See John Scott, "The Dead Sea Scrolls: Some of the Oldest Manuscripts of the Bible Ever Found are Acquired by the University," 24–5, 53–4. Two pictures are printed one above the other. The upper is the now famous picture of the scrollery with Skehan at work in the lower left corner and two others, Strugnell (upper left) and Allegro (right) working behind him [PAM 41.212]. It has often been reprinted; see *inter alia*, Shanks, *The Mystery and Meaning of the Dead Sea Scrolls*, 40; and Fields, *The Dead Sea Scrolls: A Short History*, 64. The lower picture is a plate of fragments marked "sample plate S" [PAM 41.210]. For discussion of the contents of these plates see chapter 2, nn216–19.

In a preliminary examination of these pictures I have identified parts of five chapters of the Book of Daniel,[111] of the second chapter of Jonah,[112] and of the thirty-second chapter of Deuteronomy,[113] in addition to sectarian documents. The fragment of Deuteronomy, (although it comprises only parts of three verses) is clearly of outstanding importance, for it gives the lost Hebrew original of the Septuagint Version (third century B.C.) where this differs significantly from our traditional Hebrew text.

The latest number of the Revue Biblique contains an account by Pere R. de Vaux, O. P., of the further excavation of the Covenanters' Sects' headquarters at Qumran.[114] The number of coins has risen to over 200, and the distribution of these makes it almost certain that the buildings were erected in the last decades of the second century, B.C., were temporarily abandoned from the earthquake of 31 B.C. to the first decade of our era, and then occupied until the approach of Roman armies in 68 A.D. It was at this time, evidently, that the library of the Sect was hidden in adjacent caves. The archaeological evidence for the genuineness and general period of the MSS is overwhelming. [End page 1].

---

[111] Five manuscripts of Daniel are known from Cave 4: 4QDan^a, 4QDan^b, 4QDan^c, 4QDan^d, and 4QDan^e. Which fragments Scott saw in the photographs is unclear, as they have not been preserved, and the single frame in the *McGill News* is not of high enough quality to make out more than a few words. However, Cross had made reference to McGill having a large piece of Daniel, as had Smith in his early report. According to the list compiled by Scott on his 1955 visit, as well as the distribution list eventually received from Harding, McGill expected to receive 4QDan^a, which includes portions of Dan. 1, 2, 4, 5, 7, 10, and 11. See Ulrich, "Daniel Manuscripts from Qumran. Part 1: A Preliminary Edition of 4QDan^a," 17–37; and Ulrich et al., *Qumran Cave 4.XI: Psalms to Chronicles*, 239–54.

[112] 4QXII^a (4Q76) and 4QXII^g (4Q82) both include portions of Jonah 2. However, no reference to McGill receiving Jonah fragments appears in either Scott's list (enclosed with Scott to Bentley, 2 September 1955, Letter #42, mentioned in Scott to Harding, 7 September 1955, Letter #43, and reproduced as an addendum to this book) or Harding's later list (enclosed with Harding to Scott, 6 June 1956, Letter #61) of McGill's purchases. The identification appears erroneous.

For discussion of the manuscripts, see Ulrich et al., *Qumran Cave 4.X: The Prophets*, 221–318.

[113] Likely 4QDeut^q. See Ulrich et al., Qumran Cave 4.IX: Deuteronomy, Joshua, Judges, Kings, 137–42.

[114] de Vaux, "Fouilles au Khirbet Qumrân: Rapport préliminaire sur la deuxième campagne," 206–36.

Several well-known Biblical scholars have expressed great interest in, and envy of, the McGill acquisition. Prof. Frank Cross of Chicago, who examined the fragments in Jerusalem, says that the "farsighted action" of McGill undoubtedly saved much precious material from dispersion and loss.[115] Prof. Millar Burrows of Yale is noting the acquisition in a book he is writing this summer.[116] Prof. W.D. Davies of Duke told me that he feels New Testament studies will have to wait on the fuller identification and valuation of these "very important" finds. I heard from the Secretary of the British Society for Old Testament Study that the McGill acquisition had been announced at the Jubilee meeting in Edinburgh in July.

Mr. Harding has written me[117] that since our purchase was made, a further lot has been acquired for the University of Manchester,[118] and that still further material is apparently available. But the fact that McGill was first to act means that we shall have still the outstanding collection outside of Palestine. It is all very gratifying.

Yours sincerely,
R.B.Y. Scott

LETTER #27

Archive: McGill, RG2, Container: 0179, File 6243: Divinity: DSS & Birks Donation.

4 September 1954   Montreal

Dear Professor Scott,

Thank you very much indeed for your letter of August 31st. As Mrs. McMurray has explained to you, I am completely tied up with the University principals who have come to Canada from all over the Commonwealth for the meetings

---

115 Cross to Scott, 12 August 1954, McGill University Archives, RG34, Container: 0001, File 6: Dead Sea Scrolls.

116 The announcement of McGill's purchase can be found in Burrows, *The Dead Sea Scrolls*, 69.

117 Letter not preserved.

118 By March 1954 Manchester had started to arrange funds to purchase fragments (Brown, *John Marco Allegro*, 40–3). According to Stephen Pfann the purchase took place in December 1954, but this letter to James seems to suggest that it took place in the late summer ("History of the Judean Desert Discoveries," 102).

here this month,[119] and until we get those meetings over, and the Convocation for HRH The Duchess of Kent[120] I shall not have a moment for the chat which I should very much like to have with you, so that some time after the middle of the month I shall look forward to it, and meanwhile, with renewed thanks for the report today and congratulations on the fact that McGill is well to the forefront in the matter of the Qumran Scroll Fragments, which will become the "John Henry Birks Memorial Collection".[121]

Cordially yours,
F. Cyril James

LETTER #28

Archive: McGill, RG34, Container: 0001, File 6: Dead Sea Scrolls.

6 December 1954   Montreal

Dear Dr. Thomson:[122]

As you know, McGill obtained by purchase last Spring through the Government of Jordan Department of Antiquities a quantity of ancient scroll fragments from the Judaean desert. This is to be known as the "John Henry Birks Collection", and will come to McGill after a period sufficient for the cleaning, sorting and preparation for publication of these mss. fragments.

In general terms the agreement is quite clear, and Professor Wilfred Smith last spring visited Jerusalem and saw the material which had been obtained

---

119 McGill hosted the meetings of the Association of Universities of the British Commonwealth in 1954. James was a member of the executive from 1948 to 1951 and 1960 to 1962. On the history of the association during these years, see Ashby, *Community of Universities: An Informal Portrait of the Association of Universities of the British Commonwealth, 1913-1963*.

120 HRH Princess Marina, duchess of Kent, and her daughter, Princess Alexandra, visited McGill on 14 September 1954 as part of a royal visit to Canada in August and September of that year.

121 They would eventually meet on 24 September 1954. See Scott to McMurray, 21 September 1954, McGill University Archives, RG2, Container: 0179, File 6243: Divinity: DSS & Birks Donation.

122 David L. Thomson, dean of Graduate Studies and Research at McGill University from 1942 until 1962.

for McGill; he did not, however, make any study of it. Last week I proposed to Principal James that I should try to arrange to go to Jerusalem by air next Spring, and stay six or seven weeks in order to become fully informed about the material which is to come to McGill and about the whole series of manuscript discoveries of which this is a part. I would work at the Palestine Archaeological Museum with the team of scholars who are busy with this study, and also be able to visit the sites where the mss. were found. As I shall be the person responsible for the collection, it is essential that I have all possible first-hand information. I should discuss with the Museum authorities at Jerusalem what measures should be taken for the transportation of the material, and for its proper preservation and exhibition. Most important of all, it is essential that a McGill representative be present for negotiations to exchange fragments of equal worth in order that matching pieces of the same ms. may be kept together.

The Principal said that this proposal made sense to him, and suggested that I should consult you to see if the Travel and Research funds could be drawn upon to assist in what (I think) could be called a significant piece of research in the field of the Humanities. I would have to go by air because I could not spare more time than about seven weeks, and all of that would be needed. The return fare would cost about $900.[123] and other expenses would be about $300. If you wish it, I can give a more detailed break-down. I enclose Wilfred Smith's memo., which seems relevant, for your information.[124]

Yours sincerely,
R.B.Y. Scott

---

123 Amount added in pen.

124 A grant of $1,200 was provided for Scott's travels and was approved on 21 December 1954. McGill University Research Fund Project 10, McGill University Archives, RG34, Container: 0001, File 6: Dead Sea Scrolls.

LETTER #29

Archive: McGill, RG2, Container: 0179, File 6243: Divinity: DSS & Birks Donation.

20 December 1954   Montreal

Dear Dr. James:[125]

I was tickled at this indication that McGill ran first, Manchester second, and the Vatican Library third – in the matter of the Scrolls![126]

Yours sincerely,
R.B.Y. Scott

[End page 1]

Extract from THE LISTENER, November 25th, 1954.[127]
(Broadcast talk on Dead Sea Scrolls by Professor)
(H.H. Rowley of Manchester.)[128]

From the neighbourhood of Qumran several caves have yielded texts since the first finds.

Much of the material was found first by the Bedouin, and not a little has got into the hands of dealers from whom it has had to be bought to be collected together with the fragments found by the archaeologists who have gone in the wake of the Bedouin. Much is still in the hands of the dealers, and the Jordan Government, which from its slender resources in a single year spent £15,000 in

---

125 Handwritten cover letter on university letterhead.

126 According to Stephen Pfann, the Vatican made a purchase in October and Manchester in December 1954. Rowley's talk in November of that year suggests to the contrary that the purchase took place earlier ("History of the Judean Desert Discoveries," 101–2).

Note also that John Allegro puts the Vatican contribution at £700 (*The Dead Sea Scrolls: A Reappraisal*, 47).

127 *The Listener* was a BBC magazine published weekly between 1929 and 1991. Its mandate included reproducing the content of selected radio broadcasts.

128 Harold Henry Rowley (1890–1969) was professor of Hebrew at the University of Manchester from 1945 until 1959.

buying these precious finds, is unable to complete the task. There is, therefore, great danger that pieces may be sold to tourists and be dispersed and lost, without even being properly studied. To prevent this the Jordan Government has consented to allow collections of the fragments to be bought by suitable institutions, provided they are bought through official channels and carefully examined before leaving the country. McGill University promptly sent $15,000 to be used for this purpose, and Manchester University, helped by a private gift from a public-spirited citizen, sent £2,000.[129] The Vatican Library in Rome has also made a purchase.

LETTER #30

Archive: McGill, RG2, Container: 0179, File 6243: Divinity: DSS & Birks Donation.

21 February 1955   Montreal

Dear Dr. James:

I have to report to you on two matters and feel that this is best done in writing, since you may wish to refer to them.

(i) My proposed visit to Jerusalem to examine and negotiate about the Birks Collection of the Judaean Desert Scrolls. Dean D. L. Thomson has informed me that the Committee on Research has approved my application, and has authorized an accountable grant up to $1200. I am planning to go out by air in mid-April in order to be able to see the excavations at Qumran and Jericho before the weather becomes too hot in the Jordan valley, and then to work for two months at the Palestine Museum in Jerusalem (Jordan). On the way home in July I hope to attend meetings of one, possibly two, learned societies.[130]

Since this grant by the Research Committee, though generous, will cover only transportation and a minimum of expenses for three months, I have asked Mr. Henry Birks if he would recommend to the J. H. Birks Foundation a further grant (accountable) of $1000. to provide for contingent expenses directly related

---

129 See also Brown, *John Marco Allegro*, 41–3.

130 Because of his appointment at Princeton University, Scott was in the end unable to attend any of these meetings. The planned three-month trip also had to be shortened to a month, seemingly as a result of limited funding (see Scott to Johnson, 30 March 1955, Letter #32).

to the Birks Collection. He readily agreed to propose this to the Foundation.[131] What I have in mind is the need of adequate records, photographic and other; the probability that there may be costs in arranging for shipment and insurance; and the possibility that I may have opportunities to share in other explorations or to obtain smaller items related to the discoveries (such as pottery from the caves). These things cannot be foreseen in detail, and it would be a pity if I should be unable to take full advantage of opportunities which may occur.

(ii) [Text removed. Discussion of candidate for a position in the Faculty of Divinity] ...
I am quite sure that he is the man best qualified to assist me in the Old Testament [end page 1] department <u>and</u> in the U.T.C.,[132] should it be arranged that I assume the Principalship of the latter. I have told Mr. Birks[133] that I would be willing to accept this responsibility only if I could have sufficient assistance to enable me to maintain my position in the Old Testament field.[134] So far as I am aware, no decision has yet been reached in this matter.

[Text removed explaining that the candidate's C.V. had been forwarded to the appropriate people.]

With kind regards, I remain, Sir,
Yours faithfully,
R. B. Y. Scott

---

[131] The Birks Foundation had agreed to provide up to $20,000 CAD. By this time, only $15,000 CAD had been spent on the purchase of the fragments.

[132] United Theological College. Scott was invited to apply for the position as principal of UTC on 28 November 1954 (Scott to Birks, 3 March 1955, McGill University Archives, RG2, Container: 0179, File 6243: Divinity: DSS & Birks Donation).

[133] Henry Birks, in addition to being a member of McGill's Board of Governors, also chaired the Board of Governors of the United Theological College.

[134] In the 1953 ratified agreement of the association of the theological colleges and the Faculty of Divinity, an allowance was made for principals of the colleges to remain members of the Faculty of Divinity, see Markell, *The Faculty of Religious Studies*, 34. On 3 March 1955 Scott wrote to Birks asking that his name be withdrawn from consideration for the principalship. He suggested that a younger man could focus more on directing the school. He also referred to his desire to make a greater research contribution to biblical studies (McGill University Archives, RG2, Container: 0179, File 6243: Divinity: DSS & Birks Donation).

LETTER #31

Archive: McGill, RG2, Container: 0179, File 6243: Divinity: DSS & Birks Donation.

22 February 1955   Montreal

Dear Professor Scott,

Thank you very much indeed for your letter of February 21st., with the good news that you have succeeded in obtaining accountable grants of $1,200 from Dean Thomson's fund,[135] with a further $1,000 from the J.H. Birks Foundation, to cover the costs of your visit to Palestine.

If you would send through Dean J.T. Thomson[136] a formal request for leave of absence from mid-April I shall be very glad indeed to place this before the Board of Governors at the next meeting, and I am sure that they will gladly grant it, in view of the importance of your trip.[137]

[Three lines of text removed. James indicates he will keep a copy of the candidate's c.v. on file for the position in Old Testament.]

With renewed good wishes meanwhile, I remain,

Cordially yours,
F. Cyril James

---

135 D.L. Thomson, dean of Graduate Studies at McGill.

136 J.S. Thomson, dean of the Faculty of Divinity at McGill.

137 In a letter dated 25 February 1955, Dean J.S. Thomson made the formal request to James on Scott's behalf (McGill University Archives, RG2, Container: 0179, File 6243: Divinity: DSS & Birks Donation). The leave of absence was granted on 9 March 1955 by the Board of Governors for a period from "mid-April until August 31 next" (Bentley to Scott, McGill University Archives, RG2, Container: 0179, File 6243: Divinity: DSS & Birks Donation).

LETTER #32

Archive: McGill, RG34, Container: 0001, File 6: Dead Sea Scrolls.
McGill, RG2, Container: 0179, File 6243: Divinity: DSS & Birks Donation.

30 March 1955 Montreal

Dear Mr. Johnson:[138]

As I told you in our conversation this morning, my decision to accept an invitation to Princeton University[139] means that I shall be leaving McGill at the end of August.[140] I am most anxious, however, to carry through the project of establishing the "J. H. Birks Collection of Judaean Scroll Fragments" at McGill, as the following excerpt from my letter to Principal James will make clear; -

> My one serious hesitation in accepting the Princeton invitation is the responsibility I feel to the donor and to McGill for completing the setting up of that J. H. Birks Collection. In my conversations with the head of the department at Princeton[141] I have stressed this, and he is ready to recognize that I would have a continuing responsibility at least until there is someone here ready to take it over. This seems feasible, since I plan to spend vacations at Georgeville, Quebec, and since, if other visits are needed, Princeton is only an over-night journey from Montreal.
>
> What remains to be done, as I see it, is: (i) the identification and listing of that fragments belonging to the Birks Collection, including the somewhat delicate business of trading fragments of equal value so that all known parts

---

138 Ralph R. Johnson, representative of the Birks Foundation.

139 Princeton initiated a Graduate Studies Program in Religion in 1955 (see Ramsey, "Princeton University's Graduate Program in Religion," 291–8). Scott was appointed to a newly established named professorship, the William H. Danforth Professorship of Religion.

140 Scott tendered his resignation on 18 April 1955, effective 31 August 1955 (Scott to James, 18 April 1955, McGill University Archives, RG2, Container: 0179, File 6243: Divinity: DSS & Birks Donation).

141 George F. Thomas (1899–1977), professor of religious thought, was the first faculty member hired in the field of religious studies at Princeton in 1940. He remained chair until 1959.

of one manuscript will be in one place; (ii) the completion of arrangements for packing, insurance, and shipment to Canada; (iii)[142] arrangements for reception of the material here, and for its housing, display and study; (iv) preparation of a catalogue and a popular brochure plans for use of the materiel for research and graduate study.

I will not pretend that my feeling that I should continue work on this project is dictated solely by a sense of duty. I am proud to have been instrumental in obtaining the Scroll fragments for Canada and for McGill, and I have a deep interest in carrying the project to a successful conclusion. In these circumstances I hope that arrangements [end page 1] made for my visit to Jerusalem this Spring to carry out (i) and (ii) will stand.

This visit to Jerusalem had two purposes, the completion of these arrangements about the Birks Collection, and a period of study of these and related materials in the museum there. The university had promised me a grant of $1200. from the Research Fund, and in our earlier conversations you felt that the Birks Foundation would add another $1000, to provide a reserve for expenses directly related to the Collection. Under the new circumstances McGill could hardly be expected to underwrite research which would chiefly benefit my teaching in another University. The carrying forward of the arrangements about the Birks Collection is, however, essential, and it would never do to leave these, as it were, in mid-air. My proposal is that I go to Jerusalem for this purpose as planned, but remain for a briefer time, probably four or five weeks. If the Foundation would agree to grant the $1000 as previously arranged, and add $400 or $500. for contingencies, I am prepared to give the time. I would, of course, give a full accounting of expenditures.

Yours sincerely,
R. B. Y. Scott

---

142 Number inserted in pen.

LETTER #33

Archive: McGill, RG34, Container: 0001, File 6: Dead Sea Scrolls.
McGill, RG2, Container: 0179, File 6243: Divinity: DSS & Birks Donation.

11 April 1955   Montreal

Dear Dr. James:

   As the date planned for my departure for Jerusalem (April 23) is getting near, I am trying to complete the necessary arrangements. You will remember my discussing with you the question of the amount of the grant from the Research Fund which could be considered directly applicable to work on the Birks Collection, as distinct from research as such.
   Mr. Ralph Johnson of the Birks Foundation has consulted Mrs. Birks, and they have agreed to give me the $1000 originally planned, plus $500 as a reserve for possible out-of-pocket expenses for recording, insurance or other costs in preparation for shipment. I estimate my travel expenses for six weeks, travelling by air, as $1300–1400, without any extras or reserve for contingencies. Would you be willing to have McGill contribute $400 either from the $1200 voted by the Research Fund Committee or from some other source? I think this would be a fair apportionment.
   With thanks for your continued interest, and kind rewards, I remain,

Yours sincerely,
R. B. Y. Scott

LETTER #34

Archive: McGill, RG34, Container: 0001, File 6: Dead Sea Scrolls.
McGill, RG2, Container: 0179, File 6243: Divinity: DSS & Birks Donation.

13 April 1955   Montreal

Dear Professor Scott,

   It was very good indeed to learn from your letter of April 11th that you have been able to work out such satisfactory arrangements with Mr. Ralph Johnson in regard to your projected trip to Jerusalem. Under all the circumstances I certainly think it would be appropriate for the Faculty of Graduate Studies and Research to make a grant of $400, rather than the $1200 originally proposed, towards the incidental costs of your journey since your work on the Judaean Manuscript is certainly of permanent value to McGill.[143]

With renewed good wishes, I remain,
Cordially yours,
F. Cyril James

LETTER #35

Archive: McGill, RG34, Container: 0001, File 6: Dead Sea Scrolls.

13 April 1955   Montreal

Dear Mr. Harding:

At last my plans to come out to Jordan seems to be definite, and I plan to arrive in Jerusalem (Old City) by air from Beirut on April 27 or 28. I hope to be able to stay at the American School, and in any case that will be my postal address.

My principal object in coming at this time is to examine the Qumran Four scroll fragments which were purchased last year for McGill University, and will be known as the "J.H.Birks Collection". I hope very much that it will be convenient for you to see me at Jerusalem during May, in order that we may discuss the recording of the collection and arrangements for its shipment when the necessary studies have been completed at Jerusalem. The main thing I am concerned about is the decisions as to the exchange of fragments of the McGill material which you wish to retain, for other material of equal value. I hope also to learn a good deal more than I know at present about the Qumran excavations, and I need advice about what arrangements should be planned for the proper care and preservation of the material when it reaches Montreal.

My original plan to stay in Jordan until July has had to be modified owing to my acceptance of an invitation to Princeton University, to which I expect to move in September. It is understood, however, since Princeton is only an overnight journey from Montreal, that I shall continue to be responsible for the

---

143 The letter was copied to Dean D.L. Thomson of the Faculty of Graduate Studies.

Birks Collection until someone else is here to take it over. In any case, I intend to make it a continuing interest for the rest of my academic career.

With kind regards,
Yours sincerely,
R. B. Y. Scott

LETTER #36

Archive: McGill, RG34, Container: 0001, File 6: Dead Sea Scrolls.

4 May 1955   Jerusalem

Dear Mr. Harding:

Following my conversation with you and Pere de Vaux last week and further conversations with him, I think it might be well, in order to preclude any possibility of misunderstanding, for me to put in writing my understanding concerning the Scroll fragments from Qumran Cave Four which are to come to McGill University and be known as "the J. H. Birks Collection".

The fragments purchased with the McGill contribution last year have been stamped with the letter "S", and are now in process of being identified and matched with other pieces of the same manuscripts. When this work is completed you yourself will allocate to McGill its proportionate share of the composite manuscript pieces, on the principle that a substitute piece of approximately equal value will be given for each of the "S" pieces which is retained for another collection. McGill is to accept its share of unidentifiable fragments. The remainder will be approximately one third Biblical material and two thirds non-Biblical. The study of the Biblical pieces will probably be completed by the summer of 1956 and the allocation and preparation for shipment of that part of the collection could then be made.[144] "The J.H.Birks Collection at McGill University" will be named in the official publication.[145]

In our conversation it was agreed [end page 1] that the donors and the University should now be given some idea what the Birks Collection will

---

[144] This is the first clear reference to the fact that the collection would not need to be shipped as a whole but could be sent to Montreal as sections of the collection became available upon publication.

[145] *Discoveries in the Judaean Desert* (DJD), published by Oxford University Press. See Tov, "Discoveries in the Judaean Desert," 205–8.

include.¹⁴⁶ It would be useful to both parties to have a list of the identifiable pieces which were bought with the McGill contribution,¹⁴⁷ and I have started to compile this list. I feel that on leaving McGill I should lodge in the files of the University an account of the extent and the character of the material purchased with the McGill contribution, pending the final allocation which will result in a certain amount of substitution. I should like also to have some further representative photographs to attach to the list, and to show the donor.¹⁴⁸

At the same time I want to assure you that this list will be a confidential document until such time as the allocation is made. I fully appreciate that the Museum and the scholars who are working there have prior rights of publication. I will undertake that neither the descriptive list, nor any further photographs which you may allow me to have, will be published or identified in public lectures or publications before they have been published by the Museum or the scholars working under your direction.

If there are any other points which occur to you in this connection, I should be glad to talk them over with you while I am in Jerusalem this month up to the 25th. I deeply appreciate the cordiality with which I have been received, and want to do whatever I can to ensure that the arrangements about the McGill collection are satisfactory to all concerned.

Yours sincerely,
R. B. Y. Scott

---

146 The second payment by McGill University of $10,363 had been received by 19 April 1954 the previous year. From the initial meeting with de Vaux in August 1953, until his visit to Jerusalem in May 1955, Scott knew nothing of the contents of McGill's collection except what he could make out in the four photographs Harding had sent to him. Not only were the purchases made blind, but even once the fragments were owned by McGill, their identification remained a mystery.

147 Following word scratched out in pen.

148 Scott confirms in his report on the trip (15 June 1955, Letter #40) that he received infra-red photographs. Their current whereabouts is unknown.

LETTER #37

Archive: McGill, RG34, Container: 0001, File 6: Dead Sea Scrolls.
McGill, RG2, Container: 0179, File 6243: Divinity: DSS & Birks Donation.

10 May 1955   Amman

Dear Dr. Scott,[149]

With reference to your letter of May 4, I confirm that all the proposals made therein are acceptable to us and can be carried out.

I am very glad indeed that you have been able to visit us and see the actual material being worked on, as you will now have a much better idea of our problems and difficulties than could be given in letters.

I am always ready to give what assistance I can to further your interest in the scrolls and much appreciate your help in keeping this unique collection together for study.

Yours sincerely,
G. Lankester Harding
<u>Director of Antiquities.</u>

LETTER #38

Archive: McGill, RG2, Container: 0179, File 6243: Divinity: DSS & Birks Donation.

15 May 1955   Jerusalem

Dear Dr. James:[150]

I thought you might be interested to hear how I am getting on in my work on the Birks Collection of the Qumran Scrolls. I have had a cordial reception from Mr. Harding, Director of Antiquities, Père de Vaux of L'Ecole Biblique,

---

149 This letter is the earliest known formal acknowledgement of the nature of McGill's purchase and the agreement reached with the Jordanian Department of Antiquities.

150 Handwritten aerogram.

& Mr. Saʿad, Director of the Museum.[151] Clearly they are grateful that the timely contribution from McGill enabled them to buy up a lot of material which otherwise might have found its way into private hands. In addition to McGill, Manchester, the Vatican Library and now Bonn & Heidelberg[152] have contributed but McGill still has the largest amount of fragments to go outside Palestine, though of course, much smaller than the Jordan Gov't and Museum Collections. There are thousands of pieces, from which about 300 different mss. have been identified. The material is more impressive than I had thought before seeing it, and there is no question at all about its authenticity and general dating. Even this spring three or four more small deposits were located in the vicinity of the Qumran settlement,[153] which has been almost completely excavated, and which proves to be a self-contained "monastery" of the Essenes occupied by them from late in the 2nd cent. B.C. until its destruction by the Xth legion in May or June 68. Burnt timber & Roman arrowheads were recovered. The settlement had its own pottery, smithy, kitchens, assembly hall, council chamber, and a dozen great cisterns, (some of which may have been used for "baptismal" rites – a connection with John the Baptist's movement is more than possible).[154]

I have had two good talks with Mr. Harding & Père de Vaux about the McGill Collection, & understand the situation as I could not do by correspondence. The important thing to realize is the magnitude of the problem of sorting and identifying the material in preparation for publication. Three French scholars,

---

151 Yusif Saʿad was secretary at the PAM until 1957, when he became curator. We thank Arieh Rochman-Halperin, archivist at the Israel Antiquities Authority in Jerusalem, for providing the information.

152 In the spring of 1955 a £4,500 purchase was made by Professor Karl Georg Kuhn (1906–1976) on behalf of Heidelberg University, with funds provided by the Governments of Bonn and Baden-Württemberg. See Allegro, *The Dead Sea Scrolls: A Reappraisal*, 47.

153 During the fourth season of excavations, between February and April 1955, four collapsed caves containing written remains were found and named Caves 7, 8, 9, and 10, respectively (de Vaux, "Fouilles au Khirbet Qumrân: Rapport préliminaire sur les 3e, 4e et 5e campagnes," 533–77).

154 During late April or early May 1955, that is, during Scott's visit, de Vaux was interviewed by the London *Times*. The descriptions of the fragments and of Qumran found in this letter are very similar to the information provided in the article and suggest that Scott's report to James accurately reflects the content of his discussions with de Vaux (cf., "A Jewish 'Monastery' At Khirbet Qumran: Light On Dead Sea Scrolls," *Times* (London), 9 May 1955, 13[D]).

two American and two British are doing the bulk of the work.[155] The biblical material is the easiest to deal with because there is a text to compare it with. The apocryphal material comes next, although it is in Hebrew & Aramaic rather than in Greek, Latin or Syriac translations which have been known heretofore. Some of the Essene sectarian material is known from the already published more complete documents of Cave One. But there is also a great deal of <u>new</u> apocryphal and sectarian material which has to be pieced together without any text to refer to.

The Oxford Press publication of the additional fragments from Cave One appears this month.[156] The Second volume is to contain the second cent. A.D. finds from Muraba'at, of which the McGill collection has no part,[157] the third (& possibly fourth) volumes will contain the biblical fragments, & when this is ready for the printer (autumn 1956?)[158] the allocation can be made, and that

---

[155] The Americans, Frank Cross and Patrick Skehan, and the British scholars, John Allegro and John Strugnell, are easily identified. Two of the three French representatives would appear to be József T. Milik (Polish by way of France) and Jean Starcky. The third French scholar mentioned is more difficult to identify. Dominique Barthélemy had returned to France after becoming ill in the spring of 1953 (his work focused primarily on the biblical texts from Cave 1 and then the Dodekapropheton from cave 8). During this period, Maurice Baillet worked on material from Caves 2, 3, 6, 7, and 10 and only became part of the Cave 4 editorial team in 1958. Pierre Benoit had responsibility for the publication of the Greek texts from Wadi Murabba'at.

Claus-Hunno Hunzinger (b. 1929) of the Deutsche Forschungsgemeinschaft is not mentioned in this context. He befriended Scott during his visit. His absence in Scott's listing of the team may be because Scott refers in this context to those in charge of "the bulk of the work." As Hunzinger could only remain in Jerusalem for a short while, he had requested a limited selection of material as his allotment (cf. Brown, *John Marco Allegro*, 48).

[156] Barthélemy and Milik, *Qumran Cave 1*. An advertisement from Oxford for the volume appeared in the London *Times* on 23 June 1955 (13[A]).

[157] It did not appear until 1961; see Benoit, Milik, and de Vaux, *Les Grottes de Murabba'ât*.

[158] The first volume of Cave 4 material was edited as the fifth volume of *DJD*, by John Allegro. It appeared in 1968, entitled *Qumrân Cave 4.I (4Q158–4Q186)*. The first volumes of biblical fragments did not begin to appear in *DJD* until the 1990s. The delay resulted from a number of factors, including lack of funds; the discovery of further manuscript material; the return of scholars to academic positions away from Jerusalem; and the death of de Vaux and then his successor Benoit. For discussion of these matters, see Tov, "The Publication of the Dead Sea Scrolls," 199–213.

[end page 1] part of our material shipped. Mr. Harding suggests that it be sent in "perspex",[159] through the Embassy at Amman.

The mss which have been matched will be kept together, & each institution will get a certain number of plates corresponding to its contribution. The location of these originals will be noted in the official publication. McGill will be asked to take its share of the smallest & largely unidentifiable fragments, & then will have in its share roughly 1/3 Biblical & 2/3 non-Biblical texts of the significant pieces. There is still some material in the hands of the Bedu, but no one knows how much; this uncertainty makes the scholars want to hold off publication until they can be reasonably sure almost all of it is included.[160]

It was agreed by Harding & de Vaux that it was reasonable that the donor and McGill should have some idea of the extent and character of what will be the Birks Collections, & hence that it would be useful to have a list of the fragments stamped with the letter "S" when the purchase was made on our behalf. I have been devoting my time to locating, measuring, and taking notes of identification of these pieces; so far I have listed 414 fragments from 15 books of the Old Testament,[161] and several apocryphal, sectarian & esoteric works. There is more to be listed yet. When the final allotment is made, this list will be a basis of reference, & we shall get larger sections of fewer manuscripts. I have had to give an understanding that the information given me will remain confidential until the material is published, in order not to rob the scholars of here of the fruits of their labours. I plan to lodge one copy of the list with the University, send one to Mr. Harding, & keep one for reference. I am getting photographs which I hope to make up into an album, with commentary, to give to Mrs. Birks.

With all good wishes,
Yours sincerely,
R.B.Y. Scott

---

159 Perspex is an acrylic glass brought to market in the early 1930s. The advantage over shipping the parchment fragments between glass plates is that, unlike glass, perspex will break in large pieces rather than shattering. This would prevent the fragments from severe damage in the event that plates might break during shipping.

160 The last pieces of Cave 4 fragments were only purchased from Kando in 1958.

161 A discrepancy exists: in Scott's report (Scott to F. Cyril James, et al., 15 June 1955, Letter #40) only fourteen books are listed.

LETTER #39

Archive: McGill, RG2, Container: 0179, File 6243: Divinity: DSS & Birks Donation.

30 May 1955[162] Montreal

Dear Professor Scott,

Thank you very much indeed for your long letter of May 15th which sounds very interesting indeed. As a matter of fact, since things sometimes appear in strange places, the best summary given that I have seen in print regarding the Dead Sea Scrolls and the Essene Monastery was in the <u>New Yorker</u> a couple of weeks ago where Edmund Wilson took up nearly twenty pages with a complete account of the history of the discoveries and some rather interesting comments on the content of the documents themselves.[163] If you have not seen this you may like to look at it as an interesting presentation from the layman's viewpoint.

It all sounds as though you are having a thoroughly interesting time and, also, as though the Birks Collection at McGill will be really worthwhile. I hope also that you are finding a little time to take some more photographs because I remember the records of the earlier expedition with great pleasure.[164]

Best personal wishes to you as always from,
Yours cordially,
F. Cyril James

---

162 It is unclear whether Scott ever received this letter. The only copy preserved is an unsigned duplicate. The letter was composed and addressed to ASOR Jerusalem two days after Scott had departed for Montreal.

163 Wilson, "A Reporter at Large: The Scrolls from the Dead Sea," 45–121.

164 Scott's earlier trip to Jerusalem under the aegis of ASOR from January to July 1951.

LETTER #40

Archive: McGill, RG34, Container: 0001, File 6: Dead Sea Scrolls.
McGill, RG2, Container: 0179, File 6243: Divinity: DSS & Birks Donation.

15 June 1955   Montreal

To: Dr. F. Cyril James   Mrs. J. H. Birks[165]
     Mr. Ralph R. Johnson   Henry W. Birks
     Dean D. L. Thomson   Wm. Bentley, Bursar
     Dean J. S. Thomson

Report on a Visit to Jerusalem in connection with the Acquisition of the John Henry Birks Collection of Ancient Scroll Fragments from Khirbet Qumran

R.B.Y. Scott

1. <u>General</u>: I arrived in Jerusalem (Old City) by air on April 27 and left to return to Montreal on May 28.[166] I was cordially greeted by Pere R. de Vaux, Director of the Palestine Archaeological Museum, and Mr. Lankester Harding, Director of Antiquities for the Jordan Government, and given the freedom of the manuscript room where six scholars are working on the fragments.[167] I made two visits to Khirbet Qumran and the adjacent caves where the manuscripts were discovered; the first visit was made under the guidance of Pere de Vaux, who has directed the excavations there. I had several satisfactory discussions about the Birks Collection with both these gentlemen; Mr. Harding remarked that it would have been difficult to understand the situation without a personal visit. My principal task was the listing and measurement of approximately 450 pieces of manuscripts, which, together with many small unidentifiable pieces, were purchased with the

---

165 The last three names on the list were added in pen.

166 By 2 June 1955, even before writing this report, Scott had already reported the success of his trip and the excitement surrounding McGill's collection to the local press. See Francis Allen, "Dead Sea Treasure: McGill Getting Scrolls," *Montreal Star*, 2 June 1955, 1.

167 Patrick Skehan, John Allegro, John Strugnell, Józef Milik, Jean Starcky, and Claus-Hunno Hunzinger.

Birks contribution. It was agreed that McGill should have such a master list to indicate the nature and extent of the Birks Collection, and that it would be useful for Mr. Harding to have a copy of this when the final allocation is made. I also obtained a number of infra-red photographs of the McGill fragments and other pieces which have been matched with them, and myself took colour and black-and-white pictures at Qumran and in the Museum.[168]

2. <u>Contents of the Birks Collection</u>: The material obtained by Mr. Harding with the money sent by McGill is part of the finds – partly made by the Beduin and partly by the authorities – which come from Qumran Cave Four. Unlike Cave One, where the Mss. had been preserved in jars, Cave Four contained a jumbled mass of scrolls embedded in the floor. The sorting, assembling and identifying of the thousands of fragments is a gigantic jig-saw puzzle. Nevertheless, the final result will be even more important than the finding of the seven relatively complete Mss. and some fragments in Cave One, for about three hundred different [Mss. have][169] been identified in Cave Four. About 165 of these include[170] [end page 1] one or more pieces from the McGill purchase. In several instances the McGill piece is the largest fragment of one ms.; in one instance a McGill fragment of some size is the only surviving piece of an otherwise unknown work; in another, the McGill lot contributes twenty-seven small pieces of papyrus in a "cryptic" script that has had to be "broken" like a code.[171] The following Biblical books are represented, Genesis, Exodus, Leviticus, Numbers, Deuteronomy, Joshua, Samuel, Job, Psalms, Isaiah, Jeremiah, Daniel, Hosea and Zechariah.[172] The non-Biblical works are hymns, prayers, apocalypses, apocryphal poetry

---

168 Several boxes of slides were turned over by Scott to the McGill archives. They are not preserved with the Scroll collection and, unfortunately, could not be found. Four of Scott's photographs were published in his *Treasure from Judæan Caves*:

Page 6 – A fragment of Deuteronomy which supplies the lost Hebrew original of part of the Greek translation. From Cave Four, Qumran.

Page 7 – Two openings of Cave Four as seen from the Qumran "monastery."

Page 22 – Cave One, Qumran.

Page 23 – Three of the jars, in which manuscripts were stored, and a cooking-pot; restored from fragments found in Cave One."

169 The typing has been scratched out and written over. This reading is quite certain.

170 Last five words of page added in pen.

171 On these curious scripts, see Cross, *The Ancient Library of Qumran*, 45–6.

172 Note the discrepancy: in Scott to James (15 May 1955, Letter #38) Scott refers to "15 books of the Old Testament." Here only fourteen are listed.

and prophecy, Messianic Testimonies, paraphrases, commentaries, wisdom works, and the Hebrew or Aramaic originals of the familiar "Apocrypha" which have been known previously only in translation.

3. <u>Plan and Progress of the Investigation</u>: In view of the far-reaching importance for scholarship and religion of these manuscript finds, every effort is being made (a) to secure whatever may still remain in the hands of the Beduin or their agents; (b) to concentrate the material at the Museum for preliminary study so that a team of scholars may be able to identify and assemble as much of each Ms. as survives; (c) to proceed with publication as soon as is consistent with thoroughness; and (d) to ensure that the material is properly preserved and made accessible to scholars for further study.

(a) In order to discourage sales by the Beduin to private individuals as curios and the consequent loss of it to scholarship, the Dept. of Antiquities has set out to make all purchases through a single intermediary, and has paid a good price. Opinions differ as to how much is still outstanding, – from very little to 5000 Pounds' worth. Shortly before leaving Jerusalem I was told by a dealer that he had seen a match-box of small pieces; I consulted Mr. Harding and was authorized to buy this if it appeared to be genuine Qumran material, partly in the hope that this might open up a new avenue to what is still outstanding. When the man returned with the match-box I had two of the museum scholars with me for consultation,[173] and we agreed that all but one of the tiny pieces of leather and papyrus – seventeen in all – were probably authentic, and some of them certainly so. I paid 17 Pds. ($ 45.33) for them, and turned them over to Mr. Harding to be added to the Birks Collection. The price was not out of line with what the Government had been paying, and it is just possible that the contact may be useful in clearing up the situation, and so accelerating the publication and distribution of the scrolls to institutions.

---

173 Patrick Skehan and Claus-Hunno Hunzinger. Skehan is mentioned by name in R.B.Y. Scott's 1981 recall of this story in his "Special Report: What Ever Happened to McGill's Dead Sea Scrolls?" 55–8. In the article, Scott adds that a number of common but ancient coins were also purchased and that Harding allowed him to keep these. Hunzinger was the other participant; see his letter to Scott: 17 July 1955, McGill University Archives, RG34, Container: 0001, File 6: Dead Sea Scrolls.

(b) All the known[174] scroll fragments from Cave Four are at the Palestine Museum, except for a few pieces that have found their way to Israel, and one piece to France.[175] The Government owns most of them; the rest have been bought with contributions from McGill, Manchester, Bonn, Heidelberg and the Vatican Library. The necessity of holding the material at the Museum is illustrated by the fact that a piece of Lamentations which has belonged to the Government collection for two years has been matched recently by another piece of the same manuscript which came in with the Bonn-Heidelberg purchase. McGill has the largest lot after that of the Government. If further material comes in, the Museum authorities would prefer to have it added to one of the existing collections rather than to have an additional institution involved.

(c) The Birks Collection is to be published along with the rest of the finds (except what is now owned in Israel) in a series of volumes to be issued by the Oxford Press. The Biblical Mss. are to appear in [end page 2] vols. 3 and 4 of this series, which it is expected will be ready for publication in 1956. It is anticipated by de Vaux and Harding that this part of the collection can then be shipped. The non-Biblical fragments are more difficult to identify, and it may be two or three years more before all of them are ready for publication.

(d) None of the material is at present insured, but is kept in a locked and barred room in a fireproof building; it would be difficult to insure it until it is identified and listed.[176] When the time comes to ship the Birks Collection it would be insured after packing for shipment, as well as

---

174 Word inserted above text in type.

175 In 1952 Starcky acquired a fragment including parts of Psalms 33 and 35 (4Qps98). It has been in the collection of the Musée Bible et Terre Sainte, Paris (call number CB 7162) since 1960. The text was first published by Józef T. Milik in "Deux Documents Inédit du Désert de Juda," 268. Whether this is the piece Scott had in mind remains unclear. Several fragments had appeared in private collections (cf., for example, Testuz, "Deux Fragments Inédit de la Mer Morte," 37–40) and the sale of manuscript pieces to buyers other than the PAM was recognized early on by the members of the editorial team as a problem. In a 1956 article detailing the work of the editors, Pierre Benoit was already moved to request of these purchasers: "It would be very desirable for purposes of editing if these persons would undertake to send photographs of the fragments they hold to the Palestine Archaeological Museum, Jerusalem, Jordan," ("Editing the Manuscript Fragments from Qumran," 77).

176 In September 1961 the fragments in the PAM were assessed and insured for 150,000 JD ($420,000 USD) (Pfann, "History of the Judean Desert Discoveries," 105).

being transferred from the glass plates to "Perspex" or plastic containers. The museum staff will take responsibility for preparing the shipment, and for sending it if McGill cannot have a personal representative to take custody. There will be no expense to McGill for work done by the Museum staff other than out-of-pocket expense. Mr. Harding suggests that the shipment could be made through the British Embassy at Amman and the Canadian High Commissioner's office in London; or by special arrangement with B.O.A.C.[177] which would give it into the personal custody of the captains of the aircraft.

The question of the best means for permanent preservation of the scrolls is under study, and recommendations will be made to participating institutions.

4. <u>Value of the Birks Collection</u>: I was greatly impressed with the extent and variety of the material in the Birks Collection, as a significant part of the extraordinary treasures found in Qumran Cave Four. This in turn is part of the larger picture revealed by the other eight Qumran caves which have yielded scroll fragments (a few only, except for Cave One); and revealed also by excavation of the "Essene monastery" from which they came and where most of them were copied between 125 B.C. and 68 A.D. A still larger canvas includes the finds at three other sites more distant from Qumran, from which most of the Ms. finds belong to the 2nd cent. A.D. and later.

The enormous scholarly interest in this scroll material is evidenced from the fact that three international conferences in Europe this summer are to make it their chief concern, although so far only a small part has been published and made available for discussion. The prestige accruing to McGill is manifest in the attitude of the scholars now at work on the fragments in the Museum, and in the references now beginning to appear in scholarly and popular discussions. The material of the Birks Collection will be identified as such and the location at McGill stated in the official volumes which will be standard all over the world. While no monetary value can be set on the collection I would want to see it insured for at least $50,000 when the time comes to ship it to Canada.

5. <u>My Continuing Responsibility</u>: In the next few weeks I will type out the list of the McGill scroll fragments, with detailed measurements and such notes

---

177 The British Overseas Airways Corporation. In 1971 it merged with British European Airways to form British Airways.

of identification as can now be made. One copy of this will be lodged with McGill – presumably with the Bursar – , one sent to Mr. Harding. The other I will retain until I can hand it over with other records of the Birks Collection to my successor. Meanwhile I will keep in touch by correspondence with Mr. Harding. I have given him my word that the identifications of material listed will not be published prior to publication by the Museum or the scholars who have made the identifications. The same applies to the photographs which he permitted me to have. Needless to say, I am more than willing [end page 3] to keep track of the situation until the Birks Collection comes to Montreal, and from then on to continue my interest and to collaborate with my successor in setting up the Collection here.

6. Expenses and Refund: I was able to keep the expenses of this trip to Jerusalem somewhat below the advance estimate, and expended also only $ 45.33 of the $ 500. reserve amount.
   The figures are as follows:

   A. Grant from Birks Foundation for travel - $ 1000.00
      " " McGill Research Fund " "   400.00
                                                         $ 1400.00

      Expenses: Tourist air ticket $ 868.40
                 Passport & visas   23.80
                 Inoculations   13.50
                 Photographic costs   44.00
                 Travel expenses en route both ways 49.50
                 Expenses at Jerusalem (31 days)   153.22
                                                 $1152.42

                                                              1152.42
                                          Balance $247.58*

   B. Grant from Birks Foundation for Reserve
      against expenses on Collection $500.00
      Expenses: Purchase of small additional
                  scroll fragments for Collection   45.33
                                          Balance $454.67*

   Total Balance to be refunded to the McGill University
   Special Fund (265-23) for the J.H. Birks Collection – $702.25

I am glad to have had the opportunity to make this journey which, in my view, was almost essential in the interests of the Birks Collection and has been valuable to me for such further work as I may do in this field.

I remain, Gentlemen,
Yours faithfully,
(R. B. Y. Scott
Faculty of Divinity)

LETTER #41

Archive: McGill, RG2, Container: 0179, File 6243: Divinity: DSS & Birks Donation.

22 June 1955   Montreal

Dear Professor Scott,

   Thank you very much indeed for the very interesting report on your visit to Jerusalem in connection with the John Henry Birks Collection of fragments from Khirbet Qumran. It makes very interesting reading and it is apparent that your stay in Jerusalem has been more than usually valuable in connection with the future development of the Birks Collection. I am particularly interested in your purchase of the match-box and certainly hope that it may have opened up another avenue to the purchase of the material that is still in the hands of the Arabs.

   In my own opinion transportation by B.O.A.C.[178] under personal custody of the aircraft captains might be smoother than transmission through diplomatic channels but we can reconsider this when the actual time for shipment arrives. I agree fully that the items should be insured as soon as they come into our physical custody.

   In the light of what I have already said to you in previous conversations I need scarcely add that I am very glad indeed at the further testimony of your continuing interest and responsibility outlined in paragraph 5 of the report. Your own knowledge and help will be invaluable at all times in the future and,

---

178 The British Overseas Airways Corporation.

in a more personal vein, I am happy that the Birks Collection will give us a continuing contact with you in spite of your translation to Princeton.

With best personal wishes as always,
Cordially yours,
F. Cyril James

LETTER #42

Archive: McGill, RG4, Container: 239, File: Birks, John Henry – Collection, Judean Manuscripts – Dead Sea Scrolls.

2 September 1955   Montreal

Dear Mr. Bentley:[179]

One of the main objects of my recent trip to Jerusalem was to obtain definite information as to the nature and extent of the Scroll fragments purchased for the J.H.Birks Collection. I therefore made it my business to examine all the material from Qumran Cave IV, and to list with measurements and tentative identifications all pieces purchased with the contribution from McGill University.

Enclosed is a copy of the list which I have prepared from my notes, as I think you should have a copy in your files.[180] A second copy has been sent to Mr. Johnson of Henry Birks & Sons, who acted for Mrs. Birks in this matter. A third copy goes to Mr. Lankester Harding, Director of Antiquities for Jordan. I am retaining one copy for myself, and another to be given to my successor when he is appointed.

It is understood that, when the allocation of the manuscripts assembled from pieces in different collections is made, what comes to McGill will be of equivalent extent and importance to what was purchased on McGill's account. It will coincide only partly with the list I have prepared, since manuscripts will be kept together, and allocated pro rata to the different collections out of which they have been made up. The list enclosed, however, will be of assistance to Mr. Harding in making the division, and will serve at this end as a check on what

---

179 William Bentley was McGill University bursar and secretary to the Board of Governors (Frost, *McGill University: For the Advancement of Learning*, 2: 413).

180 See a photographic reproduction of the list in the Addendum to this volume.

is done. There is no doubt whatever that Mr. Harding will act with the utmost fairness to all concerned.

With kind regards,
Yours sincerely,
R. B. Y. Scott

LETTER #43

Archive: McGill, RG34, Container: 0001, File 6: Dead Sea Scrolls.

7 September 1955   Princeton

Dear Mr. Harding:

Attached is the list of Scroll fragments from Qumran IV purchased with the contribution of the J.H.Birks Foundation and McGill University, as I listed them at the Palestine Museum last May. It is not quite complete, as some pieces were away for photographing; one plate was backed with paper and the stamps could not be seen (I did not feel justified in disturbing the plate in Mr. Allegro's absence);[181] and finally, the small pieces I obtained from Mahmud the Silwani[182] and sent you through Dr. Hunzinger, are not included. However, the list is approximately a complete list, and sets out the nature and extant of the McGill material. It is the understanding, of course, that in your final allocation McGill is to receive the equivalent of this list in assembled manuscripts, rather than the material here listed as bought with the McGill contribution. I trust that the list will be useful to you when you come to make the allocation.

One copy of this is ledged with the Bursar of McGill University, one with the Birks Foundation, and the two others with myself and my successor (as yet unnamed) at McGill University. You will note my new address above, and I shall continue to be responsible to McGill for the collection until new arrangements are made. In fact, it is my intention to maintain a direct and continuous connection with this project in the future, so that any correspondence addressed to me at Princeton in this matter will have prompt attention.

---

181 John Allegro was in Jerusalem in April and May 1955. What this absence refers to is unclear.

182 The antiquities dealer who arranged the purchase of seventeen fragments for Scott during his stay in Jerusalem (cf. Scott to F. Cyril James, et al., 15 June 1955, Letter #40).

Again, may I thank you for your cordial and helpful reception at Jerusalem last May?

Yours sincerely,
R. B. Y. Scott

LETTER #44

Archive: McGill, RG34, Container: 0001, File 6: Dead Sea Scrolls.
McGill, RG2, Container: 0179, File 6243: Divinity: DSS & Birks Donation.
McGill, RG4, Container: 239, File: Birks, John Henry – Collection, Judean Manuscripts – Dead Sea Scrolls.

18 December 1955   Jerusalem

Cher Professeur Scott,[183]

Je vous remercie de vos aimables voeux de Noël et de Nouvelle Année et je vous envoie mes meilleurs souhaits. J'ai été très heureux d'av[oir],[184] de vos nouvelles et de savoir que vous trouviez à Princeton un cadre favorable pour vos études. Je dois vous remercier aussi des récents tirés à part que vous avez bien voulu m'envoyer et que j'ai lus avec intérêt et plaisir.[185]

Il est exacte que nous avons encore besoin d'argent pour acheter ce qui reste de la Grotte 4 de Qumrân. Tout récemment, la Bibliothèque Vaticane a envoyé 3.000 dinars,[186] qui ont permis d'acheter un beau lot, mais il reste encore un certain nombre de fragments: ils sont de bonne qualité mais ils sont chers, car il

---

183   Scott only received the letter after he returned to Princeton from his Christmas holiday in Montreal. Scott forwarded the letter to James on 27 December 1955, with a short note: "It is quite clear that the further contribution from the Birks Foundation will meet an urgent need," (Scott to James, 27 December 1955, McGill University Archives, RG2, Container: 0179, File 6243: Divinity: DSS & Birks Donation).
184   Edge of letter clipped. Reconstructed word.
185   In 1955 Scott published an overview of McGill's purchase in *Canadian Journal of Theology*: "The John Henry Birks Collection of Ancient Palestinian Manuscripts," 51–2; and, in the same volume, an article entitled "Is Preaching Prophecy?" 11–18. The previous year he published, "Another Griffin Seal from Samaria," 87–90.
186   The purchase was first "officially" announced in May 1956. See Paul Hoffman, "Vatican Studies Biblical Scrolls," *New York Times*, 13 May 1956, 118. Scott had made

faut les retirer à des intermédiaires qui demandent naturellement leur ~~condition~~ commission.[187] Il y aurait cependant un gros intérêt à ce qu'ils soient achetés le plus tôt possible, d'abord parce que les prix ne peuvent que monter et surtout par ce que nous aurions ainsi en mains <u>tout</u> le materiel de la Grotte 4 et que le travail d'édition pourrait être terminé: il est actuellement bloqué, car nous ne pouvons rien publier tant que nous savons que d'autres pièces sont sur le marché et comblent certaines lacunes de nos textes. Et cela retarde d'autant la distribution des pièces déjà achetées par différents propriétaires. Vous rendriez à tout le monde un très grand service si vous pouviez obtenir, comme vous le proposez, une nouvelle contribution de McGill. D'après nos estimations, nous avons besoin de 4 à 5.000 <u>dollars</u> (soit 1.500 à 2000 <u>dinars</u>). Il est possible, mais il n'est pas certain, que le Gouvernement Hollandais donne une partie de cette somme (des démarches sont faites en ce moment à La Haye),[188] mais il vous reste de sérieuses chances et tout ce que vous pourrez obtenir pour nous sera très apprécié.

Je regrette que vous deviez renoncer à venir au Congrès de Strasbourg. Il a déjà reçu des adhésions de valeur et promet d'être fort intéressant.[189]

Avec mes meilleurs voeux, et mes remerciements pour toute l'aide que vous nous apportez, je vous prie d'accepter, cher Professeur Scott, l'assurance de mes sentiments très cordiaux,

R. de Vaux, O.P.

---

the news public earlier in January; see J. E. Belliveau, "McGill Joins Vatican Check Bible Scrolls Found in Desert Cave," *Toronto Daily Star*, 16 January 1956, 25, 27.

187 Inserted in pen above struck out word.

188 The Royal Academy of Sciences of the Netherlands would eventually purchase material from Cave 11. See notes to de Vaux to Scott, 15 May 1956, Letter #59.

189 The second international meeting of IOSOT, 27 August to 1 September 1956. De Vaux served as president of the congress, which was attended by 250 people. Both Milik and Skehan presented papers on the scrolls and the assembly was informed that the Cave 4 material would be published in 1958. Altogether, it was expected that the published material would require seven volumes (cf. Rowley, "The Second International Old Testament Congress," 443–7).

LETTER #45

Archive: McGill, RG34, Container: 0001, File 6: Dead Sea Scrolls.

23 December 1955   Montreal

Dear Mr. Johnson,-

After seeing you and Mr. Henry Birks on Wednesday I went at once to Principal James and to Mr. Bentley at the University.[190] They were both delighted to learn that the Birks Foundation was prepared to take advantage of the further opportunity to obtain Qumran Cave Four fragments for the Birks Collection.[191]

I arranged with Mr. Bentley to transit the money to Mr. Harding, Director of Antiquities at Miriam, Jordan, and he will be glad to do so on behalf of McGill and the Birks Collection on receiving the additional funds from you.

The amount of £1,500. named will come to approximately $4,200.00 and I have suggested to Mr. Bentley that this should be sent by a bank draft in U.S. currency. I myself am writing to Mr. Harding by air mail at once in order to give him further details. Yesterday I cabled the news to him that the £1,500. had been agreed to.

With renewed appreciation of your ready cooperation and interest, and with Best Christmas Wishes.

Yours sincerely,
R. B. Y. Scott

---

190 Scott was in Montreal for the Christmas holidays (see Scott to Harding, 27 December, 1955, Letter #48).

191 No letters between Harding and Scott with reference to the initial arrangements for a second McGill purchase have been preserved. From de Vaux's letter of 18 December 1955, Letter #44, and Scott to Harding, 27 December 1955, Letter #48, it is evident that other communications did take place. The latter indicates that Scott first heard from Harding about the possibility of purchasing more material on 6 December 1955.

LETTER #46

Archive: McGill, RG34, Container: 0001, File 6: Dead Sea Scrolls.
McGill, RG4, Container: 239, File: Birks, John Henry – Collection, Judean Manuscripts – Dead Sea Scrolls.

23 December 1955   Montreal

Dear Mr. Bentley,-

I have written to Mr. Johnson of the Birks Foundation telling him that you will forward to Mr. Lankester Harding the additional grant for the purchase of Qumran Scroll Fragments.[192]
Mr. Harding's full name and address are -

Mr. G. Lankester Harding, F.S.A.,
Director of Antiquities,
Post Office Box 88,
Amman,
Hashemite Kingdom of Jordan.

The amount will be approximately $4,200.00 and I think it would be wise to send it by a bank draft on New York.
My own address, should you wish to get in touch with me, is -

Murray-Dodge Hall,
Princeton University
Princeton, N.J., U.S.A.

With cordial Christmas Greetings.
Yours sincerely,
R. B. Y. Scott

---

192 On 27 December 1955, Johnson replied directly to Bentley (sending a copy to Scott) indicating that a cheque would be forthcoming as soon as the total cost for the purchase and bank fees for the draft would be submitted to the Foundation (Johnson to Bentley, 27 December 1955, McGill University Archives, RG34, Container: 0001, File 6: Dead Sea Scrolls; and RG4 Container: 239 File: Birks, John Henry – Collection, Judean Manuscripts – Dead Sea Scrolls).

LETTER #47

Archive: McGill, RG4, Container: 239, File: Birks, John Henry – Collection, Judean Manuscripts – Dead Sea Scrolls.

27 December 1955   Princeton

Dear Mr. Bentley:

I am wondering if, when you receive the $4200 from the Birks Foundation, you would see if it would be possible to cable the money to Mr. Harding at Amman, Jordan, rather than sending it by bank draft. This morning I received from Père R. de Vaux a letter (a copy of which is enclosed) which indicates that the sooner it reaches him the better.

If the money has already been sent by bank draft, that is fine. But I thought it might not be out of place to suggest cabling it, should there be a few days delay in your receipt of it.[193]

Mr. Harding's cable address is "Antique Amman".

With best New Year's wishes,
Yours sincerely,
R. B. Y. Scott

LETTER #48

Archive: McGill, RG34, Container: 0001, File 6: Dead Sea Scrolls.

27 December 1955   Princeton

Dear Mr. Harding:

When your letter of Dec. 6th[194] arrived I was soon to go to Montreal for Christmas, so I postponed writing to Mr. Birks. At the first opportunity I went

---

[193] William Bentley, the university bursar, forwarded the bankdraft for the sum of $4,200 USD to Harding on 29 December 1955, Letter #49. Copies of the bank draft and receipt dated 28 December 1955, are preserved in McGill University Archives, RG4, Container: 239, File: Birks, John Henry – Collection, Judean Manuscripts – Dead Sea Scrolls.

[194] Letter not preserved.

to see him, and he consulted Mrs. Harry Birks and Mr. R.R. Johnson of the Birks Foundation. In five minutes they had agreed to put up the additional JD 1500 for which you asked! The next day I cabled you " <u>1500</u> <u>pounds</u> <u>agreed</u> <u>writing</u> – <u>Scott</u> ", and I hope the news reached you promptly.[195]

Principal James of McGill and Wm. Bentley, Bursar, were delighted with this further munificence of the Birks Foundation. Before leaving Montreal, I arranged with Mr. Johnson to forward the money to McGill, and with Mr. Bentley to send it to you by draft on New York as soon as it is received.

Today I had a letter from Pere de Vaux in which he emphasized the importance and urgency of the additional purchase, so I had copies made and sent to Montreal as an additional check to make sure there is no unnecessary delay. I also suggested to Mr. Bentley that he enquire if it is possible to cable the money to you rather than send it by mail.

I presume that the newly purchased fragments will be marked with the same letter as those bought with McGill money in 1954. It is too much to ask that they be listed as I did with the earlier group, but you might be able to let us have some indication of the number, size and nature of the pieces. This should not be so difficult if it is done before the material has been associated in frames with other material. Perhaps the easiest way would be simply to have them photographed as they come in, or as soon as they have been treated in the humidifier.[196]

If the time should come when you feel compelled to look to a learned institution for money for the Minor Prophets scroll,[197] I wish you would let me know, as I might be able to persuade the Princeton University Library to interest itself in it.

With best wishes for the New Year,
I remain,
Yours sincerely,
R. B. Y. Scott

---

195 De Vaux confirms receipt of the telegram, and the excitement in Jerusalem upon receiving it, in de Vaux to Scott, 8 January 1956, Letter #52.

196 The humidifier was used to make the brittle fragments of parchment more pliable so that they did not crumble when flattened between glass plates. An early description of the process of preparing the fragments for study is found in Cross, "The Manuscripts of the Dead Sea Caves," 15–16.

197 A Hebrew Minor Prophets Scroll [Mur 88] was discovered in a fifth cave at Wadi Murabbaʿat in March 1955. For a description of the discovery and the text, see Benoit, Milik, and de Vaux, *Les Grottes de Murabbaʾât*, 1: 181–205.

LETTER #49

Archive: McGill, RG4, Container: 239, File: Birks, John Henry – Collection, Judean Manuscripts – Dead Sea Scrolls.

29 December 1955   Montreal

Dear Mr. Harding,

At the request of Dr. R.B.Y. Scott I enclose Bank of Montreal draft No. 34,764 for $4,200.00 in U.S. funds to purchase the balance of the Qumran Scroll Fragments which have been assigned to McGill University.[198]

With best wishes for the New Year.
Yours sincerely,
WB[199]
Bursar and Secretary of the Board of Governors

LETTER #50

Archive: McGill, RG4, Container: 239, File: Birks, John Henry – Collection, Judean Manuscripts – Dead Sea Scrolls.

29 December 1955   Montreal

Dear Professor Scott:

Your letter of December 27th arrived this afternoon and the remittance of $4200.00 U.S. funds was sent out to Mr. Harding by Air Mail this morning. A copy of my letter to Mr. Harding should reach you before this arrives. Mr. Johnson acted promptly and so did I and I trust the draft gets there soon.

With best wishes for the New Year.
Yours sincerely,
WB
Bursar and Secretary of the Board of Governors

---

198 A copy of the bank draft is preserved in McGill University Archives, RG4, Container: 239, File: Birks, John Henry – Collection, Judean Manuscripts – Dead Sea Scrolls.

199 William Bentley.

LETTER #51

Archive: McGill, RG4, Container: 239, File: Birks, John Henry – Collection, Judean Manuscripts – Dead Sea Scrolls.

5 January 1956   Amman

Dear Dr. Bentley,

I have to acknowledge with thanks your letter of the 29th. Dec. enclosing cheque for $4200 for the acquisition of Qumran scroll fragments on behalf of the McGill University.

With all good wishes
Yours sincerely,
G. Lankester Harding
<u>Director of Antiquities.</u>

LETTER #52

Archive: McGill, RG34, Container: 0001, File 6: Dead Sea Scrolls.

8 January 1956   Jerusalem

Cher Professeur Scott,

Je vous remercie de votre aimable lettre de 30 décembre.[200] Nous vos somme très reconnaissants d'avoir obtenu encore 1500 dinars de McGill University pour acheter les fragments qui restaient de la grotte 4 de Qumrân. Dès que votre télégramme a été reçu, j'ai avancé la somme nécessaire sur les fonds de l'Ecole et l'achat a été fait. Ce sont des très beaux morceaux qui appartienent tous à des groupes déjà connus et qui comblent de làcunes importantes. Je ne puis pas encore vous donner le détail. Mais c'est une aide inappreciable pour le travail d'édition. Ce fragments ont été payés nettement plus cher que les precedents parce qu'ils étaient entre les mains d'intermédiaires qui exigeaient une forte commission, mais il fallait les avoir à tous prix. La situation politique instable où nous sommes actuellement nous engageait aussi à faire vite.

Doug Tushingham est arrivé depuis quelques jours avec Miss Kenyon et nous avons parlé de vous. Les troubles actuels les ont empêches de commencer les

---

200 Letter not preserved.

fouilles de Jéricho et, à moins que la crise soit rapidement résolue, je crains qu'il ne puissant pas travailler cette année. Quelle tristesse! Nous aurions tous tant besoin de la paix!²⁰¹

Vous m'avez fait un grand honneur en me proposant comme membre d'honneur de la Society of biblical Literature and Exegesis et je vous remercie vivement. Je n'ai pas encore reçu la notificationo officielle mais je veux vous dire tout de suite combine j'apprécie cette nomination et comme je suis touché de la part que vous y avez prise.²⁰²

Je recevrai avec plaisir la brochure sur les manuscrits, que vous aves eu l'amabilité de m'envoyer et que j'ai déjà vue entre les mains de Tushingham.²⁰³ J'ai reçu déjà votre article du "Telegramm", dont je vous remercie.²⁰⁴

Avec mes meilleurs voeux de bonne année, recevez, cher Professeur Scott l'assurance de mes sentiments très cordiaux,
R. de Vaux, O. P.

---

201 The 1956 excavation was scheduled to begin in early January. Because of the tenuous political situation it was delayed until the end of the month. Tushingham had served as assistant director and as a representative of ASOR. In 1956 the Toronto *Globe and Mail* sponsored the participation of the ROM as a collaborator in the excavation and Tushingham again served as assistant director. See Kenyon, "Excavations at Jericho 1956," 67–82. In late 1955 a rise in Arab nationalism led by Egypt's 'Abd al-Nasir had captured Jordanian public opinion. This led to a wave of public protest, primarily anti-Western, to persuade King Hussein to align himself with Nasser instead of joining the pro-Western Baghdad pact. King Hussein had to use the military and needed the help of Iraqi troops to restore order. For a detailed discussion of the situation, see Dawisha, *Arab Nationalism in the Twentieth Century*, 166–73.

202 In 1955 de Vaux was made an honorary member of the society along with Joachim Jeremias (1900–1979), Georgia Augusta Professor of Theology at the University of Göttingen. The reason for the delay in officially informing de Vaux remains unclear.

203 The brief volume based on R.B.Y. Scott's August 1955 CBC radio talks on Qumran was published as *Treasure from Judæan Caves: The Story of the Dead Sea Scrolls*, in 1955.

204 A lengthy popular article: R.B.Y. Scott, "The Dead Sea Scrolls," *Star Weekend Magazine*, 15 October 1955, 2–4, 40–2.

LETTER #53

Archive: McGill, RG34, Container: 0001, File 6: Dead Sea Scrolls.
McGill, RG2, Container: 0179, File 6243: Divinity: DSS & Birks Donation.

16 January 1956   Montreal

Dear Professor Scott,

Thank you very much indeed for your kindness in sending me a copy of Père de Vaux's letter.[205] Nothing could indicate more clearly that your additional $5,000 was not only useful but, in point of fact, arrived in the nick of time. I am delighted.

Incidentally I have just been reading through Barrow's long volume on the Dead Sea Scrolls with a great deal of interest and notice, in passing, that you and McGill University are about the only names that are mentioned outside of his long and involved record of the various controversies.[206]

With best personal wishes to you as always, I remain,

Cordially yours,
F. Cyril James

---

205 De Vaux to Scott, 18 December 1955, Letter #44.
206 Burrows, *The Dead Sea Scrolls*, 69.

LETTER #54

Archive: McGill, RG34, Container: 0001, File 6: Dead Sea Scrolls.
McGill, RG2, Container: 0179, File 6243: Divinity: DSS & Birks Donation.

18 January 1956   Montreal

Dear Dr. James:[207]

I thought you would be interested to know that I have had word both from Mr. Harding and from Father de Vaux, that the purchase of the additional Scroll fragments was made as soon as my cable was received. It is quite evident, from the promptness with which the purchase was made, that the news of the additional fifteen [hundred][208] pounds was most welcome. Father de Vaux tells me that he immediately advanced the necessary sum from the funds of l'Ecole Biblique in order that the material would be available for immediate use. He tells me that there are very fine pieces included which fill in important gaps in manuscripts already on hand and being studied. The price of the latest acquisitions was somewhat higher than the earlier ones, but he says that it was essential to obtain these at any price. Certainly, in relation to the sum expended on behalf of the Hebrew Union[versity][209] and similar purchases the cost is not great, particularly in view of the growing importance of the material.

Father de Vaux says further that the present unstable political situation in Palestine made the matter more urgent, and he is greatly relieved that the material is now in safe hands.

When I have further details available I will send you the additional information. Should you wish to issue a press release, it might be added that this purchase is believed to complete the recovery of all the manuscript fragments from Qumran

---

207 A letter reproducing the first two paragraphs of this document was sent to Ralph Johnson of the Birks Foundation (Scott to Johnson, 18 January 1956, McGill University Archives, RG34, Container: 0001, File 6: Dead Sea Scrolls).
208 Inserted in pen above the line.
209 Corrected above the line in pen.

Cave four, and that the Birks Foundation for McGill and the Vatican Library are the two participants.[210]

With kind regards,
Yours sincerely,
R. B. Y. Scott

P.S. Since writing this letter, I have received yours of recent date, and from it know that you will be pleased that the purchase has gone through.[211]

LETTER #55

Archive: McGill, RG2, Container: 0179, File 6243: Divinity: DSS & Birks Donation.

24 January 1956   Montreal

Dear Dr. Scott,

Thank you very much indeed for yours of January 18th, which crossed mine to you in the mail. I am very glad indeed that the purchase of the additional Scroll fragments has now been completed, especially, as you say, in view of the present situation in Palestine.

I am just off by air to France to attend some urgent university meetings in Paris,[212] and if you have a moment and would care to draft a press release for

---

210 Scott had already made this information available to the press on 16 January 1956 in an interview with the *Toronto Daily Star*. See J.E. Belliveau, "McGill Joins Vatican Check Bible Scrolls Found in Desert Cave," *Toronto Daily Star*, 16 January 1956, 25, 27. McGill officially announced the purchase on 14 February 1956; see "From Dead Sea Cave: More Scroll Fragments Acquired for McGill," *Gazette* (Montreal), 15 February 1956, 3; and "Old Scrolls Added to By McGill," *Montreal Star*, 15 February 1956, 67.

The last of the Cave 4 fragments was only recovered from the Bedouin in 1958.

211 Note added in pen.

212 James was about to attend the annual meeting of the International Association of Universities. He served as chairperson from 1960 until 1965.

me so that I could look at it when I return next week, it might be useful to make public this additional find.

With renewed good wishes, as always,
I remain,
Cordially yours,
F. Cyril James

LETTER #56

Archive: McGill, RG34, Container: 0001, File 6: Dead Sea Scrolls.

5 February 1956   Princeton

Dear Pere de Vaux:

I was very happy to receive some time ago your letter of January 8, and to know that the additional scroll fragments were already in your hands. I have not heard from Mr. Harding that the bank draft for $4200 was received, but since it was sent by air mail before the end of December, I am sure it has arrived.

In a letter to Mr. Harding some time ago I suggested that it might be a good idea to photograph the material newly obtained for McGill before it was separated and associated with the manuscripts related to it.[213] In this way a quick record would be made of the nature and amount obtained, which would supplement the list I prepared for the original purchase, and a copy of which is in his hands. Naturally I would be glad to see such Photographs, but this is not my purpose in making the suggestion, and I shall not mind if there is any doubt about sending photos. I have been scrupulous in keeping my agreement not to identify in print or in lectures anything that has not previously been publicly identified by one of the scholars working at the Museum.

The authorities at McGill have begun to ask questions about how the fragments are to be properly cared for when they finally arrive, so that they can be kept in safety and preserved from deterioration. Have you any suggestions to make? Will it be necessary to to have them kept in a safe with automatic temperature controls, as has been suggested? My own feeling is that they should be hermetically sealed between glass plates, and kept in a safe, with trays that

---

213 Cf., Scott to Harding, 4 May 1955, Letter #36.

could be drawn out for examination.[214] Mr. Harding said he thought they should be shipped in plastic, rather than glass, to avoid damage from possible breakage of the glass.

I am sorry to hear that the Jericho dig may be postponed because of unsettled political conditions.[215] Lately things have been quieter, and let us hope this continues.

With cordial and respectful greetings,
I remain, mon pere,
Yours sincerely,
R. B. Y. Scott

---

214 While it makes sense that Scott would turn to de Vaux for advice on the storage of the fragments, it is ironic that the primitive practices employed by the men in the scrollery were responsible for much of the long-term deterioration of the material. The placement of fragments between glass plates led to the fragments sticking to the plates because of the formation of a variety of sticky deposits from trapped moisture. Fragments were also crushed under the weight of multiple plates. On attempts to remedy this, see also Libman and Boyd-Alkalay, "Restoration Techniques at the Israel Antiquities Authority," 875–80. Such practices resulted from the lack of available knowledge on any similar such discovery, again emphasizing the uniqueness of the find at the time the scrolls were discovered. As Frank Moore Cross recalls: "The procedures we used, developed in the handling of the Rockefeller fragments from Cave 1 published in DJD 1, proceeded more or less by trial and error. Advice had been sought from European museums and, I believe, the Vatican Library, on the conservation and handling of papyrus and leather documents. And we read what there was to read on such matters. But no one was brought to Jerusalem to train us. We made many mistakes which were later repaired in part by the Shrine of the Book," (Cross, "On the History of the Photography," 12).

Scott would in time turn for help to the British Library and the Vatican Library, cf., Plenderleith to Scott, 30 October 1956, McGill University Archives, RG34, Container: 0001, File 6: Dead Sea Scrolls; and Albareda to Scott, 25 January 1957, McGill University Archives, RG34, Container: 0001, File 6: Dead Sea Scrolls.

215 See de Vaux to Scott, 8 January 1956, Letter #52.

LETTER #57

Archive: McGill, RG34, Container: 0001, File 6: Dead Sea Scrolls.

7 April 1956   Jerusalem

Cher Professeur Scott,

Je m'excuse d'être si en retard avec vous. Votre lettre du 5 février m'est parvenue peu avant mon départ pour notre saison à Qumrâ[n] et je ne suis revenu de là que depuis quelques jours.[216]

Lorsque votre transfert bancaire est arrivé à G.L. Harding, les fragments étaient déjà achetés, sur une avance que l'Ecole Français[e] avait faite. Vous savez déjà que nous dû payer plus cher ces derniers fragments. Ils n'apportent à peu près aucun document nouveau mais ils complètent très heureusement les fragments des manuscrits déjà con[nus.] Notre équipe travaille actuellement à préparer une distribution provis[oi]re du matériel entre le Gouvernement et les différentes Institutions.[217] C'est un travail assez fastidieux mais qui est rendu actuellement néce[s]saire à la fois par le progrès de l'édition[218] et par l'incertitude polit[i]que où nous vivons.

Mais on ne peut pas encore prévoir le moment où ces lots p pourront être mis à la disposition des Institutions. Lesproblèmes de conservation que vous me posez sont donc un peu prématurés. L'expérie[n]ce que nous avons des quelques années où les documents ont été gardés au Palestine Museum semble indiquer qu'il suffit qu'ils soient entre deux plaques de verre hermétiquement scellées. On peut envisager aussi une monture sous plastique, qui rendrait le transport et le maniement beaucoup plus facile. Mais nous n'avons pas encore le matériel nécessaire.

Peu après votre lettre, j'ai reçu votre brochure sur les Manuscrits, que vous m'aviez annoncée. Je vous remercie de cet envoi et je vous félicite de cette présentation si vivante et si bien adaptée au grand public.

---

216 The excavation took place between 18 February and 28 March 1956. For discussion of excavation seasons three, four, and five, see de Vaux, "Fouilles au Khirbet Qumrân: Rapport préliminaire sur les 3ᵉ, 4ᵉ et 5ᵉ campagnes," 533–77.

217 Sent to McGill by Harding, 6 June 1956, Letter #61.

218 The editorial team would come to describe in their own words where they stood with respect to publication at the end of 1956. See Benoit, "Editing the Manuscript Fragments from Qumran," 75–96.

Avec mes meilleurs souhaits, recevez, cher Professeur Scott, l'assurance de mes sentiments bien amicaux,

R. de Vaux, O. P.

LETTER #58

Archive: McGill, RG34, Container: 0001, File 6: Dead Sea Scrolls.

15 April 1956   Princeton

Dear Pere de Vaux:

I have heard rumours of further discoveries at Qumran, although not what they comprise.[219] As time goes on the magnitude and importance for Biblical studies of the Scroll finds of the last nine years continually grow, and apparently "the end is not yet".

If the situation has again arisen when further sums are required to recover important materials so that they will be preserved and made available to scholarship, I think I might be able to interest the Princeton University Library,[220] and I thought you should know this. I have had a talk with the University Librarian,[221] and, while he could not promise anything definite, he thought that a special contribution might be forthcoming on the same terms as the contribution made by McGill. So if you and Mr. Harding conclude that funds are needed for a specific purchase, and will let me know, I will see what can be done. The amount in terms of which I was talkking to the Librarian was about $20,000, although of course this was an arbitrary figure chosen simply to give a general idea of what would be involved.

When you answer this, would you be so kind as to tell me if there has been any further information acquired to the question of methods for permanent preservation of the Scroll fragments. I have learned that it is possible to obtain moisture-absorbent material which can be inserted between the glass plates, and this might be a valuable aid against disintegration of leather or papyrus.

---

219 Cave 11 was discovered by the Bedouin in February 1956.

220 The agreement with the Birks Foundation was for $20,000. With this amount depleted, Scott could now freely turn to Princeton for additional funds.

221 William S. Dix (1910–1978) was Princeton University librarian from 1953 until 1975.

I am looking forward to meeting you at the Strasbourg Congress after all, as Princeton University has made me a grant which will enable me to attend. I wonder if any of the McGill fragments will by then be ready for distribution; if so, I could bring them back, if they could be brought or shipped as far as Strasbourg (or better, Paris). I shall be returning by air direct to Montreal at that time.

With kind personal regards,
Yours sincerely,
R. B. Y. Scott

LETTER #59

Archive: McGill, RG34, Container: 0001, File 6: Dead Sea Scrolls.

15 May 1956   Jerusalem

Cher Professeur Scott,

Je m'excuse de répondre seulement aujourd'hui à votre lettre du 15 avril: il faut que j'ai interroge G. Harding sur la réponse à donner aux questions que vous me posiez.

Il est exact qu'une nouvelle découverte de manuscrits a été faite aux environs de Qumrân. Nous ne savons pas encore exactement ce qu'elle comporte, mais le Gouvernement et Harding voudraient que les documents restent en Jordanie.[222] Nous cherchons donc actuellement des donateurs qui permettraient au Musée Palestinien d'acheter les documents et de les garder à Jérusalem. Sous cette forme, je pense que l'affaire n'intéresse plus la Princeton University Library. Mais nous vous sommestrès reconnaissants de votre démarche: il est possible qu'il y ait d'autres pièces, appartenant à d'autres lots et qui seraient encore à

---

[222] The majority of this material would be purchased by the PAM. The publication rights for this were sold to the Royal Academy of Sciences of the Netherlands. A list of their purchases (including 11QtgJob, for which they paid £10,000.00) is found in Stephen J. Pfann, "History of the Judean Desert Discoveries," 103. Through the generosity of the trustee, Elizabeth Hay Bechtel, ASOR would also purchase the rights to material, including a $60,000 purchase of the Psalms Scroll, published in 1965 by James A. Sanders in the fourth volume of DJD. Cf. Sanders, *The Psalms Scroll of Qumrân Cave 11 (11QPs^a)*. On the negotiations for the purchase, see Cross, "Reminiscences of the Early Days," 938–40.

vendre. Nous faisons actuellement des recherches et, s'il y avait quelque chose d'intéressant pour Princeton, je vous en avertirai.

Votre lettre s'est croisée avec celle où je répondais à votre question sur la conservation des fragments manuscrits. Nous les gardons ici entre deux verres bordées de speed-fix[223] et cela nous parait être une protection suffisante. Mais il se peut que, dans des climats plus humides que le nôtre il faille d'autres précautions. Je n'ai pas entendu parler du matériel absorbant que vous me signalez.

Je serai très heureux de vous retrouver à Strasbourg. Je ne puis malheureusement pas vous assurer que les fragments destinés à McGill University seront prêts à être distribués à ce moment, pas même en partie. Comme vous le savez, les derniers achats de la grotte 4, auxquels McGill a bien voulu contribuer, ne sont vieux que de quelques mois. Et aucune distribution ne peut être fait avant que tout ne soit étudié. Mais nous préparons une liste provisoire des fragments qui reviendront à chaque institution, et vous la recevrez bientôt.

Croyez, cher Professeur Scott, l'assurance de mes sentiments les meilleurs,

R. de Vaux, O.P.

LETTER #60

Archive: McGill, RG34, Container: 0001, File 6: Dead Sea Scrolls.

25 May 1956   Princeton

Dear Pere de Vaux:

Thank you for your letter of May 15 received a few days ago. Our previous letters had indeed crossed in the mails, as yours was delivered by the next post after I had written. How you manage to keep up your correspondence along with all your many other and important activities is an amazement.

I have showed your letter to Mr. Dix, the Princeton University Librarian, and we have agreed on a procedure. I am to prepare for him a brief memorandum on the importance of the Scrolls and the possibility of participation by Princeton University Library in the light of the information you give in your letter. This memorandum would be for Mr. Dix to have available to show to donors,

---

223 The brand name of an early form of clear cellulose tape. In addition to joining the panels of glass, it was unfortunately also used to join fragments with disastrous long-term effect.

or possible donors, and would not be otherwise circulated or published. We understand very well the distinction between funds provided for material of previous lots which might come to the University Library after previous study in Jerusalem, and funds provided as outright donations for the recently found material which is to remain permanently in Jerusalem.

It would be more difficult, but not, I think, impossible to obtain donations of the latter kind, particularly if there were some way in which the name of Princeton or of the donor could be permanently associated with the manuscript or manuscripts; for example, "the Princeton-Jerusalem Scroll of -----", and so identified in the Museum and the official publication. A complete set of photographs of the Scroll might be lodged in the University Library here on the understanding that there would be no publication prior to that in the official series already begun.

On the other hand, if you do discover that scroll fragments from previous lots is still outstanding and comes on the market, so that a contribution could obtain eventual possession of it on the same basis as the McGill scroll fragments, please let me know.[224] Of course I cannot promise that money would be forthcoming to enable us to take advantage of the opportunity, but we would do our best to interest a donor as quickly as possible.

With cordial greetings, I remain,
Sincerely yours,
R. B. Y. Scott

---

224 The last of the Cave 4 material would be purchased by a second contribution from McCormick, a donation from the Church of All Souls in New York, and one from Oxford University in July 1958 (cf. Cross, "Reminiscences of the Early Days," 938, and Stephen Pfann, "History of the Judean Desert Discoveries," 104). With regard to actual purchases of material, the preference had been that the original purchasers increase their contribution rather than distributing the collection among a larger number of institutions.

The later purchases were, in fact, donations to the PAM for the purchase of manuscripts to remain permanently in Jordan. Permission for these "foreign" sales was granted by the Jordanian prime minister, Ibrahim Hashim, in Prime Minister Order No. 26/10/548, 23 January 1958, IAA Archives, Box 73, PAM 1117: Dead Sea Scrolls (cave no. 4), jacket 1.

LETTER #61

Archive: McGill, RG2, Container: 0179, File 6243: Divinity: DSS & Birks Donation.

6 June 1956   Amman

Dear Dr. Scott

  A provisional division of the Qumran Cave IV manuscript fragments has now been made, and I enclose a list of the pieces which have been allotted to your institution. A few minor changes may be necessary as a result of further study or the acquisition of further material, but the main outline will remain unchanged. There will also be some very small, unidentified fragments which will be divided when final study is complete.

Yours faithfully,
G. Lankester Harding
<u>Director of Antiquities</u>

Enclosure:

MCGILL UNIVERSITY[225]

<u>Biblical Books</u>					<u>Non-Biblical Works, continued</u>		
Plate no.					Plate no.		
C[226]	3	Genesis, manuscript	c	M	15–17	Jubilees, ms.	a
	5	"	"	e	20	" "	d
	7	Exodus,	"	b	29–30	Enoch "	c,d
	10	"	"	e	36	" astronomical	d
	16–18	Numbers,	"	a	41	Testament of Levi, Aramaic	b
	29	Deuteronomy	"	h	43	" Naphtali	
	31	"	"	g	46	Pseudo-Daniel, ms. b	
	32	"	"	l	55	Rule of the Community f.	
	34	Joshua,	"	b	58	Damascus Document	a
	46	Samuel,	"	c	67–68	" "	c

---

  225 On the distribution lists, see Tov, ed., "The Texts from the Judean Desert and Their Negative Numbers," in *The Dead Sea Scrolls on Microfiche*, 17–19.

  226 Code letters for scholars on the editorial team responsible for each plate: A = Allegro, C = Cross, H = Hunzinger, M = Milik, Sl = Strugnell, Sn = Skehan, and Sy = Starcky. According to Frank M. Cross, the allotments to the scholars remained fluid until 1956 ("Reminiscences of the Early Days," 936).

	#	Work				#	Work	
	49	Jeremiah,	"	b		86	Barakoth (Blessings)	b
	59	Minor Prophets	"	d		88–89	Mishmaroth (Priestly courses) a	
	62	Ruth	"	a		115	Unidentified in Cryptic B	
	67–68	Daniel	"	a		122–3	Sapiental work b	
						124	" "	e
Sn	1–3	Exodus in Paleo Hebrew		b		130	List of names	
	19	Deuteronomy						
	23–4	Isaiah, manuscript	c		Sl	10	Joseph cycle	
	36–7	Psalms "		b		20–1	Psalms of the fathers	c
	47–48	Leviticus lxx version				27–8	Pseudo-Jeremiah	d
	50	Greek, non-Biblical				31–2	Proto-Mishnah	a) Purity
						35	"	e) regu-lations
Non-Biblical Works						42	Liturgical work ms.	4
						45	" "	8 (tongues of fire)
Sy	3–4	Pseudo-Enoch, b, Aramaic						
	10	Visions of Amram, b, Aramaic				50–1	Sapiental work	Ic.
	20	Visions of the 4 kingdoms		b		60	" "	3
	22–24	New Jerusalem, Aramaic				66	Hodayot (Hymns)	c.
	29	Visions, ms. c. Aramaic				73	Hymnic work, ms. 1	
	32	Halachic work				76	" ms. 5	
						80	" ms. 10	
	35	Liturgical prayers b	A			90	Commentary on Hosea	
	37	Apocalyptic work				18	Astronomical work	
	48	Unidentified Hebrew				24	Sapiental work	e
	50,51, 54d	Unidentified Aramaic	H			3a	Milhamah (War rules)	

LETTER #62

Archive: McGill, RG2, Container: 0179, File 6243: Divinity: DSS & Birks Donation.

23 July 1956   Georgeville, Quebec[227]

Dear Dr. James:

I have received from Mr. Lankester Harding, Director of Antiquities, Amman, Jordan, the enclosed list of Qumran Scroll fragments allocated to McGill, and

---

227 The Scott family continues to maintain the family home, "Dunn's Law," in the Eastern Townships of Quebec, Canada. For a description of what life was like there in 1956, see the story by Scott's son, Gavin, about Christmas 1956: "Home for Christmas: Report from the North."

[enclose also][228] a copy of Mr. Harding's explanatory letter which accompanied it.[229] The selection is gratifyingly representative and important. We now have a definite understanding of the physical extent of the collection, – eighty-six plates (c. 10" x 12"), in addition to a certain amount of unidentified small pieces.

When I return from the meetings of the Congress of Old Testament Scholars which is to be held at Strasbourg at the end of August[230] and where I am to meet Père de Vaux, I expect to have a more definite idea when and how the material is to be shipped. The scholars working on it at the Palestine Archaeological Museum have not yet completed their preparation of it for publication, but this should not be much longer delayed. I have been making enquiries about means to house and exhibit such a collection, and on this also I hope to have consultations at Strasbourg. When I return to Montreal in the second week of September I hope to be able to see you; if this is not possible I will write you fully on the matter.

Yours sincerely,
R. B. Y. Scott

LETTER #63

Archive: McGill, RG4, Container: 239, File: Birks, John Henry – Collection, Judean Manuscripts – Dead Sea Scrolls.

23 July 1956   Georgeville

Dear Mr. Bentley:

Enclosed is a copy for your files of the provisional allotment to McGill University for the John Henry Birks Collection of Judaean Desert Scrolls, as received from G. Lankester Harding, Director of Antiquities.

I have written Dr. James about this and have sent him a copy of this and also the accompanying letter from Mr. Harding.

With all good wishes,
Yours sincerely,
R. B. Y. Scott

---

228 Inserted in pen in the margin.
229 See letter and list: Harding to Scott, 6 June 1956, Letter #61.
230 IOSOT, 27 August to 1 September 1956.

LETTER #64

Archive: McGill RG4 Container: 239 File: Birks, John Henry – Collection, Judean Manuscripts – Dead Sea Scrolls

26 July 1956   Montreal

Dear Prof. Scott:

I wish to thank you for your letter of July 23rd with the copy of the Provisional Allotment of Scroll Fragments. Your present address seems to indicate that you are enjoying a well deserved holiday and I trust that this is so. I believe I noticed in the newspapers that G.Lankester Harding has resigned his position but I may be wrong.[231] With kindest regards,

Yours sincerely,
WB
Bursar and Secretary of the Board of Governors.

LETTER #65

Archive: McGill, RG34, Container: 0001, File 6: Dead Sea Scrolls.
   McGill, RG2, Container: 0179, File 6243: Divinity: DSS & Birks Donation.

11 September 1956   Georgeville, Quebec

Dear Dr. James:

When I returned from the Strasbourg Congress last week[232] I had only a few hours in Montreal and you were very busy. I expect to be back again but the times are uncertain, so it seems best to write you and then perhaps speak to you on the phone if possible when I am in the city. I want you to know the latest information about the Qumran Scroll Fragments which are to come to McGill.

---

231 The Jordanian authorities announced Harding's dismissal on 28 June 1956. See "July 1956 – Arab Legion Discussions with Britain," *Keesing's Contemporary Archives* (10 July 1956): 14965. http://www.keesings.com (accessed: 19 September 2007).

232 IOSOT, 27 August to 1 September 1956 in Strasbourg.

Princeton was sufficiently impressed with the importance of the subject that they sent me to the Congress of Old Testament Scholars at Strasbourg where de Vaux, Skehan and Milik were to give the latest information from the team working in the Palestine Museum,[233] and many other scholars working on the subject were to be present. I had a private tete-a-tete with de Vaux over lunch, talked with the others like del Medico,[234] de Boer,[235] Hunzinger; met Dupont-Sommer,[236] Driver and others. In particular, I discussed at some length with Rowley of Manchester and Kuhn of Heidelberg[237] our common concern with the effect of the political situation on the export of Cave IV fragments for which these institutions as well as McGill have contributed.

As you probably know, Lankester Harding has been dismissed as Director of Antiquities of Jordan – "Glubbed", they say – from Sept. 30th. This was due partly to the wave of Arab nationalism and partly to intrigue by a former subordinate. An emergency meeting at the Museum discussed whether it would be possible to ship out the McGill and other fragments before this date. Two things made it impossible: the work of editing for publication will require another year, and de Vaux' s judgment that an application by Harding at this time would be refused, and this would prejudice an application later when things had calmed down. De Vaux (after 23 years in the country)[238] says "We must ride out the crisis". He is not pessimistic. The main thing, he points out, is that we have official documents (i) the undertaking by the Director of Antiquities, which had been specifically authorized by a Cabinet Minister; and (ii) the allocation of specific material to McGill, according to the list of which I have already sent

---

233 For the contents of the update, see Skehan, "The Qumran Manuscripts and Textual Criticism," 148–60; and Józef T. Milik, "Le Travail d'édition des Manuscrits du Désert de Juda," 17–26.

234 Henri E. del Medico was an author of a number of books and articles on the Dead Sea Scrolls. See Trompf, "Introduction I: The Long History of Dead Sea Scrolls Scholarship," 126; and Del Medico, *The Riddle of the Scrolls*.

235 Pieter Arie Hendrik de Boer (1910–1989), Chair of Old Testament at the University of Leiden from 1938 until his retirement in 1978.

236 Epigraphist and historian, André Dupont-Sommer (1900–1983), argued for the Essene origins of Christianity (cf. Dupont-Sommer, *The Dead Sea Scrolls: A Preliminary Survey*; and Silberman, *The Hidden Scrolls*, 120–2).

237 In a letter to Harding, dated 31 July 1956, Kuhn raised similar concerns about the future of Heidelberg's allotment of Cave 4 material (Kuhn to Harding, 31 Jul 1956, IAA Archives, Box 73, PAM 1117: Dead Sea Scrolls [cave no. 4], jacket 1).

238 De Vaux arrived in Jerusalem in 1933 to teach at the École Biblique and stayed until his death in 1970.

you a copy. After I get back to Princeton I will assemble the originals of this correspondence and send them to you by registered mail.

I remarked to de Vaux that it was perhaps fortunate that the Vatican and the Bonn Government also are involved. He agreed, and added that the British and American Ambassadors[239] to Jordan are members of the Board of the Palestine [end page 1] Museum, and when the right time comes could assist in bringing pressure to bear if necessary.

Meanwhile, the primary scientific purpose of the contributions – the rescuing of priceless material from destruction or dispersal – <u>has</u> been accomplished. The significance of this is brought out in the new Pelican book on the Scrolls by Allegro (just published, and the best popular treatment),[240] where the McGill and other contributions are described as coming in the nick of time in a desperate situation.[241] I am quite proud of the fact that McGill was first, and this fact is noted in book after book.

Two other matters I should mention. The first is the arrangements made at the Museum for protection of the Scrolls should fighting break out between Israel and Jordan. Heavy wooden cases have been prepared with shelving, in which all the glass plates can be put in places already marked for them; these can be in bank vaults in Amman within a few hours of the occurrence of an emergency.[242]

The second point is the one we have mentioned before: the nature of the arrangements at McGill for preservation and availability of the fragments. There will be about 85 glass plates, 8" x 10". The curator of ancient documents at Princeton has told me of a moisture-absorbent material which can be introduced around the edges. Rowley recommended me to write to Professor Robertson of the John Rylands Library in Manchester,[243] and when in London I enquired at

---

239 Sir Charles Hepburn Johnston (1912–1986) was British ambassador to Jordan from 1956 until 1959. Lester DeWitt Mallory (1904–1994) was the American ambassador to Jordan from 1953 until 1958.

240 John M. Allegro, *The Dead Sea Scrolls: A Reappraisal*. Pelican is an imprint of Penguin Books.

241 Allegro, *The Dead Sea Scrolls: A Reappraisal*, 47.

242 The Scrolls would be moved to the vault in Amman in September 1956 as a result of the Suez Crisis. For discussion of the packing of the fragments, primarily by John Strugnell before he was pulled out of Jordan by the British authorities, see Wright, "Report of the Representative on the Board of Trustees of the American School of Oriental Studies," xvi–xviii.

243 Edward Robertson (1879–1964) was head of Semitic Languages (1934–45) at Manchester and after his retirement was appointed librarian of the John Rylands Library (1945–62).

the British Museum and was referred to Dr. H. J. Plenderleith of the laboratory. He has a book on the subject of preservation of ancient materials which is to appear shortly, and offered to reply to a written enquiry in which the situation is outlined.[244] Presumably the slides should be kept in a fireproof safe or room. I will make further enquiries and prepare more specific suggestions before the time comes when the fragments are to be shipped.

I shall be here for about another week before going back to Princeton, and when passing through Montreal I will try to have a few words with you on the telephone.

With all good wishes,
Yours sincerely,
R. B. Y. Scott

LETTER #66

Archive: McGill, RG2, Container: 0179, File 6243: Divinity: DSS & Birks Donation.

12 September 1956   Montreal

Dear Dr. Scott,

Thank you for your letter of July 23[245] and the list of scroll fragments that are to be allotted to McGill. Any information you may be able to acquire about the housing of these valuable fragments and about their susceptibility to light if exhibited will be most welcome, as I have viewed with some apprehension their arrival here, where there is certainly no provision at present for the care of such delicate and perishable material, and we shall undoubtedly have to observe whatever precautions are taken elsewhere in America for their safeguarding. I imagine that a special vault with controlled humidity and temperature will be

---

244 Harold James Plenderleith (1898–1997) was keeper of the research laboratory at the British Museum from 1949 until 1959. In 1955 three boxes of fragments were sent to him to explore possible techniques for assistance in conservation. In 1962 he came to Jerusalem to examine additional material. See Libman and Boyd-Alkalay, "Conservation," 140. Scott received a reply to his written inquiry on 30 October 1956, McGill University Archives, RG34, Container: 0001, File 6: Dead Sea Scrolls.

245 Letter not preserved.

essential; and I am inclined to think that to avoid the transport to and fro across the campus, they should be housed permanently in Divinity Hall.

Yours sincerely,
R. P.[246]
University Librarian.

LETTER #67

Archive: McGill, RG2, Container: 0179, File 6243: Divinity: DSS & Birks Donation.

21 September 1956   Montreal

Dear Dr. Scott,

    Apparently I have been unlucky on both the occasions of your visit to Montreal and I am sorry because I should have enjoyed an opportunity of chatting to you and hearing in some detail about your experiences at the Strasbourg Congress.[247] I do however appreciate the information that you gave me in your letter of September 11th and I may say, in regard to the penultimate paragraph, that Mr. Pennington[248] is already exploring with J. S. Thomson[249] the question of appropriate storage facilities when we actually receive the fragments.

With best personal wishes to you as always, I remain,
Cordially yours,
F. Cyril James

---

  246 Richard Pennington (1904–2003), McGill University librarian from 1947 until 1965.
    247 IOSOT, 27 August to 1 September 1956.
    248 McGill University librarian.
    249 Dean of the Faculty of Divinity at McGill.

LETTER #68

Archive: McGill, RG2, Container: 0179, File 6243: Divinity: DSS & Birks Donation.

26 October 1956   Montreal

Dear Mr. Pennington,

Your letter about the Dead Sea Scrolls raises a question that ought to be discussed.[250] Where are the Scrolls to repose when they come to McGill? What arrangements are to be made for their custody? I saw Dr. Scott last year and he tells me that there is a likelihood of the Scrolls being in our hands within the next 12 months. Consequently, this matter ought to be discussed.

Frankly, I know very little about the actual Scrolls; what material is to come to us or its nature, and I am not quite sure that even this has been entirely settled. So far, I think all you can do at the present time, is to send a general letter with a non-comittal reply to any enquiries, but I shall be glad to discuss the matter fully with you if you wish.

I am,
Yours sincerely,
JAMES S. THOMSON,
Dean.

LETTER #69

Archive: McGill, RG2, Container: 0179, File 6243: Divinity: DSS & Birks Donation.

29 October 1956   Montreal

Dear Dr. James,

I enclose a copy of a letter from the Dean of the Faculty of Divinity.[251] I had asked him for a statement that we could give to the too-numerous telephone inquiries we receive about the Dead Sea scrolls.

---

250 Letter not preserved, but Pennington is clearly receiving inquiries and had appealed to Dean Thomson for guidance on how to approach this. See also Pennington to James, 29 October 1956, Letter #69.

251 Thomson to Pennington, 26 October 1956, Letter #68.

If, indeed, they may come within the next twelve months, you may think it advisable to discuss the matter some time before the New Year, as provision may well involve the construction of a special receptacle or room, as I do not think that atmospheric conditions even in the new Library[252] would satisfy the exacting requirements that the preservation of such precious relics imposes upon us. Such documents are kept in electrically controlled vaults where a constant temperature and humidity are maintained, and we do not have such here.

Yours sincerely
Richard Pennington
University Librarian.

P.S. The question might arise whether, if special storage is built by general University funds for these religious relics, it could not be made large enough for our less sacred, but historically valuable, Canadian MSS.

LETTER #70

Archive: McGill, RG2, Container: 0179, File 6243: Divinity: DSS & Birks Donation.

30 October 1956   Montreal

Dear Mr. Pennington,

In response to your letter of October 29th there is on file in this Office, and available for your consultation, a memorandum by R.B.Y. Scott setting forth exactly the portions of the Dead Sea Scrolls that McGill University is to receive.
I agree that we should make appropriate provision for the proper care of these Scrolls when they come into our possession and I think that R.B.Y. Scott has already been doing some thinking about it. Would you care to get in touch with him at Princeton and follow up the matter with a view to letting me have early in 1957 a detailed report as to the arrangements that we should make (a) for the Scrolls themselves and (b) for the wider project of taking care of our valuable Canadian historical manuscripts. I should like if possible to have reasonably accurate figures as to the costs involved so that I can discuss these with the Board of Governors.

---

252 An extension was added to McGill's Redpath Library building in 1953.

One general point will need to be worked out between you and Dean J. S. Thomson. Your letter assumes that the Scrolls will be housed in the Redpath Library but I think it was R.B.Y. Scott's original intention that they should be housed in Divinity Hall. I have no strong feeling one way or the other, but quite clearly, this matter should be decided at the beginning of your study.

With best personal wishes, I remain,
Cordially yours,
F. Cyril James

LETTER #71

Archive: McGill, RG2, Container: 0179, File 6243: Divinity: DSS & Birks Donation.

11 January 1957   Princeton

Dear Dr. James:

I expect to be in Montreal during the week-end January 26th–28th, and would like to have a brief chat with you about the Birks Collection of Judaean Desert Scrolls, if this would be convenient to you. I could come any time Saturday evening, Sunday afternoon or evening, or Monday morning.

Fortunately the material has been moved from the Palestine Archaeological Museum in Arab Jerusalem to a bank vault in Amman.[253] However, the recent troubles have seriously delayed preparation of the Cave IV fragments for publication, and the prospect for the contributing institutions receiving their shares is still not immediate. I am told, nevertheless, that the agreements made with Mr. Harding have been reviewed by the Jordan Council of Ministers and confirmed.

With best wishes for the New Year,
Yours sincerely,
R. B. Y. Scott

---

253 The fragments were moved to the bank vault in Amman in September 1956 as a result of the first Suez Crisis and they were returned to the PAM in the spring of 1957 (Pfann, "History of the Judean Desert Discoveries," 104).

LETTER #72

Archive: McGill, RG2, Container: 0179, File 6243: Divinity: DSS & Birks Donation.

16 January 1957   Princeton

Dear Dr. James:

Thank you for your letter of Jan. 14th.[254] As you say, we do not seem to have much luck about meeting in Montreal. This time I have to leave for Chalk River[255] at 2 p.m. on the 28th, to talk to the Deep River Science Association on the Scrolls, so I shall be unable to keep the engagement you suggest at 3.30.

However, the matter I wanted to talk to you about – preparation for housing the Birks Collection – is not of immediate urgency, so I will try again the next time something takes me to Montreal. I have had a very helpful letter from the Keeper of the Laboratory at the British Museum, and expect to hear shortly from the Librarian of the Vatican.[256]

I suppose you saw the write-up in the Christmas number of Maclean's Magazine.[257] I imagine that when the McGill scroll fragments finally arrive there will be a good deal of public as well as scholarly interest.

With all good wishes,
Yours sincerely,
R. B. Y. Scott

---

254 A brief note indicating that James would be unavailable to meet until the afternoon of 28 January (James to Scott, 14 January 1957, McGill University Archives, RG2, Container: 0179, File 6243: Divinity: DSS & Birks Donation).

255 City in Ontario, Canada, northwest of Ottawa.

256 See Albareda to Scott, 25 January 1957, McGill University Archives, RG34, Container: 0001, File 6: Dead Sea Scrolls. Joaquin Anselmo M. Albareda (1892–1966) served as prefect of the Vatican Library under Pope Pius XI, Pope Pius XII, and Pope John XXIII. He was elevated to cardinal in 1962.

257 Eric Hutton, "What the Dead Sea Scrolls Mean to the Christian Faith," *Maclean's*, 22 December 1956, 7–9, 34–41.

LETTER #73

Archive: McGill, RG34, Container: 0001, File 6: Dead Sea Scrolls.

4 March 1957   Princeton

Dear Professor Rowley:

It was good of you to let me know at once about your disturbing news from de Vaux.[258] I have delayed replying because I have expected to hear also from de Vaux himself, but no word has come.

I find it hard to believe that the Jordan Government's refusal is final.[259] de Vaux told me at Strasbourg[260] that he was apprehensive about the effect of an application for export permits at an unpropitious time, and I am wondering if this has proved only too well founded. Certainly the anti-Western feeling must be much stronger now than it was last summer when it was bad enough. Since the Suez attack the British and French are doubtless identified with Israel as objects of implacable hatred. Canada has been regarded as pro-Israel at the U.N., and what the Arabs feel as a result of Canadian participation in U.N.E.F.[261] is problematical.

The two things that worry me are the almost certain progressive deterioration of the manuscripts if they are left indefinitely in a bank vault,[262] and the embarrassment of the institutions which have contributed and have expected

---

258 Letter not preserved.

259 On 6 February 1957, the director of antiquities informed the PAM of the government's decision (Order 27 of 1957, 6 January 1957) to keep the scrolls and to reimburse the foreign institutions. See director of antiquities to president of Board of Trustees of the PAM, 2 February 1957, Ref.: 9/4/466 IAA Archives, Box 73, PAM 1117: Dead Sea Scrolls (cave no. 4), jacket 1.

260 IOSOT, 27 August to 1 September 1956.

261 The United Nations Emergency Force (initially 6,000 strong, including Canadian troops) was created by the United Nations' General Assembly to bring about an end to the Suez Crisis. It was largely established through the efforts of the Canadian minister of external affairs, Lester Bowles Pearson (1897–1972), later prime minister of Canada (1963–68). It remained in place until 1967. On 16 May of that year Egypt ordered all UN troops out of Sinai. On Canada's participation, see Kay, *The Diplomacy of Prudence: Canada and Israel, 1948–1958*.

262 Scott's concerns proved founded. See for example, Shanks, "Leading Dead Sea Scroll Scholar Denounces Delay," 18–25.

to receive the material before this. Against this we can set the positive gain[263] that the material was recovered in large measure and has been recorded by photography;[264] and secondly, that the institutions concerned have an acknowledged stake in what is there. If this is to be discharged by payment of indemnity, only some of the embarrassment would be removed, and I don't see where the Jordanians will find the money. What we need is an official acknowledgment of the debt, with the hope that in less troubled times a new government will either pay up or permit export. One thing at least can be done, I think: if the Jordan Government will acknowledge ownership of mss by the respective institutions until indemnity is paid, this can be noted in each instance in the publications in the Oxford Press series.[265]

Since I have not heard from de Vaux, could you send me the extract from his letter as you suggested?

Thank you again for "The Faith of Israel", one of the most useful of your many useful books.[266]

With kindest regards,
Yours sincerely,
R. B. Y. Scott

---

263 Word unclear in original.

264 Much of the photography was done by Najib Anton Albina, who, supported by the Rockefeller monies, worked full time on the photography at the PAM. See Cross, "On the History of the Photography," 121–2; and John Strugnell's article in the same volume, "On the History of the Photographing of the Discoveries in the Judean Desert for the International Team," 123–34.

265 Although John Allegro's 1968 volume of DJD included the first fragments of Cave 4 material to be published in the official DJD series, discussion of the discovery and purchase of the material in the DJD series, although rather brief, would only appear in 1977, in the 6th volume. See de Vaux, "Découverte, Fouille et Achats," 5.

266 Rowley, *The Faith of Israel* (1957).

LETTER #74

Archive: McGill, RG34, Container: 0001, File 6: Dead Sea Scrolls.

4 March 1957   Princeton

Dear Pere de Vaux:

Professor Rowley tells me in a letter[267] of the refusal of the Government to permit export of any of the Qumran manuscripts. This is rather stunning news, if it is a final and irrevocable decision. However, I am not surprised that such an action should be taken at this moment, when the Arabs have good cause for resentment and suspicion of the Western powers. But I find it hard to believe that, if we are patient, the Government in happier times (if God wills) will not acknowledge its obligation undertaken on the authority of the Council of Ministers.

The present situation is embarrassing, of course, to those institutions which provided the money and to the individuals who made the arrangements. But this is less important than the danger that the material will deteriorate unless it is carefully preserved where it is, under conditions of controlled humidity. It is a great mercy that so much of it has been saved for scholarship and recorded to a great degree by photography.

Would you please let me know precisely what the situation is at this moment, and what are the prospects as you see them? Has the Government definitely said that its refusal is final? Was this with respect to a particular application by one of the institutions concerned, or is it a statement of policy? Is it admitted that an agreement was made, not simply by Mr. Harding, but with Cabinet sanction? Does ownership of the part of the manuscripts bought with money supplied by institutions rest with those institutions, whether or not it is permitted to export them? This, at least, could be acknowledged in the official publication.

I realize that some of these questions may not be easy to answer, or politic to ask of officials just now. Our thoughts and prayers are with you at a difficult time.

Yours sincerely,
R. B. Y. Scott

---

267   Letter not preserved.

LETTER #75

Archive: McGill, RG34, Container: 0001, File 6: Dead Sea Scrolls.

9 March 1957[268]   Jerusalem

Cher Professeur Scott,

Je réponds aussitôt à votre lettre du 4 mars, que je viens de recevoir. Je ne m'étonne pas que vous ayiez été ému par la lettre du Prof. Rowley et je vous dois des explications.

Au début de novembre 1956, à un moment où il y avait un réel danger de guerre à Jérusalem, les fragments manuscrits, sauf les plus fragile, ont été mis en sûreté dans les chambres fortes de la Banque Ottomane à Amman. Ce transfert s'est fait sur l'initiative du Gouvernement mais avec l' sentiment du Musée qui avait prévu cette éventualité. Mais j'ai prévenu alors, les autorités que, si ces chambres étaient tant soit peu humides et si les manuscrits y restaient trop longtemps, ils risquaient d'être endommagés. Le 8 décembre, xxxxxxxx le Conseil du Musée (où sont deux membres du Gouvernement) décida le retour des manuscrits. Mais le Directeur jordanien des Antiquités[269] n'exécuta pas cette decision. Au lieu de-céla, il fit approuver par le Ministre de l'Education,[270] en date du 6 janvier, l'acquisition par le Gouvernement de tous les manuscrits de la Mer Morte, découverts ou à découvrir. Les institutions devaient être remboursées intégralement. Aucun manuscrit ne pouvait sortir de Jordanie.

Dès que j'ai eu connaissance de cette décision, j'ai protesté en faisant valoir les engagements pris par le Gouvernement et la déception que cette mesure causerait aux institutions. D'autres difficultés ont dû être soulevées. En fait, la décision n'a pas encore été publiée officiellement, mais le Directeur des Antiquités allait repentant que le Gouvernement ne changerrait pas d'avis et que c'était pratiquement chose faite. J'ai alors essayé de faire intervenir les représentants diplomatiques intéressés à Amman, mais ils ont jugé qu'ils ne pouvaient rien faire avant qu'une pièce officielle ne soit publiée. La Délégation Apostolique a cependant fait une démarche pour le lot acheté par la Bibliothèque Vaticane, et je sais que cette démarche a eu un bon effet. J'ai alors alerté Manchester

---

268 Upon forwarding the letter to James, Scott pencilled at the top of the page, "personal and confidential," with a request that the letter be returned to him.

269 Dr Abdel Karim Ghureibeh was appointed director general of antiquities in 1956 and was succeeded the following year by Saeed Al-Durra.

270 Shafiq Rusheidat.

et Heidelberg en leur demandant d'agir de leur côté. J'allais vous écrire aussi lorsque la situation a paru changer. Le Directeur des Antiquités a enfin accepté que les manuscrits soient retirés des caves de la Banque Ottomane et ramenés à Jérusalem. Ils y sont depuis lundi dernier et le travail a déjà repris avec Hunzinger et Milik. Ce travail est placé sous le contrôle d'un comité officiellement nommé par le Ministre de l'Education[271] et qui comprend 5 membres, 3 Jordaniens,[272] le Directeur de l'École Américaine et moi-même. Ce Comité doit aider et surveiller la préservation des manuscrits, leur étude et leur publication. Dans le décret qui nomme ce Comité, rien n'est dit de la propriété des manuscrits s'il y avait eu quelque chose en ce sens, j'aurais refusé d'entrer dans le Comité. Les questions légales de propriété et d'exportation restent donc en suspens et nous pouvons peut-être encore sauver les droits des institutions en continuant de travailler avec douceur et patience.

Pour nous y aider, et pour défendre vos droits, je vous suggérrais de faire la même démarche que Manchester. L'Université McGill pourrait envoyer par l'intermédiaire officiel du Gouvernement Canadien ou du représentant de la Jordanie au Canada (Légation? Consulat?), une lettre au Directeur de Antiquités à Amman disant qu'elle a "appris" que le Gouvernement Jordanien se proposait d'acquérir les manuscrits et demandant à ce sujet une information officielle. La lettre pourrait rappeler les engagements pris par le [end page 1] Gouvernement, la somme payée par MacGill, la correspondance <u>officielle</u> avec Mr Harding, le N° référence de la letter du Ministre de l'Education autorisant l'achat par les institutions étrangères, la liste des pièces reconnues comme propriété de McGill par le partage fait par Mr Harding en juin dernier. L'Université porrait également réserver ses droits xx à une action diplomatique si ces "rumeurs" étaient confirmées. Il est vraisemblable que l'Université, si elle envoie une pareille letter, ne recevra pas de réponse. Mais l'important est qu'on connaisse ici les réactions des Institutions devant la mesure dont elles sont menacés, et ces avertissements répétés feront peut-être hésiter les autorités.

Come vous le dites vous-même dans votre lettre, l'essentiel est de gagner du temps. C'est ce que nous avons fait – et cela n'a pas été facile. Mais, les manuscrits – un peu endommagés par l'humidité – sont sauvés. Le travail a repris, et les droits des Institutions peuvent encore être sauvés. Nous ne pouvions pas faire plus.

---

271 Abdul Halim Nimer.

272 Including the mayor of Jerusalem, the director of antiquities, and the assistant director of antiquities.

Je compte parler de toutes ces questions avec le Prof. Kraeling,[273] qui doit passer ces jours ci à Jérusalem et dont j'utiliserai les bon conseils et l'autorité.

Il est inutile, je pense, de vous dire que cette lettre est personnelle et que mon nom ne doit pas paraître dans les démarches que vous ferez ou que vous provoquerez: cela pourrait détruire tout le travail que je cherche à faire à l'autre bout de la chaîne.

Croyez, cher Professeur Scott, à l'assurance de mes sentiments les meilleurs,

R. de Vaux, O.P.

LETTER #76

Archive: McGill, RG2, Container: 0179, File 6243: Divinity: DSS & Birks Donation.

19 March 1957   Princeton

Dear Dr. James:

In my letter to you of Sept. 11th last I told you of the difficulties which had arisen, with respect to the export of the Birks Scrolls Collection, owing to the dismissal of Mr. Harding, the Director of Antiquities. The work on the Scrolls was still incomplete, and Père de Vaux believed that an export licence could not be obtained at the moment.

Since then I have watched with dismay the worsening of the Palestine situation, and heard that the Scrolls had been removed to a bank vault in Amman for safekeeping[274] when fighting at Jerusalem appeared imminent. Last month I received an alarming letter from Professor Rowley (who is concerned with the Manchester purchase) saying that he had heard from de Vaux that the Jordan Government had decided to expropriate all the Dead Sea Scrolls and retain them in Jordan.[275] I waited a few days, and then wrote a careful letter to de Vaux asking what the situation is.[276] Yesterday I received the enclosed reply;[277] it is a personal and confidential letter, but I feel it is essential that you see it and draw your own conclusions.

---

273   Carl Kraeling, President of ASOR.
274   In September 1956, with the pending Suez Crisis.
275   Letter not preserved. The gist may however be deduced from Scott's reply (cf. Scott to Rowley, 4 March 1957, Letter #73).
276   Scott to de Vaux, 4 March 1957, Letter #74.
277   De Vaux to Scott, 9 March 1957, Letter #75.

As I had thought – and said to de Vaux – the situation is ticklish but all is not lost. The primary scientific objective has been largely attained, viz., the rescue and recording of priceless material which almost certainly would have been dissipated or destroyed without the aid of McGill and the other institutions. Moreover, with careful handling, a combination of tact and firmness, I think there is a good chance that the situation can be saved. The new Director of Antiquities[278] is a Jordanian who was a personal enemy of Harding. The new policy which he is trying to persuade the Government to enforce is meant, as much as anything, to discredit Harding. It also is an appeal to national pride.

McGill is entitled to ask for an accounting, in view of the official assurances, thoroughly documented, which we have. At the same time we must remember how the Arabs are feeling toward Britain and France just now, and I imagine they are pretty suspicious also of Canada and the United States. I think the line of action suggested [end page 1] by de Vaux should be followed as soon as possible, and I would underline the urgency of his request that his name be kept out of it. I have consequently composed a draft letter embodying the data of a proposed request for an official statement from the present Director of Antiquities.

You will know how to handle this. Since Jordan has no diplomatic representation in Canada (or did not until very recently)[279] I imagine the approach should be made to the Embassy of Jordan in Washington. Should it be made through the Canadian Embassy, or direct? The more impressive the approach the better, though, since the Jordan Government has not actually promulgated the decree, it would be addressed to the Director Antiquities through the Jordan Embassy. The possibility of actual diplomatic action can be held in reserve.

Please examine with particular care the wording of the final paragraph of my proposed letter enclosed, and of course redraft it in any way you see fit. Would it be well to have it signed by the Chancellor[280] as well as by yourself?

Would you please return Père de Vaux's letter when you have digested its contents? He is in a very delicate and also a key position, and it is of the utmost importance that we do not embarrass him by associating him with any action which we take.

With all best wishes, and kind regards,
Yours sincerely,
R. B. Y. Scott

---

278 Presumably, Dr Abdel Karim Ghureibeh.

279 Canada did not open an embassy in Jordan until 1982, when diplomatic relations were established at an ambassadorial level.

280 Bertie Charles Gardner, the former president of the Bank of Montreal, served as Chancellor of McGill University from 1952 until 1957.

Enclosure:
>(suggested draft letter)

The Director of Antiquities,
Amman, Hashemite Kingdom of Jordan

Dear Sir:

   McGill University, Montreal, Canada, in 1954 and 1955 made contributions totaling $19,563 (U.S. Dollars) for the purchase of scroll fragments from Qumran Cave IV, having received assurances that these could be exported after they had been retained in Jordan for about two years for study. We have now learned that that the Government of Jordan now proposes to acquire these scroll fragments and to forbid their export. I am writing to recall to you the agreement made with us by the Department of Antiquities with the specific approval of the Prime Minister[281] and the Minister of Education[282] of Jordan, and to request an official statement from you.

   On November 23, 1953 Professor R. B. Y. Scott, who had been corresponding on this matter with the Director of Antiquities, received a cable from Amman, saying:

> GOVERNMENT HAVE AGREED TO SCHEME PLEASE SEND YOUR
> CONTRIBUTION EARLIEST POSSIBLE WRITING –
>
>   (signed) HARDING

On December 30, 1953, Mr. Harding wrote as follows: (ref. 18/3/270)[283]

> The conditions as laid down in the Government's decision Are, (that the transaction of purchase and allotment Shall be entirely in my hands, and that the fragments Shall remain in the country long enough to be fully Studied before being sent to their respective purchasers. The material acquired with your funds would be marked with a special stamp....payments should be sent to me at the Department of Antiquities.

---

   281 Fawzi al-Mulki (1910–1962) served as prime minister from 5 May 1953 until 4 May 1954.
   282 Abdul Halim Nimer.
   283 Letter not preserved.

The authority on which the Director of Antiquities entered into this agreement was as follows:

(1) A letter from the Prime Minister to the Minister of Education agreeing to allow foreign institutions to acquire Scroll fragments: Ref. No. 26/1/1/8723 of 21–11–53.
(2) A letter from the Director of Antiquities to the Minister of Education asking for clearer interpretation of the above: Ref. No. 18/3/14 of 30–11–53.
(3) A reply from the Minister of Education stating that the export of Scroll fragments will be permitted: Ref. No. 39/2/12463 of 23–12–53.

On the basis of these official assurances, the following sums were sent by McGill University to the Director of Antiquites, and the receipt of them was duly acknowledged: [end page 3]

  March 4, 1954 - $ 5,000.
  April 8, 1954 -   10,363.
  December 29, 1955 -   4,200.
                       $ 19,563.[284]

In May 1955 Professor R. B. Y. Scott visited the Palestine Archaeological Museum and listed the Scroll fragments which had been purchased with these contributions from McGill University, and marked with the special stamp referred to in Mr. Harding's letter of December 30, 1953. A copy of this list was lodged with the Bursar of McGill University, and another copy was sent to Mr. Harding. The Scroll fragments purchased with the contribution of $4,200. sent subsequently were not listed. It was agreed that McGill University would receive the equivalent of the material purchased with its funds in assembled plates of manuscripts; the allocation to be made by Mr. Harding.

In June 1956 a letter was received from the Director of Antiquities, dated from Amman June 6th (Ref. 18/3/371), saying:

A provisional division of the Qumran Cave IV manuscript fragments has now been made, and I enclose a list of the pieces which have been allotted to your institution. A few minor changes may be necessary as a result of further study or the acquisition of further material, but the main outline will remain

---

284 USD.

unchanged. There will also be some very small unidentified fragments which will be divided when final study is complete.

With this letter was enclosed a list of 86 manuscript plates, headed " MCGILL UNIVERSITY ".

In light of this official correspondence McGill University believes that the Government of Jordan will feel bound to honour its agreement made in its name on the authority of its Prime Minister and Minister of Education. If this should not be so, the University reserves its right to invoke diplomatic action or to take such other measures as may seem seem necessary and advisable.

LETTER #77

Archive: McGill, RG34, Container: 0001, File 6: Dead Sea Scrolls.
McGill, RG2, Container: 0179, File 6243: Divinity: DSS & Birks Donation.

30 March 1957[285] Montreal

Dear Arnold,[286]

Some time ago McGill University, among others, was appealed to by representatives of the government of the Hashemite Kingdom of Jordan to provide money for the purchase of "Dead Sea Scrolls" then in the hands of Bedouin for which the Jordanian Government had no money available. It was agreed that the institutions supplying the funds should in due course receive portions of the Dead Sea Scrolls manuscript[s] for their libraries and archaeological collections.

McGill University, owing to the generosity of the Birks family, was one of the first to come forward in response to this appeal and an agreement was entered into. Rumours now reach my ears that the Jordanian Government is thinking of breaking these agreements and "nationalising" the manuscripts which were left in its possession for study and collation.

---

285 The letter is marked "Personal" at the top.

286 Arnold Danford Patrick Heeney (1902–1970), Canadian ambassador to the United States from 1953 to 1957 and 1959 to 1962. Heeney was a McGill alumnus. He earned a civil law degree in 1929 and had been a sessional lecturer in the Faculty of Law at McGill between 1934 and 1938. McGill honoured him with a doctor of law degree in 1961.

I do not think that we should let this decision be reached without a protest and I am wondering (since there is no Jordanian Ambassador in Ottawa) whether it would be appropriate for me to transmit through you the attached letter to the Jordanian Ambassador in Washington.

If I should use some other channel of communication I should appreciate it if you would let me know as soon as possible, since the letter, to be effective, should arrive before the Jordanian Government has publicly announced its decision.

With best personal wishes to you as always, I remain,

Cordially yours,
F. Cyril James

LETTER #78

Archive: McGill, RG34, Container: 0001, File 6: Dead Sea Scrolls.
McGill, RG2, Container: 0179, File 6243: Divinity: DSS & Birks Donation.

30 March 1957   Montreal

Your Excellency,[287]

Disturbing rumours have reached me about a possible change in the policy of your Government in the matter of the Dead Sea Scrolls and I should appreciate it very much indeed if you would be kind enough to transmit the attached letter to the Director of Antiquities in Amman in order that I can set at rest the worries of my colleagues and the board of Governors of McGill University.

With warm thanks for your assistance and best personal wishes, I remain,

Cordially yours,
F. Cyril James

---

[287] Addressed to His Excellency, Ambassador of the Hashemite Kingdom of Jordan, Washington D.C. Abdul Munim Rifai was ambassador to Washington until he was transferred to Cairo on 13 May 1957. See "Jordan Transfers Ambassador to U.S.," *New York Times*, 14 May 1957, 2.

LETTER #79

Archive: McGill, RG34, Container: 0001, File 6: Dead Sea Scrolls.
McGill, RG2, Container: 0179, File 6243: Divinity: DSS & Birks Donation.

30 March 1957   Montreal

Dear Sir,[288]

Some time ago, as you probably know, the Board of Governors of McGill University responded to the appeal of the Jordanian Government for financial assistance in order to enable your Government to purchase manuscripts of the Dead Sea Scrolls then in the possession of Bedouin. The Government of Jordan agreed in consideration of our help to earmark for the Library of McGill University a certain portion of these Scrolls and my colleagues are looking forward eagerly to the receipt of these manuscripts after the present work of study and collation has been completed.

It is therefore with very deep concern that we have during the past few weeks heard rumours that the Government of Jordan is considering the abrogation of this agreement and of similar agreements with other universities throughout the world and I have been instructed to ascertain from you whether there is any truth to these rumours.

To review the past arrangements, your record will show that there was a specific agreement made with this University by the Jordanian Department of Antiquities, with the specific approval of the Prime Minister and the Minister of Education in the years 1953–55, which is summed up in Mr. G. Lankester Harding's letter to our representative, Professor R. B. Y. Scott under date of 6th June 1956, reference 18/3/37:[289]

> "Dear Professor[290] Scott
>
> > A provisional division of the Qumran Cave IV manuscript fragments has now been made, and I enclose a list of the pieces which have been allotted to your institution. A few minor changes may be necessary as a result of further study or the acquisition of further material, but

---

288 Dr Abdel Karim Ghureibeh, director general of antiquities.
289 Harding to Scott, 6 June 1956, Letter #61.
290 The original has "Dr."; see Harding to Scott, 6 June 1956, Letter #61.

the main outline will remain unchanged. There will also be some very small, unidentified fragments which will be divided when final study is complete."

[End page 1].

I append to this letter a copy of the list which Mr. Harding's letter refers to.[291] A specific resume of the transaction is as follows:

Learning in 1953 that the Jordanian Government sought additional funds from outside Jordan to help purchase from the Bedouins the fragments discovered in Qumran Cave IV, McGill University sent $15,363 to buy a portion of this discovery, and later sent a further $4,200, for additional manuscript fragments, making a total paid of $19,563.[292]

The agreement was that we had purchased by this payment some 450 pieces of the manuscript[s] and a collection of small undeciphered pieces, that the whole collection thus acquired should be allowed to remain in your country for about two years, long enough to be studied and classified, and then exported to Canada. I refer to a cable to Professor R. B. Y. Scott by Mr. Harding on November 23, 1953:

> "Government have agreed to scheme please send your contribution earliest possible writing"

followed by his letter of December 30th, 1953, "the conditions as laid down in the Government's decision are that the transaction of purchase and allotment shall be entirely in my hands, and that the fragments shall remain in the country long enough to be fully studied before being sent to their respective purchasers. The material acquired with your funds would be marked with a special stamp ... payments should be sent to me at the Department of Antiquities." At that time I understood that Mr. Harding's authority stemmed from a letter from the Prime Minister to the Minister of Education, which agreed to allow foreign institutions to acquire Scroll fragments, and from a letter from the Minister of Education stating that export of Scroll fragments would be permitted.

---

291 See enclosure to Harding to Scott, 6 June 1956, Letter #61.
292 USD.

In May 1955 Professor Scott on our behalf visited Palestine and listed the Scroll fragments which had thus been purchased by McGill University, marking them with a special stamp in the form of a small "s".[293] [End page 2].

The Board of Governors of McGill University believes that in the light of this official correspondence the Government of Jordan will feel bound to honour the agreement made in its name on the authority of its Prime Minister and Minister of Education. The large sum of $19,563 has been paid over to the Jordanian Government by us in good faith and we confidently expect the Government to honour the agreement of sale.

Since your Country has no diplomatic representative in Canada, I am asking the Canadian Ambassador in Washington[294] to transmit this letter through His Excellency The Ambassador of the Kingdom of Jordan in Washington in the hope that it may reach you speedily. I hope to hear from you in the near future that the rumours referred to in the first paragraph are entirely false (as rumours so often are) and to have your assurance that your Government intends to transmit to McGill University in due course our collection of 82 plates.

Meanwhile with warm good wishes, I remain,
Cordially yours,
F. Cyril James

LETTER #80

Archive: McGill, RG34, Container: 0001, File 6: Dead Sea Scrolls.

3 April 1957[295]   Montreal

Dear Professor Scott,

Thank you very much indeed for letting me see Father de Vaux's letter[296] which I now return. A few days ago I sent you a copy of the letters which went

---

293 To the contrary, it was already marked as such before Scott's arrival, as Cantwell Smith reported after his visit to the scrollery in Memorandum from Wilfred Cantwell Smith for Dr. R.B.Y. Scott re McGill fragments in the Jerusalem Museum, 20 May 1954, Letter #22.
294 Arnold Heeney.
295 The letter is marked "Personal and Confidential" at the top.
296 De Vaux to Scott, 9 March 1957, Letter #75.

off to the Canadian and Jordanian Embassy in Washington. The situation looks serious but I do not know what else we can do, although I did see a rather more hopeful statement on the new regime in the Journal of the American Schools of Oriental Research[297] which I dare say caught your eye as well.

With renewed thanks and hoping you will let me know if you hear anything further, I remain,

Cordially yours,
F. Cyril James

LETTER #81

Archive: McGill, RG34, Container: 0001, File 6: Dead Sea Scrolls.

10 December 1957   Montreal

Dear Professor Scott,

Thank you very much indeed for your letter of December 6th[298] regarding the Scrolls. I had not read sufficiently between the lines to have reached the conclusion you suggest but am delighted to know that for the time being at any rate the idea of "nationalising" the Scrolls seems to have been put aside.

Incidentally I know Yighail Yadin very well since I stayed with him at his dig at Hazer when I was in Israel.[299] If there is anything that I can do to help with the question of preservation please do not hesitate to let me know. I hope too

---

297 A. Henry Detweiler, "Letter from the President's Desk," 3–4.

298 Letter not preserved.

299 Yigael Yadin excavated Hazor between 1 August and 1 November 1955. James met Yadin at the site during his visit to the Hebrew University between 26 November and 3 December 1955. See F. Cyril James, "A Visit to Israel, 1955," 26 (McGill University Archives, MG 1017, Container 75, File: James Diaries, 2 Oct 1955–3 Dec 1955). The reference to Yadin may have been inspired by the release of his *The Message of the Scrolls*, which was released in October 1957. See "Books Issued by Publishers Today," *New York Times*, 14 October 1957, 24.

that you will let me hear anything that comes to your ears regarding the twelfth cave.[300]

Meanwhile with best personal wishes, I remain,
Cordially yours,
F. Cyril James

LETTER #82

Archive: McGill, RG34, Container: 0001, File 6: Dead Sea Scrolls.

13 May 1958   Georgeville, Quebec

Dear Dr. Frost:[301]

As you see, we are back at Georgeville rather early this year, as I have leave to do some writing. Some time soon I want to drive in to Montreal to attend to the matter of finally clearing out the remains of my possessions from Divinity Hall. I regret the delay in doing this, but the accumulation of 24 years was too great to be easily absorbed in my limited housing at Princeton. Now, since Slater is leaving,[302] my old office which he has been using will have to be cleared of my remaining books, etc....
[Two paragraphs removed. Discussion of the disposal of Scott's office furniture still in his old office at McGill.]

---

300 Throughout this period rumours circulated as to the contents of the additional caves discovered in the area of Qumran. Only eleven caves contained manuscripts but, as Roland de Vaux noted, numerous additional caves were discovered and many of these contained pottery and artefacts; some related directly to the scrolls and others to the settlement at Qumran. See de Vaux, *L'Archéologie et les Manuscrits de la Mer Morte*, 40–6. The cave designated "Cave XII" by de Vaux contained the remnants of eleven items (GQ 12–1 through 12–11) including pieces of ceramic pots and lids. See Humbert and Chambon, *Fouilles de Khirbet Qumrân et de Aïn Feshka*, 344.

301 Stanley Brice Frost (b. 1913), a graduate of the University of London and Marburg, was appointed chair in Old Testament language and literature as a replacement for Scott in 1956.

302 Robert Henry Lawson Slater, chair of systematic theology from 1949 until 1958. In 1958 he left to join the faculty of Harvard University as professor of world religions.

This week I wrote de Vaux[303] for some information about the status and prospects of the McGill Birks D.S.Scoll fragments, as it is high time we had a further report. Have you heard anything from him?[304] Last year the situation with the Dept. of Antiquities was still a delicate one, but by now things seem to have settled down.

With kind regards,
Yours sincerely,
R.B.Y. Scott

LETTER #83

Archive: McGill, RG34, Container: 0001, File 6: Dead Sea Scrolls.

17 May 1958   Jerusalem

Cher Professeur Scott,

Je viens de recevoir votre lettre du 10 mai,[305] et j'y réponds aussitôt. Vous avez su qu'un Directeur des Antiquités de Jordanie, qui était insupportable, avait prétendu confisquer tous les fragments manuscrits au profit de Gouvernement. Il avait obtenu pour cela une lettre signée de son Ministre. Ce directeur a été enfin remplacé en juillet dernier et j'ai ensuite lutté beaucoup pour obtenir le retrait de cette lettre.[306]

La lettre est annulée et les engagement pris par le Gouvernement envers les Institutions qui ont acheté des lots de fragments de la Grotte 4 restent valables. Les droits de propriété de McGill sur son lot sont donc sauvegardées.

Mais conformément à ce qui avait été entendu au moment de l'achat, les pièces ne seront délivrées aux Institutions que lorsque le travail d'édition sera achevé. Ce travail a été retardé par les conditions politiques et par l'arrivée de nouveaux textes (nous allons encore racheter des fragments de la même grotte 4, les derniers, je pense!). Le travail est cependant assez avancé pour qu'on puisse prévoir que les textes originaux pourront être delivrés à leurs possesseurs respectifs d'ici deux ans.

---

303 Letter not preserved.
304 No response from Frost is preserved.
305 Letter not preserved.
306 Ghureibeh was replaced by Saeed Al-Durra.

Je regrette de vous donner un délai qui vous paraître encore très éloigné mais vous savez que j'ai tout fait et que je continuerai de tout faire pour le réduire.[307] [End page 1].

Je vous redis, cher Professeur Scott, l'assurance de mes sentiments bien cordiaux, R. de Vaux, O. P.

LETTER #84

Archive: McGill, RG34, Container: 0001, File 6: Dead Sea Scrolls.

25 May 1958   Georgeville, Quebec

Dear Dr. James:

I am sending herewith a copy of a letter just received in answer to an enquiry addressed to Father de Vaux at l'Ecole Biblique in Jerusalem.[308] It is gratifying to know that the anxieties of last year seem to have passed, and that the move to confiscate the Scroll fragments purchased for outside institutions has been dropped.

There can be no doubt, I think, that the protest lodged through the Canadian Embassy in Washington last year played some part in this, Father de Vaux has been vigilant and vigorous on our behalf, and this strengthened his hand. It looks now as if plans can go ahead now for the transportation and housing of the material within two years. With your permission, I should like to talk the matter over with Dean Frost[309] and hand to him the replies received to the enquiries I have made about the care of the fragments when received.

With kind regards, I remain,
Yours sincerely,
R. B. Y. Scott

---

307 A 1960 delivery date was already a four-year delay from the originally suggested completion date of 1956.

308 De Vaux to Scott, 17 May 1958, Letter #83.

309 James S. Thomson was succeeded by Stanley B. Frost in 1957 as dean of the Faculty of Divinity at McGill.

LETTER #85

Archive: McGill, RG34, Container: 0001, File 6: Dead Sea Scrolls.

18 June 1958   Jerusalem

Cher Professeur Scott,

  Je réponds aussitôt à votre lettre du 13 juin,[310] que je viens de recevoir.
  Comme je vous l'ai déjà écrit, je fais tous mes efforts pour que le travail sur les originaux des fragments de la Grotte 4 soit terminé à la fin de 1960, et je m'estimerai très heureux si je puis obtenir cela de mes collaborateurs...et des circonstances. Je ne puis donc rien vous promettre pour l'été de 1959. Du point de vue scientifique, il y a une certain possibilité que l'étude des fragments bibliques soit alors terminée, mais il restera à voir si, du point de vue politique, il faut demander alors leur distribution aux institutions ou s'il ne vaut pas mieux attendre que tout soit achevé. Je comprends très bien l'impatience des institutions et des donateurs, mais je leur demande de considérer que nous faisons tout ce que nous pouvons et qu'il est déjà très beau que nous ayions pu continuer le travail, dans des conditions qui, je vous l'assure, ont été et restent très difficiles.
  Je vous prie, cher Professeur Scott, de croire à l'assurance de mes sentiments bien cordiaux,

R. de Vaux, O. P.

LETTER #86

Archive: McGill, RG2, Container: 0254, File 7576: Divinity: Dead Sea Scrolls.

14 June 1959   Jerusalem

Cher Professeur Frost,

  J'ai bien reçu votre lettre de 4 juin,[311] et je comprends que McGill University soit impatiente d'avoir les manuscrits que sa générosité a permis de sauver et mettre à la disposition du monde savant.

---

310 Letter not preserved.
311 Letter not preserved.

La date de Décembre 1959 n'avait été donnée par moi au Professeur R.B.Y. Scott que comme une approximation. En fait, quelques achats de nouveau fragments ont un peu retardé l'étude. Mais il est maintenant décidé que le travail d'édition sur les originaux sera achevé à la fin de juin 1960 et qu'après cette date les manuscrits seront à la disposition des Institutions entre lesquelles ils ont été répartis. La liste que vous possédez et qui a été établie par Mr. Harding au nom du Gouvernement Jordanien reste valable et ne subira que de très menus changements, dûs à l'identification et au regroupement de certains fragments.

Lorsque viendra le moment de la distribution, après juin 1960, vous aurez à adresser une demande officielle au "Director of the Department of Antiquities", à Amman pour obtenir la délivrance de votre lot et la permissions de l'exporter hors de jordanie. Vous joindrez à cette demande une copie des documents <u>officiels</u> (et non des lettres privées que vous avez pu recevoir) de Mr. Harding, établissant votre droit.

J'ai le plaisir de revoir ici le Prof. Scott.[312] Si vous avez besoins d'autre informations, je serai heureux de vous les fournir par son intermédiaire.

Veuillez agréer, cher Professeur Frost, l'assurance de mes sentiments très distingués.
R. De Vaux, O. P.

LETTER #87

Archive: McGill, RG2, Container: 0254, File 7576: Divinity: Dead Sea Scrolls.

15 June 1959   Montreal

Dear Mr. Holton,[313]

I asked Dean Frost to let me have the attached correspondence and inventory of those portions of the Dead Sea Scrolls that are owned by McGill University, as a result of our contribution towards the cost of acquiring and processing the manuscripts. This document should I think be in your vaults since it is the only

---

312 Scott was in Jerusalem to participate in the excavations at Gibeon (see Pritchard, "Industry and Trade at Biblical Gibeon," 23–9).

For Scott's account of his visit to the scrollery, see Scott to Birks, 1 July 1959, Letter #88 and "Memorandum," 8 July 1959, Letter #89.

313 Holton succeeded Bentley as secretary to the Board of Governors at McGill after Bentley's retirement in 1957.

evidence of ownership that we have until such time as the manuscripts have been processed in Jerusalem and are sent to us.

With renewed good wishes, I remain,
Cordially yours,
F. Cyril James

LETTER #88

Archive: McGill, RG2, Container: 0254, File 7576: Divinity: Dead Sea Scrolls.

1 July 1959   Jerusalem

Dear Henry:[314]

I am in Jordan again, this time as a member of the expedition excavating Biblical Gibeon. Today I celebrated Dominion Day (or Canada Day, or whatever they call it nowadays) by visiting the "Scrollery" at the museum, and seeing a good deal of the Scroll materials allotted to the Birks Collection at McGill. When I was here four years ago I examined and listed the actual materials which had been purchased with Mrs. Harry Birks' gift.[315] Since then, as you know, this and the other material of other purchases was sorted and assembled into mss., and redivided to provide contributing institutions with the equivalents of their purchases. I have with me a copy of the list sent me subsequently;[316] Dean Frost at Divinity Hall has the original. I can assure you and Mrs. Birks that we have had a fair-deal; by passing on some remarks of Frank Cross of Harvard who was showing me round: "Great Scott, you've got a great batch!" <u>Exodus B:</u> one of the nicest, early Hasmonean, a beautiful document" "The oldest copy of Numbers, one of our earliest". <u>Samuel C</u> – a beautiful document, almost pure Septuagint text" "You won't be sorry about this – part of the short recension of <u>Jeremiah</u> – I'd rather have this than almost anything from Qumran." – <u>Daniel 9</u> – "lovely manuscript". <u>Testament of Naphtali</u> – "marvelous document" – Rule of the Community – "A beauty" – "the nicest of all copies of the <u>Mishmaroth</u>." These were all spontaneous remarks, which I noted along with more technical matters: One interesting point is that the mss. assigned to McGill have continued

---

314 Henry Birks.

315 Cf. Scott to Harding, 7 September 1955, Letter #43, as well as the transcript of the original list in the addendum to this book.

316 See Harding to Scott, 6 June 1956, Letter #61.

to grow in size, as little pieces are added here and there from the mass of fragments.

The long delay results from the right and proper decision to assemble and publish the material before letting it be scattered. When one realizes that the 'team' engaged on this is made up largely of people who come from abroad for part of the year and from local scholars who have other work on hand – and who must work extremely carefully when they can give the time – it is remarkable that so much has been finished.[317] The target date for completion is now June 1960.

Getting the stuff released and shipped is going to be a delicate business which will have to be carried on through official and diplomatic channels, and with much patience. Probably someone will have to be on the spot to see it through, and accompany the shipment. I cannot go into the whole story here, but just suggest that the delicacy required has some analogies to that needed to resolve the difficulties between Ottawa and Quebec over the Polish art treasures.[318] It is <u>very important</u> to have things handled without publicity until the stuff actually reaches Montreal.[319] The Council of Ministers has agreed to abide by the agreement made, with the Minister's permission, by the former Director of

---

317 Of the team, only John Strugnell, Józef Milik, and Roland de Vaux remained in Jerusalem full time.

318 In 1939 Polish cultural objects, including a two-volume Gutenberg Bible, a number of Chopin musical manuscripts, a medieval bejewelled sword used in the coronation of Polish kings, and large quantities of silver and gold items, were brought to Canada for safekeeping during the Second World War. The subsequent Cold War prevented their return, in part as very strong anti-Communist sentiment in Quebec prevented the federal government from acting to return the property even though it was felt that it would improve relations with Poland. It would take two decades for the material to be returned. See Balawyder, *The Maple Leaf and the White Eagle: Canadian-Polish Relations, 1918–1978*.

319 Scott and all others involved were learning from experience. On 21 September 1958, *Ad-Difaa*, for example, carried a Reuters report of the purchase of the "Oldest Version of the Ten Commandments" by the Unitarian Church of All Souls in New York ("The Oldest Version of the Ten Commandments," *Ad-Difaa*, 21 September 1958, anonymous translation preserved in: IAA Archives, Box 73, PAM 1117: Dead Sea Scrolls [cave no. 4], jacket 1). The money was, in fact, a donation to the PAM to make the purchase but the situation required a letter of explanation to the editor by Yusif Sa'ad to cool the rising political tempers. See Sa'ad to the Editor, *Ad-Difaa*, 24 September 1958 and the attached article, IAA Archives, Box 73, PAM 1117: Dead Sea Scrolls (cave no. 4), jacket 1.

Antiquities with McGill, the Vatican, Manchester and Bonn Universities[320] and McCormick Seminary.

I expect to be at Georgeville for a fortnight at the end of August and will hope to see you, Dean Frost and Dr. James about this whole matter.[321]

With kind regards,
Yours sincerely,
Bob Scott

LETTER #89

Archive: McGill, RG34, Container: 0001, File 6: Dead Sea Scrolls.

8 July 1959   Jerusalem

<u>Private & Confidential</u>

Memorandum relating to Prof. R.B.Y. Scott's conference with Pere de Vaux and Prof. F.M. Cross, Jr.[322]

1. The editorial team has agreed that editorial work on Cave IV Scrolls will be brought to a close by June 30, 1960.[323] A month or two before this de Vaux in the name of the team will notify the five contributing institutions that the purchases are ready for shipment, and that they should apply for export permits to the Director of the Jordan Department of Antiquities, Amman.

2. This application should enclose photostatic copies of the official documents relating to the purchase, the originals being retained.

---

320 Incorrect. It should read "Heidelberg University." Bonn provided funding for the purchase on behalf of Heidelberg.

321 James would be away in Paris to attend a UNESCO meeting when Scott arrived in Montreal (James to Frost, 27 July 1959, McGill University Archives, RG2, Container: 0254, File 7576: Divinity: Dead Sea Scrolls).

322 The document was produced by Scott for his own use.

323 De Vaux informed the team in March 1959 that they would need to accelerate their pace (Brown, *John Marco Allegro*, 162).

3. If no reply is received after a reasonable time, a reminder should be sent. If still no reply is forthcoming, an approach should be made through diplomatic channels, possibly in conjunction with the other institutions involved.

4. The boxes made at the Museum for temporary shipment to Amman can be used, as they are strongly built.[324] It would be advisable to have the shipment made by air freight. It would also be advantageous to have a representative on the spot to carry through the final arrangements for shipment.

5. The respective institutions will be asked to agree not to permit publication of, or to exhibit publicly, such portions of their material as have not already been published. The work of preparing Scrolls for publication by the team in Jordan should be completed by 1962; a further year or more will elapse before the volumes come from the printers.[325] Meanwhile, enough McGill materials have been published already to permit some exhibition and publicity pictures.[326]

6. A complete set of infra-red photographs of the materials shipped will be available once the materials have been published by the editorial team.
    (de Vaux added that the letter of the former Minister of Education declaring that all Scrolls would be retained in Jordan was definitely countermanded by the Council of Ministers, after strong (and risky!) representations by himself and the Museum. The Government will stand by its bargain because it cannot afford to refund the money given.)
[End page 1].

7. On July 11, 1959 the above plans were approved in principle by the editorial team at the Museum.

---

324 See Scott to James, 11 September 1956, Letter #65.

325 According to Judith Brown, in March 1959 de Vaux requested John Allegro to provide his manuscript for the fifth official volume by June 1960. He also requested that page proofs be ready for volumes 2 and 3 of DJD. It was expected that Skehan and Cross would have the fourth volume ready at the end of 1959; Milik his material by 1961; and the remaining work by Starcky, Baillet, and Strugnell, would appear semi-annually after that (Brown, *John Marco Allegro*, 161–2).
    Ultimately, only DJD 2 (2 volumes, in 1961) and DJD 3 (2 volumes, in 1962) and Allegro's work (DJD 5 in 1968) appeared before the close of the decade. The last of the volumes in the DJD series have only recently been published.

326 Presumably this refers to the state of affairs after the intended publication of volume 4 of DJD; see point 8 of this document for further elucidation.

8. On Aug. 9, 1959 Pere de Vaux told me that, if McGill agrees, the first of the Cave IV volumes (vol. 4 of 'MSS from the Judaean Desert') will be issued under the joint imprint of McGill University, the Palestine Archaelogical Museum, and the Jordan Department of Antiquities. This is the next volume to be prepared.[327]

LETTER #90

Archive: McGill, RG2, Container: 0254, File 7576: Divinity: Dead Sea Scrolls.

9 July 1959   Montreal

Dear Mr. Birks,

   Thank you very much for sending me a copy of Dr. Scott's letter dated July the 1st.[328] As you can imagine, it has pleased me very greatly. I have recently been in communication with Father de Vaux, and he too suggested that we would need to move with caution. In recent discussions with Dr. James on the matter, he has suggested that I should go to Jerusalem early next year so that I can see just what the situation is, and make the necessary arrangements. I note that Dr. Scott is going to be in Georgeville the end of August, and I think that if we could arrange to meet with him and Dr. James and talk this matter over, it would be extremely useful. I myself will not be in Montreal until the first days of September, but I would make myself available after September the 1st, at your convenience and that of Dr. James. I will wait to hear from you further with regard to this matter.

   I hope that you have had a very happy vacation in Europe and that you enjoy a very good summer.

With every good wish,
Yours sincerely,
Stanley B. Frost,
Dean,
Faculty of Divinity.

---

[327] As a result of the delays and changing political circumstances, McGill's part in the "rescue" of the material is almost nowhere explicitly acknowledged in the official publications. However, a short distribution list in homage to the participating institutions is found in Baillet, *Qumrân Grotte 4.III (4Q482–4Q520)*, ix.

[328] Scott to Birks, 1 July 1959, Letter #88.

LETTER #91

Archive: McGill, RG2, Container: 0254, File 7576: Divinity: Dead Sea Scrolls.

11 December 1959   Montreal

Dear Mr. Birks,

I promised in our hurried conversation the other day at the luncheon for the Governor General,[329] that I would let you have a memorandum on the matter of the Dead Sea Scrolls.

I have had several conversations with Professor R. B. Y. Scott who was out in the Hashemite Kingdom of the Jordan last summer, and he informs me that the work on the Scrolls should be completed by about May and that the Scrolls should be available to be sent to this country about June. But the political situation is a little difficult. There is wide spread feeling against the further dispersal of the treasures of the East to the wealthier countires of the West and this links in with Arab nationalist feelings. You may remember that there has been at least one attempt to go back on the original contract but the King and Council of Ministers have clearly indicated their intention to abide by the original agreement, but no politician in Jordan wishes to be in any way associated with the granting of permission for the Scrolls to leave the country. We may find, therefore, that we may have to make several applications for an export permit. The important thing is, however, that we are careful not to arouse any publicity about the imminent dispersal of the Scrolls until after they are in our hands. Then we can indulge in all the publicity we like.

I have on my files the papers relating to the generous gift of the Birks fund (the John Henry Birks Foundation), and it would be necessary to have photostat copies of the relevant documents to hand in order that our claim may be fully established. I have written to the professor in the States who has been most closely associated with this work, Dr. F. M. Cross and I am arranging to meet him in New York after Christmas in order to gather all the [end page 1] information I can from him as to the present situation.[330] He should know with some exactitude whether the work on the Scrolls will indeed be ready by

---

329 Governor General Georges Phileas Vanier (1888–1967) opened the McConnell Engineering Building at McGill University on 30 November 1959.

330 ASOR and SBL held their annual meetings on 28 and 29 December at Union Theological Seminary in New York City. This would have been the logical place for Frost and Cross to meet.

April or May. I have also written to the Director of the American School in Jerusalem[331] so that I may have the benefit of the latest information.

I have had several conversations with the Principal about this matter over the last year or so, and he agreed that I should make plans for a visit to Jordan, and I have been gathering information with regard to this matter also. In conversation you raised the question as to whether this was an Old Testament or New Testament matter. I think I may fairly maintain that it is an Old Testament matter[332] in that the Scrolls which are coming to us are Old Testament manuscripts in Hebrew and Aramaic and are all Old Testament books. It is true that the non-biblical manuscripts relating to the Qumran Sect are of interest to the New Testament scholars because of their content, but unfortunately, it is not these Scrolls which are included in our allocation, but rather those which are concerned with the textual authenticity of the Old Testament. We are particularly fortunate, I hear, in that we are obtaining some of the most important fragments relating to the books of Daniel and of Samuel.

My information is that tourist return fare to Israel is $960.00. My intentions are to travel about March the 25th when lectures will be almost at an end, and return at the end of April for the end-of-term Faculty Meeting, Senate and Convocation. I am making enquires as to the costs I am likely to incur while in Jordan, and my colleague, Wilfred Smith, tells me that the subsistence rate for members of the Islamic Institute traveling in the East is a maximum of $18.00 per day. As I hope to stay at the American School in Jerusalem I hope that my expenses will be considerably less than this, but I imagine that I should budget for a total expense of not less than $300.00.

I have not yet raised with the Principal as to how these expenses should be met, but in the Birks Manuscript Fund there is a balance of $702.25, and as I remarked the other day, this has been lying in the McGill general account since 1954 and interest accumulated from this amount has gone into the general operating expenses of the University. I think, therefore we might legitimately urge that the interest this sum has borne since it was deposited should be calculated and added to the capital and this would bring the total available to $900.00 or

---

331 Marvin H. Pope (1916–1997) was professor of religious studies at Yale University from 1949 until 1986. He was annual director of ASOR in Jerusalem for 1959–60.

332 For the importance of the scrolls for the New Testament, see for example, among many, the recent work by George Brooke (*The Dead Sea Scrolls and the New Testament*) and Jörg Frey ("The Impact of the Dead Sea Scrolls on New Testament Interpretation: Proposals, Problems, and Further Perspectives," 407–61).

so. I would be prepared to make a modest contribution to the expenses [end page 2] involved, and hope that other sources may be found for the balance.

I have also had in mind two other points. The first is to make provision for the safe-keeping of the Scrolls once they are in our hands. Just what museum techniques will be involved is not yet clear. This is one of the matters which I hope to discuss with Dr. Cross after Christmas. The bulk of our allocation is made up of fairly small fragments which are already set up between sheets of glass and presumably they can be stored or exhibited in this form, but I believe we have several larger fragments which are in Scroll form and those cannot be kept between glass, and for these we may need some kind of hermetically sealed container filled with argon gas. In this case we are likely to meet with a rather more expensive proposition. I hope to know a great deal more about this in the near future, and to arrive at an estimate of costs.

The second is that McGill will undoubtedly become the centre of a good deal of scholarly interest in this field, and we may expect to have scholars visiting us to examine the Scrolls and work on them. We ought, therefore, to have a member of our staff who will not only be able to deal with complete competence with all enquiries, but who is himself pursuing the kind of textual study which the Scrolls demand. This is a very specialized aspect of Old Testament studies, and I hope to raise with the Principal the possibility of a further appointment to our Faculty of a young but competent scholar who could be Curator of the Scrolls and Research Assistant In Old Testament textual matters and whose teaching would lie in the area of Hebrew and Semitic languages and post-graduate seminars.[333] I have suggested to the Principal that I might explore the various foundations to see whether they would finance a five-year initial appointment.

I trust I have now given you a clear and comprehensive picture of the present situation. If there is anything further that you wish to know, I will do my best to answer your queries. I appreciate very greatly your continued interest in this matter and in all matters pertaining to the Faculty, and will appreciate an opportunity to discuss some of these things with you.

---

[333] In 1960 Willard Gurdon Oxtoby (1934–2003) joined the faculty as lecturer in Semitics. Frost would meet Oxtoby on his visit to Jerusalem while Oxtoby was at work, as an ASOR fellow, on the concordance of scroll material at the PAM (cf. Report to the Principal, 12 May 1960, Letter #97).

You will be glad to know that I and my colleagues regard ourselves as very fortunate in the appointment of Dr. Johnston,[334] and that the students have come to [end page 3] appreciate him greatly. I think the outlook for the Faculty and for the College is encouraging.

With every good wish,
Yours sincerely,
Stanley B. Frost,
Dean, Faculty of Divinity.

LETTER #92

Archive: McGill, RG2, Container: 0254, File 7576: Divinity: Dead Sea Scrolls.

13 February 1960   Montreal

Dear Père de Vaux,

I am planning to visit Jerusalem and hope to arrive on April 2nd and stay at the American Schools of Oriental Research. I propose to remain until April the 17th, and then cross into Israel as I have to be back here by April the 29th.

The purpose of my visit is to see the Scrollery in action before it brings its operations to an end, and to get a personal knowledge of the size and nature of the McGill collection of fragments from Cave IV. When I know the amount and nature of the material I will be able to plan for its reception here when it becomes available. I understand that you hope that the work on the Scrolls will be completed by June the 30th, and that the collections which are going abroad should become available some time after that date. I also hope to make personal contacts with the Jordanian authorities so as to facilitate an application for an export permit at such time as I am advised by you that it will be appropriate to seek one. I also hope as a result of my visit to explore such matters as insurance, the method of transportation and so on. Needless to say, I shall also hope to visit Qumran and to take the opportunity of my being in Jordan to visit other interesting archaeological sites.

I would like to take this opportunity to express on my own behalf and that of the University authorities our warmest appreciation of the work which you have undertaken so skillfully and unremittingly, and to assure you that we will

---

334 George Fonds Johnston (1913–1989) joined the faculty as professor of New Testament language and literature in 1959, retiring in 1981.

seek in every way to co-operate with you and to act only in such a manner as your wisdom and great knowledge both of the Scrolls and of the local situation would advise us to follow. I hope it may be possible for me to meet with you. It will indeed be a very great pleasure for me.

With every good wish,
Yours sincerely,
Stanley B. Frost,
Dean, Faculty of Divinity.

LETTER #93

Archive: McGill, RG2, Container: 0254, File 7576: Divinity: Dead Sea Scrolls.

17 February 1960   Montreal

Dear Dean Frost,

Thank you very much indeed for your kindness in sending me a copy of the letter to Père de Vaux.

In further regard to your trip, I should be very glad, if you think it would be helpful, to write a personal note to Professor Mazar at the Hebrew University.[335]

---

335 James knew Mazar from his first visit to Israel from 26 November to 3 December 1955. Together with Mazar, Yadin, and Avigad, James undertook an archaeological tour of Israel (cf. F. Cyril James, "A Visit to Israel, 1955," 26: McGill University Archives, MG 1017, Container 75, File: James Diaries, 2 Oct 1955–3 Dec 1955). James visited Jerusalem for a second time from 23 April until 4 May 1960, after spending eight days in London. The primary purpose of his visit was to participate in a review of the Hebrew University. His report was well received and provided him the opportunity to maintain a positive relationship with Mazar, the president and rector of Hebrew University (cf. Frost, *The Man in the Ivory Tower*, 259). James provides a review of his experiences in an unpublished manuscript, "Israel Revisited, 1960: Progress and Problems" (18 May 1960, 8 pages, McGill University Archives, MG 1017, Container 75, File: James Diaries, 18 May 1960–26 Dec. 1960).

In response to James's visit, Mazar wrote to thank him: "Let me tell you again that we greatly value our friendly relations with McGill University and that we are very much indebted to you for all you are doing to strengthen the bonds that exist between our institutions," (Mazar to James, 17 May 1960, McGill University Archives, MG 1017, Container 75, File: James Diaries, 18 May 1960 – 26 Dec. 1960).

You may however prefer to handle the matter entirely yourself so that I shall be guided by your judgment.

Cordially yours,
F. Cyril James

LETTER #94

Archive: McGill, RG2, Container: 0254, File 7576: Divinity: Dead Sea Scrolls.

19 February 1960   Montreal

Dear Mr. Principal,

   Thank you very much for your offer to write a personal note to Dr. Mazar. I would appreciate this very greatly. I intend to cross into Israel on April 19th, and to leave Jerusalem on the 22nd, as my plane leaves Tel Aviv on the 23rd. I would be very glad to have an introduction to the Hebrew University such as you suggest.
   I have spoken with Mr. Holton[336] with regard to ordering the air tickets, and he has suggested that I send across the usual insurance form with an added note stating the purpose of the trip. He will then ask you to initial this document and will give me authority to pay for my tickets (roughly $800.00 in Canadian currency) on the University Air Card. I estimate that I may need not more than $500.00 in additon, and I propose, with your permission, to draw up to this amount on the Birks manuscript Fund in the expectation, however, that I shall not in fact need so large an amount.
   I will hope these arrangements commend themselves to you, but if not, I will amend them accordingly.

Yours sincerely,
Stanley B. Frost

---

336 Secretary to the board of governors at McGill.

LETTER #95

Archive: McGill, RG2, Container: 0254, File 7576: Divinity: Dead Sea Scrolls.

25 February 1960   Montreal

Dear Dr. Mazar,

I am sending over this letter of introduction now, and giving a copy to Dean Stanley B. Frost, of our Faculty of Divinity, so that he may present it to you when he gets to Jerusalem.

Dr. Frost plans to be in Jerusalem and Israel from April the 19th to the 22nd. The purpose of his visit is to see the Dead Sea Scrolls, and observe the Scrollery in action getting thus a personal knowledge of the size and nature of the McGill University collection of fragments from Cave IV. He is also anxious to visit the Hebrew University and to make your personal acquaintance.

You would find him a most interesting and charming man, and I know that you would enjoy meeting him also, so that perhaps you would write him directly and arrange a time that would be mutually convenient. A letter addressed to him at McGill University will find him.

With warmest good wishes to you, and the hope that I may also see you if I am able to arrange a trip to Israel late in April, on which Allan Bronfman[337] is now working hard, I remain, as always,

Yours cordially,
F. Cyril James

---

337 Allan Bronfman (1895–1980). The Bronfman name is best known in connection with the Seagram's distillery and related enterprises. Allan's family, however, made their fortune in real estate and became benefactors to McGill University and the Hebrew University. In 1944 Allan founded the Canadian Friends of Hebrew University (cf. Newman, *Bronfman Dynasty: The Rothschilds of the New World*, 40–5).

The day before this letter to Mazar was composed, Bronfman confirmed that James would be joining him in Israel after a week's stay in London (Bronfman to Wise, 24 January 1960, McGill University Archives, MG 1017, Container 75, File: James Diaries, 18 May 1960 – 26 Dec. 1960). Bronfman accompanied James during the entire trip to Israel in April and May of 1960, including travelling from London and back (Israel Itinerary, 1960, McGill University Archives, MG 1017, Container 75, File: James Diaries, 18 May 1960 – 26 Dec. 1960). During the visit James attended two events honouring Bronfman: a Jewish National Fund dinner on 26 April, and the laying of a cornerstone at the "Allan Bronfman Family Agricultural School for Hill-Farming in Ein Kerem," on 28 April 1960. Invitations to both are preserved in the McGill University Archives MG 1017, Container 75, File: James Diaries, 18 May 1960 – 26 Dec. 1960.

LETTER #96

Archive: McGill, RG2, Container: 0254, File 7576: Divinity: Dead Sea Scrolls.

15 April 1960   Jerusalem

Dear Mr. Principal,

The only typewriter to which I have access has so ancient a ribbon that I think you would prefer to cope with my handwriting.

My visit has proved fruitful and opportune. I have surveyed the McGill collection and discussed the question of certain desireable adjustments between the different allocations to institutions, but Pere de Vaux agreed with me that in order to avoid increasing our difficulties any such negotiations should take place after we have secured our collection. I have ordered the requisite boxes for the safe transport of the MSS & these will be adequate for their safe storage at McGill until we have decided in what manner we wish to display them.

I have paid a visit to Amman and was cordially received by the Acting Director of Antiquities[338] and by the Minister of Education.[339] I submitted copies of our correspondence & both gave me full assurances that when Pere de Vaux declared the work complete, our application for an export permit would [end page 1] not meet with any difficulties & would be facilitated by them. I sensed no tendency on their part to wish to upset the arrangement & they readily gave assurances that the export would be permitted. This is all the more important because John Allegro has bruited a scheme to raise £1 million to buy all the Scrolls (including the Government's share) & rebuild the Qumran monastery & locate them there permanently.[340] He has raised £20,000 & has obtained permission (the first ever given) to dig in the Temple=Mosque of Omar area for the treasure described in the copper scrolls.[341] Informed opinion is that he is quite irresponsible but the proposition naturally is attractive to the Jordanian Government. However, my visit has definitely re-asserted McGill's claims and de Vaux is extremely pleased that I have come just at this time. I am also having the time of [my] life, visiting sites & archaeological digs. I am omitting the Israel trip & have sent my regrets to Mazar.

Stanley B. Frost[342]

---

338 Dja Bey Rifa'i.

339 Sheikh M. Shingiti.

340 See Brown, *John Marco Allegro*, 158–64.

341 On the "enigmatic" nature of the content of the Copper Scroll (3Q15) and its references to hidden treasure, see Wolters, "Copper Scroll," 144–8.

342 No signature appears on the letter but the envelope is addressed as from Frost at ASOR Jerusalem.

LETTER #97

Archive: McGill, RG2, Container: 0254, File 7576: Divinity: Dead Sea Scrolls.

12 May 1960[343]   Montreal

John Henry Birks Collection of Dead Sea Scrolls.

Report to the Principal of Visit to
Jerusalem, by S.B. Frost.

I spent three weeks in Jerusalem during the month of April and visited the Archaeological Museum[344] frequently. I met Père de Vaux, Abbé Milik, Mr. John Strugnell and Mr. Willard Oxtoby[345] and several other members of the Scrolls Commission. I also established very friendly relationships with Mr. Yusef Saʻad, the Director of the Museum.

THE MANUSCRIPTS.

I had opportunity to examine the McGill collection in detail. It has a remarkably wide range of material, and will constitute the only major collection

---

[343] Like his predecessor, Scott, Frost went to the media with a report of his trip even before the official documentation was submitted to the university. On 4 May the *Montreal Star* reported that McGill would very soon receive its allotment because Frost, during his trip to Jerusalem, had "received assurances from the authorities concerned that every facility would be granted to the university for the export of the fragments to McGill," (D.B. Macfarlane, "Dead Sea Scroll Plates Allocated for McGill," *Montreal Star*, 4 May 1960, 55).

[344] PAM.

[345] Strictly, Oxtoby was not part of the editorial team but at the time worked on the Cave 4 concordance. He arrived in Jerusalem in October 1958 to take up a fellowship at ASOR. During that year he assembled texts for his work on Arabic epigraphy while Raymond Brown worked on the concordance (Winnett, "Report of the Director of the School in Jerusalem," 4–7). Oxtoby would remain for a second year (1959–60) to work on the concordance. He contracted hepatitis in early 1959 and was ordered to stay in bed, but continued his work on the concordance. Oxtoby would leave Jerusalem in May 1960, by which time he had already accepted the position at McGill University (Pope, "Report of the Director of the School in Jerusalem," 4–8).

of Qumran manuscripts outside Palestine. Its significance lies in three major points.

  i. It is sufficiently extensive to allow a student to familiarise himself with the whole palaeographic development of the intertestamental and early post-Christian period.
  ii. It contains material which will exercise an [end page 1] important influence on the development of theories relating to the origin and evolution of the Old Testament text and canon.
  iii. It contains a wide range of samples of non-biblical texts, which will be of the highest importance in coming to an understanding of the intellectual milieu of which Christianity arose.

The work relating to points ii and iii can be carried in the edition of the texts to be published by the Oxford University Press, in conjunction with the Museum and other authorities including this University. Point i however, requires that the MSS themselves are available for reference, and constitutes the documents as a teaching tool.

AVAILABILITY

Père de Vaux informed me that the Collection would be available for distribution on or about July 1st.

Mr. Sa'ad and I went to Amman and were received by the Acting Director of the Department of Antiquities of the Jordanian Government, Dja Bey Rifa'i. The Minister of Education, His Excellency Sheikh Shangity,[346] joined the interview at a later stage. The Director gave me assurances that when Père de Vaux announced that the manuscripts were ready for distribution, his Department would co-operate in granting the University an export permit. The Minister (who did not speak English) reiterated these assurances and I gathered the impression that there were in their minds no difficulties which would obstruct the granting of the necessary permits.

During my visit, Père de Vaux several times expressed his satisfaction that the University had evidenced its interest in this matter by sending a personal representative at so opportune a time, that is, just prior to the announcement that the manuscripts were ready for release.

---

346 Predominantly signed "Shingiti" in official correspondence. Also spelled "Shangiti," "Shangity," or "Shauqiti" in some of the letters.

He said that my visit reminded the Jordanian Government that the earlier agreements concluded by them were by no means regarded by the University as a dead letter. McGill was the only institution [end page 2] which had done this, and he really appreciated our continued interest.

PROCEDURE

As soon as Père de Vaux announces completion of the editorial work, the University should apply to the Director of Antiquities for an export permit. This may take time to secure, and persistence will be needed. To have some kind of terminal date, such as a further visit of a McGill representative would help considerably.

I have ordered the necessary transport boxes to be constructed, and someone must be given authority to receive the MSS on the University's behalf and to give the Museum a receipt for them. They should then be sealed in the presence of Jordanian Customs' officers and shipped by air-freight to Montreal and delivered sealed to Divinity Hall. This would have to be arranged with Canadian Customs here, and possibly you might think it desirable to seek the help of the Canadian diplomatic authorities in Beirut. Insurance of the scrolls should be arranged here in Montreal. Once at Divinity Hall, they should be locked in the basement Rare Books Room until a decision is made concerning their permanent storage.

COMMENT

I consider that my trip was very profitable and has done much to increase the likelihood that the University will in the near future receive this important acquisition.

Respectfully submitted,
Stanley B. Frost
Dean of the Faculty of Divinity.

LETTER #98

Archive: IAA, Box 73, PAM 1117(b): Distributions of Institutions Dead Sea Scrolls.

4 June 1960   Jerusalem

Dear Professor Frost,

McGill University with other Institutions,[347] helped to preserve the manuscripts from the 4th Cave at Qumran by offering the Funds for the purchase of a group of these fragments. These Institutions agreed that all the fragments should remain at the Palestine Archaeological Museum for so long as the work of preparing them for publication would last: for each purchase brought in mixed groups, and it was indispensable to keep these all together in order to identify and join the fragments from different purchases which belonged to the same Manuscript. It was understood that when this work of reassembling the Manuscripts was finished and the decipherment complete, each Institution would receive as its property a group of Manuscripts which would correspond, both in quantity and in quality, to the financial contribution that it made.

This work of preparing the fragments for publication has been carried on over the last seven years by an International and Interconfessional group of specialists, and it has been supported financially by Institutions other than those which contributed to the purchase of the fragments.[348] It has taken longer than we had foreseen, because we had underestimated the difficulties of the operation, and also because further fragments, which had to be identified and placed in the Manuscripts from which they came, were still being bought as late

---

347 The identical letter with the addressee's name replaced was sent to each of the participating institutions. A similar letter to the Government of Jordan, concerning their share of the material was also sent. It indicated that the work was now complete and that the Government would need to follow the same rules with regard to exhibition and publication as the foreign institutions. Copies of the letters, all dated 4 June 1960, are collected in IAA Archives, Box 73, PAM 1117(b): Distributions of Institutions Dead Sea Scrolls.

348 John D. Rockefeller, Jr, for example, through an endowment, provided funds to run the scrollery until 1960. The rush to finish by mid-1960 was partly precipitated by the fact that funds were no longer forthcoming to the museum from this source.

as 1958.³⁴⁹ The Institutions who put up money for the purchase of Manuscripts have, however, in the end gained by this delay, in that they will own rational groupings of identified and more completely restored documents.

This work in the Palestine Archaeological Museum on the fragments themselves is now drawing to an end, and the Manuscripts which fall to your Institution's lot will be at your disposal at any time after the end of the current month, June 1960. A list of the texts in your lot was sent to you in 1956 by the Department of Antiquities of Jordan.³⁵⁰ This list had a provisional character but subsequent study has necessitated very few changes in it. These will be pointed out to you at the moment when you take possession of your Manuscripts; they are the results either of a better understanding of the texts, or of the subsequent purchases of fragments, and they merely add to the value of your lot.³⁵¹ [end page 1]

The Palestine Archaeological Museum asks you to nominate a representative who will come personally to Jerusalem to take delivery of your lot, supervise its packing, and see to its dispatching. The fragments will be handed over to him in the same condition in which the museum preserves them, in other words, flattened, grouped together according to the Manuscripts to which they belong, and kept between plates of glass. This arrangement has guaranteed their preservation in good condition in the dry climate of Jerusalem, and it will suffice for their transport abroad. It has, however, a provisional character and each Institution in consultation with its technical advisers must take those measures of conservation which will suit its different climate and conditions. As for packing, the Museum has designed a kind of box which would protect the Manuscripts during transport, and it can have such boxes made at the expense of any Institution which so desires.

---

349 According to two lists in the PAM archival material (dated 9 July and 20 July 1958, respectively), the museum purchased on the 9th of July 1958, 4Q.Sl 106 – Pseudo-Jeremiah, Pseudo-Ezekiel; 4Q.C 45ᵃ – Samuelᵇ; 4Q.Sl 48ᵃ – Wisdom Text, 1st MS.; 4Q.SL 50ᵃ – Wisdom Text, 2nd MS.; 4Q.M 82ᵃ – Sectarian Work; 4Q.M 135 – Sectarian Hymnic Work; 4Q.M 136 – Daniel Cycle: Vision of the last days; 4Q.Sy 32ᵃ – Proto-Mishnah; 4Q.Sy 7ᵃ – Vision of Amram – Testament of Qohat; 4Q.M Phylactery, in pieces, with leather case; and a series of small fragments. On 20 July 1958, 4q.c. c32ᶜ Dtⁿ – an incomplete scroll of Deuteronomy (Deut 5 and 8) was purchased (IAA Archives, Box 73, PAM 1117: Dead Sea Scrolls (cave no. 4), jacket 1).

350 See Harding to Scott, 6 June 1956, Letter #61.

351 Because it was to be provided when the material finally transferred hands, McGill's representatives never saw this.

Although the purchasing Institutions accepted that the Manuscripts should stay at the Palestine Archaeological Museum for so long as the work of preparing their publication should last, your lot will be handed over to you before the volumes of the <u>editio princeps</u> of the Cave IV Manuscripts appear, in the series "Discoveries in the Judaean Desert". You will however understand that the Palestine Archaeological Museum has a duty to protect the scientific rights of the editors who have worked under its auspices. It is obliged therefore to put the following limits to the use that you will make of these Manuscripts in the immediate future. 1st) Public exhibition should only be made of texts already published. 2nd.) No other scholars should be authorised to study or publish texts until the <u>editio princeps</u> appears. 3rd.) No photographs of these unpublished texts should be given to other scholars until the the <u>editio princeps</u> appears.

These rules are not as strict as they might at first seem: your lot contains pieces which have already been edited in preliminary publications, and which are therefore exempt from the restrictions. These pieces will be indicated on the definitive list that your representative will receive. Their number will increase rapidly as each volume of the edition is published, and these volumes will not be long in appearing: the two volumes containing the Biblical Manuscripts should be given to the Printer during the coming year, and the 3 or 4 volumes of non-Biblical texts will be ready in the following two years.[352]

Your representative will take possession of your lot in return for a written declaration accepting these conditions and discharging the Palestine Archaeological Museum of its responsibilities past and future towards you.[353] [end page 2]

However, this Museum is equally responsible towards the Jordan Governement for these Manuscripts, and consequently it cannot let the Manuscripts leave the Museum except when you have obtained from the competent authorities a permit to export the same. Your Institution must make an official request for this permit to the Director of the Department of Antiquities of Jordan, Amman. The Director will submit the request to the Minister of National Education who will sign the permit. When it authorised Foreign Institutions to take part in the buying of the fragments from Cave IV, the Jordan Government explicitly committed itself to permit such export after completion of the study of the Manuscripts in Jerusalem. In support of your request you should accordingly present Photostats of your official correspondence with the Department of Antiquities

---

352 See Tov, "Discoveries in the Judaean Desert," 205–8.

353 For McGill's acceptance of these conditions, see Frost to director of antiquities, 10 June 1960, Letter #99.

in Jordan concerning a)- the purchase of the fragments, b)- the Manuscripts assigned to you, i. e. the division list; but you should not present copies of your correspondence (if any) with the Palestine Archaeological Museum, which is not an organ of the Government. We hope that no difficulty will arise in the granting of the export permit. If it does, the Palestine Archaeological Museum would not be qualified to intervene and you should request assistance from your country's Diplomatic Representative accredited to Jordan.

It may be that the conditions set to your purchase and the long delay may have appeared disagreeable to your Institution. You may be sure that the Palestine Archaeological Museum and the editors have done all in their power to limit this delay. At the moment when you are about to reap the harvest of this patient waiting, I would like to express to you, in the name of the Palestine Archaeological Museum, of those scholars who have been preparing the edition of the Manuscripts, and of all the scholars who will use their work with advantage, our sincerest thanks for the help that you have given us in the task of saving and restoring documents of such great interest.

Yours sincerely,
(Father R. de Vaux, O. P.)
PRESIDENT,
BOARD OF TRUSTEES,
PALESTINE ARCHAEOLOGICAL MUSEUM

LETTER #99

Archive: McGill, RG2, Container: 0254, File 7576: Divinity: Dead Sea Scrolls.
McGill, RG2, Container: 0179, File 6243: Divinity: DSS & Birks Donation.

10 June 1960   Montreal

Your Excellency,[354]

I have received a communication dated the 4th of June 1960, from the Rev. Fr. de Vaux, President of the Board of Trustees of the Palestine Archaeological

---

354 A copy of the letter forwarded to James on 13 June is noted as "Letter to the Director of the Department of Antiquities of Jordan," (McGill University Archives, RG2, Container: 0179, File 6243: Divinity: DSS & Birks Donation).

Museum relating to the work of editing the Qumran MSS now in the care of the Museum.

You will recall that in 1954 and 1955, McGill University made contributions totalling 19,563 U.S. dollars for the purchase of Scroll fragments from Qumran Cave IV, having received assurances that these could be exported after they had been retained in Jordan for study. On December 30th, 1953, Mr. Lankester Harding, the then Director of the Department of Antiquities, wrote as follows:

(Reference no. 18/3/270:
"The conditions as laid down in the Government's decision are, that the transaction of purchase and allotment shall be entirely in my hands, and that the fragments shall remain in the country long enough to be fully studied before being sent to their respective purchasers ... payments should be sent to me at the Department of Antiquities."

The authority on which the Director entered into this agreement was as follows:

1. A letter from the Prime Minister to the Minister of Education agreeing to allow foreign institutions to acquire Scroll fragments: Ref. no. 26/1/8723 of 21/11/53.

2. A letter from the Director of Antiquities to the Minister of Education asking for clearer interpretation of the above: Ref. no. 18/3/14 of 30/11/53.

3. A reply from the Minister of Education stating that export of Scroll fragments will be permitted: Ref. no. 39/2/12463 of 23/12/53.

[end page 1]

On the basis of these official assurances, the following sums were sent by McGill University to the Department of Antiquities, and receipt of them was duly acknowledged:

March 4, 1954	$ 5,000
April 8, 1954	10,363
December 29, 1954	4,200
	$19,563

In June 1956, a letter was received from the Director of Antiquities, dated from Amman, June the 6th, reference 18/3/371, saying:

"A provisional division of the Qumran Cave IV manuscript fragments has now been made, and I enclose a list of the pieces which have been allotted to your institution. A few minor changes may be necessary as a result of further study or the acquisition of further material, but the main outline will remain unchanged. There will also be some very small, unidentified fragments which will be divided when final study is complete".

(With this letter was enclosed a list of manuscript pieces headed, "McGill University".)[355]

In April of this year, I visited Jordan, and studied the McGill collection, and expressed myself as highly satisfied with the work of editing and the progress of the project towards publication. In the company of Mr. Yusef Sa'ad, the Director of the Palestine Archaeological Museum, I visited Amman and was granted the privilege of an interview with His Excellency, the Minister of Education, Sheikh Shangity,[356] and the Acting Director of Antiquities, Dja Bey Rifa'i. I was received with the utmost courtesy, and in conversation received assurances both from the Acting Director and His Excellency the Minister, that it was the Government's intention to issue a permit for the export of the fragments belonging to the McGill collection.

In his letter to me of the 4th of June, referred to previously, Fr. de Vaux now informs me that the MSS will be ready for distribution at any time after the end of this present month, June 1960. Fr. de Vaux says: [end page 2]

"This work in the Palestine Archaeological Museum on the fragments themselves is now drawing to an end, and the MSS which fall to your institution's lot, will be at your disposal at any time after the end of the current month, June 1960. A list of the texts in your lot was sent to you in 1956 by the Department of Antiquities of Jordan. This list had a provisional character, but subsequent study has necessitated very few changes in it. These will be pointed out to you at the moment when you take possession of your MSS; they are the results of either a better understanding of the texts, or of subsequent purchases of fragments."[357]

Fr. de Vaux also asks that we observe the following limitations of the use of the MSS allocation:

---

355 Harding to Scott, 6 June 1956, Letter #61.

356 Predominantly signed "Shingiti" in official correspondence. Also spelled "Shangiti" or "Shauqiti" in some of the letters.

357 De Vaux to Frost, 4 June 1960, Letter #98.

1. Public exhibition should only be made of texts already published.

2. No other scholar should be authorised to study or publish texts until the editio princeps has appeared.

3. No photographs of these unpublished texts should be given to other scholars until the editio princeps appears.

I wish to assure Your Excellency that McGill University agrees to such minor changes in the list of MSS allocated to this University as Fr. de Vaux himself shall advise, and that McGill University fully accepts the limitations placed on the use to be made of the MSS allotted to us.[358]

I now, therefore, make formal application for the issue of a permit for the export to Canada of the Qumran Cave IV MSS fragments allotted to this University, and in support of this application, I enclose photostat copies of the following documents:

1. Letter/
[end page 3].

1. Letter from Mr. G. Lankester Harding to Professor R.B.Y. Scott dated 30th of December 1953, reference 18/3/270.[359]

2. Letter from Mr. G. Lankaster Harding to Professor Scott dated 19th April 1954, reference 18/3/637.[360]

3. Letter from Mr. G. Lankaster Harding to Professor R.B.Y. Scott dated 6th of June 1956, reference 18/3/371, together with a list of fragments allocated to McGill University which accompanied that letter.[361]

---

358 These limitations appeared reasonable at the time when publication was assured to be imminent. However, they came to be a lightning rod in scholarly debate for the next three decades. See for example, Vermes, "Access to the Dead Sea Scrolls," 192–8. Note, however, that John Allegro was already troubled during the early years of editing by the limitations placed on the access to materials (cf. Brown, *John Marco Allegro*, 152–8).

359 Letter not preserved.
360 Harding to Scott, 19 April 1954, Letter #18.
361 Harding to Scott, 6 June 1956, Letter #61.

On receipt of the export permit, the representative of this University will accept delivery of the MSS from the President of the Board of Trustees, and from the Director of the Palestine Archaeological Museum, and will give the University's official receipt for them.

Assuring Your Excellency of the satisfaction of the University, and of myself on the happy conclusion of this matter of so great importance, I remain,

Yours truly,
Stanley B. Frost
Dean of the Faculty.

LETTER #100

Archive: IAA, Box 73, PAM 1117(b): Distributions of Institutions Dead Sea Scrolls.

13 June 1960   Montreal

Dear Father de Vaux,

Before Dean Frost left this morning for meetings in the United States, he asked me to reply to you letter of June 4th, and to say that he apologises for the fact that he himself was not able to acknowledge it.

Your letter arrived on Friday, June 10, and immediately the Dean wrote to the Director of Antiquities requesting an export permit in the terms of the enclosed copy.

Whether Principal James or the Dean or some other representative comes to Jerusalem and on what date, will depend on the reply received in answer to the request for the permit, and as soon as the Dean learns more, he will write to you at once.

In the meantime, he has asked me especially to make clear to you the sense of gratitude he feels towards you for all your kind offices undertaken on behalf of the University.

Yours sincerely,
Alice P. Baird
Secretary to Dean Frost

LETTER #101

Archive: IAA, Box 73, PAM 1117(b): Distributions of Institutions Dead Sea Scrolls.

7 July 1960   Montreal

Dear Père de Vaux,

I was very pleased to receive your recent letter telling us of the release of the fragments on July the 1st, and as I think my secretary informed you, I managed to get a letter off straight away to the Department of Antiquities before leaving home on a trip.

I have not received an answer to my letter, and I shall be away from the office from now until the end of August, and will not myself be able to pursue the matter further until I return. I am, however, writing again to the Director, and hope that by the end of August I shall have heard from his department.[362] In the meantime, I would be extremely grateful if you would watch the McGill interests, and keep us informed of any major developments. I will write you again next month and let you know where we stand in this very important matter. I trust that Mr. Sa'ad has been able to procure the necessary boxes for the transport of the fragments, and once we get the export permit, I hope that we can make arrangements for bringing them to this country.

With every good wish,
Yours sincerely,
Stanley B. Frost
Dean.

---

362 The second letter is not preserved. According to Frost to minister of education, 23 November 1960, Letter #106, the second letter was sent on 5 August 1960. On 28 September, Frost sent a telegram to de Vaux: "Have received no reply to my two letters to department seeking export permit stop Have you any information." Frost received a reply from Yusif Sa'ad indicating the de Vaux was away and that he would write (IAA Archives, Box 73, PAM 1117(b): Distributions of Institutions Dead Sea Scrolls).

LETTER #102

Archive: IAA, Box 73, PAM 1117(b): Distributions of Institutions Dead Sea Scrolls.

2 October 1960   Jerusalem

Cher Professeur Frost,

Je trouve, en venant passer le Dimanche à Jérusalem,[363] votre telegramme de 27 sept., dont Yuseif Saad vous a déjà accuse réception.[364]

Je ne suis pas étonné que vos deux lettres au Département des Antiquités soient restées sans réponse. L'affaire desfragments de la Grotte 4 acheté par les Institutions étrangères a été portée devant le Cabinet des Ministres qui a pris le décision de refuser l'exportation decesfragments, qui doivent rester en Jordanie, et de rembourser les Institutions.[365] Mais cette décision n'est pas entrée en vigueur jusqu'ici parce que l'Ambassadeur des Etats-Unis pour MacCormick Seminary et l'Ambassadeur de Grande Bretagne pour Manchester ont élevé des protestations et cherchent à faire revenir le Gouvernement sur sa décision, qui est une rupture injustifiable de la parole donnée.[366]

---

363 From 1 September until 22 October 1960, de Vaux was directing the ninth season of excavation at Tell el-Far'ah (North). See de Vaux, "Les Fouilles de Tell el-Far'ah: Rapport préliminaire sur les 7ᵉ, 8ᵉ, 9ᵉ campagnes, 1958–1960," 557–92.

364 The telegram and Sa'ad's response are preserved in IAA Archives, Box 73, PAM 1117(b): Distributions of Institutions Dead Sea Scrolls.

365 Decision Reference No. 26/A/1/6937, 28 July 1960 (IAA Archives, Box 73, PAM 1117(b): Distributions of Institutions Dead Sea Scrolls).

366 Sir Charles Hepburn Johnson (1912–1986) was the British ambassador from 1956 to 1959. He was succeeded in 1959 by Minister John Patrick Edward Chandos Henniker-Major, 8th Baron Henniker (1916–2004), who served as ambassador between 1960 and 1962. De Vaux will suggest an appeal to Johnson but he had by then already departed for a new posting.

Sheldon Tibbets Mills (1924–2007) served as U.S. ambassador to Jordan from 1959 until 1961. Mills's letters to Jordanian officials are preserved in the IAA archives. On 22 August 1960, he wrote to Jordanian prime minister, Hazza al-Majali, at his surprise on discovering a newspaper article in the *Falastin* (29 July 1960) reporting that the government would be retaining the Scrolls and not honouring its agreements with the foreign institutions. Mills met with then director of antiquities for Jordan, Dr Awni Khalil Dajani, who confirmed the report. He again wrote to the prime minister on 25 August

L'affaire n'est donc pas terminée et nous gardons un bon espoir que vos droits seront reconnus. Pour aider a ces négociations et parce que l'Ambas[sadeur] de d4Angleterre défend en Jordanie les intérets canadiens, je vous serais reconnaissant d'envoyer à l'Ambassadeur d'Angleterre à Amman une copie de la lettre que vous avez envoyée au Département des Antiquités – et qui était parfaite – avec duplicat des pièces jointes. Vous pouvez y ajouter une réference importante: j'ai retrouvé que, le 28 décembre 1957, une décision de Cabinet des Ministres a confirmé les engagements pris en 1953.[367] L'Ambassadeur actuel, Sir Charles Johnston, qui a engagé activement cette affaire, quitter Amman pour un nouveu poste le 24 octobre.[368] L'affaire sera suivie par son successeur, mais il serait avantageux que vos documents arrivent à Amman avant son départ.

Je vous prie de croire, cher Professeur Frost, à l'expression de mes sentiments distingués,

Roland de Vaux, O. P.

1960 of his disappointment, asking that the issue be reconsidered and indicating the poor sentiment that would be created for Jordan among archaeologists and educators abroad (cf. Mills to prime minister, 25 August 1960 and 28 August 1960, IAA Archives, Box 73, PAM 1117: Dead Sea Scrolls (cave no. 4), jacket 1).

The Arab language press should not be underrated as an important player in Jordan's move to nationalize the scrolls; see Silberman, *The Hidden Scrolls*, 149–50.

367 An inventory list of the contents of IAA Archives, Box 73, PAM 1117: Dead Sea Scrolls (cave no. 4), jacket 1, dated 4 December 1960, includes a reference to the resolution, but a copy of the resolution is not included. However, a copy of the minutes of a PAM trustees meeting, dated 30 December 1957, included in the file, corroborates de Vaux's statement.

368 He became governor of Aden and high commissioner of South Arabia (1959–62).

LETTER #103

Archive: McGill, RG34, Container: 001, File 6: Dead Sea Scrolls.

12 October 1960 Montreal

Dear Bob:[369]

I think I ought to keep you informed about what is happening to the Dead Sea fragments. I have received a letter today[370] from Pere DeVaux, in which he says that the Council of Ministers have definitely decided to hold them in Palestine, but that owing to representations from the Ambassador of Britain and of the U.S., the Council are giving the matter second thought, I have written to the British Ambassador at Amman[371] and given him full information with regard to our position in the matter, and also to the Canadian Ambassador at Beirut.[372] I am seeing the principal tomorrow and will discuss with him the advisability of making contact with the Jordanian Ambassador at Washington. If any further information comes to hand or the situation developes promisingly I will let you know. I have not forgotten that you said that if we do ever receive these scrolls you would like to be present at any function we have, either receiving them or putting them on show or whatever it may be. We should be certainly glad to have you with us on such an occasion.
[paragraph removed related to the activities of the Council of Graduate Studies in Religion]
I hope that you will be at the Council[373] and that I shall have the pleasure of meeting you again then, I have a very [end page 1] fine slide of you and Bob Slater,[374] looking like a couple of overworked, or perhaps out of work

---

369 R.B.Y. Scott.

370 De Vaux to Frost, 2 October 1960, Letter #102.

371 No copy of the letter is preserved.

372 In January 1958 Paul André Beaulieu became Canada's first ambassador to Lebanon and served there until 1963.

373 The excluded paragraph indicates that the meetings would be held on 12 November 1960.

374 Robert Henry Lawson Slater was a contemporary of Scott at McGill and had use of Scott's office after he left for Princeton (cf. Scott to Frost, 13 May 1958, Letter #82). Slater left McGill for Harvard in 1958.

gardeners,³⁷⁵ which does you both very great credit. I have also not yet had an opportunity to show you my Jordan slides and I would very much like to do so at some time. I hope both you and Mrs. Scott³⁷⁶ are well and we send you our friendliest greetings.

Yours sincerely,
Stanley B. Frost,
Dean of the Faculty.

LETTER #104

Archive: McGill, RG2, Container: 0254, File 7576: Divinity: Dead Sea Scrolls.
McGill, RG4, Container: 239, File: Birks, John Henry – Collection, Judean Manuscripts – Dead Sea Scrolls.

22 October 1960   Amman

To: 1. University of Manchester, England
    2. McGill University, Montreal, Canada
    3. University of Heidelberg, Germany
    4. Vatican Library, Rome
    5. McCormick Theological Seminary, Chicago, U.S.A.

Dear Sir:

It is kindly requested that you supply this Department with a statement showing the funds which your institution has paid to the account of the Department of Antiquities for the Torah-ic scrolls discovered in the caves of Qumran. This statement should also show the method of payment used, the kind of foreign currency, the name and address of the recipient. It should be backed by official vouchers. This is required in order to enter such payments in the financial registers of this Department.

We have found it difficult to gather this information because neither the registers of the Ministry of Finance, nor of the Comptroller of the Department

---

375 Scott's children, in phone interviews in July 2007, indicated that it was common for members of the Faculty of the Divinity to gather near the Scott's family home in the Eastern Townships of Quebec.

376 Kathleen Cordingley Scott (1900–1979).

of Antiquities, nor of our accounts with the Ottoman Bank show any record of any payments made by you for the above mentioned purpose.

Yours sincerely,
Minister of Education
By: Department of Antiquities
Sgd: M. Shauqiti[377]

Copy to: Ambassador of U.S.A., Amman
Ambassador of U.K., Amman
Ambassador of Germany, Amman
Ambassador of Italy, Amman[378]

LETTER #105

Archive: McGill, RG4, Container: 239, File: Birks, John Henry – Collection, Judean Manuscripts – Dead Sea Scrolls.

2 November 1960   Montreal

Dear Mr. Grimson,[379]

I am sending the copy of the translation of the letter from the Ministry of Education at Amman, Jordan.[380] Having looked through our files, I can at least give you the following information.

1. The cheque for $5,000.00 described as "a university cheque" was sent on the 4th of March, 1954, by R.B.Y. Scott to G. Lankester Harding, the then Director of the Department of Antiquities of Jordan.

2. A bank draft for $10,363.00 described as "on New York" was similarly sent on April the 8th, 1954.

---

377 Predominantly signed "Shingiti" in official correspondence. Also spelled "Shangiti" or "Shangity" in some of the letters.

378 Canada did not have an embassy in Jordan at the time, hence the lack of a copy to a Canadian ambassador in Amman.

379 Comptroller's office at McGill.

380 Previous letter preserved only in translation. Original most likely in Arabic.

3. A "draft number 34764" for $4,200.00 was sent on December 29, 1955.

4. A letter dated the 16th of March, 1954, from Mr. Harding acknowledges receipt of the cheque for $5,000.00[381]

5. A letter from R.B.Y. Scott says that Mr. Bentley wishes to have receipts showing what McGill has paid so far and Scott's letter is dated April 8th, 1954.[382]

6. Correspondence of 19th of April, 1954, mentions a receipt being enclosed in a letter from Harding to Scott.[383]

These are all the facts that I can ascertain from the files but we appear to have no actual receipts. I hope the University records for 1954 are still intact and that you will be able to provide what the Minister is asking for.

Yours sincerely,
Stanley B. Frost, Dean.

LETTER #106

Archive: McGill, RG4, Container: 239, File: Birks, John Henry – Collection, Judean Manuscripts – Dead Sea Scrolls.

23 November 1960   Montreal

TO: Dean S. B. Frost   FROM: Comptroller's Office
      Faculty of Divinity   SUBJECT: Judean Manuscripts

In reply to your letter of November 2nd, I enclose herewith two sets of photocopies including all information available in our office covering payments and receipt of payments to the Director of the Department of Antiquities of Jordan.[384] I trust this will constitute adequate support for the receipt of the Manuscripts.

---

381 Harding to Scott, 16 March 1954, Letter #15.
382 Scott to Harding, 8 April 1954, Letter #17.
383 Harding to Scott, 19 April 1954, Letter #18.
384 Included in each set were, in the following order: Frost to Grimson, 2 November 1960, Letter #105; Shingiti to 1. University of Manchester, England, et al., 22 October 1960, Letter #104; Harding to Bentley, 5 January 1956, Letter #51; Bentley to Harding,

LETTER #107

Archive: McGill, RG2, Container: 0254, File 7576: Divinity: Dead Sea Scrolls.

23 November 1960   Montreal

Your Excellency,[385]

I am in receipt of your letter of the 22nd of October 1960, reference number 21-2-2-1492 in which you requested details of the payments made by this University to the Department of Antiquities in connection with the allocation of Scroll fragments discovered in the caves of Qumran. I submit the following information together with copies of the relevant documents.

1. In a letter dated the 4th of March 1954, Professor R.B.Y. Scott sent a cheque for $5,000. (U.S. funds) to Mr. G. Lankester Harding, then Director of Antiquities in the Kingdom of Jordan.[386] Attached sheet numbered 'McGill 1' is a copy of the counterfoil of the cheque issued on March 4th, 1954 in favour of 'G. Lankester Harding'. On the 16th of March 1954, Mr. Harding acknowledged receipt of the cheque, the copy of which acknowledgement is attached, numbered 'McGill 2'.[387]

2. On the 8th of April 1954, Professor Scott sent a further draft in favour of Mr. Harding in the amount of $10,363.52 (U.S. currency).[388] A copy of the requisition for this draft is attached, numbered 'McGill 3'. A copy of the University cheque which underwrote the draft is attached numbered 'McGill 4'. The difference in the two amounts arises from the exchange rate between Canadian and American dollars at that time.

---

29 December 1955, Letter #49; Bank of Montreal bank draft for $4200 USD in favour of Harding, 28 December 1955; receipt for same; receipt for $15,363.52 USD from Harding, 19 April 1954, Letter #18; Bank of Montreal bank draft for $10,156.25 USD in favour of Harding, 8 April 1954; receipt for same; Harding to Scott, 16 March 1954, Letter #15; Harding to Scott, 19 April 1954, Letter #18. These copies are preserved in the McGill University Archives (RG4, Container: 239, File: Birks, John Henry – Collection, Judean Manuscripts – Dead Sea Scrolls).

385 Sheikh M. Shingiti, minister of education for Jordan.
386 Letter not preserved.
387 Harding to Scott, 16 March 1954, Letter #15.
388 Scott to Harding, 8 April 1954, Letter #17.

3. On the 19th of April 1954, Mr. Harding wrote to Professor Scott acknowledging receipt of the cheque for $10,363.00,[389] the copy of which letter is numbered 'McGill 5'. He also enclosed a receipt for the total sum received by him up to that date, which was for $15,363.52 (U.S. currency). This is numbered 'McGill 6'. [end page 1]

4. On December the 29th, 1955, the Bursar and Secretary of the Board of Governors of this University, William Bentley, wrote to Mr. Harding[390] enclosing a Bank of Montreal draft, number 34764, in the amount of $4,200.00 in U.S. funds. The copy of Mr. Bentley's letter to Mr. Harding is numbered 'McGill 7'. The copy of the counterfoil of the University cheque on the Bank of Montreal is numbered 'McGill 8'. The copy of the Bank of Montreal requisition for the draft is numbered 'McGill 9'. On the 5th of January 1956, Mr. Harding wrote acknowledging receipt of the cheque for $4,200.00, and the copy of his letter is numbered 'McGill 10'.[391]

I trust that Your Excellency will find here all the information which he needs in order that the requisite export permit may be issued.[392] Your Excellency will recall that I wrote to the Department of Antiquities on June 10, 1960 requesting the issue if such a permit,[393] and that I wrote again on August 5, 1960 saying that I had received no reply to my previous letter.[394] Your letter of the 22nd of October[395] makes no reference to my previous letters nor to the issuance of a permit, but I trust that you now have full and sufficient information in order that such a permit may be issued forthwith.

Yours truly,
Stanley B. Frost,
Dean, Faculty of Divinity

---

389 Harding to Scott, 19 April 1954, Letter #18.
390 Bentley to Harding, 29 December 1955, Letter #49.
391 Harding to Bentley, 5 January 1956, Letter #51.
392 The previous day, the national press had reported that McGill would not be getting its fragments (cf. Stanley Twardy, "No Fragments for McGill: The Missing Link Between Judaism and Jesus," *Globe and Mail* (Toronto), 22 November 1960, 7).
393 Frost to the director of antiquities, 10 June 1960, Letter #99.
394 Letter not preserved.
395 Shingiti to 1. University of Manchester, England, et al., 22 October 1960, Letter #104.

LETTER #108

Archive: McGill, RG2, Container: 0254, File 7576: Divinity: Dead Sea Scrolls.

25 November 1960   Montreal

Dear Mr. Green,[396]

I am writing at the Principal's request on behalf of McGill University in the matter of the University's purchase of Dead Sea Scroll fragments in the years 1954 and 1956. The Principal, Dr. F. Cyril James, has been called to Quebec and will follow the matter up upon his return.

When the Scrolls were first discovered, the need arose for funds whereby they could be purchased from the Bedouin, housed in the Jerusalem Archaeological Museum,[397] photographed, edited and published by an international team of scholars. By the generosity of the Birks Manuscript Fund, McGill was able to contribute 19,363 U.S. dollars to the fund set up by the Museum and in return was allocated certain fragments of scrolls from Cave Four, with the clear understanding that export of the fragments to this country would be permitted. It was agreed that all the scroll fragments should remain in Jerusalem until the work of editing was complete, which was expected to be some time in 1956. The President of the Board of Governors of the Museum, Père de Vaux, was, however, not able to declare the work finished until June 30th, last.

I myself visited Jerusalem in April of this year and had a cordial interview with the Acting Director of Antiquities and with the Minister of Education, H.E. Sheikh Shangiti,[398] at which I was assured once again that export of the McGill allocation of fragments would be permitted once the editorial work was complete.

I wrote on June 10th requesting the permit and again in August but received no reply until on November 12th I received a letter asking for details of all our financial transactions with regard to the Scrolls.[399] I have furnished the Minister with complete details and have again requested an export permit.

---

396 Howard Green (1896–1989), Canadian minister of external affairs from 1959 to 1963.

397 PAM.

398 Predominantly signed "Shingiti" in official correspondence. Also spelled "Shangiti," "Shangity," or "Shauqiti" in some of the letters.

399 Dated 22 October 1960, Letter #104.

There have been strong and persistent rumours that the [end page 1] Jordanian Government intends to renege on the agreement and pay the five institutions (the universities of Manchester, Heidelberg, McCormick Seminary Chicago, McGill and the Vatican) the amounts they subscribed to the Scrolls fund.

The University has a full legal claim to the allocation made to it in 1954 and does not intend to forgo its right to these fragments. They are of considerable interest to Biblical scholars throughout the world and to have this collection in Canada would greatly increase the quality of the work done here, besides attracting scholars and visitors from far afield. McGill's contribution was prompt and timely when it was greatly needed, and was I believe the largest made. Without this help, the Museum authorities would not have been able to recover the scrolls from the Bedouin. We have therefore not only a legal but also a strong moral right to our allocation of fragments.

I raised the matter with Mr. Arnold Smith,[400] before he returned to Cairo recently, and he advised me to communicate with M. Paul Beaulieu, who has already been extremely helpful. Copies of the correspondence are attached to this letter.

The University is prepared to give the firmest undertaking that once the allocation has been received it will not part with any of the fragments to any other person or institution whatsoever. Since McGill has the only Islamic Institute in North America, and since the Faculty of Divinity has seen fit to appoint a practising Muslim as Visiting Fellow to write a critique of Christian Ethic from the Muslim point of view, it will be readily recognised that we have a deep and sympathetic appreciation for the situation of the Arab nations.[401] We believe, however, that this partial distribution of the Scrolls will in no way lessen the importance of the Jerusalem Collection and will be of immense service to Biblical studies in North America.

I am therefore writing to request that if it see fit, the Canadian Government should make representations to the Jordanian Government on behalf of this University to the end that a permit should be issued for the export of the

---

400 Arnold Cantwell Smith (1915–1994), Canadian ambassador to the United Arab Republic from 1958 to 1961 and the first secretary-general of the Commonwealth (1965–1975). His relationship to McGill was firmly established as his brother, Wilfred Cantwell Smith, was long a member of the Faculty of Divinity.

401 McGill's Institute of Islamic Studies was founded in 1952 by Wilfred Cantwell Smith. The visiting scholar was Isma'il Raji al-Faruqi.

fragments allocated to it at the time of the considerable contribution from the Birks Manuscript Fund.

Yours truly,
Stanley B. Frost,
Dean, Faculty of Divinity

A response from Green was received on 7 December 1960. He recommended "quiet diplomacy" in connection with representatives of the other purchasing institutions. Mostly, it appears, he was trying to avoid the lodging of a formal challenge by the Government of Canada. He was of the opinion that in considering how McGill's "concern to secure delivery of the Scroll fragments [could] best be furthered [it could be assumed] that the Jordanian authorities [were] prepared to be co-operative in working out mutually satisfactory arrangements, provided that special considerations which they regard[ed] as essential to their interests [could] be met." Given that their "special considerations" were maintaining ownership of the scrolls in Jordan, Green's response was not particularly helpful to Frost, (Green to Frost, 7 December 1960, McGill University Archives, RG2, Container: 0179, File 6243: Divinity: DSS & Birks Donation).

LETTER #109

Archive: IAA, Box 73, PAM 1117(b): Distributions of Institutions Dead Sea Scrolls.

30 March 1961   Montreal

Your Excellency,[402]

I wrote to you last on November 23, 1960 in reply to your letter of October 22, 1960, reference number 21-2-2-1492. Your Excellency will recall that I enclosed copies of all the documents relating to the financial transactions which took place between this University and the then Director of Antiquities.[403]

I earnestly hope that the Government of the Hashemite Kingdom is now in a position to issue an export permit which would enable this University to receive the Dead Sea Scroll fragments allotted to it in 1954. I am planning to travel to your country in July next, and would be glad to receive an assurance that the

---

402 Sheikh M. Shingiti, minister of education for Jordan.
403 Frost to Shingiti, 23 November 1960, Letter #107.

necessary permit will be made available so that I may arrange for the transport of the fragments to this country. I wish to repeat that the University is ready to give a solemn undertaking never to dispose of these fragments to any other party whatsoever.[404]

Yours faithfully,
Stanley B. Frost
Dean of the Faculty

LETTER #110

Archive: IAA, Box 73, PAM 1117(b): Distributions of Institutions Dead Sea Scrolls.

30 March 1961   Montreal

Dear Père de Vaux,

I enclose a copy of a letter which I have today written to His Excellency, the Minister of Education enquiring whether if I travel to Jordan during the summer I may hope to receive an export permit for the McGill Scroll fragments.[405] I have had no communication from the Minister since I sent him copies of the financial transactions between this University and Mr. Lankester Harding. The purpose of my letter is to seek a response of some sort from the Government, but if they should reply that the permit will be forthcoming I should most certainly be prepared to go and fetch the Scrolls. If you have any fresh information or any advice to give I would be very happy to receive it.

I trust that you are in good health and assure you of my continued cordial good wishes.

Yours sincerely,
Stanley B. Frost
Dean of the Faculty

---

404 The tone of this, and the previous letter (Frost to Green, 25 November 1960, Letter #108), clearly indicates that Frost suspects fear on the part of the Jordanian government that McGill would consider disposing of the fragments in favour of the State of Israel.

405 Frost to Shingiti, 30 March 1961, Letter #109.

LETTER #111

Archive: IAA, Box 73, PAM 1117(b): Distributions of Institutions Dead Sea Scrolls.

30 March 1961   Montreal

Dear Mr. Sa'ad,

I am happy to greet you at this Easter season of the year and I trust that you continue in good health. I have several times during this past year looked back on my visit to Jerusalem a year ago and I recall my visit to Amman in your company with the very greatest pleasure. I hope that the affairs of the Museum are in good order and that all goes very well with you.

In order that you may be informed as to what I am doing in an attempt to procure the much desired export permit for the McGill fragments, I am enclosing a copy of a letter which I have today written to His Excellency, the Minister of Education.[406] I have also written to Père de Vaux in order to keep him informed. Any further information or advice which you have to give I would be happy to receive.

With renewed assurances of my good wishes for you and for the Museum,
I am,
Yours sincerely,
Stanley B. Frost
Dean of the Faculty

---

[406] Frost to Shingiti, 30 March 1961, Letter #109.

LETTER #112

Archive: McGill, RG2, Container: 0274, File 8260: Divinity: Dead Sea Scrolls.

13 June 1961   Amman

To: University of Manchester, England
     McGill University, Canada
     Heidelberg University, Germany
     Vatican Library, Rome
     McCormick Theological Institute, America.

Gentlemen:

Greetings!
   Enclosed herewith please find an exact copy of the resolution of the Cabinet as communicated to me by the Prime Minister's letter No. 26/1/2/5691 dated 8 May 1961, regarding the Dead Sea Scrolls, in answer to your un-numbered letters dated 3 March 1961, 10 June 1960[407] and 5 August 1960.[408] I shall be grateful if you will kindly inform me in which manner you would like to be refunded and furnish me with a complete address.

Yours sincerely,
M. SHINGITI[409]
Minister of Education and Antiquities[410]

Enclosure:

Department of Antiquities
Amman
Ref.No. 26/1/2/5691
Date: 8 May 1961

---

   407 Frost to the director of antiquities, 10 June 1960, Letter #99.

   408 Second letter sent by Frost, but not preserved (cf. reference to it in Frost to Shingiti, 23 November 1960, Letter #107).

   409 Predominantly signed "Shingiti" in official correspondence. Also spelled "Shangiti," "Shangity," or "Shauqiti" in some of the letters.

   410 The Department of Antiquities fell under the authority of the Ministry of Education.

H.E. The Minister of Education and Antiquities.

The Cabinet has reviewed all the resolutions passed by them since 1953 on the subject of the Dead Sea scrolls. After study, the Cabinet arrived at the following conclusions:

1. Because of their antiquity-importance as well as their scientific, historical and religious value, it is necessary to keep these scrolls in the Kingdom.

2. The funds, which have been previously paid by educational establishments for the purpose of exporting the scrolls, shall be returned.

3. Financial assistance for the collection of the scrolls in the Kingdom shall henceforth be accepted as free offer in exchange for such facilitation as the Government may grant to the giver for the study of the scrolls, their photography or their publication in general service to history and knowledge. The Jordanian Government shall, however, be entitled to prevent, in such time and circumstances as it sees fit, the exposition of these scrolls outside the Hashemite Kingdom of Jordan, in agreement with the offering institutions.

The reason for this is that these scrolls constitute an indivisible part of the history of Jordan in particular and of the spiritual legacy of all mankind. This being the case, neither the antique treasure as a whole nor any part thereof shall be allowed to be lost through transfer of property rights to any party.

Yours truly,
THE PRIME MINISTER[411]

---

[411] Bahjat al-Talhouni (1913–1994) served four terms as Jordanian prime minister: 1960–62; 1964–65; 1967–March 1969; and August 1969–1970.

LETTER #113

Archive: McGill, RG2, Container: 0274, File 8260: Divinity: Dead Sea Scrolls.

6 July 1961   Montreal

Your Excellency,[412]

I acknowledge the receipt of your letter 21/2/8/1698 enclosing a copy of a memorandum from the Prime Minister numbered 26/1/2/5691, communicating a resolution of the Jordanian Cabinet relating to the Dead Sea Scrolls.[413]

I note in particular the wording of the last sentence of the first paragraph of section 3: 'The Jordanian Government shall, however, be entitled to prevent, in such time and circumstance as it sees fit, the exposition of these scrolls outside the Hashemite Kingdom of Jordan, in agreement with the offering institutions'.

I wish to enquire whether the interpretation is correct that the Jordanian Government, while retaining full legal possession of the fragments originally allotted to this University, would be prepared in lieu of returning the money paid by us in 1954–55 to allow the collection to come to McGill on long loan, in order that it may be displayed to the public and further studied at this University.

I would remind Your Excellency that Canada as a young and growing nation needs the help in cultural affairs of older peoples with a richly endowed past. We are distant from the Near East and our scholars cannot easily travel to Jordan and spend long periods there in this study. With the help of this collection, we could train students in the initial stages of Dead Sea Scroll scholarship, and while they would certainly have to complete their education in Jerusalem they could make a very good beginning here, by familiarising themselves with these fragments.

We should, of course, take adequate steps to ensure the safety and well-being of the fragments sent to us on loan by the Jordanian authorities. I shall await Your Excellency's reply with interest.

Yours sincerely,
Stanley B. Frost, Dean.

---

412 The letter is addressed at the top of the page to: "His Excellency M. Shingiti; Minister of Education and Finance; The Hashemite Kingdom of Jordan; Amman, Jordan."

413 Shingiti to Manchester et al., 13 June 1961, Letter #112.

LETTER #114

Archive: McGill, RG2, Container: 0274, File 8260: Divinity: Dead Sea Scrolls.

6 October 1961   Montreal

Dear Sir,[414]

Your letter of August 16th last arrived during my absence from the University,[415] and since my return I have been waiting for a reply to my last letter to the Government of Jordan.[416] I enclose a copy of that letter from which you will see that I have proposed on behalf of the University that if the Government felt itself unable to relinquish legal title to the McGill collection, it might consider retaining legal title but allow McGill to house the collection on a permanent loan, or long loan basis. As you will see, I wrote that letter on July 6, but still have not received a reply.

I enclose also a copy of a further letter to the Jordanian Minister of Education in which I renew the proposal, and request the decision of the Authorities.[417] If the Ambassador at Beirut, or anyone else who is charged to conduct Canadian affairs in Amman, could be informed of our requests to the Jordanian Authorities and could draw their attention to the desirability of a settlement of this matter, we would welcome this help very greatly.

We appreciate the interest which the Department has taken in this matter.

Yours sincerely,
Stanley B. Frost, Dean

---

414 The under-secretary of State for External Affairs, Canada.

415 The letter from the under-secretary for External Affairs indicated that the Canadian government understood from the Jordanians that the scroll material would be kept in Jordan and the institutions reimbursed. The Canadian government hoped that the process of settling the financial matters was under way (Under-Secretary of State for External Affairs to Frost, 16 August 1961, McGill Archives, RG 2, Container: 0274, File 8260: Divinity: Dead Sea Scrolls).

416 Frost to Shingiti, 6 July 1961, Letter #113.

417 Letter not preserved. According to Frost to Shingiti (19 March 1962, Letter #115), the letter was dated the previous day, 5 October 1961.

A response was received on 18 October 1961 from the office of the Under-Secretary of State for External Affairs indicating that Frost's suggestions of a loan of material for exhibit was in line with Jordan's decision but that "'permanent' or 'long-term' loan of the fragments may perhaps go farther than the Government intended," (Department of External Affairs to Frost, 18 October 1961, McGill Archives, RG2, Container: 0274, File 8260: Divinity: Dead Sea Scrolls).

LETTER #115

Archive: McGill, RG34, Container: 0001, File 6: Dead Sea Scrolls.
       McGill, RG2, Container: 0274, File 8260: Divinity: Dead Sea Scrolls.

19 March 1962   Montreal

Your Excellency,[418]

    I received from your office on June 13th, 1961 (Reference Number 21/2/8/1698 and 26/1/2/5691) the letter in which you informed this University of the decision of your Government to retain the Dead Sea Scrolls in the Hashemite Kingdom of Jordan.[419] I replied on July 6th suggesting an alternative arrangement whereby the Jordanian Government, while retaining full legal possession of the fragments originally allotted to this University would allow the collection to come to McGill on long-loan.[420] On October 5th, since I had received no reply to my letter of July 6th, I wrote again, asking for your Government's reply to my proposal.[421]
    I have not received any reply either to the letter of July 6th or that of October 5th, and therefore I have no alternative to request the return of the monies paid by this University. In my letter of November 23rd, 1960, I detailed the amounts as being:

4th March 1954	$ 5,000.00
8th April 1954	10,363.52
29th December 1955	4,200.00.

---

  418 The letter is addressed to: "His Excellency M. Shingiti; Minister of Education and Finance; The Hashemite Kingdom of Jordan; Amman, Jordan."
  419 Shingiti to Manchester et al., 13 June 1961, Letter #112.
  420 Frost to Shingiti, 6 July 1961, Letter #113.
  421 Letter not preserved.

At the same time, I enclosed full documentation together with copies of the requisite receipts.

I now request that the full amount of $19,563.52 be paid into the account of McGill University, the Bank of Montreal in U.S. funds, in Montreal, or an equivalent amount in Sterling at the Bank of Montreal, London. Since we have important educational projects for which these funds are urgently needed, we would be grateful if Your Excellency would expedite this payment.[422]

Yours sincerely,
Stanley B. Frost, Dean.

LETTER #116

Archive: McGill, RG34, Container: 0001, File 6: Dead Sea Scroll.

20 March 1962   Montreal

Dear Bob,[423]

You will, I know, be very disappointed to hear that McGill has given up hope of negotiating further with the Jordanian Government and that we are now asking for the return of the monies paid through you in 1954 and '55. Since you are to be out there this year[424] I want you to be kept fully informed of the situation, and I enclose a copy of my latest letter to the Minister of Education. If I receive a reply I will let you know and if I have heard nothing by the time you get out there, I will ask you to explore whether anything can be done from that end of things. I have also written to the Under Secretary of State for External Affairs and hope that we may have the assistance of the Ambassador at

---

422 The public would be informed that the wait for the scrolls was over, on 21 March 1962: "Worth Thousands: Dead Sea Scrolls Now Dead Secret," *Montreal Star*, 21 March 1962, 10.

423 R.B.Y. Scott.

424 Scott was annual professor at ASOR Jerusalem in 1962–63. During that period he participated in the third season of excavation at 'Arâq el-Emîr. He arranged to have the excavation funded, in part, by Princeton. See Lapp, "The Second and Third Campaigns at 'Arâq el-Emîr," 8–39.

Damascus.[425] I suspect if we do receive our money that it will not be for a long time yet.

I hope very much that you are fully recovered from your recent illness and that you are looking forward to your Palestine trip. Please give my very warm greetings to your wife, and say that we would be very glad if during the summer we were able to see her.

With every good wish,
Yours,
Stanley[426]

LETTER #117

Archive: McGill, RG34, Container: 0001, File 6: Dead Sea Scrolls.

March 26, 1962   Princeton

Dear Stanley,

Thank you for your letter of March 20,[427] enclosing a copy of your letter of March 19 addressed to the Minister of Education and Finance of Jordan.[428] There has recently been a change in the composition of the Cabinet, but I do not remember if this particular ministry remained in the same hands.[429]

I am glad you are going to keep me informed of the situation, and I am hoping that during my expected stay in Jordan of six or seven months I may at least be able to get the picture clear. The failure of the minister to reply to your letters is annoying, to put it mildly, and I am not surprised that McGill has decided to press for the return of the monies sent under an express agreement to permit export of the scroll materials after a specified time. At the same time, I find it hard to believe that the Jordan Government will be able to find the money for repayment, even granted (which I doubt) that they should be willing to do so.

The plain fact is that the whole business has been caught up in Jordanian politics, and especially in the nationalist re-action which resulted in the ousting

---

425 The comment is erroneous. In this period the Canadian ambassador in Beirut, Paul Beaulieu, was the representative to Jordan, Lebanon, and Syria.

426 Stanley B. Frost.

427 Frost to Scott, 20 March 1962, Letter #116.

428 Frost to Shingiti, 19 March 1962, Letter #115.

429 Ibrahim Quattan became minister of education following the election.

of Harding and Glubb. It is a little like the situation of the Canadian authorities with respect to the Polish art treasures, so long as Duplessis was alive.[430] I have come round to the view that the best we can hope for is the acknowledgement that the scrolls purchased with the Birks gift belong to McGill University, though retained in Jordan; that they will be exhibited (or samples of them) in the Palestine Archaeological Museum as the McGill collection; and that McGill have a complete set of photographs of them. Finally, you will remember that de Vaux proposed (and, I think, the committee in charge agreed) that one of the volumes of <u>Discoveries in the Judaean Desert</u> should be published under the joint auspices of the Dept. of Antiquities, the Palestine Arch. Museum and McGill University. I would like to know what would be your view and that of Dr. James and Mr. Birks on such an arrangement, if it seems unlikely that the money paid will be repaid.

Thank you for your personal good wishes. I am back to full time work, but it will be some months yet before I am in full vigor. Incidentally, Kathleen[431] is going to accompany me to the Near East this time, and we shall be at Georgeville only briefly before sailing for England from Montreal on July sixth.

All best wishes,
R. B. Y. Scott.

LETTER #118

Archive: McGill, RG34, Container: 0001, File 6: Dead Sea Scrolls.

17 April 1962   Montreal

Dear Bob:[432]

[First paragraph deleted. Discussion of candidate for a position at McGill]

With regard to the affair in Jordan, our last communication to the Jordanian Government was to request the repayment of the monies.[433] Frankly I don't think we would be very interested in having the fragments displayed in the Jerusalem museum as the McGill collection at a cost of $20,000. I feel that the Government have treated us rather scurvily and if they do not wish to stand by

---

430 See notes to Scott to Birks, 1 July 1959, Letter #88.
431 Kathleen Cordingley Scott, R.B.Y. Scott's wife.
432 R.B.Y. Scott.
433 Frost to Shingiti, 19 March 1962, Letter #115.

their agreement then I think they should return the money which I could use very helpfully in other ways. I hope that I may yet hear from them in reply to my last letter, and as I sent copies to External Affairs perhaps they too will be delicately probing to see what the future holds,[434] I would, of course, still like to have the collection here, but failing that, it seems to me that we might well use the money in other ways.

I think you said you might be passing through Montreal before you go to Jordan, if so, I should of course be very glad to have discussion with you,

Yours as ever,
Stanley[435]

LETTER #119

Archive: McGill, RG34, Container: 0001, File 6: Dead Sea Scrolls.
McGill, RG2, Container: 0274, File 8260: Divinity: Dead Sea Scrolls.

20 June 1962

Your Excellency,[436]

In the year 1954 following upon the discovery of the Dead Sea Scrolls at Qumran, McGill University entered into an agreement with the then Director of Antiquities, Mr. G. Lankester Harding, whereby in return for contributions made towards the cost of editing the Scroll fragments in the possession of the Palestine Museum of Archaeology, this University was to receive a collection of the fragments.

The amounts paid were on the 4th of March 1954, $5,000.; on the 8th of April 1954, $10,363.52; and on the 29th of December 1955, $4,200. all in U.S. funds. When the Jordanian Government decided to retain the manuscripts in Jordan I wrote on November 23, 1960, giving full documentation of these payments together with copies of the requisite receipts.[437] In reply I received

---

434 By this point the letter from External Affairs dated 16 April 1962 had not yet arrived at McGill.

435 Stanley B. Frost.

436 The letter is addressed to: "His Excellency M. Shingiti, Minister of Education and Finance, The Hashemite Kingdom of Jordan, Amman, Jordan," yet, the content of this letter indicates that a new minister is intended to be addressed.

437 Frost to Shingiti, 23 November 1960, Letter #107.

from the office of the then Minister of Education and Finance, His Excellency M. Shingiti, a letter of June 13, 1961 (reference number 21–2–8–1698 and 26–1–2–5691) in which this University was formally informed of the decision of the Jordanian Government.[438] I replied on July 6th 1961, suggesting an alternative arrangement whereby the Jordanian Government while retaining full legal possession of the fragments originally allocated to this University would nevertheless allow the collection to come to McGill on long loan.[439]

Since I had received no reply I wrote again on October 5th 1961, requesting your Government's reaction to my proposal.[440] On March 19, 1962 again having received no reply I wrote requesting that the monies subscribed, by this University, that is, $19,363.52 U.S.[441] funds be paid into the account of McGill University either at the Bank of Montreal in Montreal, or in Sterling at the Bank of Montreal, London.[442] [end page 1]

Since we have important educational projects for which these funds are urgently needed, I would be grateful if Your Excellency would expedite this payment.

Yours sincerely,
Stanley B. Frost, Dean.

---

438 Shingiti to Manchester et al., 13 June 1961, Letter #112.

439 Frost to Shingiti, 6 July 1961, Letter #113.

440 Letter not preserved.

441 Erroneous calculation. The total was, in fact, 19,563.52 (cf. Dajani to Frost, 27 June 1962, Letter #123).

No mention is ever made of the money spent by Scott for the seventeen fragments purchased on his 1955 visit and turned over to Harding (cf. Scott to F. Cyril James et al., 15 June 1955, Letter #40).

442 Frost to Shingiti, 19 March 1962, Letter #115.

LETTER #120

Archive: McGill, RG34, Container: 0001, File 6: Dead Sea Scrolls.
McGill, RG2, Container: 0274, File 8260: Divinity: Dead Sea Scrolls.

20 June 1962   Montreal

Dear Dr. Dajani,[443]

You may remember that during your recent visit to Canada we met briefly in a television studio in Toronto and I recall our conversation with pleasure.

I am enclosing copies of letters which I have written to His Excellency Sheikh Ibrahim Quattan and to His Excellency Izziddin Mufti[444] asking that since it has become apparent that McGill will not be receiving the Scroll fragments the University should receive the return of the monies paid in 1954 and '55.

Anything that you can do to assist us in this matter will be very greatly appreciated.

Dr. R.B.Y. Scott who was active in this matter and who negotiated the payments while he was Professor of Old Testament Studies in this University is to be Visiting Professor at the American School of Oriental Studies in Jerusalem this year and will, I understand, be arriving in Jordan shortly. He is fully acquainted with the whole matter and would, I am sure, be ready to assist you with any further information which you may find helpful.

With every good wish,
Yours sincerely,
Stanley B. Frost, Dean.

---

443   Awni Dajani, director of antiquities, Jordan.

444   The minister of finance received an identical copy with a cover letter indicating that Frost wished that the minister "may become fully acquainted with the matter" (Scott to Minister of Finance, 20 June 1956, McGill University Archives, RG34, Container: 000, File 6: Dead Sea Scrolls; and RG2, Container: 0274, File 8260: Divinity: Dead Sea Scrolls).

LETTER #121

Archive: McGill, RG34, Container: 0001, File 6: Dead Sea Scrolls.

20 June 1962   Montreal

Dear Mr. Robertson,[445]

Thank you very much for your letter of June 13, 1962[446] referring to the negotiations between this University and the Jordanian Government in which we are seeking to obtain the return of funds paid by us in expectation of receiving a collection of Dead Sea Scroll fragments.

I am very happy to avail myself of the offer you make to despatch these letters by way of diplomatic bag to Beirut for forwarding to Jordan and I enclose copies of the letters together with the two originals for despatch.[447] I have also written to Dr. Dajani giving him copies of my letters to the two Ministers.

On behalf of the University I would like to express our appreciation of your interest in this matter.

Yours sincerely,
Stanley B. Frost, Dean.

---

445 Canadian under-secretary of state for External Affairs.

446 Letter not preserved.

447 Letters to Jordanian minister of education (Frost to Shingiti, 20 June 1962, Letter #119) and the minister of finance. The minister of finance received an identical copy with a cover letter indicating that Frost wished that the minister "may become fully acquainted with the matter" (Scott to Minister of Finance, 20 June 1956, McGill University Archives, RG34, Container: 000, File 6: Dead Sea Scrolls; and RG2, Container: 0274, File 8260: Divinity: Dead Sea Scrolls).

LETTER #122

Archive: McGill, RG34, Container: 0001, File 6: Dead Sea Scrolls.

20 June 1962   Montreal

Dear Bob,[448]

I do not know when you expect to arrive in Jerusalem, but I am sending this letter to await your arrival and with it copies of correspondence relating to the McGill Scroll fragments.[449]

The file of letters I enclose is as follows: a letter to the Minister of Education; a letter to the Minister of Finance; a letter to Dr. Awni Dajani and a letter to the Under-Secretary of State for External Affairs.[450]

I know that you will be disappointed to know that the fragments will not come to McGill but there does not now seem to be any possibility of obtaining them, and we can put the money to good use in other ways. I thought you would like to be kept up to date with the correspondence. I shall, of course, have to consult with the Birks Family Foundation to see what they would like done with the money if and when we receive it.

Will Oxtoby received his degree at your Spring Convocation the other day and is now turning his mind to fresh research. If you have any suggestions to make as to what we might put up to him I am sure he would be glad to receive them, or I would be happy to pass them on. I hope you have a thoroughly enjoyable year in Palestine and if you can find time to scribble a note, we shall look forward to hearing from you.

With every good wish,
Yours,
Stanley

---

448   R.B.Y. Scott.

449   Letter addressed to Scott at ASOR, Jerusalem.

450   All dated 20 June 1962 (Letters #119–21). The letter to the minister of finance was an identical copy with a cover letter indicating that Frost wished that the minister "may become fully acquainted with the matter" (Scott to Minister of Finance, 20 June 1956, McGill University Archives, RG34, Container: 000, File 6: Dead Sea Scrolls; and RG2, Container: 0274, File 8260: Divinity: Dead Sea Scrolls).

LETTER #123

Archive: McGill, RG34, Container: 0001, File 6: Dead Sea Scrolls.

27 June 1962   Amman

Dear Dr. Frost,

The monies your University had paid to Mr. Harding for buying Dead Sea Scrolls are ready since few months. The fragments are still in the hands of the Palestine Archaeological Museum up till now, but we are going to have them very soon, after which I will refund your money amounting 19,563.52$, and not 19,363.52$, a slight mistake in addition which is in your favour.

Since Prof. Scott is now in Jerusalem, I will negotiate with him, and ask his help in all matters relating to the subject.

I assure you that payment will be done us soon as we receive the fragments from the P.A.M. which will be done I hope sooner so as to let you use the money in important educational projects.

Yours sincerely,
Dr. Awni Dajani
Director of Antiquities

LETTER #124

Archive: McGill, RG2, Container: 0274, File 8260: Divinity: Dead Sea Scrolls.

7 September 1962   Montreal

Dear Sir:[451]

Thank you for your letter of August 30th last,[452] informing me that Mr. Munro of the Embassy in Beirut had delivered my letters to the Deputy Minister of Education in the Jordanian Government.

---

451 The under-secretary of state for External Affairs Canada.
452 Letter not preserved.

I very much appreciate the active interest of the External Affairs Department in the concerns of the University, and I will continue to keep you informed of further developments in the matter.

Yours sincerely,
Stanley B. Frost,
Dean.

LETTER #125

Archive: McGill, RG34, Container: 0001, File 6: Dead Sea Scrolls.

17 December 1962   Jerusalem

Dear Dr. Dajani:

You were good enough to send me a copy of your letter to Dean Frost, McGill University, dated 27th June 1962 (ref. 21/2/8/843), to which I replied[453] at once offering any help I could give in relation to the repayment to McGill University of $ 19,563.52 advanced for the purchase of scrolls from Qumran Cave IV.

Nearly six months have passed since then and, so far as I have been informed, the refund has not yet been sent, I have now learned that the McGill scrolls have been taken over from the Palestine Archaeological Museum on behalf of the Government, so that there is no longer any obstacle to the prompt repayment to McGill which you promised in your letter of June 27th.[454] I hope that you will give this matter your attention at the earliest possible time, in view of the long delay since that date. If I can be of assistance in any way, please let me know.

Yours sincerely,
R. B. Y. Scott

---

453 Letter not preserved.

454 The Jordanian authorities announced that the scroll material was to be moved from Jerusalem to Amman in September 1962 (cf. "Scrolls to Amman," *New York Times*, 30 Sept 1962, 30).

LETTER #126

Archive: McGill, RG34, Container: 0001, File 6: Dead Sea Scrolls.

8 April 1963   Montreal

Dear Bob,[455]

Thank you for finding time in the midst of clearing your business up in Jerusalem to write to me.[456] You will be glad to hear that the money has indeed arrived and I have had conversations with Mr. Birks as to what should be done with it.

He has decided that $5,000. of it should stay in the Faculty to gather a special collection of books, mss., photographs et cetera relating to the Dead Sea Scrolls and that the remainder amounting to some $15,000. should be paid into the United Theological College Building Fund. This was not quite what I had in mind as the best disposition of the money, but clearly the Birks Family Foundation had every right to decide, and I am very pleased indeed about the $5,000. for the D.S.S. Library. The other half of my mind is also very happy at the thought of the U.T.C. Building Fund being increased, since I am sure that it is becoming a matter of urgency that U.T.C. should be properly and worthily housed. Now that the Presbyterian College on the corner of University and Milton is nearing completion and the Diocesan College are launching an appeal to provide married quarters on the rear of their building, U.T.C. cannot afford to be left provided for as it is at present rather inadequately.[457]

Thank you very much indeed for all the care and trouble you have taken about this. We know in some ways it represents a personal disappointment that the fragments never came to McGill but the initiative you took eight years ago meant a very great deal for the Scrolls' project at that time and has continued to mean a great deal for the Faculty ever since. We appreciate your efforts most warmly and I am glad to have this opportunity of saying thank you. [end page 1]

I hope you have enjoyed a thoroughly profitable year in Jerusalem and that your European trip will be an enrichment both of mind and spirit. Owing to the Faith and Order Commission meeting at McGill in July[458] we shall be remaining

---

455 R.B.Y. Scott.

456 Letter not preserved.

457 UTC began its partnership with McGill in 1929. On the relationship between UTC and McGill University, see Markell, *The Faculty of Religious Studies*.

458 Meeting of the World Council of Churches.

put this summer, and have vague plans of finding a cottage in Georgeville and in this case I hope we may see something of you. In the meantime, I send my best regards to Mrs. Scott and wish you well in your further journeyings.

Yours sincerely,
Stanley

Appendix

Transcription of R.B.Y. Scott's Handlist of Qumran Cave Four Fragments purchased by McGill University as of May 1955

SCROLL FRAGMENTS from QUMRAN CAVE FOUR

Purchased with a contribution from McGill University, 1954, as the John Henry Birks Collection; listed by R.B.Y. Scott at the Palestine Archaeological Museum, Jerusalem, Jordan, May 1955.

- - - - - - - - - - - - - - - -

(NOTE: Sizes given are measurements in centimeters of rectangles which would contain pieces specified. Fragments noted as "matched" had been matched with pieces from other collections of Cave Four fragments at the time of listing)

	Plate Label	Size	Tentative Identification	Remarks
(1)	4Q Ex.^{e} (Plate 10) (*seder pesach?*)	6.5 x 8.5	Ex. 13:3, 5	Photo 41.163
(2)	4Q Num.^{a} (Plate 13b)	6.2 x 4.5	Num. 10:14-22	
(3)	4Q Gen.^{e}? (Plate 5)	4 x 2	-	
(4)	" " " "	2.5 x 2.2	Gen. 30:35-36	
(5)	4Q Gen.^{c} (Plate 3)	5 x 8	Gen. 41:6-11	Photo 41.151 matched
(6)	4Q Ex.ª (Plate 6)	4 x 3.4	Ex. 5:3-8	matched
(7)	4Q Lev.^{b} (Plate 12)	7.2 x 4.6	Lev. 3:8-11	Photo 41.187
(8)	4Q Isa.^{c}	14.5 x 6.5	((Isa. 23:10 (-24:15 (	matched Photo 41.676
(9)	" "	12.2 x 7.5		matched Photo 41.176 In 24:3 *YHVH* In palaeo-Heb.
(10)	4Q Isa.^{c}	6.2 x 3	Isa. 45:1-5	

(11)	4Q Deut.	10.7 x 7.5	Deut. 32; 40, 41c, 42d-43	matched
(12)	4Q Job (pal.Heb.)	4.5 X 3.5	Job 13:24-27	
(13)	4Q Isa.^{b}	7.2 x 3	Isa. 57:18-58:2	matched
(14)	4Q Isa.^{f}	4.7 x 4.7	Isa. 48:8-16	
(15)	4Q Deut. (palaeo-Heb.)	4.5 x 5	Deut. 23:13-14	Photo 645
(16)	" " " "	2.5 x 2.5	Deut. 18:14?	
(17)	" " " "	about 1 x 1	Deut. 32:10-11 OR Deut. 32:13-14	
(18)	" " " "	3 x 1.7	unidentified	
(19)	" " " "	about 1 x 1	"	
(20)	" " " "	about 1 x 1	"	
(21)	4Q Isa.^{a}	4.7 x 4.7	Isa. 12:5-14	matched
(22)	4Q Isa.^{b} (first plate)	3.2 x 1	Isa. 39:1-2	
(23)	" " " "	5 x 6	Isa. 39:5-40:4	
(24)	4Q Isa.^{b} (second plate)	8.5 x 8.7	Isa. 43:12-15 AND 44:19-28	Photo 41.281
(25)	" " " "	3.7 x 4	Isa. 42:2-7	" "
(26)	4Q Ps.^{c}	5 x 1.2	Ps. 52:10-11	
(27)	4Q Ex. ^{Bet} (palaeo-Heb.) (first plate)	8 x 8	Ex. 10:1ff.	Photo 41.388
(28)	" " " "	2 x 5	Ex. 18:19	" "
(29)	" " " "	2 x 2.2	Ex. 26:24-26	" "
(30)	" " " "	5.5 x 9	Ex. 23:5ff.	" "
(31)	" " " "	2.5 x 2.5	Ex. 16:18-20	" "
(32)	" " " "	3 x 2.5	Ex. 14:17?	" "
(33)	4Q Ex. ^{Bet} (palaeo-Heb.) (second plate)	4 x 1.7	unidentified	
(34)	4Q Ex. ^{Alef} (palaeo-Heb.) (first plate)	2 x 1.2	Ex. 18:4-5	Samaritan text Photo 41.513 matched
(35)	" " " "	2 x .7	Ex. 32:28-29	" " " "
(36)	" " " "	2.5 x .7	unidentified	Samaritan text Photo 41.513
(37)	" " " "	1.2 x 1.2	"	" " " "
(38)	" " " "	.5 x .5	"	" " " "
(39)	4Q Ex. ^{Alef} (palaeo-Heb.) (second plate)	1 x 1	"	Samaritan Text Photo 41.641
(40)	" " " "	1 x 1	"	" " " "
(41)	" " " "	1 x 1	"	" " " "
(42)	" " " "	1 x 1	"	" " " "
(43)	" " " "	2 x 1	"	" " " "
(44)	" " " "	1.5 x 1	"	" " " "
(45)	" " " "	1.7 x 1	"	" " " "
(46)	4Q Ps.^{b}	17 x 5	Pss. 103:12-14, 20-21; AND 11:4-113:1	four columns
(47)	" "	1 x 1.5	Ps. 116:8-12	matched
(48)	4Q Ps.^{a}	6 x 7.2	Ps. 33:2-12 with traces of Pss. 35 and 36	Photo 41.188

(49)	" "	2.7 x 1.5	From Ps. 104	
(50)	4Q Jos.ª	2.7 x 1.5	Jos. 3:6 or 6:6	
(51)	" "	2.5 x .7	Jos. 8:8	
(52)	4Q Dan.	2.5 x 1.2	Dan. 5:13	
(53)	4Q Ex. (miscell. mss.)	2.8 x 5.5	Ex. 12:46-51	matched
(54)	" " " "	1.8 x 1.7	Ex. 21:6-8	
(55)	4Q Deut. (miscell. mss.)	3.6 x 3	Deut. 25:16-18	
(56)	4Q Num. (miscell. mss.)	3 x 2.5	Num. 11-17-18	
(57)	4Q Deut. (miscell. mss.) (second plate)	1.7 x 1.2	Deut. 33:8	
(58)	4Q Paraphr. (Paraphr. Is.)	4.5 x 2.8		
(59)	4Q Jer.	4.2 x 4.6	Jer. 8:2-3	thread at join of sheets
(60)	4Q Jer.ᶜ	8 x 6.7	from Jer. 30-31	almost illegible matched
(61)	4Q Dan.ª	14.5 x 10	Dan. 2:19ff.	matched Photo 52
(62)	4Q Dan.ᵇ	13 x 9.7	Dan. 6:8-10, 15-22	matched Photos 53 and 41.183
(63)	4Q Gen. (miscell. mss.)	7 x 3	Gen. 2:15-19	
(64)	" " " "	2.4 x 2.5	Gen. 48:5-7	
(65)	" " " "	4 x 2.5	unidentified	
(66)	4Q Sam.ª (Plate 38)	5.1 x 5	II Sam. 16:17-18	matched
(67)	4Q Sam.ª (Plate 39)	9.2 x 6.6 OR 13.7x 6.6	II Sam. 22:30-23:6	uncertain if this is one piece or two Photo 41.200
(68)	4Q Sam.ª (Plate 32)	2.2 x 1.6	I Sam. 14:28-30 (part of)	matched
(69)	4Q Sam.ª (Plate 35)	7 x 4.7	II Sam. 8:1-2 AND 10:4-5	matched many holes Photo 41.147
(70)	4Q Sam.	4 x 3.6	II Sam. 4:1-3	Photo 288
(71)	" "	2.6 x 1.8	unidentified	
(72)	Papyrus backing of 4QSam.ª (Plate 42)	8.7 x 6.4		
(73)	4Q Deut.ᶠ (Plate 23)	4.7 x 2.3	Deut. 4:25-26	
(74)	" " " "	2.8 x 4.5	Deut. 18:6-9	matched
(75)	4Q Deut.ʰ (Plate 24a)	5 x 4.7	Deut. 2:28-29	matched
(76)	4Q Crypª (6 JMA)	11 x 7.2	unidentified	matched Photo 41.314
(77)	4Q pIsa.ᵇ (21 JMA)	1.2 x 2.2	"	
(78)	4Q Misc. S/curs. (22 JMA)	2.1 x 1.6	"	
(79)	" " " "	1.9 x 1.3	"	
(80)	4Q pPs (Isa) (15 JMA)	3.5 x 2.9	"	
(81)	4Q pHos. (27 JMA)	4.2 x 4.3	Hos. 8:6-8	
(82)	4Q (?)	3.4 x 4.5	unidentified	Catena?
(83)	4Q Catena (16 JMA)	7.7 x 5.5	Ps. 2:1 in last line	
(84)	4Q pap pIsa. (4 JMA)	1.1 x .8	unidentified	
(85)	" " " "	2 x .8	"	
(86)	" " " "	1.9 x 1.4	"	
(87)	4Q pIsa. (3 JMA)	4.6 x 1.8	cf. Isa. 58:13	

(88)	4Q Sam.ᶜ (Plate 28)	4 x 4.1	II Sam. 14:20-21	matched Photo 41.171
(89)	4Q Sam.ᶜ (Plate 28)	9 x 3.2	(II Sam. 14:14-15,)...... (22-31 (	matched Photo 41.171
(90)	" " " "	8.5 x 2.7	(	
(91)	4Q Gen.	9.3 x 6.5	Gen. 4:2-7ff.	plate not labeled
(92)	" "	4.5 x 5.7	(Gen. 41:3 etc. (Gen. 41:42-44 etc.	
(93)	" "	5.6 x 5.3	Gen. 41:38-41	
(94)	4Q Ex. & Lev.	9 x 5.6	unidentified	Photo 41.425
(95)	4Q Lev.ᶜ	4.1 x 2.4	Lev. 4:13-14	
(96)	4Q xiiᵈ/ᴱ/Zech.	1.6 x 1.3	Zech. 5:10	matched
(97)	pap 4QH(odayot)	3.1 x 4.5	unidentified	Nos. (97)-(249) are non-Biblical works being studied by J. Strugnell
(98)	" "	2.1 x 2.1	"	
(99)	4QHᵉ	5.2 x 5.7	"	
(100)	4Q Mispate hayahhad	7.2 x 2.3	"	two columns
(101)	4Q "merkaba" (apocalyptic work) (Plate 1)	3.1 x 1.7	"	
(102)	" " " "	2.3 x 2	"	
(103)	(Ditto, Plate II)	2.9 x 2.4	"	
(104)	" " " "	4.7 x 4.9	"	
(105)	" " " "	3.2 x 3.8	"	
(106)	" " " "	3.8 x 3.2	"	
(107)	(" , Plate III)	4.3 x 2.7	"	)) joined)
(108)	" " " "	7.7 x 5	"	
(109)	4Q "merkaba" (Plate III con.)	5.6 x 6))	unidentified	joined to (110)
(110)	" " " "	5.4 x 6.1)		" " (109)
(111)	4Q Pent. paraphr.ᵃ (Plate I)	3.3 x 3.9	cf. Ex. 39:17-19	
(112)	" " (Plate II)	7.1 x 3.5	cf. Ex. 30:31-31:3	
(113)	" " " "	6.3 x 2.7	cf. Ex. 15:17-19	
(114)	" " (Plate III)	3.2 x 1.7		Photo 286
(115)	" " (Plate IV)	4.8 x 3	cf. Deut. 3:20-21	
(116)	" " " "	6.8 x 7	cf. Deut. 11:7	matched
(117)	" " " "	2.2 x 3.1	unidentified	
(118)	4Q Pent. paraphr.ᵇ	4.7 x 4.5	cf. Lev. 25:29-42	Photo 41.102
(119)	" " " "	1.8 x 1.6		
(120)	4Q "Three Tongues of Fire" (liturgical work)	17.7 x 9.7		Photo 41.421 Fragment of different ms. in Cave One
(121)	4Q "Purity" Document (Plate I)	)) joined;	unidentified	matched
(122)	" " " "	) total size		
(123)	" " " "	) 13.8 x 11.5		
(124)	" " (Plate II)	14 x 13	"	

(125)	4Q Sapiential Work[a]	8.4 x 8.4	"	Photo 41.504
(126)	4Q Sapiential Work[c] (Plate I)	1.8 x 1.4	"	
(127)	" " " "	2.5 x .7	"	
(128)	" " " "	4.4 x 1.6	"	matched
(129)	4Q Sapiential Work[c] (Plate II)	1.5 x 1.4	unidentified	
(130)	" " " "	1.5 x 1.2	"	
(131)	" " " "	1.3 x 1.4	"	
(132)	" " " "	1.9 x 1.3	"	
(133)	" " " "	1 x 1.9	"	
(134)	" " " "	1.5 x 1.9	"	
(135)	" " " "	2.4 x 3	"	
(136)	" " " "	1.4 x 1.5	"	
(137)	" " " "	1.6 x 2.3	"	
(138)	" " (Plate III)	3 x 2.9	"	
(139)	" " " "	2.9 x 2.9	"	
(140)	" " " "	1 x 2.3	"	
(141)	" " " "	1.8 x .9	"	
(142)	" " " "	1.8 x 1.2	"	
(143)	" " (Plate IV)	11 x 3.8	"	
(144)	" " " "	2 x 1.6	cf. Lam. 1:18	
(145)	" " " "	5 x 1.8	unidentified	
(146)	" " " "	5.5 x 4.1	"	
(147)	" " " "	4.8 x 2	"	
(148)	" " (Plate V)	2 x 2.3	"	
(149)	4Q Sapiential Work[c] (Plate V)	1.9 x 2.3	unidentified	
(150)	" " " "	1 x .5	"	
(151)	" " (Plate VI)	2.3 x .8	"	
(152)	4Q Pseudo-Jer.[b] (Plate I)	3.1 x 1.6	"	
(153)	" " (Plate II)	4.4 x 6.6	"	
(154)	" " " "	5.4 x 6.1	"	
(155)	pap 4Q Pseudo-Jer.	1.4 x .7	"	
(156)	" " " "	1.1 x 1.7	"	
(157)	" " " "	2.1 x 1.9	"	
(157b)	" " " "	2.5 x 1.9	"	
(158)	" " " "	2.4 x 1.8	"	
(159)	" " " "	2.2 x 2.9	"	
(160)	" " " "	2.5 x 1.4	"	
(161)	4Q Tehillot Jehoshua' (Plate I)	7.7 x 3.7	"	
(162)	" " " "	4.9 x 2.1	"	
(163)	" " " "	6 x 5.2	"	
(164)	" " (Plate II)	7.1 x 5.7	"	
(165)	4Q Tehillot Nebiim (2nd ms.)	1.9 x 1.4	"	(Pl.5 [o]Tehillot Neb[n])
(166)	4Q H(odayot)[h]	4.7 x 3.5	n 12:2-4	
(167)	pap 4Q H(odayot)[h] (1st ms.)	1.8 x 1.9	unidentified	
(168)	" " " "	2.9 x 1.4	"	

313

(169)	pap 4Q H(odayot)ᵇ (1ˢᵗ ms.)	1.1 x 1.3	unidentified	
(170)	" " " "	2.1 x 1.1	"	
(171)	" " " " (2ⁿᵈ ms.)	1.1 x 1.1	"	
(172)	" " " "	1.3 x .7	"	
(173)	" " " "	2.5 x 1.4	"	
(174)	" " " "	1.3 x .9	"	

4Q (UNIDENTIFIED MATERIAL IN JOHN STRUGNELL'S LOT)

(175)	"J.Str.1"	2.4 x 2.3		
(176)	"J.Str.2"	6 x 4.4		
(177)	"J.Str.2"	12.2 x 7.1		On McGill photo
(178)	" "	5 x 5.7		" " " " matched
(179)	" "	7 x 4.5		
(180)	"J.Str.3"	8.7 x 8.6		matched
(181)	" "	2.5 x 1		
(182)	"J.Str.4" (ms. 2)	4.5 x 3.4		
(183)	"J.Str.5"	one piece		"Heavenly Liturgy"
(184)	"J.Str.6"	12 x 2.7		Liturgical prayer or hymn; McGill photo
(185)	"J.Str.7" (plate I)	3.5 x 2		hymnic composition
(186)	" " " "	2.5 x 1.3		" "
(187)	" " (Plate II)	4 x 1.8		" "
(188)	" " (Plate III)	5.1 x 5.6		
(189)	"J.Str.8" (1ˢᵗ ms.)	5.9 x 7.1	unidentified	
(190)	" " (2ⁿᵈ ms.)	2 x 2.7	"	
(191)	"J.Str.9"	3.9 x 3.4	"	matched
(192)	Unlabeled, (1ˢᵗ plate)	8.2 x 3.7	"	McGill Photo
(193)	" " " "	2 x 1.3	"	
(194)	" " " "	2.2 x 2.7	"	
(195)	" " " "	4.3 x 1.1	"	
(196)	" " " "	2.2 x .6	"	
(197)	Unlabeled, (2ⁿᵈ plate)	1.3 x 1.3	"	
(198)	" " " "	1.5 x 1.3	"	
(199)	Unlabeled, (3ᵈ plate)	1.5 x 1.2	"	
(200)	" " " "	1.3 x 1.2	"	
(201)	" " " "	1.8 x 2.3	"	
(202)	" " " "	2.5 x 1.4	"	
(203)	" " " "	1.5 x 1.7	"	
(204)	" " " "	1 x 1.4	"	
(205)	" " " "	1.5 x 1.6	"	
(206)	Unlabeled, (4ᵗʰ plate)	1.1 x 2.8	"	
(207)	Unlabeled, (5ᵗʰ plate)	1.5 x .6	"	
(208)	Unlabeled, (6ᵗʰ plate)	1.9 x 1.3	"	
(209)	Unlabeled, (6ᵗʰ plate)	1.4 x 1.2	"	
(210)	" " (7ᵗʰ plate)	2.2 x 1.5	"	
(211)	" " " "	2.4 x 1	"	
(212)	" " (8ᵗʰ plate)	1.8 x 1.9	"	
(213)	" " (9ᵗʰ plate)	1.6 x 1.6	"	
(214)	" " (10ᵗʰ plate)	2 x 4.5	"	

(215)	" " " "		1.8 x 2.2	"	
(216)	" " " "		4.9 x 4.2	"	
(217)	" " " "		4 x 1.7	"	
(218)	" " " "		3 x 1.2	"	
(219)	" "	(11th plate)	1.8 x 1.1	"	Photo 371
(220)	" " " "		3 x .8	"	
(221)	" " " "		2.3 x 2.5	"	
(222)	" " " "		1.6 x 1.9	"	
(223)	" " " "		2 x 3.3	"	
(224)	4Q Tephillot "J.Str."		2.3 x 3.4	"	
(225)	" " " "		8.3 x 7.7	"	Photo 41.401
(226)	"J.Str.10"		6.2 x 2	"	
(227)	" "		4.8 x 3	"	
(228)	" "		2.6 x 1.3	"	
(229)	" "		1.5 x 1.3	"	
(230)	"J.Str.11"		4.6 x 3	unidentified	
(231)	4Q Pseudo-Jer.c (1st plate)		4.1 x 2.9	"	See no. 247
(232)	" " " "		5.7 x 2.8	"	
(233)	pap 4Q "J.Str.12" (Plate I)		1.3 x 1.9	A wisdom work	
(234)	" " " "		4.6 x 1.8	" " " "	
(235)	" " " "		1.8 x .6	" " " "	
(236)	" " " "		1.6 x 1.1	" " " "	
(237)	" " " "		1.6 x 2.2	" " " "	
(238)	"J.Str.13"		3.2 x 3.2	unidentified	
(239)	" "		1.5 x 1	"	
(240)	" "		2 x 2.8	"	
(241)	" "		2.2 x 1.5	"	
(242)	" "		4.9 x 2.2	"	
(243)	" "		2 x 1.5	"	
(244)	" "		2 x 3.2	"	
(245)	"J.Str.14"		6 x 5.5	"	non-Biblical
(246)	"J.Str.15"		2.3 x 2.9	"Adamic" work	
(247)	4Q Pseudo-Jer.c (2nd plate)		12.7 x 8.7	- - - - -	See no. 231
(248)	"J.Str.16"		6.1 x 3	Sapiential work?	
(249)	"J.Str.17"		6.4 x 3.7	Milhamah?	
(250)	pap 4Q ms.Alef "Hunz" (Plate I)		3 x 2.8	liturgical work	Nos. 250-300 are mss. studied by Dr. Hunzinger
(251)	" " " "		1.8 x 2.5	" "	
(252)	" " " "		1.3 x 2.2	" "	
(253)	" " (Plate II)		2.1 x 2.5	" "	
(254)	" " " "		2.5 x 1.9	" "	
(255)	" " " "		2.8 x 1.4	" "	
(256)	" " " "		2.8 x .8	" "	
(257)	" " " "		2.3 x 1.5	" "	
(258-272)	" " " "		small fragments	" "	
(273)	" " (Plate III)		1.8 x 1	" "	
(274)	" " " "		1.9 x 1.6	" "	
(275)	" " " "		3 x 1.3	" "	
(276)	" " " "		2.2 x 1.9	" "	

(277)	" " " "	2.5 x 1.6	" "	
(278)	pap 4Q ms.^{Bet} "Hunz"	1.9 x 2.3	Second liturgical work or 2nd ms. of same	
(279)	" " " "	1.7 x 1	" " " "	
(280)	" " " "	3.2 x 1	" " " "	
(281)	pap 4Q "Hunz"	1.9 x 1.1	Unidentified	
(282)	" " " "	1.9 x .9	"	
(283)	4Q Milhamot "Hunz"	) total area	- - - - -	matched
(284)	(1st ms.)	) 7.2 x 5.3		
(285)	4Q Milhamot "Hunz" (2nd ms.) (Plate I)	5.2 x 6.6		
(286)	" " " " (Plate II)	2.1 x 1.1		
(287)	4Q "Hunz"	4.6 x 7	ritual work	matched
(288)	" " " "	1.7 x 1.4	" "	
(289)	" " " "	3.3 x 2.7	" "	
(290)	4Q "Hunz. Sap. work"	3.2 x 4.8		matched
(291)	" " " "	2.6 x 6.4		
(292)	" " " "	5.6 x 7.8		
(293)	pap 4Q Berakhot	1.2 x 1.4		
(294)	" " " "	1.7 x 2.4		
(295)	pap 4Q "Hunz" (Plate 1)	3.7 x 2.8	Liturgical work	
(296)	" " " "	1.4 x 2.2	" "	
(297)	" " " "	2.3 x 1.3	" "	
(298)	" " " "	1.4 x .9	" "	
(299)	" " (plate II)	2.4 x 1.6	" "	
(300)	" " " "	1.9 x 1	" "	
(301)	pap 4Q "Milik 5"	3 x 1.6	Tobit in Aramaic	matched
(302)	" " " "	3.5 x 1.2	" "	"
(303)	" " " "	2.5 x 1.1	" "	"
(304)	" " " "	1.6 x .9	" "	"
(305)	pap 4Q "Milik 5"	4.8 x 1.1	Tobit in Aramaic	
(306)	" " " "	2.9 x 1.2	" "	
(307)	pap 4Q "Milik 6"	2.4 x 1.5	" "	
(308)	" " " "	1.6 x 1.3	" "	
(309)	" " " "	2.6 x 3	" "	
(310)	" " " "	1.6 x .9	" "	
(311)	" " " "	1.2 x .7	" "	
(312)	pap 4Q "Milik 7"	3 x 1.8	" "	
(313)	" " " "	4.3 x 1.8	" "	
(314)	" " " "	1.6 x .8	" "	
(315)	" " " "	2 x .8	" "	
(316)	" " " "	1.9 x .8	" "	
(317)	4Q "Milik 8"	2.4 x 1.7	Jubilees in Hebr., 1st ms.	
(318)	4Q "Milik 9"	1.6 x 2.2	" " " "	
(319)	pap 4Q "Milik 12"	1.4 x 1.9	" " " "	
(320)	" " " "	1.3 x 1.7	" " " "	
(321)	pap 4Q "Milik 13"	1.8 x 1	" " " " 2nd ms. (col. 5)	
(322)	" " " "	2.5 x 2	" " " " (col. 7)	
(323)	4Q "Milik 19"	4.8 x 4.2	Enoch in Aramaic	no. 2, matched

(324)	4Q "Milik 22"	3.1 x 1.6	Enoch-like work, 1ˢᵗ ms.	matched nos. 6-10
(325)	4Q "Milik 22"	2.8 x 1.6	Enoch-like work, 1ˢᵗ ms.	matched nos. 6-10
(326)	4Q "Milik 23"	4.6 x 1.9	" " " "	no. 11
(327)	" " " "	6.1 x 4.3	" " " "	no. 13
(328)	4Q "Milik 25"	4.3 x 6	" " 2ⁿᵈ ms.	
(329)	" " " "	6.3 x 8.9	" " " "	
(330)	" " " "	2.8 x 2.2	" " " "	
(331)	" " " "	2.1 x 2.5	" " " "	matched
(332)	4Q "Milik 28"	5.8 x 5.3	Testament of Levi, Aramaic	Matched (published Rev. Bib. '55) Photo 41.405
(333)	4Q "Milik 30"	6.3 x 5	Unidentified work, Aramaic	
(334)	pap 4Q "Milik 31"	1.4 x 1.1	" " pseudepigraph, Hebr.	matched
(335)	" " " "	3 x .6	" " " "	
(336)	" " " "	1.6 x .9	" " " "	
(337)	" " " "	1.2 x .7	" " " "	
(338)	" " " "	1.7 x .7	" " " "	
(339)	" " " "	1 x 1.4	" " " "	
(340)	" " " "	3 x .7	" " " "	
(341)	" " " "	1.8 x .9	" " " "	
(342)	" " " "	1.5 x 1.5	" " " "	
(343)	" " " "	1.7 x .6	" " " "	
(344)	pap 4Q "Milik 32"	1.7 x 1.3	" " " "	same as 334-343
(345)	pap 4Q "Milik 32"	1.8 x 2.7	Unidentified pseudepigraph, Hebrew	
(346)	pap 4Q "Milik 33"	1.8 x 1	" " " "	same as 334-345
(347)	" " " "	1.2 x 1.9	" " " "	
(348)	4Q "Milik 37"	1.5 x 1	Manual of Discipline, 1ˢᵗ ms. (different recension from 1Q ms.)	matched col. 1
(349)	" " " "	2.5 x 1.4	" " " "	col. 5
(350)	4Q "Milik 38"	4.9 x 4.1	" " " "	same as 348-349
(351)	4Q "Milik 39"	5.4 x 3.3	" " 2ⁿᵈ ms	
(352)	" " " "	6.3 x 3.7	" " " "	
(353)	4Q "Milik 42"	6.3 x 3.7	Damascus Document, 1ˢᵗ ms. (different recension)	Matched
(354)	4Q "Milik 43"	4.4 x 5.2	Damascus Document, 2ⁿᵈ ms. (different recension)	
(355)	4Q "Milik 44"	1.5 x 1.4	unidentified	
(356)	4Q "Milik 45"	4.3 x 5.9	"	
(357)	4Q "Milik 50"	7.3 x 6	Damascus Document, 3ᵈ ms.	

(358)	4Q "Milik 52"	6.2 x 6.5	" "	matched
(359)	4Q "Milik 55"	6.2 x 8.6	" "	(additional material not in Cairo ms.)
(360)	4Q "Milik 59"	2.2 x 1.3	" . "	" " " "
(361)	4Q "Milik 61"	1.3 x 2.5	unidentified	
(362)	" " " "	4.8 x 2.9	"	
(363)	4Q "Milik 62"	2.9 x 4.6	legal work	
(364)	" " " "	2.9 x 3.6		
(365)	4Q "Milik 63"	5.2 x 6.5	legal work	same as 364
(366)	" " " "	2.2 x .9	" "	
(367)	" " " "	6.8 x 2.9	" "	
(368)	4Q "Milik 67"	4.3 x 2.9	legal work	matched
(369)	4Q "Milik 71"	5.1 x 3.4	Berakhot	matched
(370)	4Q "Milik 73"	7.3 x 4	Book of Mysteries	same work as 1Q 27
(371)	4Q "Milik 77"	8.5 x 5.5	Zodiacal work	matched
(372)	" " " "	7.2 x 5.9	" " " "	"
(373)	4Q "Milik 82" (possibly a second piece, 4.4 x 4.3; stamp not clear)	2.4 x 2.6	unidentified	
(374)	4Q "Milik 90"	2.8 x 1.7	"Cryptic A", 1st ms.	
(375)	4Q "Milik 91"	3.4 x 4.1	"Cryptic A", 2nd ms.	
(376)	pap 4Q "Milik 97" (plate I)	1.3 x 1.7	Midrash Moshe[d] (cryptic)	
(377-378)	" " " "	Two smaller pieces	" " " "	
(379)	" " " " (plate II)	2.4 x 1.2	" " " "	
(380)	" " " "	2.5 x 1	" " " "	
(381-392)	" " " "	twelve smaller pieces	" " " "	
(393)	4Q "Milik 99"	1.5 x 1.3	"Cryptic A", 3d ms.	written on verso
(394)	4Q "Milik 103"	3.8 x 3.2	Proper names, with numerals	register?
(395)	Unlabeled	2.8 x 4.4	unidentified	with Milik material
(396)	Unlabeled	2.5 x 1.9	unidentified	with Milik material
(397)	4Q "h 1 Starcky" (Plate I)	4.3 x 2.3	"	Photo 280; same work as 1Q 34
(398)	" " (plate II)	5 x 4.5	"	photo 438
(399)	" " " "	2.8 x 1.1	"	
(400)	4Q "h 7 Starcky" (4Q JS hebr. no. 7) (plate I)	3.8 x 3.9	hymnic work	photo 424
(401)	" " (plate II)	6 x 8.4	" "	photo 41.678
(402)	4Q "h 8 Starcky" (JS hebr. no. 8 4Q)	5.4 x 9.2	unidentified	
(403)	" " " "	10.5 x 8	"	matched
(404)	4Q "h 10 Starcky"	5.7 x 8.9	"	
(405)	" " " "	3.9 x 2.5	"	
(406)	4Q "h 12 Starcky" (4Q eschatologique JS hebr. no. 12)	8.2 x 5.8	eschatological work	matched photo 41.675
(407)	" " " "	2.9 x 2.2	" "	" " " "
(408)	" " " "	4.5 x 3	" "	photo 41.675

(409)	4Q "JS aram no. 6"	7 x 5.7	unidentified	Photo 41.512
(410)	4Q "JS aram no. 14"	7 x 2.5	"	
(411) and	4Q "JS aram no. 23"	)) total size	"	)) matched with
(412)	" " " "	)13.4 x 9.3	"	) each other
(413)	" " " "	5.7 x 3	"	Matched
(414)	4Q "JS aram no. 1"	7.7 x 6	"	
(415)	4Q "JS aram no. 2"	7.5 x 6.4	"	
(416)	4Q "JS aram no. 4"	1.1 x 1.7	unidentified	matched
(417)	" " " "	1.8 x .8	"	
(418)	" " " "	2.6 x 2.3	"	matched
(419)	4Q "JS no. 24"	3.2 x 1.4	"	
(420)	" " " "	3.3 x 4.9	"	
(421)	4Q "JS no. 30"	2 x 2.4	"	
(422)	4Q "JS no. 33"	2.9 x 1.7	"	
(423)	4Q "JS no. 40"	7.5 x 4.4	"	
(424)	" " " "	3.3 x 2.2	"	
(425)	4Q "no. 41" (Starcky)	4.1 x 6.2	"	
(426)	4Q "no. 42" (Starcky)	3.6 x 6.1	"	
(427)	4Q "no. 48" (Starcky)	2.4 x 1.7	"	
(428)	4Q "no. 49" (Starcky)	1.4 x 1.7	"	
(429)	4Q "no. 56" (Starcky)	2.3 x 1	"	
(430)	" " " "	2 x 1.8	"	
(431)	4Q "no. 57" (Starcky)	2.6 x 1.1	"	matched
(432)	" " " "	2.2 x 1	"	"
(433)	4Q "no. 59" (Starcky)	4.5 x 2.5	"	
(434)	4Q "no. 68" (Starcky)	3.3 x 3	"	
(435)	4Q "pcs Starcky"	4.9 x 2.3	"	
(436)	4Q "Starcky"	10 x 3.8	liturgical work	Photo 41.677

Notes

ACKNOWLEDGMENTS

1 It became the Faculty of Religious Studies in 1970. See Markell, *The Faculty of Religious Studies*, McGill University, 53–4.

PREFACE

1 Harry Orlinsky, undated manuscript identified from contents of the text, Harry Meyer Orlinsky Papers, American Jewish Archives, Cincinnati, Ohio. MSS Col. No. 601, Sub-series 4: Writings, File 4:18, Dead Sea Scrolls Intro.
2 Canadian copyright law prohibits the publication of archival material without permission from the literary heirs or copyright holders.

CHAPTER ONE

1 "I should perhaps recall to you that the first find of ancient scrolls near the Dead Sea was made in 1947, and has aroused world-wide interest. These were Biblical and non-Biblical works in Hebrew, apparently coming from the library of the first century Jewish sect of the Essenes. The new finds are both more abundant and more fragmentary. They came to light between November 1951 and September 1952" (Scott to James, 28 September 1953, Letter #2).
2 This assessment of date is that of Scott. Most recent handbooks date the various manuscripts to between 250 BCE and 68 CE when the Qumran community was destroyed by the Roman military. For a survey of methods of dating and their results see VanderKam and Flint, *The Meaning of the Dead Sea Scrolls*, 20–33.

3 Peter Mellors, "Canada's Big Biblical Bargain," *Star Weekend Magazine*, 26 November 1960, 10–11, 37.
4 "Rev. R.B.Y. Scott, 88, Old Testament Scholar," *New York Times*, 5 November 1987, 10(B).
5 Fields, *The Dead Sea Scrolls: A Short History*, 43.
6 Roland de Vaux (1903–1971) was director of the French-Dominican École Biblique et Archéologique Française in Jerusalem and a trustee of the Palestine Archaeological Museum. At the request of the director of the Jordanian Department of Antiquities, G. Lankester Harding, he would become the chief excavator at Khirbet Qumran. From 1954 until 1970 he served as the editor-in-chief for the publication of the manuscripts. See Briend, "De Vaux, Roland," 202–4 and Strugnell, "In Memoriam – Roland Guérin de Vaux, O.P.," 3–5.
7 Burrows, *The Dead Sea Scrolls*, 69. Millar Burrows (1889–1980) was professor at both Brown (1925–34) and Yale Divinity School (1934–58). He was annual director of ASOR Jerusalem in February 1948 when Mar Athanasius Samuel brought scrolls from the Cave 1 find to ASOR for assistance in valuation and identification. Although away in Baghdad at the time, Burrows was largely responsible for the publication of the scrolls from Cave 1, which were later offered to McGill by Charles Manoog (cf. Burrows, Trever, and Brownlee, eds, *The Dead Sea Scrolls of St. Mark's Monastery*; and also, Trever, *The Dead Sea Scrolls: A Personal Account*.
8 John Allegro (1923–88) early on turned out to be the most controversial of the initial members of the Cave 4 editorial team. A short biographical sketch is provided by Davies, "Allegro, John Marco," 18; see also the recent biography by his daughter, Judith Brown, *John Marco Allegro: The Maverick of the Dead Sea Scrolls*.
9 Allegro, *The Dead Sea Scrolls: A Reappraisal*, 47.
10 Józef T. Milik (1922–2006), a Polish-born Dominican priest, was an original member of the Dead Sea Scrolls Cave 4 editorial team. He is described by many as the most gifted of the scholars who assembled in Jerusalem for this task. See Puech, "Milik, Józef T.," 552–4.
11 Milik, *Ten Years of Discovery in the Wilderness of Judaea*, 17.
12 Scott, *Treasure from Judæan Caves*, 13–14.
13 Gerald Lankester Harding (1901–1979) was director of the Department of Antiquities of Jordan from 1936 until 1956 when, in a wave of Arab nationalism, as a Briton he was summarily removed from office and retired to Beirut. See, Winnett, "Tribute: Gerald Lankester Harding 1901–1979," 127.

14 Michael Specter, "Dead Sea Scrolls: Open to Whom? – Biblical Scholars Clash on Access; Many Documents Still Closely Held," *Washington Post*, 15 November 1989, 3(A).
15 Cf. Shanks, "Is the Vatican Suppressing the Dead Sea Scrolls?" in *Understanding the Dead Sea Scrolls*, 275–90.
16 Baigent and Leigh, *The Dead Sea Scrolls Deception*.
17 Eisenman and Wise, *The Dead Sea Scrolls Uncovered: The First Complete Translation and Interpretation of 50 Key Documents Withheld for Over 35 Years*.
18 John Noble Wilford, "New Accusations Erupt over Dead Sea Scrolls," *New York Times*, 13 December 1992, 28.
19 John Noble Wilford, "Scrolls Scholars Resolve Dispute: Authors of Book on Dead Sea Fragments Apologize for Any Slights to Others," *New York Times*, 18 December 1992, 15(A). Transcripts of a discussion about the book by Eisenman and Wise in response to the accusations, along with their formal statements, are recorded in "Ethics of Publication of the Dead Sea Scrolls: Panel Discussion," in *Methods of Investigation of the Dead Sea Scrolls and the Khirbet Qumran Site: Present Realities and Future Prospects*, Michael O. Wise et al., eds, 455–97.
20 See, for example, John Noble Wilford, "Israelis Try, Again, to Limit Access to Scrolls," *New York Times*, 23 January 1992, 7(A); and also Nimmer, "Copyright in the Dead Sea Scrolls," 1–222.
21 For an account of Abegg and Wacholder's efforts and the response of scholars inside and outside the inner circle of editors, see Kalman "Optimistic, Even with the Negatives," 63–71.
22 The photographs were deposited at the Huntington as a precaution should anything happen to the originals in the wartorn Middle East.
23 See John Noble Wilford, "Officials in Israel Ease Stand on Access to Ancient Scrolls," *New York Times*, 27 September 1991, 14(A) and Clyde Haberman, "Israel to Revise Rules on Scrolls," *New York Times*, 28 October 1991, 3(A).
24 Shanks, *The Mystery and Meaning of the Dead Sea Scrolls*, 36; and VanderKam and Flint, *The Meaning of the Dead Sea Scrolls*, 17.
25 For an account of possible early and medieval references to discoveries, see Driver, *The Judaean Scrolls*, 7–15.
26 This claim is derived from a telegram sent to John Trever by the father of Biblical Archaeology, William Foxwell Albright. Albright received photographs of the first Dead Sea Scrolls in the mail from Trever in Jerusalem on 15 March 1948 and responded: "My heartiest congratulations on the greatest MS discovery of modern times!" For the entire communication, see Trever,

The Dead Sea Scrolls: A Personal Account, 79; see also Albright, "Notes from the President's Desk," 3.

27 "Ancient MSS. Found in Palestine: Earliest Known Copy of Isaiah," *Times* (London), 12 April 1948, 4.

28 Eleazar Lipa Sukenik (1889–1953), a Lithuanian-born but American-trained archaeologist, joined the faculty of Hebrew University in the late 1920s and became involved with the scrolls as the curator of the National Museum of Antiquities at the Hebrew University. See Silberman, "Sukenik, Eleazar L.," 902–3.

29 "Isaiah Find Described: Bible manuscript 2,000 Years Old," *Palestine Post*, 27 April 1948, 3.

30 Julius Louis Meltzer, "10 Ancient Scrolls Found in Palestine," *New York Times*, 25 April 1948, 6.

31 See, for example, "Biblical Papers 2,000 Years Old Reported Found," *Daily Star* (Toronto), 27 April 1948, 3; and, "Find Hebrew Biblical Manuscripts in Earthenware Jars Near Dead Sea," *Globe and Mail* (Toronto), 27 April 1948, 3. The delay may have resulted in part from the fact that Canadian newspapers at this time, by and large, did not publish Sunday editions.

32 G. Lankester Harding, "A Bible Discovery: Earliest Known Texts of the Hebrew Bible," *Times* (London), 9 August 1949, 5, 10.

33 Albright's official stamp was of immense importance and his influence on twentieth-century scholarship in the field cannot be overestimated.

William Foxwell Albright (1891–1971) of Johns Hopkins University is rightly described by Seymour Gitin as the "driving force behind a revolution in biblical studies and in the study of the history and religion of ancient Israel" ("The House That Albright Built," 5). For biographical details and further elaboration see, among many, the work of Running and Freedman, *William Foxwell Albright: A Twentieth-Century Genius*; van Beek, ed., *The Scholarship of William Foxwell Albright: An Appraisal*; and Long, *Planting and Reaping Albright: Politics, Ideology, and Interpreting the Bible*.

34 Albright, "Notes from the President's Desk," 2–3. Although it was the April edition of BASOR it had been delayed and Albright's article is dated 19 May 1948.

35 Trever, "The Discovery of the Scrolls," 45–57. Trever (1916–2006), at the time a young American scholar, was at ASOR in Jerusalem when the Cave 1 scrolls were brought there for assessment. He examined and photographed the scrolls and, on 25 February 1948, sent some images of the Isaiah Scroll to his teacher, William F. Albright, at Johns Hopkins University. For Trever's account of studying and photographing the scrolls, and Albright's response, see Trever, *The Dead Sea Scrolls: A Personal Account*, especially 56–89.

36 See, for example, William G. Weart, "Bible Scroll 'Find' suspected Hoax: Dr. Zeitlin of Dropsie College Splits With Other Scholars on Dead Sea Discovery," *New York Times*, 4 March 1949, 19, and the response by Eleazar Sukenik among the Letters to the Editor: "Antiquity of Hebrew Scrolls: Scholar Presents Evidence for View That Manuscripts are Authentic," *New York Times*, 19 March 1949, 19. This matter will receive more attention later on in this narrative.

37 For the announcement of the Cave 4 finds, see "70 Ancient Scrolls Found at Dead Sea – Manuscripts in Cave Identified as Books of Old Testament and History of Essenes – Discovered by Shepherds – Documents Will Keep Scholars Busy For Generation, Says Expert," *New York Times*, 2 April 1953, 29.

38 The word "biblical" here refers exclusively to the Jewish Bible or Christian Old Testament.

39 Schiffman, *Reclaiming the Dead Sea Scrolls*, 54. See also the complete list of the manuscripts divided according to genre in Lange with Mittmann-Richert, "Annotated List of the Texts from the Judaean Desert Classified by Content and Genre," 115–64.

Almost 25 percent of the materials discovered in the eleven caves at Qumran were copies of biblical books. A detailed list of the biblical manuscripts has been compiled by Emanuel Tov, "Categorized List of the 'Biblical Texts,'" 165–83.

40 "Of all the caves, cave 4 has yielded the most valuable finds, which have provided keys to unlocking the entire library. Here were found parts of 223 biblical scrolls; numerous apocryphal compositions, many of them previously unknown; many types of unknown sectarian writings; and some economic documents. These materials, because of their fragmentary condition, have posed a tremendous challenge to scholars. In fact, the bulk of the work on the scrolls in our generation will be directed at conserving, piecing together, editing, analyzing, and translating the documents," (Schiffman, *Reclaiming the Dead Sea Scrolls*, 54, 56).

41 Hence the alternative appellation for the scrolls, a reference to the wadi and the adjacent settlement ruins. The proximity of the caves where the scrolls were discovered to the nearby ruins at Khirbet Qumran also represents a possible link used to explain the origin of the scrolls.

For an elaboration on the statistics, see Shanks, "Chief Scroll Editor Opens Up," 32–5, 62; but also Dimant, "The Qumran Manuscripts: Contents and Significance," 23–58.

42 Cross, "Reminiscences of the Early Days," 933.

43 Frank Moore Cross (b. 1921), a student of William F. Albright, was appointed in 1953 to join Józef T. Milik in working on the fragments from Cave 4. They

became the first of the international Cave 4 editorial team. Cross, today "in the opinion of many, the world's leading Bible scholar" (Gitin, "The House That Albright Built," 6) and also a leading expert on epigraphy and palaeography, became a respected Dead Sea Scrolls scholar and would be appointed to Harvard University in 1957, where he remained until he retired in 1992. See, Ulrich, "Cross, Frank Moore," 157–8.

44 Cross, *The Ancient Library of Qumran*, rev. 3rd ed., 38.
45 The best known version of the discovery is related in Cross's *The Ancient Library of Qumran*. For bibliographic references to a list of fairly recent introductions to this topic, see Schuller, *The Dead Sea Scrolls,* xvi, and Fields, "Discovery and Purchase," 208–12.
46 "I [Frank M. Cross] was the first of the Cave 4 team to arrive on the scene, starting to work in the scrollery in May, 1953. I was nominated by the American Schools. My task was to prepare and identify the fragments unearthed from Cave 4 by scholars after the ravages of the Taʿâmireh Bedouin were halted. J.T. Milik, a Pole attached to the École Biblique and later to CNRS, arrived in September, 1953," (Cross, "Reminiscences of the Early Days," 932). At the time of appointment Cross was professor at McCormick Theological Seminary in Chicago and the Annual Professor at ASOR in Jerusalem (cf. Pfann, "History of the Judean Desert Discoveries," 100).
47 Cross, "Reminiscences of the Early Days," 932.
48 John Strugnell (1930–2007) joined the editorial team in 1954 while still a graduate student at Oxford. Between 1984 and 1990 he served as editor-in-chief. During the 1950s, Milik and Strugnell would prove the "most consistent" workers in the scrollery in Jerusalem (Pfann, "History of the Judean Desert Discoveries," 101). Strugnell would teach at Duke University from 1960 until 1967; he then joined the faculty at Harvard as professor of Christian origins and remained there until his retirement in 1991. Although Strugnell opened the team to Israeli scholars, he would be forced to resign as editor-in-chief after an unfortunate interview with the Israeli press in which he condemned Judaism as a "horrible religion" (Katzman, "Interview with Chief Scroll Editor John Strugnell," 261). See also Collins, "Strugnell, John," 895–6; John Noble Wilford, "Dead Sea Scroll Editor's Exit Tied to Anti-Jewish Remarks," *New York Times*, 12 December 1990, 14(A); and John Noble Wilford, "John Strugnell, Scholar Undone by His Slur, Dies at 77," *New York Times*, 9 December 2007, 41.
49 Strugnell, "The Original Team of Editors," 178–92.
50 Hershel Shanks's chapter describing Weston Fields's search for the Bedouin boy (by then a man in his seventies) credited with discovering Cave 1 is a

51 Meyer, *Joachim Prinz*, xi.
52 See, for example, de Vaux, "Fouille au Khirbet Qumrân: Rapport préliminaire," 83–106; and de Vaux, "Chronique Archéologique: Khirbet Qûmran," 567–8.
53 Harding and Reed, "Archaeological News from Jordan," 9–10.
54 Cross, "The Manuscripts of the Dead Sea Caves," 1–21.
55 Cross, "A Report on the Biblical Fragments of Cave Four in Wâdī Qumrân," 9–13.
56 Pierre Benoit (1906–1987) was born in France and joined the Dominican Order at eighteen. He came to the École Biblique in Jerusalem in 1932. Benoit would act as editor of the *Revue biblique* from 1953 until 1968. He was responsible for editing the Greek texts from Wadi Murabba'at and became editor-in-chief of the Dead Sea Scrolls editorial committee after the death of de Vaux in 1971. This responsibility was transferred to John Strugnell before his death. Cf. Murphy-O'Connor, "In Memoriam: Pierre Benoit, O.P.," 1–2, and also Benoit, Milik and de Vaux, *Les Grottes de Murabba'ât*.
57 Benoit, "Editing the Manuscript Fragments From Qumran," 75–96.
58 Athanasius Yeshue Samuel (1907–1995) was the Turkish-born archbishop of the Syrian Orthodox Church in Jerusalem until he left for the United States, settling in New Jersey in 1949. He would eventually sell his Cave 1 scrolls in 1954. They were purchased for the State of Israel by Yigael Yadin (1917–1984), son of the eminent Hebrew University scholar Eleazar Sukenik. Samuel recounts the tale of his involvement with the scrolls in his autobiography, *Treasure of Qumran: My Story of the Dead Sea Scrolls*.
59 Allegro, *The Dead Sea Scrolls: A Reappraisal*, 52–8.
60 Milik, *Dix ans de découvertes dans le désert de Juda* and *Ten Years of Discovery in the Wilderness of Judaea*.
61 Cross, *The Ancient Library of Qumran*, 10–46. See also pages 47–53 for the supplement to the first chapter added to the third edition: "Discovery of an Ancient Library and Related Discoveries (1960–1993)."
62 See Schuller, *The Dead Sea Scrolls*, 29–30.
63 Silberman, *The Hidden Scrolls: Christianity, Judaism, and the War for the Dead Sea Scrolls*. All of Silberman's interviews were carried out between 1990 and 1993 – cf. his list of interviewees, 285–6.
64 Pfann, "History of the Judean Desert Discoveries," 97–108.
65 Brown, *John Marco Allegro: The Maverick of the Dead Sea Scrolls*.
66 Kiraz, *Anton Kiraz's Archive on the Dead Sea Scrolls*.

(continued from previous page) good example of this ephemeral quality in which much of the history of discovery is cloaked. See Shanks, *The Mystery and Meaning of the Dead Sea Scrolls*, 3–23.

67 On the significant influence of the media, see the 2005 *DSD* volume (12, no. 1) devoted to "The Dead Sea Scrolls in the Popular Imagination."
68 A volume entitled *Manchester and the Dead Sea Scrolls*, edited by George J. Brooke, is in the offing.
69 This statement counters Hershel Shanks's claim to the contrary: "By 1961, however, Jordan decided it did not like the arrangement that allowed foreign institutions to acquire some of the fragments; it nationalized the scrolls ... Although Jordan offered to repay the institutions that had contributed to the purchase price, it has yet to do so," (*The Mystery and Meaning of the Dead Sea Scrolls*, 36).
70 Scott, "Special Report," 55–8.
71 Du Toit and Kalman, "Great Scott!," 6–23.
72 Established as the PAM in 1927 with a $2 million grant from John D. Rockefeller, Jr, this museum was later renamed in honour of Rockefeller (Reed, "Survey of the Dead Sea Scrolls Fragments and Photographs at the Rockefeller Museum," 45). The museum, although private, acted in concert with the Jordanian Government and became host to the central collection of Dead Sea Scrolls. After the Six Day War in 1967, the PAM was renamed the Rockefeller Museum as a nod to the Rockefeller grant. For history and background on the PAM/Rockefeller Museum, see Zias, "Palestine Archaeological Museum," 634–5; Sussman and Reich, *L'Toldot Muzaon Rockefeller B'Yirushalaim*, 83–92; and Yusif Sa'ad, *The Palestine Archaeological Museum and the Dead Sea Scrolls*.
73 Most important in this regard was the invaluable access we had to the F. Cyril James correspondence. James was principal of McGill University from 1940 until 1962. As will become apparent, he was also a key participant in negotiations for the purchase of the Dead Sea Scrolls. A rich correspondence with R.B.Y. Scott and others at the time of the purchase of the Dead Sea Scrolls for the university and thereafter was found in the McGill archives. For more on James, see Frost, *The Man in the Ivory Tower: F. Cyril James of McGill*.
74 On the across the board interest of role players (collectors, museum professionals, and scholars) in this topic in recent years, see, for example: Cuno, *Who Owns Antiquity? Museums and the Battle over our Ancient Heritage*; Robson, Treadwell, and Gosden, eds, *Who Owns Objects? The Ethics and Politics of Collecting Cultural Artefacts*; Barkan and Bush, eds, *Claiming the Stones, Naming the Bones: Cultural Property and the Negotiation of National and Ethnic Identity*; Renfrew, *Loot, Legitimacy and Ownership*; Vitelli, ed., *Archaeological Ethics*; and Greenfield, *The Return of Cultural Treasures*; to name but a few.

75 "The story of the Faculty of Divinity [at McGill University – after 1970 known as the Faculty of Religious Studies] epitomizes the fortunes of religion in North American society, and so has a larger significance than the relatively small numbers involved would suggest. In the postwar years, the quickened interest in studies of man's many and diverse cultures drew considerable attention to the religious aspects of those cultures," (Frost, *McGill University: For the Advancement of Learning*, 2:286).

76 Scott to Frost, 13 May 1958, Letter #82. James S. Thomson (1949–57) and Stanley B. Frost (1957–62) succeeded Scott as dean. For a comprehensive early history of the faculty, see Markell, *The Faculty of Religious Studies*. Note that the official history of McGill University, where the establishment of the Faculty of Divinity is concerned, neglects to mention R.B.Y. Scott's tenure as dean. For the history of the Faculty of Divinity as rendered in McGill's official history, see Frost, *McGill University: For the Advancement of Learning*, 2: 286–90.

77 Cf. R.B.Y. Scott, *Memorandum*, 2 March 1954, Letter #12.

78 "Since McGill was a prestige university and had joined in the common pledge that no duly qualified veteran would be denied a place, its resources came under tremendous pressure ... Since a student's fees covered only a part of the cost of the education, each veteran admitted by McGill would constitute an additional burden on the endowment. Provincial institutions, such as the University of Toronto or l'Université de Montréal, could expect provincial funds to cover the balance of costs but as a private university, McGill would have to meet them from its own resources," (Frost, *The Man in the Ivory Tower*, 130–1).

79 Frank Cyril James (1903–1973) was principal of McGill from 1939 until 1962. Born in London, he received his PhD in Economics from the University of Pennsylvania and was appointed to the faculty of the Wharton School of Business in 1927. He was invited to McGill as head of the Commerce Department in 1939 by the recently appointed principal, Lewis Williams Douglas. Douglas planned to reform the Commerce Department as his first official act and scouted James. Douglas had been Chancellor Sir Edward Beatty's candidate of choice. As a result of this relationship, James quickly formed a friendship with Beatty as well. Very soon after James's arrival, Douglas resigned as principal to return to his native United States and Beatty tapped James as his replacement. See Frost, *The Man in the Ivory Tower*.

80 Frost, *The Man in the Ivory Tower*, 130.

81 Nevertheless, strong indications exist that some of the Dead Sea Scrolls, despite all efforts, are in private hands to this day. In the John Strugnell

interview with Avi Katzman, Strugnell alludes to this: "Strugnell claims at least four other scrolls have been found that have not yet come to light: 'I've seen, with my own eyes, two.' One of the two is a complete copy of the book of Enoch ... These scrolls, like the Temple Scroll, came from Cave 11 at Qumran, according to Strugnell. The manuscripts are now somewhere in Jordan. Various people own them. Several of them have been sold to big bankers. They're investments for these people. There's no point in forcing a sale ... As for the other two scrolls – the ones Strugnell has not seen – '[Lankester] Harding [the director of Jordan's Department of Antiquities] on his death bed told me he'd seen three, only one of which I've seen – so that makes four," (Katzman, "Interview with Chief Scroll Editor John Strugnell," 262).

82 For a recent discussion of the looting of the Baghdad Museum and attempts to retrieve lost and stolen artefacts, see, for example, Bogdanos, *Thieves of Baghdad*.

83 Only recently has this issue been taken up; see Bernhardsson, *Reclaiming a Plundered Past: Archaeology and Nation Building in Modern Iraq*. For a similar discussion of archaeology in the formation of Egyptian national identity, see Reid, *Whose Pharaohs? Archaeology, Museums, and Egyptian National Identity from Napoleon to World War I*.

84 Bogdanos, *Thieves of Baghdad*, 223.

85 See, for example, the 25 June 2009 press release from Palestine House requesting a boycott of the exhibit of Dead Sea Scrolls at the Royal Ontario Museum (ROM) in Toronto (Canada) from the end of June 2009 until early January 2010: "There remains an unfortunate impression that the ROM is profiting from its involvement with a collection of archeological artifacts acquired by Israel in violation of international conventions and law. As such, and to address this issue, Palestine House boycotts the exhibition unless that ROM admits the factual history, that these scrolls are Palestinian property," (Palestine House, "Palestine House Calls to Boycott the Dead Sea Scrolls Exhibition at the ROM," [25 June 2009]. http://www.marketwire.com/press-release/Palestine-House-1009412.html [accessed: 8 July 2009].

86 Carson, "Raiders of the Lost Scrolls," 309.

CHAPTER TWO

1 Cross, "Reminiscences of the Early Days," 932.
2 On the discovery and sale, see the overview provided by Frank, "How the Dead Sea Scrolls Were Found," 7–19.

3 Kando (1910–1993) was a Syrian Orthodox Christian who, although he began as a cobbler, later opened an antiquities shop. In addition to arranging these sales, he would eventually act as the intermediary between the Bedouin and the Jordanian Department of Antiquities for the sale of the ancient materials discovered in other caves. See Briend, "Shahin, Khalil Iskandar (Kando)," 869–70.
4 Sukenik describes the events in his *The Dead Sea Scrolls of the Hebrew University*, 13–21. He does not mention the antiquities dealer by name (cf. Silberman, "Sukenik, Eleazar L.," 902). See also Silberman, *The Hidden Scrolls*, 43–6.
5 According to Harding the news did not reach him until November 1948 [Harding, "Introductory. The Discovery, the Excavation, Minor Finds," 6]. In November 1955 Trever, who had first photographed the scrolls, wrote to Scott that Harding's claim was not true:

> The truth of the matter is that I risked my life and the possibility of doing anything to the scrolls in 1948 in order to report to the Department of Antiquities exactly what had been discovered and their importance. I had to make my visits to the department secretly in view of what I knew was the antagonistic attitude of the Syrian Archbishop. I have documented evidence to prove what was done, but it has been more convenient for the Department to perpetuate the lie that has been circulating. The evidence has been presented to Mr. Harding, but in spite of it he came out in QUMRAN CAVE I (Harding, "Introductory. The Discovery, the Excavation, Minor Finds," 6) with his previously stated position, even stronger. [Trever to Scott, 3 November 1955, R.B.Y. Scott Papers, 89.112c, file: 1–6 United Church of Canada Archives, Toronto, Ontario.]

The letter continues with a description of Trever's visits with Harding's predecessor as director of antiquities, Robert William Hamilton, and describes the find. He recounts the first visit, which he dates to early February 1948, in *The Untold Story of Qumran*, 66–7, although there he notes that in recounting the story of the discovery to Hamilton: "The fact that it was my understanding that the scrolls had been in the Syrian Monastery for many years, of course, was included," 66. This may explain why the Department of Antiquities did not see this as a formal report of a recent archaeological discovery in its territory.

On the nature of antiquities law in this period as it related to the Dead Sea Scrolls see, for example, Carson, "Raiders of the Lost Scrolls," 299–348.
6 Cave 2 was discovered in February 1952 by the Bedouin. Although Caves 3 and 5 were found by archaeologists, Caves 4 and 6 were discovered by the

Bedouin that same year. The interchange of discovery between archaeologists and Bedouin, indicated by the naming of the caves by number in sequence of discovery, clearly reveals the close race between the discoverers to find additional caves. Caves 7, 8, 9, and 10 were found in 1954 by the archaeologists. But, in 1956, Cave 11, again a source of significant and relatively intact material, was discovered by the Bedouin.

7 On the reliability of the story and the efforts of scholars to validate it, see Shanks, *The Mystery and Meaning of the Dead Sea Scrolls*, 3–23. Shanks's notes to the chapter provide a useful bibliography of interviews with those in later years claiming to be the legendary Edh-Dhib.

8 Milik, *Ten Years of Discovery*, 16–17.

9 For an overview of the discovery and purchase of these early finds, see Fields, *The Dead Sea Scrolls: A Short History*, 17–54.

10 Ibid., 46.

11 The editorial team consisted of members representing each of the four archaeological schools who also had trustees on the Board of the PAM: the British School of Archaeology; the American Schools of Oriental Research; the Deutschen Evangelischen Instituts für Altertumswissenschaft des Heiligen Landes; the École Biblique; and the Jewish Palestine Exploration Society. The latter did not have representation on the editorial team as the PAM was still in Jordanian territory at the time of the composition of the group. See Cross, "Reminiscences of the Early Days," 933, and Fields, *The Dead Sea Scrolls: A Short History*, 63. The membership of the original international Cave 4 editorial team receives further attention later in this narrative.

12 Letter dated, 3 February 1954, cited in Brown, *John Marco Allegro*, 40–1.

13 IOSOT was founded in 1950, see Clines, "From Copenhagen to Oslo," 194–221.

14 The first conference participation in the program was by invitation only. Scott offered to fill in if any of the invited speakers could not attend, but no place in the schedule opened for him. See Bentzen to Scott, 9 January 1953 and 13 February 1953, R.B.Y. Scott Papers, 89.112c, file: 1–6, United Church of Canada Archives, Toronto, Ontario.

15 Scott, "The Original Language of the Apocalypse."

16 "Rev. R.B.Y. Scott, 88, Old Testament Scholar," *New York Times*, 5 November 1987, 10(B).

17 Scott's most enduring works are most probably *Towards the Christian Revolution* and the Anchor Bible volume *Proverbs and Ecclesiastes*.

18 McGill University Archives, M.G. 2005, Scott, Robert Balgarnie Young.

19 According to the course catalogues, this course was required for students earning a Bachelor of Divinity, and Scott offered it each year from 1948

Notes to pages 24–7

until 1955 (McGill University, *Catalogue of Courses, 1953–1954*, 2,652, and McGill University, *Catalogue of Courses, 1954–1955*, 2,653).

20 McGill University, *Catalogue of Courses, 1953–1954*, 2,652, and McGill University, *Catalogue of Courses, 1954–1955*, 2,653. The course was possible because of the publication of the Isaiah material from Qumran in Sukenik, *Megilot Genuzot*, and the two volume publication by Burrows, Trever, and Brownlee, eds, *The Dead Sea Scrolls of St. Mark's Monastery*.

21 Scott to James, 28 September 1953, Letter #2.

22 See Rowley, "The International Old Testament Conference in Copenhagen," 423–8. Harold Henry Rowley (1890–1969) was professor of Hebrew at the University of Manchester from 1945 until 1959. By this time he had published a series of lectures on the Dead Sea Scrolls: *The Zadokite Fragments and the Dead Sea Scrolls* (1952).

23 Godfrey Rolles Driver (1892–1975) was professor of Semitic philology at Oxford from 1928 and an influential scholar in a wide range of matters related to the study of the languages of the ancient Near East. He challenged the antiquity of the scrolls in his *The Hebrew Scrolls from the Neighbourhood of Jericho and the Dead Sea* and queried their date and purpose in *The Judaean Scrolls: The Problem and a Solution*. Later, Driver modified his earlier stance on dating the scrolls and would allow for a possible first century CE date of composition. Cf., for example, Driver, "Mythology of Qumrân," 241–81. See also Wiseman, "Obituary: Sir Godfrey Driver," 160–3.

24 Harold H. Rowley, "The International Old Testament Conference in Copenhagen," 426.

25 Fields, *The Dead Sea Scrolls: A Short History*, 37.

26 Ibid., 39.

27 Cross, "Reminiscences of the Early Days," 937.

28 Harding to Scott, 23 November 1953, Letter #4. The transcription by Scott is misdated as 27 November. A letter from F. Cyril James to the director of antiquities of Jordan, 30 March 1957, Letter #78, cites the cable as dating from the 23rd. Furthermore, a letter from Scott to a prospective donor, Mr Lazarus Phillips, dated 25 November 1953, Letter # 5, cites the cable in full. Scott uses 27 November as *terminus a quo* in his recounting of his participation in McGill's scrolls purchase in Scott, "Special Report: What Ever Happened to McGill's Dead Sea Scrolls?" 55–8. It is fairly certain that Scott incorrectly reproduced this date from the earlier transcription.

29 On this point Stephen Pfann's timeline is therefore somewhat misleading ("History of the Judean Desert Discoveries," 100). Although Jordanian Government agreement to this arrangement was only reached in November 1953, it was prompted by an already existing offer from McGill University

to purchase Cave 4 materials arising from de Vaux's talk in Copenhagen (cf. the cables sent between Scott and Harding, 25 September 1953 to 2 October 1953, Letter #1 and Scott to James, 28 September 1953, Letter #2).

30 Cross, *The Ancient Library of Qumran*, 38–9.
31 Carl H. Kraeling (1897–1966), of the University of Chicago, was President of ASOR from 1949 to 1954 (King, *American Archaeology in the Mideast*, 121–2, 275). Largely as a result of his efforts, the work in the "scrollery" where the editorial team met in Jerusalem was, and remained, funded by John D. Rockefeller, Jr, from 1954 through 1960. See King, *American Archaeology in the Mideast*, 122–3. See also below for further discussion of the Kraeling-Rockefeller funding arrangement.
32 Kraeling to Harding, 8 November 1952, IAA Archives, Box 73, PAM 1117: Dead Sea Scrolls (cave no. 4), jacket 1.
33 Kraeling to Harding, 8 October 1952, IAA Archives, Box 73, PAM 1117: Dead Sea Scrolls (cave no. 4), jacket 1.
34 Frank Moore Cross has noted several reasons for the Bedouin's success: "During the labors of the scholars in the desert, the Bedouin bided their time. When the scholars left, they set back to work. The terrain of the Judaean desert is too wild to police adequately, and while the archaeologist can survive brief forays in its wilderness, the Bedouin alone can search systematically its desolate crags and canyons. The Bedouin have no expedition expenses; they have an almost unlimited number of workers; and they have the infinite time and knowledge required to seek out each cranny of the wilderness," (Cross, "The Manuscripts of the Dead Sea Caves," 6).
35 Brown, *John Marco Allegro*, 48. The real threat of indiscriminate purchase on the black market is illustrated by the fact that in 1955 Scott was able to buy seventeen fragments from a Jerusalem antiquities dealer. This incident is discussed in greater detail further on in this narrative.

Joseph Fitzmyer reports that during his year in Jerusalem (1957–58): "[The editors] constantly heard rumors that fragments, supposedly from Cave 4, had been sold by antiquities dealers in East Jerusalem to tourists who were often anxious to acquire a fragment of the DSS. In fact, one such fragment had been bought by an American, who had enough sense to send it back to the Museum. When the curator brought the fragment to the scrollery, J.T. Milik looked at it and recognized immediately that it belonged to one of his texts. He went to the plate where other fragments of the text were preserved, and it fitted in exactly, making a perfect join with about five or six other fragments," (Fitzmyer, *Responses to 101 Questions*, 10). The tourist was Cecil Osborne, minister of the First Baptist Church in Burlingame, California, who visited during the summer of 1957. He turned over a fragment from

a manuscript of the "Manual of Discipline" (4Q260, photograph: 42.490, taken October 1957). See, Osborne to Saʻad, 25 October 1957 and Saʻad to Osborne, 23 November 1957, IAA Archives, Box 73, PAM 1117: Dead Sea Scrolls (cave no. 4), jacket 1.
36 Cable, Scott to Harding, 25 September 1953, Letter #1.
37 Cable, Harding to Scott, 28 September 1953, Letter #1.
38 Cable, Scott to Harding, 28 September 1953, Letter #1.
39 Harding to Scott, 3 October 1953, Letter #3.
40 For background on the American School of Oriental Research in Jerusalem (now the Albright Institute of Archaeology) and ASOR in general, see King, *American Archaeology in the Mideast*.
41 Fred Winnett (1903–1989) and Scott were classmates while pursuing their doctorates at the University of Toronto in the late 1920s. Winnett was the director of the American School in Jerusalem in 1950–51 when Scott visited for the first time and again in 1958–59. He served on the faculty of the University of Toronto from 1930 until his retirement in 1969. See Tushingham, "In Memoriam: Frederick Victor Winnett, 1903–1989," 1–4. Winnett, Scott, and Tushingham together formed a core group of close friends, colleagues, and University of Toronto alumni. Our thanks are extended to the Scott family for sharing with us their recollections of these men in personal interviews during July 2007.
42 Scott, "More Treasure Trove: Dead Sea Region Discoveries," 5, 28.
43 de Vaux, "Fouille au Khirbet Qumrân: Rapport préliminaire," 83–106.
44 Arlotte Douglas Tushingham (1914–2002) was educated at the University of Toronto and the Oriental Institute, Chicago. Tushingham served as professor of theology at Queen's from 1953–55. In 1956 he joined the Royal Ontario Museum (ROM) where he became director of archaeology and chief archaeologist until his retirement in 1981. He was among the first Canadians to make a name in Near Eastern archaeology, and is perhaps best known for assisting Dame Kathleen Kenyon during her excavations in Jerusalem and eventually publishing the results after her death, see Tushingham, *Excavations in Jerusalem 1961–1967*, vol. 1. Scott contributed a study of the weights and measures found during the excavations to this volume. See, "Weights from the 1961–1967 Excavations," 197–212.
45 On Winnett, Tushingham, and the Dead Sea Scrolls, see also Schuller, "The 40th anniversary of the Dead Sea Scrolls," 61–2.
46 Yusif Saʻad (in correspondence and publications spelt alternatively as: Yusef, Yussef, Yuseif or Joseph Saʻad/Saʼad) (b. 1908–unknown) began his career as chief clerk grade I at the British Mandate's Department of Antiquities in 1935. With the end of the British Mandate, he became the secretary of the

PAM. From 1957, until his retirement due to poor health in 1966, he was curator of the PAM. We thank Arieh Rochman-Halperin, archivist at the IAA in Jerusalem, for providing the biographical information. See also Zias, "Palestine Archaeological Museum," 635.

47 See Burrows, *The Dead Sea Scrolls*, 62–4.
48 Tushingham, "Report of the Director of the School in Jerusalem," 43. As to de Vaux's presence at the opening tea and Tushingham's response to the new discoveries, G. Ernest Wright relates: "At the annual tea in the American School in Jerusalem on Oct. 4th Father de Vaux of the French Dominican School rushed up to tell Dr. Tushingham, the successor of Professor Reed as our Director for this year, that new caves had been discovered and new manuscripts were pouring forth. A new search expedition was promptly organized, but nothing was found. The whole area is now patrolled by mounted police, but the region has always been too wild to be controlled by the authorities. The Bedouin are now manuscript-conscious; they are indefatigable, and they are making discoveries. Dr. Tushingham reports that 'the new manuscripts coming out – to judge by pieces already acquired by the Palestine Archaeological Museum – are most important. They are absolutely unique and they make the initial discoveries of the Dead Sea Scrolls seem rather 'tame' by comparison,'" (Wright, "Archaeological News and Views," 17).
49 At the time the sales to the University of Manchester and the other institutions had not yet taken place; material was still available.
50 Scott only knew that material for McGill would be acquired from the Cave 4 cache. He did not yet have any idea of the extent or true nature of the collection.
51 Winnett to Scott, 9 March 1954, McGill University Archives, RG34, Container: 0001, File 6: Dead Sea Scrolls.
52 Tushingham would continue to hope for an opportunity to purchase scrolls. He tried again in July 1956 while employed by the ROM but was informed by de Vaux that no fragments were immediately available for purchase. He was offered a jar and lid instead. Writing to Harding about de Vaux's offer, he commented: "About the cover and the jar he mentioned. I think we shall let it go for the present. I do hope that later on we shall be able to acquire some fragments – no great quantity but just enough to have something to show – and then we shall consider the jar," (Tushingham to Harding, 17 July 1956, IAA Archives, Box 73, PAM 1117: Dead Sea Scrolls [cave no. 4], jacket 1). According to John Strugnell, in 1966 Tushingham finally succeeded in purchasing Qumran material. He donated three pitch-black fragments of leather to the Rockefeller Museum. With the help of infra-red photography the fragments were identified as belonging to the collection of non-biblical

Thanksgiving psalms (Schuller, "The 40th anniversary of the Dead Sea Scrolls," 62).

53 Tushingham to Scott, 12 February 1954, McGill University Archives, RG34, Container: 0001, File 6: Dead Sea Scrolls.

54 Tushingham to Scott, 12 February 1954, McGill University Archives, RG34, Container: 0001, File 6: Dead Sea Scrolls. As noted above, Tushingham was present in Jerusalem when significant scroll discoveries were made. His knowledge of the negotiations seems to have been firsthand, as he had established a relationship with de Vaux.

55 Tushingham knew the two men from the period he served as director of the American School in Jerusalem (1952–53).

56 Inserted in pen by Tushingham above the struck-out word.

57 Although in his earlier correspondence with James and donors Scott appears to have been quite certain as to the authenticity of the material being purchased, it is clear from this letter that he was not operating on instinct alone. His friendship with Tushingham provided him the opportunity to hear about the discoveries at Qumran from someone who was in Jerusalem at the time and intimately involved. The pertinent discussion of authenticity of the finds seems to indicate that Scott was by no means naïve in his dealings with Harding and de Vaux.

58 Scott has "why?" pencilled in the margin in response to this statement.

59 Scott heeded the advice and cabled Harding on 15 February 1954. Further discussion of this matter follows later in the narrative.

60 The manuscript discoveries by Bedouin at Khirbet Mird in July 1952 (excavated by a Belgian team in February and March of 1953), dating to the sixth to seventh centuries CE, may have raised some concerns about the dates of other finds. See Patrich, "Mird, Khirbet," 563–6.

61 Scott had only dealt in person with de Vaux when they met in Copenhagen. He may have met Harding during his visit to ASOR in 1950–51.

62 Antiquities Law #24 of 1934 was the first Jordanian legislation protecting cultural property.

63 The Department of Antiquities discovered letters relating to a land lease in the name of Bar Kokhba in excavations at Wadi Murabba'at in 1952. Unlike the Cave 4 fragments, these were found by the department and did not have to be purchased from the Bedouin. For more on this see Eshel, "Murabba'at, Wadi," 581–6.

64 This would be the basis for the purchase agreement. Lots purchased would be identified but the final allotment would be manipulated so fragments from individual manuscripts could be kept together.

65 Winnett to Scott, 9 March 1954, McGill University Archives, RG34, Container: 0001, File 6: Dead Sea Scrolls.
66 Litt, *The Muses, the Masses, and the Massey Commission*, 105.
67 Clokie, "Canada's National Status in Recent Years," 23.
68 In the post-war period the popular media of magazines and film were dominated by New York and Hollywood, and Canadians proved eager consumers. The United States also represented one-third of the investment in Canadian industry (Finlay, *The Force of Culture*, 207).
69 Clokie, "Canada's National Status in Recent Years," 23.
70 Among other Canadian supporters, F. M. Heichelheim, a University of Toronto classicist, corresponded with Scott concerning the McGill purchase. While he had been very pleased that Canadians would own these materials, he came to be quite disappointed when he learned that no Canadians would be permanently appointed to the editorial team. Heichelheim to Scott, 3 March 1955, R.B.Y. Scott Papers, 89.112c, file: 1–6, United Church of Canada Archives, Toronto, Ontario.
71 D.B. Macfarlane, "Professor Back from Holy Land: 3,500-year-old Objects Found," *Montreal Star*, 9 July 1951, 3.
72 "McGill Buys Priceless Scraps of Old Testament Manuscripts," *Gazette* (Montreal), 22 May 1954, 19.
73 Father James Terence Forestell (1925–2000). The information supplied by the journalist is not entirely correct. Forestell, a Basilian father, ordained in Toronto in 1951, began graduate studies in Rome in 1951 and received his licence in Sacred Scripture at the Pontifical Biblical Insitute in 1955. From there he travelled to Jerusalem to study at the École Biblique, returning in 1956 to take up an appointment at St Basil's Seminary in Toronto. The Seminary in the 1950s was independent of the Pontifical Institute of Medieval Studies, although both were administered by the Basilian Fathers and they sometimes shared faculty. Forestell defended his doctoral dissertation, "The Presentation of Salvation in the Fourth Gospel," before the Pontifical Biblical Commission in 1969. Our thanks to Father James Rent, archivist of the Basilian Fathers in Toronto, Ontario, for sharing this information. Cf. Platt, "Forestell, James Terence," 227–30.
74 Harry Meyer Orlinsky (b. 1908, Owen Sound, Ontario, d. 1992) earned his Ph.D. at Dropsie College in Philadelphia. He taught at Baltimore Hebrew College (1936–44) and later at the Jewish Institute of Religion. After the latter merged with Hebrew Union College in 1950, Orlinsky continued to teach at HUC-JIR for another three decades. For a brief biography and an examination of Orlinsky's contribution to Dead Sea Scroll studies see, Kalman,

"Optimistic, Even with the Negatives," 15–25.
75 Although Orlinsky published a number of early articles on the Isaiah material from Qumran, he was not the first to translate it. See, for example, Orlinsky, "Studies in the St. Mark's Isaiah Scroll," 149–66.
76 J.E. Belliveau, "McGill Joins Vatican Check Bible Scrolls Found in Desert Cave," *Toronto Daily Star*, 16 January 1956, 25, 27. More on Orlinsky's participation in Israel's acquisition of the Dead Sea Scrolls follows in this narrative.
77 Cited in Scott to Johnson, 30 March 1955, Letter #32.
78 Frost, *The Man in the Ivory Tower*, 225.
79 In August 1955 Scott left McGill to join the faculty of Princeton University. He recognized clearly what he was giving up. Scott approached Princeton with the hope that they might also be induced to purchase scroll material, but such an arrangement never came to fruition. In a letter to Harding after his arrival at Princeton, he commented that he might be able to interest his new home institution in purchasing the Minor Prophets scroll from Wadi Murabba'at [Mur 88] in the event that the Museum needed foreign funds to acquire it (see Scott to Harding, 27 December 1955, Letter #48). In this particular case, had the arrangements been made, ironically, Princeton would have acted as the "McGill of the south."
80 In Harding's October 1953 letter, he indicates that there is more material than first appreciated and that a sum of approximately £10,000 to £12,000 will be needed for purchase – nearly triple the sum Scott was able to raise. For conversion rates, see PACIFIC Exchange Rate Service, "Foreign Currency Units per 1 British Pound, 1948–2006," http://fx.sauder.ubc.ca (accessed 18 July 2007). $12,000 to $15,000 CAD in 1953 is worth approximately $96,800 to $121,000 CAD today, see Bank of Canada, "Rates and statistics: inflation calculator," http://www.bankofcanada.ca/en/rates/inflation_calc.html (accessed 8 July 2007).
81 Brown, *John Marco Allegro*, 42.
82 As for the relative values of the purchase price at the time, Hershel Shanks points out: "In 1933 the Codex Sinaiticus, a fourth-century Bible in Greek, was purchased by the British Museum for £100,000 (then about $335,000). At about the time Yadin purchased these four [Cave 1] scrolls for Israel [from Mar Samuel], Yale University paid $50,000 for a first edition of *Alice's Adventures in Wonderland*, only a little less than the price of one of the four scrolls," (*The Mystery and Meaning of the Dead Sea Scrolls*, 22).
83 Scott to James, 28 September 1953, Letter #2.
84 Frost, *The Man in the Ivory Tower*, 7–11.

85 Tushingham to Scott, 12 February 1954, McGill University Archives, RG34, Container: 0001, File 6: Dead Sea Scrolls.
86 Harding to Kendrick, 23 October 1952, IAA Archives, Box 73, PAM 1117: Dead Sea Scrolls (cave no. 4), jacket 1. From an incomplete letter preserved in the archives of the PAM it would seem that a similar offer was made to the Library of Congress (letter to John D. Jernegan of the US Department of State, author unknown [at American Embassy in Amman], 20 October 1952, IAA Archives, Box 73, PAM 1117: Dead Sea Scrolls [cave no. 4], jacket 1).
87 Alexander Strathern Fulton was the director of the Department of Oriental Manuscripts and Printed Books of the British Museum from 1940 to 1953.
88 Kendrick to Harding, 8 November 1952, IAA Archives, Box 73, PAM 1117: Dead Sea Scrolls (cave no. 4), jacket 1.
89 Brown, *John Marco Allegro*, 42.
90 Scott to James, 28 September 1953, Letter #2.
91 Massolin, "Modernization and Reaction," 131.
92 Here the Canadian experience very much mimicked that of the United States. In general, Canadian intellectuals criticized this change in Canadian society as reflecting the influence of Canada's bigger southern neighbour. See Kuffert, *A Great Duty: Canadian Responses to Modern Life and Mass Culture in Canada, 1939–1967*.
93 Ibid., 110–16.
94 Massolin, *Canadian Intellectuals*, 155. We have relied heavily on Massolin for describing the situation in Canada. See especially chapters 4 and 5, 112–215.
95 The address entitled, "Have You Anything to Declare?" is cited in Manning, "Conflicting Views in Higher Education," 30. The article provides a useful overview of the debates concerning the role of the university in Canada, the United States, and Great Britain in the period following World War II.
96 Kuffert, *A Great Duty*, 107–9.
97 Massolin, *Canadian Intellectuals*, 129.
98 The Congregational College of Canada (affiliated in 1865), the Presbyterian College (affiliated in 1868), the Wesleyan College (affiliated in 1879), and the Montreal Diocesan Theological College (affiliated in 1880). The former three colleges merged in 1925 and became the United Theological College (UTC). The UTC in turn became an affiliate of McGill in 1929 (Markell, *The Faculty of Religious Studies*, 1).
99 Markell, *The Faculty of Religious Studies*, 15.
100 William Massey Birks (1868–1950). The Birks family made their fortune expanding a jewellery business established by Henry Birks (1840–1928).
101 Henry Guifford Birks (1892–1985).

102 Scott, "The Living Interest of the Old Testament," 66–7.
103 Quoted in Kuffert, *A Great Duty*, 134.
104 Markell, *The Faculty of Religious Studies*, 32.
105 R.B.Y. Scott, *Memorandum*, 2 March 1954, Letter #12. See especially number 4.
106 Markell, *The Faculty of Religious Studies*, 21.
107 For further exploration of the donors, see the discussion to follow.
108 Canadian Jewish Congress, *Inter-Office Information*, No. 2004, 25 October 1955 and No. 2012, 22 November 1955. Documentation provided by the Canadian Jewish Congress Charities Committee National Archives, Montreal, Quebec.
109 "Dr. R.B.Y. Scott Will Lecture on the Dead Sea Scrolls," *Gazette* (Montreal), 12 November 1955, 29.
110 "'Foundations Not Undermined': Dead Sea Scrolls Help Bible's Understanding," *Gazette* (Montreal), 22 November 1955, 3.
111 "Dead Sea Scrolls: Sharp Divergences in Scholarly Views," *Montreal Star*, 9 February 1956, 12.
112 "Spiritual Barriers Being Lowered," *Gazette* (Montreal), 7 February 1961, 11. On the contents of Golb's lecture and the participants in the institute, see also: "Dead Sea Scrolls Subject of Talk," *Montreal Star*, 7 February 1961, 13.
113 David Rome (1910–1996), director of Montreal's Jewish Public Library from 1953 until 1972, was the first Jewish member of the faculty. He served as part-time lecturer in Judaistic Studies from 1964 until 1972 (Markell, *The Faculty of Religious Studies*, 41, 67). McGill established the present Department of Jewish Studies in 1968 (Frost, *McGill University: For the Advancement of Learning*, 2: 284). Professor B. Barry Levy would become the first Jewish dean of the Faculty of Religious Studies of McGill University [formerly the Faculty of Divinity] in January 1997. He served as dean until 2007.
114 Frost, *McGill University: For the Advancement of Learning*, 2: 254–5.
115 Wilson, "A Reporter at Large: The Scrolls from the Dead Sea," 45–121. Neil Asher Silberman calls the 1955 book, *The Scrolls from the Dead Sea* by Edmund Wilson, based on this article: "the most popular and influential book on the Dead Sea Scrolls ever written," (*The Hidden Scrolls*, 119). For background and an inkling of its influence on the popular (and scholarly) imagination, see also pages 119–37 of the same.
116 Scott, "Methods and Objectives of Biblical Scholarship." The original article was entitled, "Biblical Scholarship; Like the Dead Sea Scrolls the Graduate Program in Religion Raises Questions for the Liberal Arts." It appeared in the *Princeton Alumni Weekly*, 15 April 1960, 10–15, 19. Erroneously it states in the pamphlet that it is reprinted from the weekly for 15 May 1960. This is a typographical error.

117 Scott, "Methods and Objectives of Biblical Scholarship."
118 This appreciation of the power of the press for purposes of attracting donors was by no means unique to Scott. John Allegro expressed similar sentiments and attributed the same sentiments to Frank Cross: "There is probably one third as much [fragments] again in the hands of the Bedu [sic], and it seems Harding and de Vaux are losing hopes of ever being able to get them. Frank [Cross] and I are shocked, and are sure that, given sufficient publicity, the funds would be forthcoming ... Probably something like £10–£15,000 is required – this is not an impossible figure. The trouble probably is that neither Harding nor de Vaux can spare time for a publicity tour, but I feel that this is just what is needed, complete with a short film, lots of slides, and samples from the fragments themselves. I wouldn't mind doing it myself!" (Brown, *John Marco Allegro*, 40–1).
119 See, Scott to James, 1 February 1954, Letter #8 and R.B.Y. Scott, "More Astonishing Discoveries Have Been Made in Palestine," *Montreal Star*, 23 January 1954, 21.
120 Scott to James, 1 February 1954, Letter #8.
121 Scott to Phillips, 25 November 1953, Letter #5.
122 R.B.Y. Scott, "More Astonishing Discoveries Have Been Made in Palestine," *Montreal Star*, 23 January 1954, 21.
123 Johnson to James, 26 February 1954, McGill University Archives, RG34, Container: 001, File 6: Dead Sea Scrolls.
124 James to Mrs J.H. (Elizabeth) Birks, 15 March 1954, Letter #14.
125 R.B.Y. Scott, "More Astonishing Discoveries Have Been Made in Palestine," *Montreal Star*, 23 January 1954, 21.
126 In the years immediately preceding the war the collective budget of Canadian universities was approximately $15,000,000. Government sources were responsible for 43 per cent of the budget and student fees 32 per cent. The remainder came from endowment investments and other sources. By 1948 the collective budget had risen to $36,000,000. Student fees were raised to match the government contribution but the difference could not be made up by the other sources. Cf. Pilkington, "A History of the National Conference of Canadian Universities 1911–1961," 508.
127 For a discussion of James's efforts as president of the Conference see Frost, *The Man in the Ivory Tower*, 180–4.
128 Maurice Le Noblet Duplessis (1890–1959) served as Quebec premier, 1936–39 and 1943–59. His many policies moved to maintain the distinction between federal and provincial legislative jurisdictions of which the matter of university funding was only one of many. Cf. *Canadian Encyclopedia*, s.v. "Duplessis, Maurice Le Noblet" (by Conrad M. Black), http://www.

thecanadianencyclopedia.com/index.cfm?PgNm=TCE&Params=A1A
RTA0002468 (accessed 20 February 2008).
129 For a review of these matters, see Frost, *The Man in the Ivory Tower*, 179–90. On the impact of the changing structure of university funding on McGill University in particular, see Frost, *McGill University: For the Advancement of Learning*, 2: 247–53.
130 Scott to Harding, 8 December 1953, Letter #6.
131 Ibid.
132 Harding's letter to Scott is not preserved; that it was sent and received can be confirmed by references to it in other documents such as the *Memorandum to the Board of Governors of McGill* dated 2 March 1954, Letter #12.
133 Scott to Harding, 27 January 1954, Letter #7.
134 The three cables are transcribed in Letter #10.
135 Cross, "Reminiscences of the Early Days," 932.
136 Frank Moore Cross perhaps most succinctly encapsulates the entire dating debacle from past until present:
> Driver, after three years of study in 1951 dated the scrolls to the period between the Mishnah and the Talmud, 'between AD 200 and AD 500.' After another fourteen years he had refined his dates to AD 70–73 for the Habakkuk Commentary, AD 73–81 for the Thanksgiving Hymns (a modest question mark is put here), and AD 96–132 for the Zadokite Document and the War Scroll. In fact, Albright's date for the Isaiah Scroll, the second century BCE, stands. The great Israeli epigraphist, Nahman Avigad dated the manuscript to the second half of the second century. I have dated it to 125–100 BCE. A recent carbon$_{14}$ dating yields the range 202–107 BCE. There have been many attempts to ignore palaeographical and carbon$_{14}$ dating, most recently by scholars who wish to see the sectarian documents reflecting the events of early Christian history. The speculations of these scholars are implausible enough in themselves, but by ignoring hard scientific evidence they guarantee that their views, like those of older scholars who refused to take seriously archaeological and palaeographical data, will end up on the trash heap of the history of scholarship ("Reminiscences of the Early Days," 932–3).

137 Solomon Zeitlin, (1886–1976) was Professor of Rabbinics and History at Dropsie College in Philadelphia.
138 See a selection of some of these articles in the bibliography to this book.
139 Zeitlin, "More Hebrew Scrolls," 406–8; "The Fiction of the Recent Discoveries near the Dead Sea," 85–115; "The Antiquity of the Hebrew Scrolls and the Piltdown Hoax. A Parallel," 1–29; and "A Note on the Fiction of the 'Bar Kokba' Letter," 174–80.

140 The Cairo Genizah, a rich depository of some 220,000 medieval Jewish writings discovered in the Ben Ezra Synagogue in Old Cairo in the nineteenth century. For elaboration on possible connections between the genizah and the Dead Sea Scrolls, cf. Reif, "Cairo Genizah," 105–8.

141 Zeitlin, "The Fiction of the Recent Discoveries near the Dead Sea," 100.

142 The available biographical information for Wechsler is limited. In retellings of this story he is occasionally addressed as doctor or professor and more often as mister. Sometimes he is described as a professor and at times as a journalist. According to his own account, he was a "researcher of ancient Israel history" born in Libau, Latvia, in 1889. Wechsler received his higher education in Tübingen and Hamburg and made *aliyah* to Israel in 1935. See, "Wechsler, Tovia," in *Who's Who in Israel, 1966–67*, col. 653.

143 The Jewish Sabbath liturgy includes two scriptural readings. The first is Pentateuchal and is read from the Torah scroll. The second consists of one of a series of specially selected portions from the Prophets or Hagiographa. Called the "Haftorah" ("haftorot" is the plural), these portions were sometimes hand copied on parchment scrolls like the Torah for ritual use. This kind of scroll is what Wechsler claimed to have seen. He first reported on his activities at St Mark's in a newspaper article, "*HaGenizah haGluyah v'ha Genizah haGnuzah*," *Ha'Olam*, 1 December 1949, 156–7. See also Wechsler, "The 'Hidden Geniza' Once More or Mr. Trever *versus* Mr. Trever," 247–50; and "The Origin of the So Called Dead Sea Scrolls," 121–39. A collection of his work appeared in *Tsfunot baMasoret Yisrael* (Jerusalem: Ruben Mass, 1968).

144 Zeitlin, "Where is the Scroll of the Haftarot?," 291–6.

145 The suspicion may also have found traction in circumstantial evidence. In an article in the *New York Times* the scholars working on the scroll material complained of a growing black market in "ancient" biblical texts. Much of the material traded consisted of pieces of later Torah scrolls: "'Black Market' in Biblical Documents Rises as Result of Finds in Judean Desert Caves," *New York Times*, 21 February 1953, 15.

146 The majority of these are cited in Burrows, "Concerning the Dead Sea Scrolls: A Reply to Professor Zeitlin," 105–32.

147 Ibid., 123.

148 Scott summarizes the history of authenticating the scrolls (and his own reasoning for accepting the authentication) in *Treasure from Judæan Caves*, 31–7.

149 Schuller, "The 40th anniversary of the Dead Sea Scrolls," 62.

150 Brown, *John Marco Allegro*, 41.

151 Driver, *The Hebrew Scrolls from the Neighbourhood of Jericho and the Dead Sea*, 26–50.
152 Albright, "The Dead Sea Scrolls of St. Marks Monastery," 6. As early as 1949 Albright let his feelings for Zeitlin's scholarship on these matters be known. In a private letter to Harry Orlinsky, he elaborates: "This morning I received the new JQR, with Zeitlin's blast against Sukenik's publication. I wish he hadn't taken the flyer into paleography, since I had no conception how ignorant of this field he turns out to be. This article will cook his scholarly goose for good, in so far as discussions of this type of material are concerned. I am sorry, since I like him personally and we have always got along well together. Birnbaum is right: nothing will induce Zeitlin to change his mind," (William F. Albright to Harry Orlinsky, 9 May 1949, Harry Meyer Orlinsky Papers, American Jewish Archives, Cincinnati, Ohio. MSS Col. No. 601, Sub-series I Personal and Organizational Correspondence, File 1:11 Albright, William). For additional discussion of Albright's distaste for Zeitlin's ideas, see Running and Freedman, *William Foxwell Albright*, 250–67.
153 Albright to Scott, 1 March 1954, R.B.Y. Scott Papers, 89.112c, file: 1–7, United Church of Canada Archives, Toronto, Ontario.
154 Interdepartmental Memorandum, 4 March 1954, McGill University Archives, RG34, Container: 0001, File 6: Dead Sea Scrolls.
155 Harding to Scott, 16 March 1954, Letter #15.
156 Scott to Harding, 8 April 1954, Letter #17. A copy of the bank draft made out in Harding's name for $10,363.52 USD is preserved in McGill University Archives, RG4 Container: 239, File: Birks, John Henry – Collection, Judean Manuscripts – Dead Sea Scrolls.
157 We could find no evidence for the preservation of such a physical record in the archives of McGill University, the Rockefeller Museum, or the Department of Antiquities of Jordan.
158 Scott, "Special Report: What Ever Happened to McGill's Dead Sea Scrolls?" 56.
159 Harding to Scott, 11 March 1954, Letter #13.
160 Wilfred Cantwell Smith (1916–2000) came to McGill's Faculty of Divinity in 1949 as Professor of Comparative Religion. He established the Institute of Islamic Studies in 1951 and remained its director until he left in 1964 for Harvard Divinity School's Center for the Study of World Religions. Smith's involvement, as a revered member of McGill's faculty, is important, as it establishes the project as institutionally important, rather than the mere pet project of an Old Testament scholar (Scott) and an indulgent university principal (James). See also Markell, *The Faculty of Religious Studies*, 29.

161 Scott to Harding, 27 March 1954, Letter #16.
162 Memorandum from Wilfred Cantwell Smith for Dr. R.B.Y. Scott re McGill fragments in the Jerusalem Museum, 20 May 1954, Letter #22.
163 Memorandum from Wilfred Cantwell Smith for Dr. R.B.Y. Scott re McGill fragments in the Jerusalem Museum, 20 May 1954, Letter #22. On the arrival of McGill's fragments, see Harding to Scott, 19 April 1954, Letter #18.
164 Memorandum from Wilfred Cantwell Smith for Dr. R.B.Y. Scott re McGill fragments in the Jerusalem Museum, 20 May 1954, Letter #22.
165 In speaking to the press, Smith would reiterate much of what would appear in his memorandum to Scott about his visit (Letter #22), including the number of plates McGill would receive and a description of interesting pieces in the collection. Cf. "McGill Buys Priceless Scraps of Old Testament Manuscripts," *Gazette* (Montreal), 22 May 1954, 19. Discussion of the contents of Smith's report follows further on in this narrative.
166 See Scott's notes on his interview with James, 24 March 1954, McGill University Archives, RG34, Container: 0001, File 6: Dead Sea Scrolls.
167 James Sutherland Thomson (1892–1972), formerly principal of the University of Saskatchewan, was appointed dean of the Faculty of Divinity at McGill following R.B.Y. Scott in 1949. He remained with the faculty until he was appointed moderator of the United Church of Canada in 1956.
168 McGill University, *Annual Report, 1953–1954*, 48, 201.
169 The contents of the "Notes for Press Release" are faithfully reflected in four consequent newspaper articles: "McGill Buys Priceless Scraps of Old Testament Manuscripts," *Gazette* (Montreal), 22 May 1954, 19; "McGill Gets Part of Rare Bible Find," *Montreal Star*, 22 May 1954, 3–4; "McGill University Buys Ancient Bible Scrolls," *New York Times*, 24 May 1954, 21; and "Biblical Manuscripts $15,000 purchase by McGill University," *Times* (London), 24 May 1954, 6(G).
170 See Press Release: "Montreal Professor Broadcasts on Dead Sea Scrolls," McGill University Archives, RG34, Container: 0001, File 6: Dead Sea Scrolls; and "Discovery of the Dead Sea Scrolls," CBC *Times* (14–20 August 1955), n.p., photocopy in McGill University Archives, RG34 Container: 0001 File 6: Dead Sea Scrolls. Scott's appearances on CBC Radio were published in December of the same year as *Treasure from Judæan Caves: The Story of the Dead Sea Scrolls*.
171 Scott, "Acquisition of Dead Sea Scroll Fragments by McGill University," 8.
172 Albright to Scott, 28 May 1954, R.B.Y. Scott Papers, 89.112c, file: 1–7, United Church of Canada Archives, Toronto, Ontario.
173 John Scott, "The Dead Sea Scrolls: Some of the Oldest Manuscripts of the Bible Ever Found are Acquired by the University," *McGill News* 4 (Autumn 1954), 24–5, 53–4.

174 John Scott, "The Dead Sea Scrolls: Some of the Oldest Bible Manuscripts," 3.
175 Frank Cross was at the time teaching at McCormick Theological Seminary in Chicago.
176 Cross to Scott, 12 August 1954, McGill University Archives, RG34, Container: 0001, File 6: Dead Sea Scrolls.
177 The announcement of McGill's purchase can be found in Burrows, *The Dead Sea Scrolls*, 69.
178 William David Davies (1911–2001) was professor of Biblical Theology at Duke from 1950 to 1955. He left for Princeton and Union Theological Seminary, returning to Duke in 1966, where he remained until 1981. He would eventually assert the usefulness of the Qumran finds for understanding the historical background to the New Testament. See for example: "Paul and the Dead Sea Scrolls: Flesh and Spirit," 157–82.
179 The Society has two secretaries: home and foreign. From 1946 to 1960, the home secretary was G. Henton Davies of Durham University and the foreign secretary was H.H. Rowley of Manchester. Who was responsible for the announcement is not clear. As is apparent from later letters, Scott knew and corresponded with Rowley. The official minutes of the meeting, preserved at the archives of the British Society for Old Testament Study, University of Wales, Bangor, include no mention of this announcement. We extend our thanks to the archivist, Edward Ball, for checking the material on our behalf.
180 Scott to James, 31 August 1954, Letter #26.
181 See, for example, Pfann, "History of the Judean Desert Discoveries," 97–108. No mention of it is made in Fields's *The Dead Sea Scrolls: A Short History*, although his entry in the *Encyclopedia of the Dead Sea Scrolls* (Weston Fields, "Discovery and Purchase," 1: 211) acknowledges a purchase of Cave 4 documents by McGill University but does not provide a chronological listing of institutions who funded the purchase of Cave 4 fragments and the consequent status of McGill as the "first foreign institution to purchase scroll fragments" is therefore underplayed.
182 Pfann, "History of the Judean Desert Discoveries," 101.
183 Frost to the Director of Antiquities, 10 June 1960, Letter #99.
184 James to the Director of Antiquities, 30 March 1957, Letter #79.
185 Frost to the Director of Antiquities, 10 June 1960, Letter #99.
186 Scott to Harding, 27 January 1954, Letter #7.
187 Frank Cross joined the team in May 1953; Milik followed in the fall of that year. In December 1953, John Marco Allegro arrived and Jean Starcky joined in January 1954, with Patrick Skehan following in June 1954. John Strugnell came to the team in July 1954 and Claus-Hunno Hunzinger in October 1954 (Pfann, "History of the Judean Desert Discoveries," 100–1).
188 Harding to Scott, 3 October 1953, Letter #3.

189 For a short history of the unintended role of the Cave 4 concordance would later play in freeing the scrolls from editorial monopoly in the early 1990s, see Shanks, *The Mystery and Meaning of the Dead Sea Scrolls*, 45, 54–6.
190 In 1960 Willard Gurdon Oxtoby (1933–2003) joined the faculty as lecturer in Semitics. Dean Stanley Frost would meet Oxtoby on his visit to Jerusalem while Oxtoby was at work on the concordance of scroll material at the museum (cf. Report to the Principal, 12 May 1960, Letter #97). Oxtoby was annual fellow in 1958–1959 at ASOR and remained an additional year in Jerusalem. For brief reference to Oxtoby's duties in Jerusalem, cf. Winnett, "Report of the Director of the School in Jerusalem," 4–7; and Pope, "Report of the Director of the School in Jerusalem," 5. Completing his Ph.D. at Princeton in 1962, Oxtoby was appointed assistant professor at McGill, but left the university in 1964 to pursue post-doctoral work at Harvard. See also, "In Memoriam: Willard Gurdon Oxtoby," *News@UofT*, 5 May 2003. http://www.newsandevents.utoronto.ca/bin5/030505h.asp (accessed: 23 November 2007); and Ron Csillag, "Scholar was Hooked on Religion," *Globe and Mail* (Toronto), 31 March 2003, 7(R).
191 Scott to Harding, 27 March 1954, Letter #16.
192 De Vaux to Scott, 23 April 1954, Letter #21.
193 As an aside, Frank Moore Cross indicated to the authors during a personal interview at his home on 22 May 2000 that the job at Princeton awarded to Scott was first offered to him. Cross had declined and one wonders the degree to which Scott's own involvement with the scrolls made him a worthwhile candidate to his prospective new employer.
194 Harding to Kendrick, 23 October 1952, IAA Archives, Box 73, PAM 1117: Dead Sea Scrolls (cave no. 4), jacket 1.
195 Kendrick to Harding, 8 November 1952, IAA Archives, Box 73, PAM 1117: Dead Sea Scrolls (cave no. 4), jacket 1. Jacob Leveen (1891–1980) was assistant keeper in the Department of Oriental Printed Books and Manuscripts in the British Museum, later Keeper (1953–56). Between 1949 and 1951, a significant number of articles and letters to the editor in the *Times* (London), by G.R. Driver and others, challenged the antiquity of the scrolls. Leveen, to the contrary, published in defence of dating the scrolls to the period before the birth of Jesus. See, for example, "Hebrew Scrolls' Age: Evidence for a B.C. Date," *Times* (London), 26 August 1949, 5; "Hebrew Scrolls' Age: The Use of Ruling," *Times* (London), 5 September 1949, 7; and, "Dead Sea Scroll of Isaiah: Examination of the Evidence of Date," *Times* (London), 7 May 1951, 5.

On the implications of Kendrick's letter for understanding the political motives for keeping Jews off the editorial team, see Silberman, *The Hidden Scrolls*, 84–5. On anti-Semitism and the absence of Jewish members of the

196 Fields, *The Dead Sea Scrolls: A Short History*, 63.
197 Elsewhere Fields has more to say about the very limited discussion of Harding in various histories of the Dead Sea Scrolls:

> Just one example illustrates the need for this book. Anyone who reads the first eight chapters of the book, or who looks at the Palestine Archaeological Museum archive, or speaks with the remaining members of the Cave 4 Team will understand that the greatest share of the credit for saving the Cave 4 fragments for posterity goes to Gerald Lankester Harding. Yet one scarcely hears his name on the lips of scrolls scholars today despite the fact that he was pivotal in every aspect of early research, whether documentary or archaeological. This leads inevitably to the conclusion that something has gone amiss, that the written and oral tradition took a wrong turn somewhere. This sort of thing will be observed again and again: there is frequently a skewed view of who made what important decisions, or took significant actions, even of when, and why. (Fields, *Dead Sea Scrolls: A Full History*, 17).

198 Cross, "Reminiscences of the Early Days," 934.
199 "Bible Scrolls Found in Cave to Go on Sale," *New York Times*, 14 April 1949, 21. The following week an article appeared describing the contents of the scrolls. It commented on the fact that the scrolls were being examined by biblical scholars at Yale University under the auspices of ASOR. The article includes a photograph of the archbishop holding a scroll, surrounded by Millar Burrows, John Trever, and an official of the Syrian Orthodox Church. The article also reminded the reader that "it is reported that he [Samuel] plans to sell them [the scrolls] to some institution," ("A 2,000-Year-Old 'Mystery' at Yale: Old-Scroll Cache Widens Bible Lore," *New York Times*, 21 August 1949, 19).
200 After Mar Athanasius Samuel brought the scrolls he had purchased to ASOR for examination they were photographed by John Trever. ASOR, over the next year, negotiated the rights to publish the photographs along with transcriptions of the texts. The two-volume publication appeared in 1950 and 1951 and made the content of these scrolls available to the public. See Burrows, Trever, and Brownlee, eds, *The Dead Sea Scrolls of St. Mark's Monastery*.
201 Wilson, *The Scrolls from the Dead Sea*, 30, 149–50.
202 Shanks, *The Mystery and Meaning of the Dead Sea Scrolls*, 22–3.
203 In fact, the sale had been interrupted by American attempts (ASOR) to negotiate the rights to publish them and, as a result, to increase their commercial value. Sukenik described his efforts to purchase the scrolls in January and

February 1948 in his private journal. A translation of this is found in Yadin, *The Message of the Scrolls*, 21–9.
204 Ted R. Lurie, "Judean Scrolls in Danger of being Sold Abroad," *Palestine Post*, 21 April 1949, 2.
205 Zeitlin, "The Dead Sea Scrolls: 1. The Lamech Scroll: A Medieval Midrash. 2. The Copper Scrolls. 3. Was Kando the Owner of the Scrolls?" 264–8. Harding reiterated Jordan's claim in the first volume of DJD, even after the archbishop's scrolls had been sold to Israel. He insisted that the Department of Antiquities had never been informed of the scrolls in the archbishop's possession despite Mar Samuel's claim to the contrary (cf. Harding, "Introductory. The Discovery, the Excavation, Minor Finds," 4–5).
206 Zeitlin, "When Were the Hebrew Scrolls 'Discovered' – in 1947 or 1907?" 373–8.
207 Charles Manoog (1903–1989) was a Worcester, Mass., businessman who founded a wholesale plumbing business in 1927. His parents were members of St Mary's Assyrian Orthodox Church in Worcester, the first church built in the American diocese. When Athanasius Samuel became the head of the Archdiocese, he befriended Manoog, who became a confidant and helped support the archbishop financially. For a number of years he preserved the scrolls in his home and helped arrange the placement of the now famous classified ad in the *Wall Street Journal* on 1 June 1954. See, "Archbishop Leading His Flock – Syrian Orthodox Church Cleric," *Worcester Telegram & Gazette*, 4 July 1993, 5(B); and the Archbishop's description of Manoog and his role in the Dead Sea Scrolls story in Samuel, *Treasure of Qumran*, 185–201.
208 Word inserted in pen above the line.
209 See Manoog to James, 3 June 1954, McGill University Archives, RG34, Container: 0001, File 6: Dead Sea Scrolls. The "enclosed pamphlet" is not preserved in the McGill archives. A copy of the same pamphlet seemed to have been offered via a middleman to Yigael Yadin when he began to arrange the purchase of these scrolls. See Yadin, *The Message of the Scrolls*, 42–43.
210 Yigael Yadin (1917–1984) was the son of Eleazar Sukenik. As archaeologist he would make an invaluable contribution to archaeology in Israel. In the present context, he is best remembered for his acquisition and publication of one of the "most important manuscripts from Qumran," the Temple Scroll (11Q19), in 1967 (Silberman, "Yadin, Yigael," 999–1000). See also Yadin, *The Temple Scroll: The Hidden Law of the Dead Sea Sect*.
211 This is erroneous. As the call was received in response to McGill's public announcement of purchase, this could only have happened on the day, or some time after 22 May 1954.
212 Samuel, *Treasure of Qumran*, 197–8.

213 The letter of 3 June 1954 is ink-stamped with the date of receipt and the insignia of the principal's office.
214 Therefore, Manoog wrote to McGill on 3 June 1954 having not yet received Yigael Yadin's representative's letter dated 2 June 1954.
215 For Yigael Yadin's description of the events of the purchase, see *The Message of the Scrolls*, 39–52. The archbishop provides his version of the events in *Treasure of Qumran*, 197–201. Professor Harry Orlinsky, of the Hebrew Union College–Jewish Institute of Religion in New York, authenticated the materials for Yadin using the alias, "Mr. Green." For his account of these events, see Orlinsky, "The Dead Sea Scrolls and Mr. Green," 245–56. On the participation of William F. Albright, see Running and Freedman, *William Foxwell Albright*, 265–7. The advertisement was brought to Yadin's attention by journalist Monty Jacobs, the New York correspondent for the London-based *Jewish Chronicle*. Jacobs described his assistance to Yadin in an extensive article in the *Chronicle* that appeared a few days following Israel's announcement of the purchase on 18 February 1955 (Monty Jacobs, "Israel's Purchase of the Dead Sea Scrolls: Initiative of the 'J.C.' Correspondent," *The Jewish Chronicle*, 18 February 1955, 19, 29). Despite Orlinsky's active involvement, his personal papers include only one reference to the event. In a letter to Albright, he notes that he spoke to Yadin by phone on 15 June 1954 and was scheduled to meet with him the coming Friday (18 June). It appears that although both men knew of each other's participation, they limited any oblique discussion thereof (cf. Harry Orlinsky to William Albright, 15 June 1954 and William Albright to Harry Orlinsky, 23 June 1954, Harry Meyer Orlinsky Papers, American Jewish Archives, Cincinnati, Ohio. MSS Col. No. 601, Sub-series I Personal and Organizational Correspondence, File 1:11 Albright, William).
216 Scott to Manoog, 9 June 1954, Letter #25.
217 "Price: $250,000. Israel Buys 4 Scrolls Once Offered McGill," *Gazette* (Montreal), 14 February 1955, 3.
218 Memorandum from Wilfred Cantwell Smith for Dr. R.B.Y. Scott re McGill fragments in the Jerusalem Museum, 20 May 1954, Letter #22.
219 Scott to Harding, 8 June 1954, Letter #24.
220 Letter not preserved, the date and contents derived from Frank Cross's response dated 12 August 1954.
221 Cross to Scott, 12 August 1954, McGill University Archives, RG34, Container: 0001, File 6: Dead Sea Scrolls.
222 According to Scott, he received four pictures of plates of fragments and one of scholars at work in the scrollery [Scott to James, 31 August 1954, Letter #26]. The plates can be identified certainly as PAM 41.208, 41.209, and

41.210. These are all marked "Sample Plate S" in the lower left corner. (NB: 41.211 is marked "Sample Plate A" for Manchester.) A fourth fragment plate which includes the large piece of Daniel is not marked as belonging to McGill but seems, based on sequence and content, to be PAM 41.207, which includes 4Q112 Dan[a]. The scholars at work are found in PAM 41.212. It was first published in Burrows, *The Dead Sea Scrolls*, plate VIII. Only PAM 41.209 is preserved in the McGill archives, although it is marked generically as PR015862 – Document: Pieces of Ancient Syrian Papyrus in the Palestine Archaeological Museum.

According to Reed and Lundberg (*The Dead Sea Scrolls Catalogue*, 313), PAM 41.208 includes fragments 4Q299 Myst[a], 4Q385 psEzek[a], 4Q394 MMT[a] (4 fragments), 4Q436 Barki Nafshi[c], 4Q477 Decrees, 4QM PsHis B and three unidentified fragments. PAM 41.209 includes 4QGen[b], 4Q44 Deut[q], 4Q84 Ps[b], 4Q205 En[d], 4Q261 S[g], 4Q372 apocrJoseph[b], 4Q385 psEzek[a], 4Q425 Sap Work C, 4QM PsHis A, 4QM127A, and four unidentified fragments. PAM 41.210 includes 4Q57 Isa[c] frg 48, 4Q118 Chr, 4Q216 Jub[a], 4Q247 Apoc Weeks, 4Q374 apocrMoses, 4Q388 psEzek[d], 4Q423 Sap Work A[e], 4Q423a Sap Work E, 4Q434 Barki Nafshi[a], 4Q434a Grace After Meals, 4Q443 Prayer, 4Q457 Prayer, 4Q481 UnclassFragment, 4Q527 Hebrew Frg D, and twelve unidentified fragments.

223 The photographer, Najib Albina, kept a log of his work. It is reproduced in Tov and Pfann, *Companion Volume*, 155–62. For the photographs discussed here, see 158.

224 PAM 41.210 and 41.212, 24 of the article. The caption with the former reads: "Not all McGill's Old Testament fragments are as small as the ones in this lot. But the scraps here convey the difficulty facing scholars attempting to identify, match and read their horde of hundreds of scraps. It is estimated that it will probably take two years for the job of identification to be completed." The caption with the latter reads: "In the Jerusalem Museum a fascinating 'jigsaw puzzle' with the Bible progresses day by day. Here Biblical scholars pore over literally hundreds of fragments of Old Testament books found in caves at Khirbet Qumran, trying to identify and match them. McGill's fragments are among the pieces shown." The captions point to Scott's concern that some might be underwhelmed by McGill's purchase of scraps (as shown in the photo) and the need to justify the delay before their arrival in Montreal.

225 Five manuscripts of Daniel are known from Cave 4: 4QDan[a], 4QDan[b], 4QDan[c], 4QDan[d], and 4QDan[e]. Together, portions of all the chapters of Daniel are represented, except for chapter 12. Frank Cross had made reference to McGill's purchase of a large piece of Daniel, as had Smith in his earlier report. According to the list compiled by Scott on his 1955 visit, as well

as the distribution list eventually received from Harding, McGill expected to receive 4QDan[a], which includes portions of Dan. 1, 2, 4, 5, 7, 10, and 11 (cf. Ulrich, "Daniel Manuscripts from Qumran. Part 1: A Preliminary Edition of 4QDan[a]," 17–37). The *editio princeps* has since been published; see Ulrich et al., *Qumran Cave 4.XI: Psalms to Chronicles*, DJD, 16:239–54. PAM 41.207 includes a high quality photo of 4Q112 Dan[a]. None of the three other plates include a fragment from Daniel.

226 4QXII[a] and 4QXII[g] both include portions of Jonah 2. However, no reference to McGill receiving Jonah fragments appears in Scott's or Harding's lists. For discussion of the manuscripts, see Ulrich et al., *Qumran Cave 4.X: The Prophets*, DJD, 15:221–318. Scott seems to have erred in his identification, as none of the photos he received includes material from Jonah.

227 Based on this description and the information in Scott's list, it would appear to be part of 4QDeut[q]. For discussion of this manuscript, see Ulrich et al., *Qumran Cave 4.IX: Deuteronomy, Joshua, Judges, Kings*, DJD, 14:137–42.

228 Scott to James, 31 August 1954, Letter #26.

229 The list was included as an attachment to a letter from Scott to Harding, 7 September 1955, Letter #43. It appears in the addendum to this book, entitled: "Scroll Fragments from Qumran Cave Four purchased with a contribution from McGill University, 1954."

230 Scott to Thomson, 6 December 1954, Letter #28.

231 The UTC had been an affiliate of the Faculty of Divinity at McGill since 1929. See Scott to Henry G. Birks, 3 March 1955, McGill University Archives, RG2, Container: 0179, File 6243: Divinity: DSS & Birks Donation.

232 Scott to Johnson, 30 March 1955, Letter #32.

233 See Ramsey, "Princeton University's Graduate Program in Religion," 291–8.

234 Scott would continue to communicate with the Birks family as the story of McGill's scrolls purchase unfolded. See, for example, Elizabeth Birks to Scott, 18 May 1955, McGill University Archives, RG34, Container: 0001, File 6: Dead Sea Scrolls. Birks wrote the letter thanking Scott for updating her on his work in Jerusalem. The letter makes clear that the family was grateful for the opportunity to participate in the project and took an interest in Scott's discoveries: "I appreciate your great kindness in writing me such an interesting and informative account of your visit to the Museum. I do hope the 'Fragments' will be sufficiently plentiful to repay you for your work in connection with them. It is strange to think that it is possible in this day and age to see the remains of writings, furniture, and other articles in use so long ago."

235 Scott to James cited in Scott to Johnson, 30 March 1955, Letter #32.

236 Scott to Harding, 13 April 1955, Letter #35.

237 James, the other important figure in these events, would resign as principal of McGill University in February 1962.
238 James to Scott, 13 April 1955, Letter #34. The Birks Foundation forwarded a cheque for $1,500 CAD on 19 April 1955 to cover Scott's expenses (Johnson to Bentley, 19 April 1955, McGill University Archives, RG34, Container: 001, File 6: Dead Sea Scrolls).
239 The fourth season's excavation under de Vaux's direction was carried out between 2 February and 6 April 1955 (cf. de Vaux, "Fouilles au Khirbet Qumrân: Rapport préliminaire sur les 3e, 4e et 5e campagnes," 533). Scott gave a lively account of his visit to the site with de Vaux in, "The Dead Sea Scrolls," *Star Weekend Magazine*, 15 October 1955, 2–4, 40, 42.
240 Scott, "The Dead Sea Scrolls," 40. The nature of the relationship between the Qumran settlement and the adjacent caves has proved contentious, though the majority view is in favour of a link. However, Dead Sea Scrolls scholarship is unanimous in agreement that no connection between the settlement and a monastery, in the Christian sense of the word, can be supported. On the unfortunate preconceived notions brought to the table by the early team of predominantly Christian scholars, cf., for example, Schiffman, *Reclaiming the Dead Sea Scrolls*.
241 Scott, "The Dead Sea Scrolls," 40.
242 Scott to Harding, 4 May 1955, Letter #36 and Harding to Scott, 10 May 1955, Letter #37.
243 This step was confirmed prior to Scott's visit by Frank Moore Cross in a handwritten letter dated 12 August 1954 (McGill University Archives, RG34, Container: 0001 File 6: Dead Sea Scrolls). Wilfred Cantwell Smith, in his memorandum of May 1954, Letter #22, explained that "S" (for Scott) was chosen instead of "M" (for McGill) in order not to confuse McGill's purchase with that of the museum: "M."
244 Scott to Harding, 4 May 1955, Letter #36.
245 Harding to Scott, 10 May 1955, Letter #37.
246 Scott to James, 15 May 1955, Letter #38.
247 Scott to F. Cyril James et al., 15 June 1955, Letter #40.
248 Scott to Harding, 7 September 1955, Letter #43.
249 McGill University Archives, RG34, Container: 0001, File 6: Dead Sea Scrolls.
250 Patrick Skehan, John Allegro, John Strugnell, Józef Milik, Jean Starcky, and Claus-Hunno Hunzinger (Scott to F. Cyril James et al., 15 June 1955, Letter #40).
251 Scott to James, 15 May 1955, Letter #38.
252 Scott to Harding, 7 September 1955, Letter #43.
253 Ibid.

254 Scott, "Special Report: What Ever Happened to McGill's Dead Sea Scrolls?" 57.
255 Scott to F. Cyril James et al., 15 June 1955, Letter #40.
256 Claus-Hunno Hunzinger (b. 1929), a Lutheran scholar, now emeritus professor of New Testament at the University of Hamburg. He was sent to Jerusalem as the representative of the Deutsche Forschungsgemeinschaft and worked primarily on the War Scroll and papyrus manuscript fragments. According to Stephen J. Pfann's timeline, Hunzinger would withdraw his membership from the editorial team in April 1971. His assigned allotments of texts were added to that of Baillet ("History of the Judean Desert Discoveries," 106).
257 Patrick W. Skehan (1909–1980), a New York-born Roman Catholic priest with a doctorate from the Catholic University of America, was in Jerusalem as an annual professor at ASOR in 1954 when he was appointed to the editorial team. He was responsible for editing biblical manuscripts in Paleo-Hebrew script (cf. Ulrich, "Skehan, Patrick W.," 880).
258 Hunzinger's participation is evidenced in a letter he wrote to Scott following Scott's departure from Jerusalem (Hunzinger to Scott, 17 July 1955, McGill University Archives, RG34, Container: 0001 File 6: Dead Sea Scrolls, described below). Skehan is described by Scott in his 1981 retelling of the story: "Special Report: What Ever Happened to McGill's Dead Sea Scrolls?" 55–8.
259 Scott, "Special Report: What Ever Happened to McGill's Dead Sea Scrolls?" 55–8.
260 Scott to F. Cyril James et al., 15 June 1955, Letter #40.
261 Most likely the reference is to Philip C. Hammond and his wife. They were at the end of a two year stint at ASOR in Jerusalem, where Hammond had been a fellow. During his tenure he also excavated at Jericho and Dhiban. Hammond's "A Note on a Seal Impression From Tell es-Sultân," is based on material discovered during his excavation at the site with Kathleen Kenyon in 1955.
262 From his return until 1957, Philip Hammond was in New Haven, Connecticut, completing his Ph.D. at Yale.
263 Hunzinger to Scott, 17 July 1955, McGill University Archives, RG34, Container: 0001 File 6: Dead Sea Scrolls.
264 James to Scott, 22 June 1955, Letter #41.
265 In a no longer extant letter dated 6 December 1955. It is referred to in later correspondence between Scott and Harding, 27 December 1955, Letter #48.
266 De Vaux to Scott, 18 December 1955, Letter #44.
267 Scott to Johnson, 23 December 1955, Letter #45.

268 The contents of the telegram are quoted in Scott to Harding, 27 December 1955, Letter #48.
269 De Vaux to Scott, 18 December 1955, Letter #44.
270 The Royal Academy of Sciences of the Netherlands would in due course purchase material from Cave 11 (see annotations to de Vaux to Scott, 15 May 1956, Letter #59).
271 Just like McGill, the Vatican Library made at least two purchases of Cave 4 material. The first was made in October 1954 and the second in December 1955. De Vaux is here clearly referring to the second, and more substantial, purchase (cf. Pfann, "History of the Judean Desert Discoveries," 101–2). According to John Allegro, the first purchase amounted to approximately £700 (*The Dead Sea Scrolls: A Reappraisal*, 47).
272 Paul Hofmann, "Vatican Studies Biblical Scrolls," *New York Times*, 13 May 1956, 118. The article's purpose was to report on Ernst Vogt's announcement that the Vatican did not fear the scrolls and that they proved "the substantial faithfulness of the sacred texts transmitted to us." Vogt's own interest in the scrolls preceded the Vatican's purchase of any part of them. See, for example, Vogt, "'Pax Hominibus Bonae Voluntatis' Lc 2:14" ("Peace Among Men of God's Good Pleasure" Lk. 2:14), 427–9.
273 The purchase was officially announced in May 1956. Cf. Paul Hoffman, "Vatican Studies Biblical Scrolls," *New York Times*, 13 May 1956, 118. See also, J.E. Belliveau, "McGill Joins Vatican Check Bible Scrolls Found in Desert Cave," *Toronto Daily Star*, 16 January 1956, 25, 27.
274 J.E. Belliveau, "McGill Joins Vatican Check Bible Scrolls Found in Desert Cave," *Toronto Daily Star*, 16 January 1956, 27.
275 Unless what Vogt was referring to was emergency funding provided by the École Biblique as a Roman Catholic institution, via the agency of de Vaux. From de Vaux's response to Scott's confirmation of funding for a second purchase of materials, the use of an advance by the École Biblique was clearly not out of the question (De Vaux to Scott, 8 January 1956, Letter #52).

The Jordanians agreed to allow foreign institutions to buy and export the fragments in three documents, all dated late 1953: 1) A letter from the prime minister to the minister of education including agreement to allow foreign institutions to acquire scroll fragments: Ref. No. 26/1/1/8723 of 21 November 1953; 2) a letter from the director of antiquities to the minister of education asking for clearer interpretation of the previous letter: Ref. No. 18/3/14 of 30 November 1953; and 3) a reply from the minister of education including a statement that the export of scroll fragments would be permitted: Ref. No. 39/2/12463 of 23 December 1953 (cf. Scott to James, 19 March 1957, Letter #76).

276 On the Manchester Purchase, see Brown, *John Marco Allegro*, 41–3. Scott had been informed of Manchester's negotiations in May 1954 by William Albright. Albright to Scott, 28 May 1954, R.B.Y. Scott Papers, 89.112c, file: 1–7, United Church of Canada Archives, Toronto, Ontario.
277 Extract from BBC Radio's *The Listener*, 25 November 1954, included with Scott to James, 20 December 1954, Letter #29.
278 Stephen J. Pfann ("History of the Judean Desert Discoveries," 101) dates the purchase to October 1954 and lists as his source the archival distribution list from the PAM archives and John Allegro's *The Dead Sea Scrolls: A Reappraisal*. Neither the preliminary list nor the final division appear to include the exact dates of purchase. John Allegro did note that the Vatican made two purchases, a first contribution of about £700, and a second of several thousand pounds (*The Dead Sea Scrolls: A Reappraisal*, 47); he does not provide an exact date for the purchases.
279 Scott to Bentley, 27 December 1955, Letter #47.
280 Harding to Bentley, 5 January 1956, Letter #51.
281 De Vaux to Scott, 8 January 1956, Letter #52.
282 De Vaux to Scott, 7 April 1956, Letter #57.
283 F. Cyril James, "A Visit to Israel, 1955," 26 (McGill University Archives, MG 1017, Container 75, File: James Diaries, 2 Oct 1955–3 Dec 1955).
284 Ibid., 19.
285 Ibid.
286 J.E. Belliveau, "McGill Joins Vatican Check Bible Scrolls Found in Desert Cave," *Toronto Daily Star*, 16 January 1956, 25, 27.
287 James to Scott, 24 January 1956, Letter #55. On James's participation in the International Association of Universities, see Frost, *The Man in the Ivory Tower*, 214–18 and 259–71.
288 For a broader discussion of Scott's media presence and the history of the Canadian press's treatment of the scrolls, see du Toit and Kalman, "Great Scott!," 6–23.
289 "Archaeological Trip Planned," *Montreal Star*, 7 December 1950, 3; "McGill Professor to Visit Mid-East to Join in Archaeological Research," *Gazette* (Montreal), 27 December 1950, 15; D.B. Macfarlane, "Professor Back from Holy Land: 3,500-year-old Objects Found," *Montreal Star*, 9 July 1951, 3; and D.B. Macfarlane, "Holy Land Study Fruitful, Says McGill Prof. R.B.Y. Scott," *Montreal Star*, 9 July 1951, 3.
290 "McGill Professor to Visit Mid-East to Join in Archaeological Research," *Gazette* (Montreal), 27 December 1950, 15.
291 R.B.Y. Scott, "More Treasure Trove: Dead Sea Region Discoveries," *United Church Observer*, 15 July 1953, 5, 28.

292 R.B.Y. Scott, "More Astonishing Discoveries Have Been Made in Palestine," *Montreal Star,* 23 January 1954, 21.
293 Wilson, "A Reporter at Large: The Scrolls from the Dead Sea," 45–121. On the importance of Wilson's work in shaping the public discourse on the scrolls, see Schiffman, "Inverting Reality," 25–9. Schiffman asserts that Wilson's interpretation of the scrolls (in his article and subsequent work), "because of his substantial reputation, influenced all subsequent development of the depiction of the scrolls in the popular media," ("Inverting Reality," 27). For its reception by the scholarly world, see Goldman, "A Long Affair," 119–20.
294 James to Scott, 30 May 1955, Letter #39.
295 For Scott's radio programs, see Press Release: "Montreal Professor Broadcasts on Dead Sea Scrolls," McGill University Archives, RG34, Container: 0001, File 6: Dead Sea Scrolls; and "Discovery of the Dead Sea Scrolls," CBC *Times* (14–20 August 1955), n.p., photocopy in McGill University Archives, RG34 Container: 0001 File 6: Dead Sea Scrolls.
296 A contemporary discussion of the laity's concerns is provided in "Laity Said to Think Scrolls Hurt Creed," *New York Times,* 26 March 1956, 33.
297 "'Foundations Not Undermined': Dead Sea Scrolls Help Bible's Understanding," *Gazette* (Montreal), 22 November 1955, 3.
298 Transcripts of the three talks are preserved in the R.B.Y. Scott papers in the United Church of Canada archives, 89.112c, files: 3–22, 3–23, and 3–24, United Church of Canada Archives, Toronto, Ontario. The book was well received by de Vaux, who, in thanking Scott on receipt of a copy, commented: "I congratulate you on this especially lively presentation and particularly well adapted to the public at large," (de Vaux to Scott, 7 April 1956, Letter #57). In the dedication of the book, which was an expansion of several talks Scott gave to CBC radio (see above), Scott thanks de Vaux and Frank Moore Cross, who took him to see Cave 4 and the Qumran excavations during his Spring visit to Israel. Scott sent a copy of the book to Cross as well. Cross's copy, now in the possession of the authors, includes a note indicating it was a gift from Scott.
299 Scott, *Treasure from Judæan Caves,* v.
300 Brown, *John Marco Allegro,* 76–112.
301 Ibid., 78.
302 Jean Starcky (1909–1988) was one of the original members of the international Cave 4 editorial team, for more on his contribution to Dead Sea Scroll scholarship, see Puech, "Starcky, Jean," 891–2.
303 These phrases appear explicitly in the coverage of Allegro's broadcast provided by *Time* ("Crucifixion Before Christ," *Time* [6 February 1956]. http://

www.time.com/time/magazine/article/0,9171,893345,00.html?iid=chix-sphere [accessed: 10 December 2007]).

304 "Letters to the Editor," *Times* (London), 16 March 1956, 11.

305 "The Dead Sea Scrolls, Their Significance to Religious Thought: A Symposium," *The New Republic*, 9 April 1956.

306 "The Dead Sea Scrolls: How Do They Affect Traditional Beliefs?" *The New Republic*, 9 April 1956, 12.

307 Wilson, *The Scrolls from the Dead Sea*.

308 R.B.Y. Scott, "Christianity not Born in a Vacuum," *The New Republic*, 9 April 1956, 22–3.

309 Ibid, 24.

310 "Dead Sea Scrolls: Sharp Divergences in Scholarly Views," *Montreal Star*, 9 February 1956, 12; and Douglas J. Wilson, "Biblical Study Intensified: Debate Goes on About the Dead Sea Scrolls," *Montreal Star*, 11 February 1956, 10.

311 On Edmund Wilson directly, Samuel Sandmel was quoted as stating, "seldom have so many readers been led astray by one man," ("Dead Sea Scrolls Held Overvalued," *New York Times*, 6 February 1956, 25; the same article was reprinted in the Canadian national press as, "Caution Urged by Theologians," *Globe and Mail* [Toronto], 7 February 1956, 10). It was not just Wilson who might have concerned Sandmel. During the same week, on 5 February 1956, the *New York Times* carried a report on John Allegro's arguments that the Qumran community's Teacher of Righteousness had likely been persecuted and crucified in Christ-like fashion at the hands of gentiles incited by a wicked Jewish priest and that Paul's teachings descended from traditions already evidenced among the Dead Sea sectarians (John Hillaby, "Christian Bases Seen in Scrolls," *New York Times*, 5 February 1956, 2). Allegro's comments were cited from the third of the aforementioned series of lectures he did for the BBC. For elaboration on the lecture and the response to it, see Brown, *John Marco Allegro*, 76–82.

312 Samuel Sandmel's files, preserved at the American Jewish Archives, Cincinnati, Ohio (Sandmel, Samuel, 1911–1979, Nearprint), include a copy of the lecture and dozens of press clippings about his comments. On 6 February 1956 references to Sandmel's talk appeared in the *New York Times, Des Moines Tribune, Baltimore Sun,* and *Rochester Times Union*. In the days following, reports also appeared in the *Springfield Ohio News, Omaha Morning World-Herald, Two-Rivers Wisconsin Reporter,* Toronto's *Globe and Mail,* the *Worcester Mass. Gazette, Flint Michigan Journal,* the *Montreal Jewish Chronicle,* Cincinnati's *The American Israelite,* Philadelphia's *Jewish Exponent,* and Baltimore's *Jewish Times*. It also seems as though Sandmel's comments may have troubled the president of HUC-JIR, where he taught.

Just a few months prior, Nelson Glueck suggested in a book review for the *New York Times* that readers of the scrolls, "will browse in this library for generations to come, studying the full significance of its treasures for the trials and the temper of the times of Hillel and Jesus, for the spirit and variety of the religious gropings and groupings of the Jews and for the fuller understanding of the major and minor currents of thought of the Judaism of their times," (Nelson Glueck, "New Light on the Dim Past," *New York Times*, 20 November 1955, 54[BR]). At this time, Glueck had also assigned to Harry Orlinsky of HUC-JIR's New York Campus the task of coordinating an international conference to include Roland de Vaux, Millar Burrows, William Albright, and others in celebration of the tenth anniversary of the discovery of the scrolls to be held in September 1957 (Harry Orlinsky to Nelson Glueck, 20 April 1956, Harry Meyer Orlinsky Papers, American Jewish Archives, Cincinnati, Ohio. MSS Col. No. 601, Sub-series I Personal and Organizational Correspondence, File 6:15 Glueck, Nelson). The conference was eventually cancelled because of a conflict with another that would be convened in Israel by Ben Zion Dinur. A core group of scholars, including Albright, Zeitlin, Edward Y. Kutscher, and Patrick Skehan would nevertheless meet at Dropsie College in Philadelphia on 20 May 1957 to celebrate the tenth anniversary of the scrolls' discovery and the first jubilee of the college (cf. Zeitlin, "Review: The Dead Sea Scrolls: Fantasies and Mistranslations," 75–6, and Kutscher, "Dating the Language of the Genesis Apocryphon," 288). For a thorough examination of the attitudes of Sandmel, Glueck, and Orlinsky towards the scrolls as well as discussion of the conferences see Kalman, "Optimistic, Even with the Negatives."

313 "From Dead Sea Cave: More Scroll Fragments Acquired for McGill," *Gazette* (Montreal), 15 February 1956, 3, and "Old Scrolls Added to By McGill," *Montreal Star*, 15 February 1956, 67.

314 Scott was also making his voice heard by the public in Princeton on the matter of the scrolls. See, for example, his review of Charles T. Fritsch's *The Qumran Community* in the Princeton Seminary Bulletin for 1956. Scott points especially to why the book is valuable for the lay person.

315 "Dead Sea Scrolls: Sharp Divergences in Scholarly Views," *Montreal Star*, 9 February 1956, 12.

CHAPTER THREE

1 "As you probably know, Lankester Harding has been dismissed as Director of Antiquities of Jordan – 'Glubbed', they say – from Sept. 30th ... An emergency meeting at the Museum discussed whether it would be possible to

ship out the McGill and other fragments before this date. Two things made it impossible: the work of editing for publication will require another year, and de Vaux's judgment that an application by Harding at this time would be refused, and this would prejudice an application later when things had calmed down. De Vaux (after 23 years in the country) says 'We must ride out the crisis'. He is not pessimistic," (Scott to James, 11 September 1956, Letter #65).

2 Fields, *The Dead Sea Scrolls: A Short History*, 47.
3 Scott to de Vaux, 15 April 1956, Letter #58.
4 De Vaux to Scott, 15 May 1956, Letter #59.
5 Scott to de Vaux, 25 May 1956, Letter #60.
6 On Bechtel's participation in the purchase of the scrolls, see King, *American Archaeology in the Mideast*, 121. Elizabeth Bechtel was the wife of Kenneth K. Bechtel, son of Warren A. Bechtel, the founder of the Bechtel Corporation, which, among other projects, had directed the construction of the Hoover Dam.
7 Fields, "Discovery and Purchase," 211.
8 Scott to de Vaux, 5 February 1956, Letter #56.
9 De Vaux to Scott, 7 April 1956, Letter #57.
10 Harding to Scott, 6 June 1956, Letter #61, and Scott to James, 23 July 1956, Letter #62. The list is included with both letters.
11 A = Allegro, C = Cross, H = Hunzinger, M = Milik, Sl = Strugnell, Sn = Skehan and Sy = Starcky.
12 This, however, is not the first inkling of potential difficulties resulting from the tenuous political situation. De Vaux informed Scott in January 1956 of troubles related to the Jericho excavation: "Doug Tushingham arrived a few days ago with Miss Kenyon and we spoke of you. The real troubles have begun to prevent the excavations of Jericho and, unless the crisis is quickly resolved, I fear that they will not be able to dig this year. How unfortunate! We're all in need of peace," (de Vaux to Scott, 8 January 1956, Letter #52).
13 On the growth of Arab nationalism in Jordan and the move to limit British power in the Middle East, see Oren, "A Winter of Discontent: Britian's Crisis in Jordan, December 1955–March 1956," 171–84, and Massad, *Colonial Effects: The Making of National Identity in Jordan*.
14 See "July 1956 – Arab legion Discussions with Britain," *Keesing's Contemporary Archives* 10 (July 1956): 14965. http://www.keesings.com (accessed: 19 September 2007).
15 Scott to James, 11 September 1956, Letter #65.
16 "Dead Sea Scrolls Reported Stolen," *Washington Post*, 25 May 1956, 34.

17 "No Dead Sea Scrolls Lost, Aide Reports," *Washington Post*, 27 May 1956, 4(A). See also "Dead Sea Scrolls All Safe," *New York Times*, 26 May 1956, 11. Unfortunately, fragments would indeed be stolen later on. On 26 April 1960, Starcky and Strugnell would report the disappearance of a fragment purchased for the PAM by McCormick (the largest piece in photograph 41.894). Strugnell would find three pieces missing from David^c on 30 April 1960 (cf. the statements of Strugnell, 29 and 30 April 1960, and Starcky, 26 April 1960 in IAA Archives, Box 73, PAM 1117: Dead Sea Scrolls [cave no. 4], jacket 1).

18 See, Harding to Bridson, 8 June 1956, IAA Archives, Box 73, PAM 1117: Dead Sea Scrolls (cave no. 4), jacket 1.

19 The undated letter makes reference to a number of events, including a loan from the Economic Development Fund in March 1956, which allow for dating (cf. Director of Antiquities to Minister of Education, August 1956, IAA Archives, Box 73, PAM 1117: Dead Sea Scrolls [cave no. 4], jacket 1).

20 On 19 March 1956, Harding and the appropriate Jordanian cabinet minister signed a loan agreement with the Jordanian-American Joint Fund for General Economic Development to the amount of 7,000 JD. A copy of the signed contract is preserved in the IAA Archives, Box 73, PAM 1117: Dead Sea Scrolls (cave no. 4), jacket 1. It would prove difficult to repay this a year later (cf. Underwood, acting co-director of EDF to The Board of Trustees, PAM, 16 April 1957, IAA Archives, Box 73, PAM 1117: Dead Sea Scrolls [cave no. 4], jacket 1). In May 1956, the Board of Trustees, with Harding's support, agreed to ask for a loan of an additional 10,000 JD to place a deposit on recently discovered manuscripts ("Extract of the Minutes of the Eleventh Ordinary Meeting … . May 5th, 1956," 13 May 1956, IAA Archives, Box 73, PAM 1117: Dead Sea Scrolls [cave no. 4], jacket 1).

21 Harding to Scott, 9 July 1956, R.B.Y. Scott Papers, 89.112c, file: 1–7, United Church of Canada Archives, Toronto, Ontario.

22 Bentley to Scott, 26 July 1956, Letter #64. William Bentley joined the McGill staff in 1926, and became bursar in 1945. He held a dual appointment by also acting as secretary to the Board of Governors, from 1947 until 1956. He officially retired in 1957, but served as assistant to the principal until 1960. On his contribution to McGill, see Grimson, "The Bursar Retires," 12.

23 Bentley to Scott, 26 July 1956, Letter #64.

24 Tushingham to Harding, 17 July 1956, IAA Archives, Box 73, PAM 1117: Dead Sea Scrolls (cave no. 4), jacket 1.

25 Harding to Scott, 9 July 1956, R.B.Y. Scott Papers, 89.112c, file: 1–7, United Church of Canada Archives, Toronto, Ontario.

26 In a letter from John Allegro to Frank Cross, dated 16 July 1956, the importance of Strasbourg as a meeting point to discuss difficulties with the scrolls editorial team and the lag in publication was also stressed, albeit in a manner of almost gleeful anticipation of the expected confrontation: "I am frankly glad at the moment that *The Times* letter has drawn a distinction between myself and those in Jerusalem of the team, because I hear growlings along the grapevine from world scholarship about the way this stuff is being handled, and I am not particularly keen to be caught up in the storm which is blowing up. I have a feeling that de Vaux, Milik and Co are in for a warm time at Strasbourg, and I am not sorry that I shall not be there. Happily my mass publication of the messianic material in the next *JBL* ought to put me in the right with the lads who are waiting impatiently for the stuff, and if you take my tip you'll get just as much stuff out as you can a.s.a.p.," (Brown, *John Marco Allegro*, 101–2).

27 Rowley, "The Second International Old Testament Congress," 443–7.

28 Scott to James, 23 July 1956, Letter #63.

29 At the Strasbourg meeting Milik reported on the publication schedule. He suggested that publication would require a minimum of seven volumes (only one had appeared by this point): one for the Murabba'at material, one for Cave 5 and the Copper Scroll, and one or two volumes for material of unknown provenance. It was expected that the Cave 4 material would appear in approximately two years' time. Milik could provide little detail on the content and nature of the Cave 11 finds that had only recently come to light (Rowley, "The Second International Old Testament Congress," 445). Józef Milik's report was published in the congress volume as, "Le Travail d'édition des Manuscrits du Désert de Juda," 17–26.

30 Scott to James, 11 September 1956, Letter #65.

31 De Vaux to Scott, undated letter in response to Scott's letter of 23 July 1956, R.B.Y. Scott Papers, 89.112c, file: 1–7, United Church of Canada Archives, Toronto, Ontario.

32 Harding to Scott, 9 July 1956, R.B.Y. Scott Papers, 89.112c, file: 1–7, United Church of Canada Archives, Toronto, Ontario.

33 Fields, *The Dead Sea Scrolls: A Short History*, 47.

34 Harding to Scott, 27 September 1956, R.B.Y. Scott Papers, 89.112c, file: 1–7, United Church of Canada Archives, Toronto, Ontario.

35 Henri E. del Medico was a biblicist in Paris and author of a number of books and articles on the Dead Sea Scrolls. He was among the first to challenge de Vaux's contention that the Dead Sea Scroll caves and the ruins at Qumran were related. See Trompf, "Introduction I: The Long History of

Dead Sea Scrolls Scholarship," 126; and Del Medico, *The Riddle of the Scrolls*.

36 André Dupont-Sommer (1900–1983) was a French epigraphist and historian. His work, *The Dead Sea Scrolls: A Preliminary Survey*, argued for the Essene origins of Christianity. For more background, see also Silberman, *The Hidden Scrolls*, 120–2.

37 Scott to James, 11 September 1956, Letter #65.

38 Ibid.

39 The University of Heidelberg made the purchase with funds provided by the Governments of Bonn and Baden-Württemberg. See Allegro, *The Dead Sea Scrolls: A Reappraisal*, 47.

40 Kuhn to Harding, 31 July 1956, IAA Archives, Box 73, PAM 1117: Dead Sea Scrolls (cave no. 4), jacket 1.

41 Scott to James, 11 September 1956, Letter #65.

42 Wright refers to Strugnell three times in the article by the title "Dr." Although Strugnell began graduate work in Semitics at Oxford, he never earned his doctorate.

43 Wright, "Report of the Representative on the Board of Trustees of the American School of Oriental Studies," xvi–xviii.

44 Fitzmyer started this project in July 1957 (cf. Schiffman and Brooke, "The Past: On the History of Dead Sea Scrolls Research," 15).

45 Shanks, "Leading Dead Sea Scroll Scholar Denounces Delay," 25.

46 Scott to James, 11 September 1956, Letter #65.

47 Pennington to James, 29 October 1956, Letter #69.

48 Thomson to Pennington, 26 October 1956, Letter #68.

49 In contradiction to Thomson's stated ignorance as to the matter of McGill's scroll fragments, James indicated intimate and exact knowledge of the current state of affairs (cf. James to Pennington, 30 October 1956, Letter #70). The contrast proves both James's enthusiastic support of and keen interest in the project but may also indicate the collateral damage of the agreement to secrecy reached with Harding as to the exactitudes of the purchase (cf. Scott to Harding, 4 May 1955, Letter #36).

50 At the time, the only scrolls known to be housed outside Jordan were the complete scrolls purchased by Sukenik and Yadin. The preserved archival material does not evidence any communications between Scott and the Israelis about their management of the material in their possession. Given James's previous interaction with Yadin and other scholars at the Hebrew University, it is strange that Scott never approached them for information. The decision may have been political, as Israel understood the scroll materials as part of their cultural heritage. Scott may have wished to avoid any conflict

with a third party over the nature of the purchase. It may also have resulted from Scott's perception that the preservation of complete scrolls (as in the hands of the Israelis) differed from the preservation practices required for the conservation of hundreds of small fragments, such as the Cave 4 collection represented.

51 Scott turned to Plenderleith for advice as the author of *The Conservation of Antiquities and Works of Art: Treatment, Repair, and Restoration*. Cf. also Scott to James, 11 September 1956, Letter #65. Scott's letter to Plenderleith, dated 2 October 1956, is not preserved. Its date is provided in Plenderleith's reply to Scott (Plenderleith to Scott, 30 October 1956, McGill University Archives, RG34, Container: 0001, File 6: Dead Sea Scrolls).
52 Scott to James, 11 September 1956, Letter #65.
53 Plenderleith added a note in the margin of his letter indicated by an asterisk: "recondition [the gel] periodically by heating in an oven."
54 Plenderleith to Scott, 30 October 1956, McGill University Archives, RG34, Container: 0001, File 6: Dead Sea Scrolls.
55 Wright, "Archaeological News and Views," 64.
56 "Old Testament Finds: Difficulties of Inspection," *Times* (London), 12 August 1949, 4. An image of Plenderleith examining the fragments appears on page 10.
57 Among the issues to explore was a build-up of a pitch-like substance that had formed on the scrolls. Plenderleith confirmed that the material was coagulated parchment resulting from the natural decay of the organic material. He suggested that the best way to treat the coated fragments was to expose them to eighty-percent humidity to relax the parchment so it could be separated and arranged. The humidity caused the black material to become sticky but this could be treated by refrigerating the fragments ("Old Testament Finds: Difficulties of Inspection," *Times* [London], 12 August 1949, 4). See also Wright, "Archaeological News and Views," 64.
58 Libman and Boyd-Alkalay, "Conservation," 140–2.
59 See the reports by Plenderleith, 23, 27, and 29 March 1962, and the report on the description of his visit dated, 21 March 1962, in IAA Archives, Box 73, PAM 1117(c), W. Harold James Plenderleith on Dead Sea Scrolls. For discussion of Plenderleith's contribution, see Libman and Boyd-Alkalay, "Conservation," 140–1.
60 Scott to James, 16 January 1957, Letter #72.
61 Joaquin Anselmo M. Albareda (1892–1966) served as prefect of the Vatican Library under Pope Pius XI, Pope Pius XII, and Pope John XXIII. He was elevated to cardinal in 1962.
62 Albareda to Scott, 25 January 1957, McGill University Archives, RG34, Container: 0001, File 6: Dead Sea Scrolls.

63 "Dead Sea Scrolls Purchased," *New York Times,* 30 November 1956, 35.
64 Cross, "Reminiscences of the Early Days," 938.
65 Richard Philbrick, "9 of Dead Sea Scrolls to be Brought Here," *Chicago Tribune,* 30 November 1956, 11. According to a handwritten note (possibly Frank Cross's hand) dated 27 July 1956, McCormick's allotment included 4QJer[b], 4QDan[c], 4QDan[e], 4QQoh[a]. Also identified on the list are the Paraphrase of Genesis and the papyrus apocalyptic assigned to Milik, a liturgical work (ms 3) and hymnic work #11, assigned to Strugnell, and sapiential work Wisdom "A", assigned to Allegro – cf. McCormick Allocation, 27 July 1956, IAA Archives, Box 73, PAM 1117(b): Distributions of Institutions Dead Sea Scrolls.
66 Dr Abdel Karim Ghureibeh (b. 1923) was appointed director general of antiquities in 1956 and was later professor of history and dean of the faculty of arts at the University of Jordan. He was succeeded later that same year by Saeed Al-Durra, who remained until 1959, when he was replaced by Dr Awni Khalil Dajani (1917–1968), the first Jordanian to earn a Ph.D. in archaeology. He had previously served as assistant director. Dajani wrote his University of London dissertation, "The Hyksos Period in Palestine" under the supervision of Kathleen Kenyon. Dajani served as director until his death. Little biographical information is available for the directors; cf. however, the website of the Jordanian Department of Antiquities: http://images.jordan.gov.jo/wps/wcm/connect/eGov/Government+Ministries+&+Entities/Department+of+Antiquities/General+Information/. Dajani's biography here has been compiled from references to his cooperation with various excavations in Jordan, as described in final reports. See, for example, Sellers et al., *The 1957 Excavation at Bet-Zur.*
67 Cross to Scott, 26 March 1957, McGill University Archives, RG34, Container: 0001, File 6: Dead Sea Scrolls.
68 De Vaux to Scott, 9 March 1957, Letter #75.
69 First Ordinary Meeting, 23 March 1957, IAA Archives, Box 73, PAM 1117: Dead Sea Scrolls (cave no. 4), jacket 1.
70 On 25 March 1957 the director of antiquities took from the PAM: Plate #1 (Deuteronomy from Cave 1 in Hebrew), Plate #2 (Isaiah from Cave 1 in Hebrew), Plate #3 (Apocryphal Books from Cave 1 in Hebrew), Plate #4 (A Deed of Redemption from the Judaean Wilderness in Nabatean), Plate #13 (two fragments of the Manual of Discipline from Cave 1 in Hebrew), Plate #35 (text from Khirbet Mird in Arabic), along with an amulet in Arabic from Wadi Marraba'at, a jar with a cover and a juglet (cf. "Received from the Palestine Archaeological Museum, 25 March 1967," IAA Archives, Box 73, PAM 1117: Dead Sea Scrolls [cave no. 4], jacket 1).

The material was returned on 21 July 1957. See, "Received from the Director of Antiquities (Dr. Awni Dajani), 21 July 1957", IAA Archives, Box 73, PAM 1117: Dead Sea Scrolls (cave no. 4), jacket 1.

71 The letter is not preserved but it is discussed by Scott in his reply to H.H. Rowley, 4 March 1957, Letter #73.

72 Only later would the matter of reimbursement be raised. Here, it appears, the minister was simply making a claim to all the material in such a manner that export would be prohibited.

73 The minister of education (Shafiq Rusheidat) to the director of antiquities, 6 January 1957, Reference #18/3/27, IAA Archives, Box 73, PAM 1117: Dead Sea Scrolls (cave no. 4), jacket 1.

74 Scott to De Vaux, 4 March 1957, Letter #74.

75 De Vaux to Rowley as cited in Rowley to Scott, 7 March 1957, McGill University Archives, RG34, Container: 0001, File 6: Dead Sea Scrolls:

J'ai actuellement de très gros soucis concernant les manuscrits de la Mer Morte. Le Gouvernement a l'intention de s'approprier tous les fragments trouvés ou à trouver, y compris ceux qui ont été acquis par des institutions étrangères. Toute exportation sera interdite, et le Gouvernement se réserve tous les droits d'étude et de publication. On promet sans doute d'indemniser les Institutions mais je ne sais pas quand et comment cela sera fait. C'est une histoire folle et, malheureusement, je n'ai aucun moyen de m'opposer à cette enterprise: aucune raison ne vaut contre ce qui leur apparaît comme un devoir national. Le seul recours est une action diplomatique, que j'ai mise en route ici, mais qui aurait besoin d'être appuyée de l'extérieur. J'ai cru nécessaire de vous mettre en garde contre le grave danger qui menace ces documents et les droits que Manchester a acquis sur eux. Vous jugerez peut-être opportun de mettre votre Gouvernement au courant et de demander son intervention. Il faudrait alors lui fournir les documents que vous avez et que ne possède pas votre Ambassadeur à Amman: votre correspondence avec Mr. Harding, établissant le montant de votre contribution, la validité légale de l'achat fait avec agrément du Gouvernement jordanien et par l'entremise du Directeur des Antiquités, la liste officielle du lot qui vous revient avec la promesse qu'il vous sera laissé après étude. N'oubliez pas la référence au N° de la lettre du Ministre de l'Education autorisant ces achats et en fixant les conditions. Je ne sais pas si une intervention sera efficace, mais il faut au moins la tenter. Nous aurons fait alors tout ce que nous pouvons.

76 The committee was established by Order nr. 5 of 1957, 25 February 1957. This was an order, "for the establishment of a board to supervise the study, the preservation, the printing and the publication of the manuscripts." It

became effective on 25 February 1957. Article 2 states: "The Board shall be constituted of the following Members: – i) His Worship the Mayor of Jerusalem – President. ii) Director of Antiquities and Curator of the Jerusalem Museum – Treasurer. iii) Asst.-Director of Antiquities. iv) Director of the American School of Oriental Research at Jerusalem. v) Director of Ecole Biblique et Archèologique at Jerusalem." Article 5 indicates that in the event of disagreement among members of the board, the minister of education would make the final decision (IAA Archives, Box 73, PAM 1117: Dead Sea Scrolls [cave no. 4], jacket 1). See also Silberman, "Department of Antiquities of Jordan," 193.

77 De Vaux to Scott, 9 March 1957, Letter #75.
78 Ibid.
79 Rowley to Scott, 7 March 1957, McGill University Archives, RG34, Container: 0001, File 6: Dead Sea Scrolls.
80 Scott to James, 19 March 1957, Letter #76.
81 James to the Jordanian ambassador to the United States, 30 March 1957, Letter #78 and James to the director of antiquities, 30 March 1957, Letter #79.
82 James to Heeney, 30 March, 1957, Letter #77.
83 James to Scott, 3 April 1957, Letter #80.
84 A. Henry Detweiler of Cornell University was president of ASOR from 1955 until 1966. See King, *American Archaeology in the Mideast*, 146–7 and 275. See also Albright, "Albert Henry Detweiler: In Memoriam," 2–4.
85 Kraeling's reassuring presence is particularly relevant in this context. King refers to William Albright's comments about Kraeling noting his "remarkable ability to take a neutral position on political and other critical issues. It is not too much to say that he saved both institutions [the Oriental Institute and ASOR] from *debacle*." King continues: "One can only conjecture about the meaning of Albright's last comment. Academe is filled with single-minded scholars, who at times are a mixed blessing; their expertise is indispensable, their tenacity insufferable. Situations sometimes require a Solomonic diplomat if any institution is to survive. To take political sides in the Mideast, for example, is the shortest route to destroying a scholarly organization like ASOR. All would agree with Albright that Kraeling was a good diplomat; he was also a capable administrator and an excellent scholar," (King, *American Archaeology in the Mideast*, 122).

That Kraeling would act here at least indirectly to defend the status quo on the scrolls is also an ironic twist. In his letter in February 1954, Tushingham advised Scott on finding a representative in Jerusalem to protect McGill's interests and warned him of the difficulties of having Kraeling involved: "I can see how you would like to have someone representing your interests there for the division [of scroll fragments to institutions], and that is only right. But who? I have been wracking my brains. I would suggest Kraeling who is going out there very soon, but I can understand it if you don't want him and the ASOR mixed up in this. Kraeling has shown no enthusiasm for raising money for the scrolls and this should remain as a purely Canadian venture – unchannelled in any way through the ASOR," (Tushingham to Scott, 12 February 1954, McGill University Archives, RG34, Container: 0001, File 6: Dead Sea Scrolls).

86 Detweiler, "Letter from the President's Desk," 3.
87 Frost, *The Man in the Ivory Tower*, 213–14.
88 James to Scott, 10 December 1957, Letter #81.
89 In April and May 1960 James would again visit Israel. His schedule would not allow this kind of archaeological tour. In writing to thank James for his visit, Mazar comments somewhat disappointedly, "I am very sorry that owing to innumerable conferences, meetings and unofficial conversations, which kept you busy from the early morning till late at night, you had no time for relaxation. I hope that on your next visit we shall be able to take some time off for an archeological excursion," (Mazar to James, 17 May 1960, McGill University Archives, MG 1017, Container 75, File: James Diaries, 18 May 1960 – 26 Dec. 1960).
90 Walton to James, 8 December 1955, James to Walton, 12 December 1955, Walton to James, 15 May 1956, and James to Walton, 17 May 1956. The letters are assembled in McGill University Archives, RG2, Container: 0179, File 6243: Divinity: DSS & Birks Donation.
91 Walton to James, 15 May 1956, and James to Walton, 17 May 1956. The letters are assembled in McGill University Archives, RG2 Container: 0179 File 6243: Divinity: DSS & Birks Donation.
92 James to Scott, 3 April 1957, Letter #80.
93 Burrows, *The Dead Sea Scrolls*.
94 James to Scott, 16 January 1956, Letter #53. For the reference to McGill and Scott, see Burrows, *The Dead Sea Scrolls*, 69.
95 "Stanley Frost: A Cool Look at History," *McGill Reporter* 35, no. 10 (13 February 2003). http://www.mcgill.ca/reporter/35/10/kaleidoscope/ (accessed: 22 July 2007).
96 Scott to Frost, 13 May 1958, Letter #82.
97 De Vaux to Scott, 17 May 1958, Letter #83.
98 Minutes of the Fourteenth Ordinary Meeting, 30 December 1957, IAA Archives, Box 73, PAM 1117: Dead Sea Scrolls (cave no. 4), jacket 1.
99 Scott to James, 25 May 1958, Letter #84.

100 Scott to James, 25 May 1958, Letter #84.
101 De Vaux to Scott, 18 June 1958, Letter #85.
102 De Vaux to Scott, 18 June 1958, Letter #85. In November 1958 Scott wrote to Patrick Skehan, an American member of the editorial team, to get a better idea of how the publication efforts were proceeding: "Is there any hope that Vol. II of 'Discoveries' will be out soon? Is work on the remaining Cave 4 stuff progressing? Can we ever hope to see the McGill purchase? ... If you can satisfy my curiosity on any of these points, I shall be most grateful." Scott to Skehan, 21 November 1958, cited in Fields, *Dead Sea Scrolls: A Full History*, 424.
103 De Vaux to Scott, 18 June 1958, Letter #85.
104 The excavations, directed by James Pritchard, took place between 28 May and 6 August 1959. For discussion of the discoveries of that season, see Pritchard, "Industry and Trade at Biblical Gibeon," 23–9.
105 "Memorandum relating to Prof. R.B.Y. Scott's conference with Pere de Vaux and Prof. F.M. Cross, Jr.," 8 July 1959, Letter #89.
106 The retrospective statistics, as an indication of the misplaced optimism as to the task ahead, are staggering. Under de Vaux's editorial leadership only four volumes of DJD would eventually be published and, although the vast majority of the matching and identification of fragments would be completed by mid-1960, the last volumes of the material would only reach the press in 2009, more than fifty years after their discovery. See, for example, Shanks, "Chief Scroll Editor Opens Up," 32–5, 62.

On 11 July 1959, the schedule was approved officially by the editorial team ("Memorandum," 8 July 1959, Letter #89). The discrepancy in the dates results from the fact that Scott began writing the memorandum on 8 July and dated it as such. It is clear from the latter half of the memorandum that he completed it some time after 9 August 1959.
107 Strugnell, "The Original Team of Editors," 184–5.
108 They expected that the preparations for publication would be completed by 1962 and that the printer would require another year ("Memorandum," 8 July 1959, Letter #89).
109 Although no volume would appear under the imprint of McGill University, the university's contribution, and that of the other institutions, is alluded to in Roland de Vaux's posthumous contribution to the sixth volume of DJD: "Il demeure que l'autorisation initiale donnée par le Gouvernement Jordanien et la réponse qu'elle a reçue à l'extérieur ont permis de sauver d'une dispersion certaine et d'une perte éventuelle des textes dont l'importance exceptionnelle est universellement reconnue et apparaîtra aux usagers de ces volumes," ("Découverte, Fouille et Achats," 5). ["It remains that initial authorization

given by the Jordanian Government and the response that it received outside (of Jordan) allowed us to save from a certain dispersion and from an eventual loss the texts whose exceptional importance is universally recognized and will be apparent to the users of these volumes." Our Translation.]

In *DJD*, vol. 7, Maurice Baillet provided a distribution list for the fragments included in the edition. Three of these, 493, 508, and 513 (4Q493 War Scroll^c; 4Q508 Festival Prayers^b; and 4Q513 Ordinances^b [Halakhic text]) are listed as allotted to McGill University. Baillet notes that the inclusion of this list, despite the fact that other distribution arrangements were made, was a tribute to the institutions: "Que cette liste serve du moins à rendre hommage aux diverses institutions dont la générosité a permis de les acquérir," (*Qumrân Grotte 4.III [4Q482–4Q520]*, *DJD*, 7:ix). ["That this list serves at least to pay homage to the diverse institutions whose generosity allowed us to acquire them (the scrolls fragments)." Our Translation.]

110 Scott to Birks, 1 July 1959, Letter #88.
111 Sa'ad to President Mckay, 21 July 1958, IAA Archives, Box 73, PAM 1117: Dead Sea Scrolls (cave no. 4), jacket 1. For a description of McCormick's participation, see Cross, "Reminiscences of the Early Days," 937–939. On 9 July 1958, the PAM purchased the fragments preserved in the PAM photo archive as photographs 42.597 – 42.604. See "List of Manuscript Fragments Purchased on Wednesday, 9 July 1958", IAA Archives, Box 73, PAM 1117: Dead Sea Scrolls (cave no. 4), jacket 1.
112 See "List of Manuscript Fragments Purchased on Sunday, 20 July 1958", IAA Archives, Box 73, PAM 1117: Dead Sea Scrolls (cave no. 4), jacket 1.
113 Kring to Cross, 15 July 1958, IAA Archives, Box 73, PAM 1117: Dead Sea Scrolls (cave no. 4), jacket 1. See also George Dugan, "Unitarians Acquire Dead Sea Decalogue," *New York Times*, 19 September 1958, 1, 25; and "The Oldest Decalogue," *Time* (29 September 1958). http://www.time.com/time/magazine/article/0,9171,821184,00.html (accessed: 14 November 2007).
114 Sa'ad to Cross, 24 September 1958, IAA Archives, Box 73, PAM 1117: Dead Sea Scrolls (cave no. 4), jacket 1.
115 "The Oldest Version of the Ten Commandments," *Ad-Difaa*, 21 September 1958, anonymous translation preserved in: IAA Archives, Box 73, PAM 1117: Dead Sea Scrolls (cave no. 4), jacket 1.
116 Sa'ad to the editor, *Ad-Difaa*, 24 September 1958; IAA Archives, Box 73, PAM 1117: Dead Sea Scrolls (cave no. 4), jacket 1.
117 Sa'ad to Cross, 24 September, 1958; IAA Archives, Box 73, PAM 1117: Dead Sea Scrolls (cave no. 4), jacket 1.
118 "The Oldest Decalogue," *Time* (29 September 1958). http://www.time.com/time/magazine/article/0,9171,821184,00.html (accessed: 14 November 2007).

119 Prime Minister Order No. 26/10/548, 23 January 1958, IAA Archives, Box 73, PAM 1117: Dead Sea Scrolls (cave no. 4), jacket 1.
120 More than twenty-five years later, in the mid-1980s, this optimistic attitude was still in place, as is best illustrated by Lawrence Schiffman's anecdotal rendering of John Strugnell's presentation of the schedule for completion at New York University: "'John [Strugnell] gave his report on where things stood at that time, which everybody believed like suckers. That's the other thing: We always believed that it was coming out next year. You know, it's like the messiah' … Schiffman recalled in amusement at his own naivete. 'He said it and we believed it,'" (Silberman, *The Hidden Scrolls*, 180).
121 As discussed above, the publishing of the material took more than forty years. The process might have been shortened had the restrictions on access to the material not been as strict. James Robinson has suggested rules for future discoveries that would limit the period of restricted access to such material. As for the Dead Sea Scrolls, he surmised that: "If the scholars involved [in publishing the scrolls] had been asked then [in the 1950s] whether they should be given 40 years or more to complete their assignments, certainly these sensible and decent people would have said no. But there was no contingency plan envisaged then for the situation that has actually evolved," (Robinson, "Commentary: Handling Future Manuscript Discoveries," 236).
122 De Vaux to Allegro, 22 March 1959, cited in Brown, *John Marco Allegro*, 162.
123 See also Libman and Boyd-Alkalay, "Restoration Techniques at the Israel Antiquities Authority," 875.
124 Silberman, *The Hidden Scrolls*, 158.
125 Cross, "Reminiscences of the Early Days," 937.
126 Frost to Birks, 11 December 1959, Letter #91. In a January 2000 interview with Professor Stanley Frost, he indicated to us that he had John Strugnell in mind for such an appointment. Instead, Oxtoby was appointed, as he had a broader range of interests, including Persia and Zoroastrianism. Frost met both men in person during his visit to the scrollery in April 1960 (see, "Report to the Principal," 12 May 1960, Letter #97).
127 Frost to de Vaux, 13 February 1960, Letter #92. In an interesting side note, James again visited Jerusalem in April 1960. The trip allowed him to renew his friendship with the president and rector of Hebrew University, the well-known archaeologist, Benjamin Mazar (Frost, *The Man in the Ivory Tower*, 259). When Frost visited Jerusalem in 1960, he carried with him a letter of introduction to Mazar from James for when he crossed from Jordan into Israel (James to Mazar, 25 February 1960, Letter #95). The letter indicates to Mazar that Frost's intention was to visit the scrollery at the PAM to view

McGill University's collection. How the Israeli university president perceived McGill's purchase of disputed national treasures remains unknown.
128 Predominantly signed "Shingiti" in official correspondence. Also spelled "Shangiti," "Shangity," or "Shauqiti" in some of the letters.
129 Frost to James, 15 April 1960, Letter #96, and Frost, "Report to the Principal," 12 May 1960, Letter #97.
130 Frost to James, 15 April 1960, Letter #96. Although Scott had little to say to his McGill colleagues about Allegro, his impatience with him was already evident in a letter he wrote to Patrick Skehan in late November 1958: "So Allegro is off the rails again – or was he ever on them?" Scott to Skehan, 21 November 1958, cited in Fields, *Dead Sea Scrolls: A Full History*, 424.
131 Brown, *John Marco Allegro*, 158–64.
132 Ibid., 160.
133 Ibid., 162. See also "Dead Sea Scrolls for London," *Times* (London), 19 December 1961, 9, which includes a photograph of King Hussein making the announcement.
134 Frost, "Report to the Principal," 12 May 1960, Letter #97.
135 D.B. Macfarlane, "Dead Sea Scroll Plates Allocated for McGill," *Montreal Star*, 4 May 1960, 55.
136 Albright, "Carl Herman Kraeling: In Memoriam," 5.
137 Silberman, *The Hidden Scrolls*, 100–1.
138 That this was of serious concern is evidenced by the fact that, for example, the Temple Scroll from Cave 11 (11Q19), probably discovered in 1956, was confiscated by Yigael Yadin from Kando as late as 1967 (cf. Yadin, *The Temple Scroll: The Hidden Law of the Dead Sea Sect*, 8–55).
139 Concerning the Bedouin and Kando's treatment of the scrolls, Emanuel Tov has reported, "However, it was simply bad fortune that the fragments were handed over to the scholars in complete disarray, often after having been maltreated by Bedouin. For example, according to Père Barthelémy, the Greek Minor Prophets scroll from Nahal Hever was kept under the *kefiyyeh* of one of the Bedouin ... and according to Strugnell, one of the copies of 4Q416, the so-called 4QInstruction[a], was 'hidden under Kando's shirt and absorbed his perspiration, as he hid it there to prevent its discovery during a police search' ... These external conditions did not improve the quality of the Scrolls, to say the least. Likewise, the Temple Scroll from Cave 11 was hidden for many years in a shoe box in Kando's garden in Bethlehem, and the present decay of the top part of that Scroll probably could have been prevented had it been stored in better conditions," ("The Publication of the Dead Sea Scrolls," 201–2).

140 Peter Mellors, "Canada's Big Biblical Bargain," *Star Weekend Magazine*, 26 November 1960, 37. The latter part of a suggested agreement as outlined here reflects the arrangements that would be made with ASOR and the Dutch with regard to publication of Cave 11 material. According to the draft agreement with the Koninklijke Nederlandse Akademie van Wetenschappen in Amsterdam, in exchange for a donation of £10,000, equivalent to the cost of purchasing 11QTargum of Job, the academy would purchase the rights to study and publish the manuscript while its ownership would remain permanently in the hands of the PAM. The PAM had initially purchased it with funds from their endowment. The draft agreement is preserved in, IAA Archives, Box 73, PAM 1117(a): Mrs. Kenneth K. Bechtel (Dead Sea Scrolls). By contrast, the draft agreement with ASOR transferred ownership, as well as rights to study and publication (in the *DJD* series), of the Psalms Scroll from Cave 11 to ASOR Jerusalem in exchange for $60,000 USD donated by the Bechtels. However, the scroll would remain in the PAM for permanent exhibit. The draft agreement is preserved in IAA Archives, Box 73, PAM 1117(a): Mrs. Kenneth K. Bechtel (Dead Sea Scrolls). In the final agreements, ownership in both cases was transferred not to the academy, ASOR, or the PAM, but to the Government of Jordan with study and publication rights to ASOR and the academy and exhibition rights to the PAM. See de Vaux to the prime minister of Jordan, 21 April 1962 and "Revised Agreement by the American School, 1961," both preserved in IAA Archives, Box 73, PAM 1117(a): Mrs. Kenneth K. Bechtel (Dead Sea Scrolls).

141 De Vaux to director of antiquities, Frost, Father Dom Albereda of the Vatican Library, president of McCormick Theological Seminary, rector of Heidelberg University, vice chancellor of the University of Manchester, 4 June 1960, IAA Archives, Box 73, PAM 1117(b): Distributions of Institutions Dead Sea Scrolls.

142 De Vaux to Frost, 4 June 1960, Letter #98.

143 Frost to director of antiquities, 13 June 1960, Letter #99.

144 Cooper to de Vaux, 23 June 1960, IAA Archives, Box 73, PAM 1117(b): Distributions of Institutions Dead Sea Scrolls.

145 De Vaux to director of antiquities, Frost, Father Dom Albereda of the Vatican Library, president of McCormick Theological Seminary, rector of Heidelberg University, vice chancellor of the University of Manchester, 4 June 1960, IAA Archives, Box 73, PAM 1117(b): Distributions of Institutions Dead Sea Scrolls.

146 The division list is preserved in IAA Archives, Box 73, PAM 1117(b): Distributions of Institutions Dead Sea Scrolls. McGill's allotment is provided below.

147 De Vaux to director of antiquities, 4 June 1960, IAA Archives, Box 73, PAM 1117(b): Distributions of Institutions Dead Sea Scrolls.
148 The archival material came into the possession of Israel after the capture of East Jerusalem during the Six-Day War in 1967. These records of the discovery of the scrolls along with the work of the editorial team had been in the PAM, along with the Cave 4 fragments, when on 7 June 1967, just two days after the Battle for Jerusalem began, Israeli paratroopers took control of the museum. Harding had a plan in place for the removal of the scrolls from Jerusalem and their transportation to Amman in 1956 with the Suez Crisis and it was followed then. According to Silberman, a similar plan was in place for 1967, but, "due to a missed or misunderstood instruction, the truck dispatched from Amman to pick up the scroll crates at the Palestine Archaeological Museum never arrived," (Silberman, *The Hidden Scrolls*, 151–2). While for most of its history the museum had been controlled by an independent and private trusteeship, on 28 November 1966 it had been nationalized by the Jordanians and the trusteeship dissolved. In an ironic twist the museum and its contents were transferred to Jordanian possession and then to that of Israel less than a year later.
149 IAA Archives, Box 73, PAM 1117(b): Distributions of Institutions Dead Sea Scrolls.
150 The abbreviated labels indicate the scholar responsible for the study and therefore also the publication of a particular portion of the collection: A = Allegro, Bt = Baillet, C = Cross, H = Hunzinger, M = Milik, Sl = Strugnell, Sn = Skehan and Sy = Starcky.
151 See Skehan, "A Fragment of the 'Song of Moses' (Deut. 32) from Qumran," 12–15.
152 See Skehan, "The Qumran Manuscripts and Textual Criticism," 148–60.
153 Added in pen, preceding the column. Number of plates changed from "2" in type, to "4" in pen.
154 See Milik, "Henoch au pays des aromates (ch. XXVII a XXXII)," 70–7.
155 The lists are collected in IAA Archives, Box 73, PAM 1117(b): Distributions of Institutions Dead Sea Scrolls; and IAA Archives, Box 73, PAM 1119: Dead Sea Scroll Scholars to work on fragments.
156 Frost to de Vaux, 28 September 1960, IAA Archives, Box 73, PAM 1117(b): Distributions of Institutions Dead Sea Scrolls.
157 Saʿad to Frost, 29 September 1960, IAA Archives, Box 73, PAM 1117(b): Distributions of Institutions Dead Sea Scrolls.
158 This (1 September until 22 October 1960) represented the ninth season of excavation at Tell el Farʾah. See de Vaux, "Les Fouilles de Tell el-Farʾah: Rapport préliminaire sur les 7ᵉ, 8ᵉ, 9ᵉ campagnes, 1958–1960," 557–92.

159 De Vaux to Frost, 2 October 1960, Letter #102. Frost described the contents of the letter to Scott, 12 October 1960, Letter #103.
160 De Vaux to director of antiquities, 19 August 1960, IAA Archives, Box 73, PAM 1117(b): Distributions of Institutions Dead Sea Scrolls.
161 Frost, "Report to the Principal," 12 May 1960, Letter #97.
162 De Vaux to Frost, 2 October 1960, Letter #102.
163 As Silberman has appropriately noted, by mid-1960 the Arab language press had adopted these ancient manuscripts as a symbol for fomenting anti-Hashemite sentiment. On 30 May 1960 *Ad-Difaa*, for example, carried the explosive headline, "The Scrolls at the Jerusalem Museum are the Property of the Government and Should Not be Allowed to Leave the Country," (*The Hidden Scrolls*, 149–50).
164 Mills to prime minister, 22 August 1966, IAA Archives, Box 73, PAM 1117(b): Distributions of Institutions Dead Sea Scrolls.
165 The letter to the prime minister is described in Mills to Walstrom, 25 August 1960, IAA Archives, Box 73, PAM 1117(b): Distributions of Institutions Dead Sea Scrolls.
166 Mills to Walstrom, 25 August 1960, IAA Archives, Box 73, PAM 1117(b): Distributions of Institutions Dead Sea Scrolls.
167 Letter not preserved. See, however, Frost to Scott, 12 October 1960, Letter #103. The date of the letter is derived from the Canadian ambassador's response: Beaulieu to Frost, 20 October 1960, McGill University Archives, RG2, Container: 0254, File 7576: Divinity: Dead Sea Scrolls.
168 Donald Wallace Munro (1916–1998) was posted to Beirut between 1960 and 1963. He would later be elected a member of the Canadian parliament (1972–84).
169 Beaulieu to Frost, 20 October 1960, McGill University Archives, RG2, Container: 0254, File 7576: Divinity: Dead Sea Scrolls.
170 Beaulieu [erroneously transcribed as *Beaubien*] to Frost, 1 November 1960, McGill University Archives, RG2, Container: 0254, File 7576: Divinity: Dead Sea Scrolls. A letter to the various purchasing institutions, from the Department of Antiquities, indicates that it was copied to the ambassadors of the United States, United Kingdom, Germany, and Italy, suggesting that de Vaux's advice had been heeded by all the institutions involved (22 October 1960, Letter #104).
171 Beaulieu [erroneously transcribed as *Beaubien*] to Frost, 1 November 1960, McGill University Archives, RG2, Container: 0254, File 7576: Divinity: Dead Sea Scrolls.
172 Beaulieu [erroneously transcribed as *Beaubien*] to Frost, 1 November 1960, McGill University Archives, RG2, Container: 0254, File 7576: Divinity: Dead Sea Scrolls.

173 Stanley Twardy, "No Fragments for McGill: The Missing Link Between Judaism and Jesus," *Globe and Mail* (Toronto), 22 November 1960, 7.
174 Following the loss of the war with Israel in 1948, Nasser founded a group consisting of junior military officers who sought to unseat King Farouk I, the Egyptian monarchy, and its British supporters and advisors. On 23 July 1952 a successful *coup d'état* was launched, leading to the establishment of an Egyptian republic. For elaboration, see Dawisha, *Arab Nationalism in the Twentieth Century*, 135–60.
175 French control of the service began in the 1850s. In 1850 Auguste Mariette (1821–1881) was sent to Egypt by the Louvre to regulate Egyptian excavations and he was appointed director of the Egyptian Antiquities Service in 1858. For a full discussion of the place of Egyptian antiquities in the shaping of national identity, see Reid's *Whose Pharaohs?* For a treatment of the end of French control over the Egyptian Antiquities Service, see especially pages 292–7.
176 Reid, *Whose Pharaohs?*, 257.
177 See "New Aid for Egyptologists in Act of Recording – Temples Threatened By Aswan Dam," *Times* (London), 19 May 1959, 5; and "Egypt Offers Treasures of the Past – International Aid in Exchange – Work on Sites Due for Submersion," *Times* (London), 2 October 1959, 12.
178 "Sale of Treasures to Aid Currency? Unthinkable, says Cairo," *Times* (London), 18 March 1957, 6.
179 See Peter Mellors, "Canada's Big Biblical Bargain," *Star Weekend Magazine*, 26 November 1960, 10.
180 Frost to Shingiti, 30 March 1961, Letter #109.
181 On the "passionate attachment" to antiquities and the "emotional involvement" of all concerned with cultural heritage, see Tubb, "Artifacts and Emotion," 284–302.
182 See letter from Jordanian prime minister, dated 8 May 1961, attached to Shingiti's letter of 13 June 1961, Letter #112.
183 It is interesting that no discussion appears in any of the correspondence as to whether the reimbursement should be corrected for inflation or paid with interest.
184 "Memorandum," 8 July 1959, Letter #89.
185 "Dead Sea Scrolls for London?" *Times* (London), 29 November 1960, 12.
186 "Jordan Ready to Exhibit Scrolls," *Gazette* (Montreal), 30 November 1960, 34.
187 Incidentally, in September 1961, Stephen J. Pfann records, the "scrolls at the PAM were evaluated for insurance purposes and their commercial value was set at JD 150,000," ("History of the Judean Desert Discoveries," 105).
188 For discussion of the organization of the exhibit, particularly the role of John Allegro, see Brown, *John Marco Allegro*, 174–84. Allegro had been

canvassing at least since 1961 to get the government to agree to allow the scrolls to leave the country for exhibit abroad. He had planned to have them exhibited during a visit by King Hussein to Britain in December 1961. The plan was then to move the event to August 1962, when the British Museum Laboratory would work to preserve some of the fragments. In May 1962 it was announced that the August exhibit would be further delayed: "Delay in Exhibiting Dead Sea Scrolls," *Times* (London), 23 May 1962, 5. The delay may have resulted in part from the interference of Harold James Plenderleith. In March 1962 he was in Jerusalem studying the conservation of the scrolls. Concerned with Allegro's lack of attention to the poor condition of the scrolls and fragments, Plenderleith wrote to Frank Francis, the director of the British Museum, in the hope that he could influence a reconsideration of the exhibition: "The sinister aspect in all this is that Allegro is alleged to have received the approval of the king for the scheme which no doubt is admirable as a long-term project but I can imagine the Sunday times [*sic*] is blundering ahead with the best of intentions without thinking to take expert advice on the condition of the material which is the very aspect that should come up for first consideration," (Plenderleith to Francis, undated [March 1961], IAA Archives, Box 73, PAM 1117(c), W. Harold James Plenderleith on Dead Sea Scrolls).

189   William H. Brownlee eventually published 11QEzekiel in 1963 (cf. "The Scroll of Ezekiel from the Eleventh Qumran Cave," 11–28). Through the generosity of the trustee, Elizabeth Hay Bechtel, ASOR purchased the publication rights to the Psalms Scroll, published in 1965 by James Sanders for $60,000 (cf. Sanders, *The Psalms Scroll of Qumrân Cave 11 [11QPs^a]*). On the negotiations for the purchase, see Cross, "Reminiscences of the Early Days," 938–40.

190   As to national interests in movable cultural property, the anthropologist Jaime Litvak King, rather cynically, has observed: "National legislation is, by definition, self-serving. Governments do not graciously give up their rights or their power and this, in the case of antiquities, can hurt research and knowledge. UNESCO Conventions notwithstanding, countries consider their antiquities property, in the Roman sense, for *usere et abutere*. Many national legislations are good examples of chauvinistic thought. They look into cultural property solely as material that proves a politically convenient ethnogenetical theory, or as assets, whose monetary value can be added to a total in a national budget. They do not take into consideration that cultural property is a highly perishable, nonrenewable resource for international research and scholarship," ("Cultural Property and National Sovereignty," 199).

191   See, for example, Merryman, "The Public Interest in Cultural Property," 354–5.

192 Fechner, "The Fundamental Aims of Cultural Property Law," 376. This pragmatic, though cynical, approach to cultural property law illustrates that the questioning of the ethics of individuals, governments, and institutions comes with the territory and that this is not limited to the actions and decisions of any one government. In this context Silberman provides an account of the questionable ethics of the Israel Antiquities Authority in their timing of "Operation Scroll" in November 1993, to look for fragments on the western shore of the Dead Sea and in the vicinity of Qumran before a staged withdrawal of Israeli troops from the region: "The urgency of Operation Scroll was certainly hard to fathom: though this was the area where the Dead Sea Scrolls and other ancient documents had been discovered, the last major manuscript find in this region took place in the early 1960s ... Though the IAA spokeswoman denied that Operation Scroll had any political implications, its timing, at least, was awkward. 'The French did the same thing before they left Algeria,' charged Nazmi Jubeh, a technical advisor to the Palestinian delegation to the Washington peace talks," ("Operation Scroll," 133). On the Palestinian view of the same matter, see also, for example, El-Haj, *Facts on the Ground: Archaeological Practice and Territorial Self-Fashioning in Israeli Society*, 244–8.

193 Shingiti to 1. University of Manchester, England, et al., 22 October 1960, Letter #104.

194 This possibility was of definite concern to Scott as early as March 1957, as is revealed in his list of questions to de Vaux for clarification on the state of affairs vis-à-vis scroll ownership and the Jordanian Government: "Would you please let me know precisely what the situation is at this moment, and what are the prospects as you see them? Has the Government definitely said that its refusal is final? Was this with respect to a particular application by one of the institutions concerned, or is it a statement of policy? Is it admitted that an agreement was made, not simply by Mr. Harding, but with Cabinet sanction?" (Scott to de Vaux, 4 March 1957, Letter #74).

195 See, for example, the letter addressed to Harding by Scott confirming the second payment and requesting official confirmation thereof: "When you acknowledge receipt of this second amount, would you kindly enclose for the University Bursar a note of the total amount received from McGill University 'for the purchase on behalf of McGill University of a collection of ancient scroll fragments from the Judaean desert'. The Bursar needs this for accounting purposes," (Scott to Harding, 8 April 1954, Letter #17). On 19 April 1954 Harding acknowledges receipt of funding and provides McGill in return with a receipt enclosed (Harding to Scott, 19 April 1954, Letter #18).

196 The delay in responding to the government's request for proof occurred because no copies of the receipts had been preserved in the files of the Faculty of Divinity. Frost was therefore dependent on the university comptroller to track their whereabouts (see Frost to Grimson, 2 November 1960, Letter #105; and Comptroller to Frost, 23 November 1960, Letter #106).
197 Frost to Shingiti, 23 November 1960, Letter #107.
198 Green to Frost, 12 December 1960, McGill University Archives, Container: 0179, File 6243: Divinity: DSS & Birks Donation.
199 Frost to Green, 25 November 1960, Letter #108; and Green to Frost, 12 December 1960, McGill University Archives, Container: 0179, File 6243: Divinity: DSS & Birks Donation.
200 Under-secretary of state for External Affairs to Frost, 16 August 1961, McGill University Archives, Container: 0274, File 8260: Divinity: Dead Sea Scrolls. The Canadian government did, however, continue to monitor the situation well into 1962. See Department of External Affairs Canada to Frost, 16 April 1962, McGill University Archives, Container: 0274, File 8260: Divinity: Dead Sea Scrolls. The government also dispatched letters through diplomatic channels on McGill University's behalf. See, for example, Frost to Under-Secretary of State Robertson, 20 June 1962, Letter #121.
201 Frost to Green, 25 November 1960, Letter #108.
202 Shingiti to Manchester et al., 13 June 1961, Letter #112.
203 See letter from Jordanian prime minister, dated 8 May 1961, attached to Shingiti's letter of 13 June 1961, Letter #112.
204 Frost to Shingiti, 19 March 1962, Letter #115.
205 Henniker-Major to Prime Minister Talhouni, 3 June 1961. See also Talhouni to Henniker-Major, 3 July 1961. Both letters are preserved in IAA Archives, Box 73, PAM 1117(b): Distribution of Institutions Dead Sea Scrolls.
206 Under-secretary of state for External Affairs to Frost, 18 October 1961, McGill University Archives, RG2, Container: 0274, File 8260: Divinity: Dead Sea Scrolls.
207 Under-secretary of state for External Affairs to Frost, 18 October 1961, McGill University Archives, RG2, Container: 0274, File 8260: Divinity: Dead Sea Scrolls.
208 Frost to Shingiti, 19 March 1962, Letter #115.
209 Frost to Scott, 20 June 1962, Letter #118.
210 Scott to Frost, 26 March 1962, Letter #117 and Frost to Scott, 17 April 1962, Letter #118.
211 Frost to Robertson, 20 June 1962, Letter #121; and Frost to under-secretary of state for External Affairs Canada, 7 September 1962, Letter #124.
212 Dajani to Frost, 27 June 1962, Letter #123.

213 Dajani to Saʻad, 27 June 1962, Reference #21/2/8/831, IAA Archives, Box 73, PAM 1117(b): Distributions of Institutions Dead Sea Scrolls.
214 Saʻad to Trustees of the Museum, 10 July 1962, Reference #PAM/1/4, IAA Archives, Box 73, PAM 1117(b): Distributions of Institutions Dead Sea Scrolls.
215 Dajani to Saʻad, 21 August 1962, IAA Archives, Box 73, PAM 1117(b): Distributions of Institutions Dead Sea Scrolls.
216 Scott to Dajani, 17 December 1962, Letter #125.
217 "Jordan Given Title to Dead Sea Scrolls," *Globe and Mail* (Toronto), 3 October 1962, 9. See also "Scrolls to Amman," *New York Times*, 30 September 1962, 30.
218 No accompanying cover letter from the Jordanian government or official acknowledgement of receipt from McGill was found in the archives. But Frost confirmed that McGill had received full reimbursement in a letter to Scott on 8 April 1963 (Letter #126). The reimbursement seemed to have taken place shortly before the writing of this letter. In an e-mail exchange dated 28 November 2007, Professor George Brooke of the University of Manchester confirmed that Manchester was also reimbursed. We thank Professor Brooke for his kind assistance in this regard.
219 Frost to Scott, 8 April 1963, Letter #126.
220 "Worth Thousands: Dead Sea Scrolls Now Dead Secret," *Montreal Star*, 21 March 1962, 10.
221 Scott, "Special Report: What Ever Happened to McGill's Dead Sea Scrolls?" 57.
222 Ibid.
223 As early as 1954 their heroic efforts had been recognized: "As a matter of fact, the chief problem has not been lack of available material to buy from [the] Bedouin, or to excavate in the caves, but the limitation of funds for purchase and exploration. It has been by means of heroic efforts by Mr. G. Lankester Harding, director of antiquities, and Père R. de Vaux, Director of the *Ecole Biblique et Archeologique Française* [sic], that so much of this priceless material is now safely in Jordan's museums and available for scholarly study," (Cross, "The Manuscripts of the Dead Sea Caves," 4).

CHAPTER FOUR

1 "... *Who Owns Antiquity?* This is the real question, the one that lies behind the recent arguments between museums and archaeologists, and between museums and 'source' countries' nationalist governments," Cuno, *Who Owns Antiquity? Museums and the Battle over our Ancient Heritage*, 146.

2 Title adapted from Merryman, "The Nation and the Object," 61.
3 Lyons, "Objects and Identities: Claiming and Reclaiming the Past," 116.
4 Zias, "Palestine Archaeological Museum," 635. The nationalization of the PAM by Jordan in early November received limited international press attention and then only by mid-December 1966. The move was pushed by the Jordanian director of antiquities, Awni Dajani, whose criticism of the museum trustees set him against his doctoral supervisor, Kathleen Kenyon, who "accused him of incompetence or worse" (Patrick Seale, "Dead Sea Scrolls Dispute Settled in Jordan," *Washington Post*, 11 December 1966, 14[L]).
5 See letter from Jordanian prime minister, dated 8 May 1961, attached to Shingiti's letter of 13 June 1961, Letter #112. We take the letter from the prime minister as date for final nationalization rather than the 27 July 1960 date offered by Stephen J. Pfann ("History of the Judean Desert Discoveries," 105) or the 5 August 1961 date suggested by Weston Fields (*The Dead Sea Scrolls: A Short History*, 51).
6 Allegro, in his role as "Honorary Adviser to H.M. Government of Jordan on the Dead Sea Scrolls," singled these out as the major challenges for "urgent attention" and then proceeded to describe each in detail in a memorandum to the Jordanian Prime Minister in September 1966: "The main problems requiring urgent attention fall into two sections: I. The physical care of the manuscripts; II. The arrangements for speedy publication of the texts," (Brown, *John Marco Allegro*, 165–7).
7 Ibid., 167.
8 Ibid., 164–5. Although Allegro's concern for the conservation of the fragments was no doubt genuine, he had also proved in the past not above using the fragments to forward his own agenda, without necessarily considering preservation and conservation. Note further on in this narrative that it was only Harold Plenderleith's intervention, at the behest of de Vaux, that would prevent the fragile fragments from transport for exhibit in the United Kingdom in the early 1960s – a move strongly supported by John Allegro.
9 Ibid., 168.
10 Ibid., 169–70.
11 Yigael Yadin provides a description of the capture of the museum and the acquisition of the scrolls in *The Temple Scroll: The Hidden Law of the Dead Sea Sect*, 44–55.
12 Dever, "Archaeology and the Six Day War," 104–5. For discussion of the exploration and repair of the museum, see also Glueck, *Dateline: Jerusalem*, 26–7. Glueck was in Jerusalem from 12 June to 27 August 1967.
13 Fields, *The Dead Sea Scrolls: A Short History*, 52.

14 Yadin by now was not only an important archaeologist but also security advisor to Israeli Prime Minister Levi Eshkol.
15 "Already on Tuesday morning, June 6, when the fighting in Jerusalem was at its heaviest, I [William Dever] ran across Dr. Avraham Biran, Director of the Israel Department of Antiquities, who mentioned that he was headed for the Palestine Archaeological Museum in the Old City," (Dever, "Archaeology and the Six Day War," 103).
16 For Biran's firsthand description of the events, see his comments in "Captured Museum Yields Scrolls Bits," *New York Times*, 17 June 1967, 19, and also James Feron, "Israel Repairing Ravaged Museum," *New York Times*, 9 July 1967, 11.
17 For a complete list of the scrolls housed in the National Archaeological Museum in Amman, see Brooke, "Amman Museum," 22–3. A number of other institutions and private collections around the world play host to Dead Sea Scrolls; for a summary see Fields, "Museums and Collections," 586–7.
18 The conservation of the fragments did benefit from the change in management: "In 1967, one of the first major changes implemented after the reunification of Jerusalem was to remove the approximately 1,300 glass plates that held the scroll fragments to a specially built room where environmental and security conditions could be controlled and carefully monitored ... Conservators were brought in from the Israel Museum, who initiated the painstaking process of removing the cellophane tape and rebacking the fragments with acid-free materials," (Zias, "Palestine Archaeological Museum," 635). See also, Libman and Boyd-Alkalay, "Conservation," 140–2.
19 "The volumes are produced by Oxford University Press, under the (often joint) auspices of the Jordan Department of Antiquities (vols. 1–3), École Biblique et Archéologique Française (vols. 1–3, 5), Palestine Archaeological Museum (vols. 1–5), and the American Schools of Oriental Research (vols. 3–4). No such auspices are listed for volume 6 (1977) and subsequent volumes. Volume 8 and all subsequent volumes were and are published under the auspices of the Israel Antiquities Authority, which has been actively involved in the publication effort since 1990. Throughout, the series has been named *Discoveries in the Judaean Desert*, with an interlude (1962–68) during which volumes 3–5 were titled *Discoveries in the Judaean Desert of Jordan*, (Tov, "Discoveries in the Judaean Desert," 205).
20 Yadin, *The Temple Scroll: The Hidden Law of the Dead Sea Sect*, 45–6.
21 "Jerusalem News Briefs," *Jerusalem Post*, 27 July 1967, 6.
22 By June 1961, a year after the Rockefeller funding ended, "511 manuscripts from cave 4 had been identified on 620 museum plates with fragments on 25 plates still unidentified. The final series of photographs was completed at this

time," (Stephen J. Pfann, "History of the Judean Desert Discoveries," 105). See also the sixth volume of DJD, de Vaux and Milik, *Qumrân Grotte 4.II. I. Archéologie. II. Tefillin, Mezuzot et Targums (4Q128–4Q157)*.

23 Schiffman, "The Many Battles of the Scrolls," 161.
24 Frank Moore Cross had been appointed Hancock Professor of Hebrew and Other Oriental Languages at Harvard University in 1957 (Ulrich, "Cross, Frank Moore," 157–8).
25 Patrick Skehan taught in the Department of Semitic and Egyptian Languages and Literatures from 1938 until his retirement in 1979 (Ulrich, "Skehan, Patrick W.," 880).
26 John Strugnell taught at Duke University from 1960 until 1967, when he left for Harvard (Collins, "Strugnell, John," 2: 896).
27 Brown, *John Marco Allegro*, 170.
28 Puech, "Milik, Józef T.," 552–4.
29 Allegro, *Qumrân Cave 4.I (4Q158–4Q186), DJD*, vol. 5. On de Vaux's delay, see also Brown, *John Marco Allegro*, 152–8.
30 See the reports by Plenderleith 21, 23, 27, and 29 March 1962, IAA Archives, Box 73, PAM 1117(c), W. Harold James Plenderleith on Dead Sea Scrolls.
31 Shor and Libman, "Conservation of the Dead Sea Scrolls," 20. See also Plenderleith's report dated 23 March 1962, IAA Archives, Box 73, PAM 1117(c), W. Harold James Plenderleith on Dead Sea Scrolls; and Brownlee, "The Scroll of Ezekiel from the Eleventh Qumran Cave," 11–28.
32 Report dated 23 March 1962, IAA Archives, Box 73, PAM 1117(c), W. Harold James Plenderleith on Dead Sea Scrolls.
33 Copy of undated letter from Plenderleith to Francis preserved with Plenderleith's reports on conservation activities in the scrollery. Plenderleith opens the letter indicating that he was writing while at work in the scrollery of the PAM on an Ezekiel fragment, IAA Archives, Box 73, PAM 1117(c), W. Harold James Plenderleith on Dead Sea Scrolls.
34 Plenderleith's report dated 21 March 1962, IAA Archives, Box 73, PAM 1117(c), W. Harold James Plenderleith on Dead Sea Scrolls.
35 Plenderleith to de Vaux, 29 March 1962, IAA Archives, Box 73, PAM 1117(c), W. Harold James Plenderleith on Dead Sea Scrolls.
36 De Vaux to Francis, 26 July 1962, IAA Archives, Box 73, PAM 1117(c), W. Harold James Plenderleith on Dead Sea Scrolls.
37 Francis to Dajani, 19 September 1962, IAA Archives, Box 73, PAM 1117(c), W. Harold James Plenderleith on Dead Sea Scrolls.
38 De Vaux to Francis, 8 October 1963, IAA Archives, Box 73, PAM 1117(c), W. Harold James Plenderleith on Dead Sea Scrolls.

39 A copy of Foulkes's report is preserved in IAA Archives, Box 73, PAM 1117(c), W. Harold James Plenderleith on Dead Sea Scrolls. For discussion of her activities, see Libman and Boyd-Alkalay, "Restoration Techniques at the Israel Antiquities Authority," 876–8; and VanderKam and Flint, *The Meaning of the Dead Sea Scrolls*, 64–5.

40 See list of fragments marked "Negative numbers identifying fragments which have been permanently mounted," in IAA Archives, Box 73, PAM 1117(c), W. Harold James Plenderleith on Dead Sea Scrolls.

41 John Strugnell to Prince Hassan of Jordan, 28 November 1966, quoted in Brown, *John Marco Allegro*, 165.

42 Zias, "Palestine Archaeological Museum," 2: 635.

43 "Founded on April 1, 1990, the Israel Antiquities Authority (IAA) assumed the role and functions of the Israel Department of Antiquities and Museums (IDAM), which had operated since the founding of the State of Israel (1948) as an integral part of the Israel Ministry of Education and Culture … In this respect it continued the function of the Department of Antiquities of the British Mandate over Palestine (1920–1948)," (Reich, "Israel Antiquities Authority," 391).

44 See Lim, MacQueen and Carmichael, eds, *On Scrolls, Artefacts and Intellectual Property*.

45 "The treaties and methods used by countries in at least the past century and a half teach us that, both in the matter of ceding territory and in that of the break-up of multinational states, the dominant element in deciding the status of movable cultural property is the principle of the territorial link. The criterion of a given country's closeness to *patrimoine intellectuel* comes second … it is enough to say that in assessing [the Scrolls'] situation the general guideline should also be that of the territorial link to the place where the object was found," (Kowalski, "Legal Aspects of the Recent History of the Qumran Scrolls," 145–7).

46 Fitz Gibbon, "Chronology of Cultural Property Legislation," 3–8.

47 Merryman, "The Nation and the Object," 64.

48 At the time of purchase, Jordan still adhered to the *Antiquities Ordinance 1929* of the Palestinian Mandate (Prott and O'Keefe, *Discovery and Excavation*, vol. 1 of *Law and the Cultural Heritage*, 50). Currently, the West Bank's cultural heritage is under the jurisdiction of the Law of Antiquities Jordan, 1966. Morag Kersel classifies both this law and the Antiquities Ordinance No. 51 of 1929, which still governs the Gaza Strip, as "holdovers from the British Mandate," ("From the Ground to the Buyer," 195). The status quo for the region, in this regard, has therefore not changed much. See

also Prott and O'Keefe (*Discovery and Excavation*, 73), as well as Bentwich ("The Antiquities Law of Palestine," 251–4) for background on the history of the establishment and the nature of antiquities legislation in the former British Mandate.

49 Scott to Henry Birks, 1 July 1959, Letter #88.
50 "In an object-oriented cultural property policy, the emphasis is on three conceptually separate but, in practice, interdependent considerations: preservation, truth and access, in declining order of importance," (Merryman, "The Nation and the Object," 64). See also Merryman, "The Public Interest in Cultural Property," 355–61.
51 Renfrew, *Loot, Legitimacy and Ownership*, 39.
52 Harding to Scott, 19 April 1954, Letter #18. See also Harding to Bentley, 5 January 1956, Letter #51, for confirmation from Harding of the receipt of a further payment.
53 Harding to Scott, 6 June 1956, Letter #61.
54 ASOR. "ASOR Policy on Preservation and Protection of Archaeological Resources," http://www.asor.org/policy.htm (accessed: 20 June 2008).
55 For a retrospective of the value of the Hague Convention over the past fifty years, see Gerstenblith, "Recent Developments in the Legal Protection of Cultural Heritage," 68–92.
56 "Some of the Scrolls were found in Israeli-controlled areas, others were ultimately sold to the government of Israel, and some came to Israel as spoils of war," (Carson, "Raiders of the Lost Scrolls," 309). Note also Kowalski's objection to the term "spoils of war" in favour of "succession" on the part of the State of Israel, as "it is generally accepted that removing cultural property as spoils of war is forbidden, at least, since 1815," (Kowalski, "Legal Aspects of the Recent History of the Qumran Scrolls," 147).
57 "Dead Sea Scrolls Still a Puzzle after 50 Years," CNN *Interactive* (26 July 1997). http://www.cnn.com/WORLD/9707/26/dead.sea.scrolls/ (accessed: 29 November 2006).
58 Kowalski, "Legal Aspects of the Recent History of the Qumran Scrolls," 145.
59 Yadin, *The Message of the Scrolls*, 15–30.
60 Prott and O'Keefe, *Discovery and Excavation*, 24.
61 Letter from Jordanian prime minister, dated 8 May 1961, attached to Shingiti's letter of 13 June 1961, Letter #112.
62 Merryman, "Cultural Property Internationalism," 11–39. This changing pattern has also been described by Jeanette Greenfield (*The Return of Cultural Treasures*, 254–6).
63 Frost to Henry Birks, 11 December 1959, Letter #91. This response echoed Scott's conclusion in an earlier missive to de Vaux when first confronted

with the spectre of nationalization: "Professor Rowley tells me in a letter of the refusal of the Government to permit export of any of the Qumran manuscripts. This is rather stunning news, if it is a final and irrevocable decision. However, I am not surprised that such an action should be taken at this moment, when the Arabs have good cause for resentment and suspicion of the Western powers. But I find it hard to believe that, if we are patient, the Government in happier times (if God wills) will not acknowledge its obligation undertaken on the authority of the Council of Ministers," (Scott to de Vaux, 4 March 1957, Letter #74).

64 Merryman, "The Nation and the Object," 64.
65 Merryman, "The Public Interest in Cultural Property," 358.
66 Renfrew, *Loot, Legitimacy and Ownership*, 22.
67 "Frank Cross of Harvard was showing me round: 'Great Scott, you've got a great batch!'" (Scott to Birks, 1 July 1959, Letter #88).
68 For a reprint of the original newspaper article, see Katzman, "Interview with Chief Scroll Editor John Strugnell," 260–3.
69 Lawrence H. Schiffman ("The Many Battles of the Scrolls," 164) on open access after the publication of a set of microfiches of the entire collection in 1993.

POSTSCRIPT

1 "It may be that the conditions set to your purchase and the long delay may have appeared disagreeable to your Institution. You may be sure that the Palestine Archaeological Museum and the editors have done all in their power to limit this delay. At the moment when you are about to reap the harvest of this patient waiting, I would like to express to you, in the name of the Palestine Archaeological Museum, of those scholars who have been preparing the edition of the Manuscripts, and of all the scholars who will use their work with advantage, our sincerest thanks for the help that you have given us in the task of saving and restoring documents of such great interest," de Vaux to Frost, 4 June 1960, Letter #98.
2 A critical publication on the fragments is forthcoming.
3 Barbara Lawson, e-mail message to authors, 17 March 2008. Lawson is curator of ethnology at the Redpath Museum, McGill University, Montreal.
4 From an interview with Donna Runnals, former dean of the Faculty of Religious Studies, in February 2000. Runnals facilitated the purchase, visiting Scott in Toronto to view and acquire the collection.
5 Scott to F. Cyril James et al., 15 June 1955, Letter #40.
6 Scott, "Special Report: What Ever Happened to McGill's Dead Sea Scrolls?" 57.

7 Postscript by Donna Runnals to R.B.Y. Scott, "Special Report: What Ever Happened to McGill's Dead Sea Scrolls?" 57.

The written material from Wadi Murabba'at was found by the Bedouin in caves near the Dead Sea 18 km south of Khirbet Qumran at the time of the discoveries at Wadi Qumran. The documents discovered date from the First Temple period to the Middle Ages. For an overview of the archaeological finds and a discussion of the nature and content of the written material, see Eshel, "Murabba'at, Wadi," 581–6.

Bibliography

NEWSPAPERS

Ad-Difaa (Jordan), 21 September 1958–24 September 1958.
Chicago Tribune, 30 November 1956.
Gazette (Montreal), 27 December 1950–7 February 1961.
Globe and Mail (Toronto), 27 April 1948–31 March 2003.
Ha'Olam, 1 December 1949.
Jerusalem Post, 27 July 1967.
Jewish Chronicle (London), 18 February 1955.
McGill Reporter, 13 February 2003.
Montreal Star, 27 December 1950–21 March 1962.
New York Times, 25 April 1948–9 December 2007.
Palestine Post, 27 April 1948–21 April 1949.
Princeton Alumni Weekly, 15 April 1960.
Times (London), 23 December 1933–23 May 1962.
Toronto Daily Star, 27 April 1948–16 January 1956.
United Church Observer, 15 July 1953.
Washington Post, 25 May 1956–15 November 1989.
Worcester (Mass.) Telegram and Gazette, 4 July 1993.

GENERAL BIBLIOGRAPHY

Albright, William F. "Notes from the President's Desk." *Bulletin of the American Schools of Oriental Research* 110 (April 1948): 1–3.
– "The Dead Sea Scrolls of St. Marks Monastery." *Bulletin of the American Schools of Oriental Research* 118 (April 1950): 5–6.

- "Albert Henry Detweiler: In Memoriam." *Bulletin of the American Schools of Oriental Research* 198 (April 1970): 2–4.
- "Carl Herman Kraeling: In Memoriam." *Bulletin of the American Schools of Oriental Research* 198 (April 1970): 4–7.

Allegro, John M. *Qumrân Cave 4.I (4Q158–4Q186). Discoveries in the Judaean Desert*, vol. 5. Oxford: Clarendon Press, 1968.

- *The Dead Sea Scrolls: A Reappraisal*. 1956. Reprint, rev. ed. London: Penguin Books, 1990.

Ashby, Eric. *Community of Universities: An Informal Portrait of the Association of Universities of the British Commonwealth, 1913–1963*. Cambridge: Cambridge University Press, 1963.

ASOR. "ASOR Policy on Preservation and Protection of Archaeological Resources." http://www.asor.org/policy.htm (accessed 20 June 2008).

Baigent, Michael, and Richard Leigh. *The Dead Sea Scrolls Deception*. London: Corgi, 1991.

Baillet, Maurice. *Qumrân Grotte 4.III (4Q482–4Q520). Discoveries in the Judaean Desert*, vol. 7. Oxford: Clarendon Press, 1982.

Baillet, Maurice, Józef T. Milik, and Roland de Vaux. *Les "Petites Grottes" de Qumrân*. 2 vols. *Discoveries in the Judaean Desert*, vol. 3. Oxford: Clarendon Press, 1962.

Balawyder, Aloysius. *The Maple Leaf and the White Eagle: Canadian-Polish Relations, 1918–1978*. Boulder: East European Monographs, 1980.

Bank of Canada. "Rates and statistics: inflation calculator." http://www.bankofcanada.ca/en/rates/inflation_calc.html (accessed 8 July 2007).

Barkan, Elazar, and Ronald Bush, eds. *Claiming the Stones, Naming the Bones: Cultural Property and the Negotiation of National and Ethnic Identity*. Los Angeles: Getty Research Institute, 2002.

Barthélemy, Dominique, and Józef T. Milik. *Qumran Cave 1. Discoveries in the Judaean Desert*, vol. 1. Oxford: Clarendon Press, 1955.

Benoit, Pierre. "Editing the Manuscript Fragments from Qumran." *Biblical Archaeologist* 19, no. 4 (1956): 75–96.

Benoit, Pierre, Józef T. Milik, and Roland de Vaux. *Les Grottes de Murabba'ât*. 2 vols. *Discoveries in the Judaean Desert*, vol. 2. Oxford: Clarendon Press, 1961.

Bentwich, Norman. "The Antiquities Law of Palestine." *Journal of Comparative Legislation and International Law* 6, no. 4 (1924): 251–4.

Bernhardsson, Magnus T. *Reclaiming a Plundered Past: Archaeology and Nation Building in Modern Iraq*. Austin: University of Texas Press, 2006.

Bisheh, Ghazi. "One Damn Illicit Excavation After Another: The Destruction of the Archaeological Heritage of Jordan." In *Trade in Illicit Antiquities*, Neil

Brodie, Jennifer Doole, and Colin Renfrew, eds, 115–18. Cambridge: McDonald Institute for Archaeological Research, 2001.

Bogdanos, Matthew. *Thieves of Baghdad*. New York: Bloomsbury, 2005.

Briend, Jacques. "De Vaux, Roland." In Lawrence H. Schiffman and James C. Vanderkam, eds, *Encyclopedia of the Dead Sea Scrolls*, vol. 1. Oxford: Oxford University Press, 2000, 202–4.

– "Shahin, Khalil Iskandar (Kando)." In Lawrence H. Schiffman and James C. Vanderkam, eds, *Encyclopedia of the Dead Sea Scrolls*, vol. 2. Oxford: Oxford University Press, 2000, 869–70.

Brooke, George. "Amman Museum." In Lawrence H. Schiffman and James C. Vanderkam, eds, *Encyclopedia of the Dead Sea Scrolls*, vol. 1. Oxford: Oxford University Press, 2000, 22–3.

– *The Dead Sea Scrolls and the New Testament*. Minneapolis: Fortress, 2005.

Brown, Judith A. *John Marco Allegro: The Maverick of the Dead Sea Scrolls*. Studies in the Dead Sea Scrolls and Related Literature. Grand Rapids: William B. Eerdmans, 2005.

Brownlee, William H. "The Scroll of Ezekiel from the Eleventh Qumran Cave." *Revue de Qumran* 4, no. 13 (1963): 11–28.

Burrows, Millar. "Concerning the Dead Sea Scrolls: A Reply to Professor Zeitlin." *Jewish Quarterly Review* 42, no. 2 (October 1951): 105–32.

– *The Dead Sea Scrolls*. New York: Viking Press, 1955.

– *More Light on the Dead Sea Scrolls*. New York: Viking Press, 1955.

Burrows, Millar, John C. Trever, and William H. Brownlee, eds. *The Dead Sea Scrolls of St. Mark's Monastery*. 2 vols. New Haven: American Schools of Oriental Research, 1950–51.

Cadbury, Henry J. "Annual Meeting of the Corporation." *Bulletin of the American Schools of Oriental Research* 133 (February 1954): 4.

– "December Meeting of the Board of Trustees." *Bulletin of the American Schools of Oriental Research* 133 (February 1954): 2–3.

– "Members and Contributor." *Bulletin of the American Schools of Oriental Research* 133 (February 1954): 4–5.

Carson, Cindy A. "Raiders of the Lost Scrolls: The Right of Scholarly Access to the Content of Historic Documents." *Michigan Journal of International Law* 16, no. 2 (1995): 299–348.

Clark, Kenneth W. "The Posture of the Ancient Scribe." *Biblical Archaeologist* 26, no. 2 (1963): 63–72.

Clines, David J.A. "From Copenhagen to Oslo: What has (and has not) Happened at Congresses of the IOSOT." In David J.A. Clines, ed., *On the Way to the Postmodern: Old Testament Essays, 1967–1998*. 194–221. Sheffield: Sheffield Academic Press, 1998.

Clokie, H. McDowall. "Canada's National Status in Recent Years." *Annals of the American Academy of Political and Social Science* 253 (1947): 22–31.

Collins, John J. "Strugnell, John." In Lawrence H. Schiffman and James C. Vanderkam, eds, *Encyclopedia of the Dead Sea Scrolls*, vol. 2. Oxford: Oxford University Press, 2000, 895–6.

Cross, Frank Moore. "A New Qumran Biblical Fragment Related to the Original Hebrew Underlying the Septuagint." *Bulletin of the American Schools of Oriental Research* (December 1953): 15–26.

– "The Manuscripts of the Dead Sea Caves." *Biblical Archaeologist* 17, no. 1 (1954): 2–21.

– "A Report on the Biblical Fragments of Cave Four in Wâdī Qumrân." *Bulletin of the American Schools of Oriental Research* 141 (February 1956): 9–13.

– *The Ancient Library of Qumran*. 1958. Rev. 3rd ed. Minneapolis: Fortress Press, 1995.

– "On the History of the Photography." In Emanuel Tov, ed., with collaboration of Stephen J. Pfann, *The Dead Sea Scrolls on Microfiche: A Comprehensive Facsimile Edition of the Texts of the Judean Desert. Companion Volume*. Leiden: E.J. Brill, 1993, 121–2.

– "Reminiscences of the Early Days in the Discovery and Study of the Dead Sea Scrolls." In Lawrence H. Schiffman, Emanuel Tov, and James C. Vanderkam, eds, *The Dead Sea Scrolls: Fifty Years after their Discovery*. Jerusalem: Israel Exploration Society, 2000, 932–43.

"Crucifixion Before Christ." *Time*, 6 February 1956. http://www.time.com/time/magazine/article/0,9171,893345,00.html?iid=chix-sphere (accessed 10 December 2007).

Cuno, James. *Who Owns Antiquity? Museums and the Battle over our Ancient Heritage*. Princeton: Princeton University Press, 2008.

Dajani, Awni Khalil. "The Hyksos Period in Palestine." Ph.D. diss., University of London, 1956.

Davies, Philip R. "Allegro, John Marco." In Lawrence H. Schiffman and James C. Vanderkam, eds, *Encyclopedia of the Dead Sea Scrolls*, vol. 1. Oxford: Oxford University Press, 2000, 18.

Davies, William David. "Paul and the Dead Sea Scrolls: Flesh and Spirit." In Krister Stendahl, ed., *The Scrolls and the New Testament*. New York: Harper, 1957, 157–82.

Dawisha, Adeed. *Arab Nationalism in the Twentieth Century*. Princeton: Princeton University Press, 2003.

"The Dead Sea Scrolls: How Do They Affect Traditional Beliefs?" *The New Republic* (9 April 1956) 12.

"Dead Sea Scrolls Still a Puzzle after 50 Years." CNN *Interactive* (26 July 1997). http://www.cnn.com/WORLD/9707/26/dead.sea.scrolls/ (accessed 29 November 2006).
"The Dead Sea Scrolls, Their Significance to Religious Thought: A Symposium." *The New Republic* (9 April 1956).
Del Medico, Henri E. *The Riddle of the Scrolls*. H. Garner, trans. London: Burke, 1958.
Detweiler, A. Henry. "Letter from the President's Desk." *Bulletin of the American Schools of Oriental Research* 146 (April 1957): 3-4.
De Vaux, Roland. "Fouille au Khirbet Qumrân: Rapport préliminaire." *Revue biblique* 60, no. 1 (1953): 83-106.
- "Fouilles au Khirbet Qumrân: Rapport préliminaire sur la deuxième campagne." *Revue biblique* 61, no. 2 (1954): 206-36.
- "Chronique Archéologique: Khirbet Qûmran." *Revue biblique* 61, no. 4 (1954): 567-8.
- "Fouilles au Khirbet Qumrân: Rapport préliminaire sur les 3ᵉ, 4ᵉ et 5ᵉ campagnes." *Revue biblique* 63, no. 4 (1956): 533-77.
- *L'Archéologie et les Manuscrits de la Mer Morte*. Schweich Lectures 1959. London: British Academy, 1961.
- "Les Fouilles de Tell el-Far'ah: Rapport préliminaire sur les 7ᵉ, 8ᵉ, 9ᵉ campagnes, 1958-1960." *Revue biblique* 68, no. 4 (1961): 557-92.
- "Découverte, Fouille et Achats." In *Qumrân Grotte 4.II. I. Archéologie. II. Tefillin, Mezuzot et Targums (4Q128-4Q157)*. Roland de Vaux and Józef T. Milik, *Discoveries in the Judaean Desert*, vol. 6. Oxford: Clarendon Press, 1977, 3-5.
De Vaux, Roland, and Józef T. Milik. *Qumrân Grotte 4.II. I. Archéologie. II. Tefillin, Mezuzot et Targums (4Q128-4Q157)*. *Discoveries in the Judaean Desert*, vol. 6. Oxford: Clarendon Press, 1977.
Dever, William G. "Archaeology and the Six Day War." *Biblical Archaeologist* 30, no. 3 (1967): 73, 102-8.
Dimant, Devorah, "The Qumran Manuscripts: Contents and Significance." In Devorah Dimant and Lawrence H. Schiffman, eds, *Time to Prepare the Way in the Wilderness: Papers on the Qumran Scrolls*. Leiden: E.J. Brill, 1995, 23-58.
"Discovery of the Dead Sea Scrolls," CBC *Times* (14-20 August 1955), n.p.
Driver, Godfrey Rolles. *The Hebrew Scrolls from the Neighbourhood of Jericho and the Dead Sea*. London: Oxford University Press, 1951.
- *The Judaean Scrolls: The Problem and a Solution*. New York: Schocken, 1965.
- "Mythology of Qumrân." *Jewish Quarterly Review* 61, no. 4 (April 1971): 241-81.

Dupont-Sommer, André. *The Dead Sea Scrolls: A Preliminary Survey*. E. Margaret Rowley, trans. Oxford: Basil Blackwell, 1952.

Du Toit, Jaqueline S. and Jason Kalman. "Great Scott! The Dead Sea Scrolls, McGill University, and the Canadian Media." *Dead Sea Discoveries* 12, no. 1 (2005): 6–23.

Eisenman, Robert and Michael Wise. *The Dead Sea Scrolls Uncovered: The First Complete Translation and Interpretation of 50 Key Documents withheld for over 35 Years*. New York: Penguin, 1993.

El-Haj, Nadia Abu. *Facts on the Ground: Archaeological Practice and Territorial Self-Fashioning in Israeli Society*. Chicago: University of Chicago Press, 2002.

Eshel, Hanan. "Hever, Nahal." In Lawrence H. Schiffman and James C. Vanderkam, eds, *Encyclopedia of the Dead Sea Scrolls*, vol. 1. Oxford: Oxford University Press, 2000, 357–9.

– "Murabba'at, Wadi." In Lawrence H. Schiffman and James C. Vanderkamm, eds, *Encyclopedia of the Dead Sea Scrolls*, vol. 1. Oxford: Oxford University Press, 2000, 581–6.

"Ethics of Publication of the Dead Sea Scrolls: Panel Discussion." In Michael O. Wise, et al., eds, *Methods of Investigation of the Dead Sea Scrolls and the Khirbet Qumran Site: Present Realities and Future Prospects*. New York: New York Academy of Sciences, 1994, 455–97.

Fechner, Frank G. "The Fundamental Aims of Cultural Property Law." *International Journal of Cultural Property* 7, no. 2 (1998): 376–94.

Fields, Weston W. "Discovery and Purchase." In Lawrence H. Schiffman and James C. Vanderkam, eds, *Encyclopedia of the Dead Sea Scrolls*, vol. 1. Oxford: Oxford University Press, 2000, 208–12.

– "Museums and Collections." In Lawrence H. Schiffman and James C. Vanderkam, eds, *Encyclopedia of the Dead Sea Scrolls*, vol. 1. Oxford: Oxford University Press, 2000, 586–7.

– *The Dead Sea Scrolls: A Short History*. Leiden: E.J. Brill, 2006.

– *The Dead Sea Scrolls – A Full History: Volume One, 1947–1960*. Leiden: E. J. Brill, 2009.

Filson, Floyd V. "Some Recent Study of the Dead Sea Scrolls." *Biblical Archaeologist* 13, no. 4 (1950): 96–9.

Finlay, Karen A. *The Force of Culture: Vincent Massey and Canadian Sovereignty*. Toronto: University of Toronto Press, 2004.

Fitz Gibbon, Kate. "Chronology of Cultural Property Legislation." In Kate Fitz Gibbon, ed., *Who Owns the Past? Cultural Policy, Cultural Property, and the Law*. New Brunswick: Rutgers University, 2005, 3–8.

Fitzmyer, Joseph A. *Responses to 101 Questions on the Dead Sea Scrolls*. New York: Paulist Press, 1992.

"Forestell, James Terence." In *Dictionary of Basilian Biography: Lives of Members of the Congregation of Priests of Saint Basil from its Origins in 1822 to 2002*, 2nd ed. Rev. Philip Wallace Platt. Toronto: University of Toronto Press, 2005, 227–30.

Frank, Harry Thomas. "How the Dead Sea Scrolls Were Found." In *The Dead Sea Scrolls*. Washington, D.C.: Biblical Archaeology Society, 2007, 7–19. Originally published in Harry Thomas Frank, "How the Dead Sea Scrolls Were Found," *Biblical Archaeology Review* 1, no. 4 (December 1975): 1, 7–16, 28–30.

Frey, Jörg. "The Impact of the Dead Sea Scrolls on New Testament Interpretation: Proposals, Problems, and Further Perspectives." In James H. Charlesworth, ed., *The Bible and the Dead Sea Scrolls: The Second Princeton Symposium on the Dead Sea Scrolls*, vol. 3. The Scrolls and Christian Origins. Waco: Baylor University Press. 2006, 407–61.

Frost, Stanley B. *McGill University: For the Advancement of Learning*. 2 vols. Montreal: McGill-Queen's University Press, 1980–84.

– *The Man in the Ivory Tower: F. Cyril James of McGill*. Montreal: McGill-Queen's University Press, 1991.

Gerstenblith, Patty. "Who Owns the Past: Introduction." In Neil Asher Silberman and Ernest S. Frerichs, eds, *Archaeology and Society in the 21st Century: The Dead Sea Scrolls and Other Case Studies*. Jerusalem: Israel Exploration Society, 2001, 128–31.

– "Recent Developments in the Legal Protection of Cultural Heritage." In Neil Brodie et al., eds, *Archaeology, Cultural Heritage, and the Antiquities Trade*. Gainesville: University Press of Florida, 2006, 68–92.

Gitin, Seymour. "The House that Albright Built." *Near Eastern Archaeology* 65, no. 1 (2002): 5–10.

Glueck, Nelson. *Dateline: Jerusalem*. Cincinnati: HUC Press, 1968.

Goldman, Shalom. "A Long Affair: Edmund Wilson on Judaism, the Hebrew Language and the American Jewish Community." *Modern Judaism* 21, no. 2 (2001): 108–24.

Government of Jordan. Department of Antiquities: General Information. http://images.jordan.gov.jo/wps/wcm/connect/eGov/Government+Ministries+&+Entities/Department+of+Antiquities/General+Information/ (accessed 20 June 2008).

Greenfield, Jeanette. *The Return of Cultural Treasures*. 2nd ed. Cambridge: Cambridge University Press, 1995.

Grimson, George A. "The Bursar Retires." *McGill News* 38 (Autumn 1957): 12.

Hammond, Philip. "A Note on a Seal Impression From Tell es-Sultân." *Bulletin of the American Schools of Oriental Research* 147 (October 1957): 37–9.

Harding, G. Lankester. "Introductory. The Discovery, the Excavation, Minor Finds." In Dominique Barthélemy and Józef T. Milik, *Qumran Cave I. Discoveries in the Judaean Desert*, vol. 1. Oxford: Clarendon Press, 1955, 3–7.

Harding, G. Lankester, and William L. Reed. "Archaeological News from Jordan." *Biblical Archaeologist* 16, no. 1 (1953): 1–17.

Hirschfeld, Yizhar. *Qumran in Context*. Peabody: Hendrickson, 2004.

Humbert, Jean Baptiste, and Alain Chambon. *Fouilles de Khirbet Qumrân et de Aïn Feshka*. Göttingen: Vandenhoeck & Ruprecht, 1994.

Hutton, Eric. "What the Dead Sea Scrolls Mean to the Christian Faith." *Maclean's* (22 December 1956): 7–9, 34–41.

"In Memoriam: Willard Gurdon Oxtoby." *News@UofT* (5 May 2003). http://www.newsandevents.utoronto.ca/bin5/030505h.asp (accessed: 23 November 2007).

"July 1956 – Arab Legion Discussions with Britain." Keesing's Contemporary Archives 10 (July 1956): 14965. http://www.keesings.com (accessed 19 September 2007).

Kalman, Jason. "Optimistic, Even with the Negatives: HUC-JIR and the Dead Sea Scrolls, 1948–1993" *American Jewish Archives Journal* 61, no. 1 (2009): 1–114.

Katzman, Avi. "Interview with Chief Scroll Editor John Strugnell." In Hershel Shanks, ed., *Understanding the Dead Sea Scrolls: A Reader from the Biblical Archaeology Review*. New York: Vintage Books, 1993, 260–3.

Kay, Zachariah. *The Diplomacy of Prudence: Canada and Israel, 1948–1958*. Montreal: McGill-Queen's University Press, 1996.

Kenyon, Kathleen. "Excavations at Jericho 1956." *Palestine Exploration Quarterly* 88, no. 2 (1956): 67–82.

Kersel, Morag M. "From the Ground to the Buyer: A Market Analysis of the Trade in Illegal Antiquities." In Neil Brodie et al., eds, *Archaeology, Cultural Heritage, and the Antiquities Trade*. Gainesville: University Press of Florida, 2006, 188–205.

King, Philip J. *American Archaeology in the Mideast: A History of the American Schools of Oriental Research*. Philadelphia: American Schools of Oriental Research, 1983.

Kiraz, George A., ed. *Anton Kiraz's Archive on the Dead Sea Scrolls*. Piscataway: Gorgias, 2005.

Kowalski, Wojciech. "Legal Aspects of the Recent History of the Qumran Scrolls: Access, Ownership Title and Copyright." In Timothy H. Lim, Hector L. MacQueen and Calum M. Carmichael, eds, *On Scrolls, Artefacts and Intellectual Property*. Journal for the Study of the Pseudepigrapha: Supplement Series, Lester L. Grabbe and James H. Charlesworth, eds., no. 38. Sheffield: Sheffield Academic Press, 2001, 128–58.

Kuffert, Leonard B. *A Great Duty: Canadian Responses to Modern Life and Mass Culture in Canada, 1939–1967*. Montreal: McGill-Queen's University Press, 2003.

Kutscher, Edward Y. "Dating the Language of the Genesis Apocryphon." *Journal of Biblical Literature* 76, no. 4 (1957): 288–92.

Lange, Armin with Ulrike Mittmann-Richert. "Annotated List of the Texts from the Judaean Desert Classified by Content and Genre." In Emanuel Tov, ed., *The Texts from the Judaean Desert: Indices and an Introduction to the* Discoveries in the Judaean Desert Series. *Discoveries in the Judaean Desert*, vol. 39. Oxford: Clarendon Press, 2002, 115–64.

Lapp, Paul W. "The Second and Third Campaigns at 'Arâq el-Emîr." *Bulletin of the American Schools of Oriental Research* 171 (October 1963): 8–39.

Libman, Elena, and Esther Boyd-Alkalay. "Conservation." In Lawrence H. Schiffman and James C. Vanderkam, eds, *Encyclopedia of the Dead Sea Scrolls*, vol. 1. Oxford: Oxford University Press, 2000, 140–2.

– "Restoration Techniques at the Israel Antiquities Authority." In Lawrence H. Schiffman, Emanuel Tov and James C. Vanderkam, eds, *The Dead Sea Scrolls: Fifty Years after their Discovery*. Jerusalem: Israel Exploration Society, 2000, 875–80.

Lim, Timothy H., Hector L. MacQueen, and Calum M. Carmichael, eds. *On Scrolls, Artefacts and Intellectual Property*. Journal for the Study of the Pseudepigrapha: Supplement Series, Lester L. Grabbe and James H. Charlesworth, eds., no. 38. Sheffield: Sheffield Academic Press, 2001.

Litt, Paul. *The Muses, the Masses, and the Massey Commission*. Toronto: University of Toronto Press, 1992.

Litvak King, Jaime. "Cultural Property and National Sovereignty." In Phyllis M. Messenger, ed., *The Ethics of Collecting Cultural Property*. Albuquerque: University of New Mexico, 1989, 199–208.

Long, Burke O. *Planting and Reaping Albright: Politics, Ideology, and Interpreting the Bible*. University Park, PA: Pennsylvania State University, 1997.

Lufkin, Martha B.G. "End of the Era of Denial for Buyers of State-Owned Antiquities: United States v. Schultz." *International Journal of Cultural Property* 11, no. 2 (2002): 305–22.

Lyons, Claire L. "Objects and Identities: Claiming and Reclaiming the Past." In Elazar Barkan and Ronald Bush, eds, *Claiming the Stones, Naming the Bones: Cultural Property and the Negotiation of National and Ethnic Identity*. Los Angeles: Getty Research Institute, 2002, 116–37.

Magness, Jodi. "Two Notes on the Archaeology of Qumran." *Bulletin of the American Schools of Oriental Research* 312 (November 1998): 37–44.

- *The Archaeology of Qumran and the Dead Sea Scrolls.* Grand Rapids: William B. Eerdmans, 2002.
Manning, John. "Conflicting Views in Higher Education." *Journal of Higher Education* 21, no. 1 (1950): 26–56.
Markell, Keith H. *The Faculty of Religious Studies, McGill University, 1948–1978.* Montreal: McGill Faculty of Religious Studies, 1979.
Massad, Joseph A. *Colonial Effects: The Making of National Identity in Jordan.* New York: Columbia University Press, 2001.
Massolin, Philip. *Canadian Intellectuals, the Tory Tradition, and the Challenge of Modernity, 1939–1970.* Toronto: University of Toronto Press, 2001.
- "Modernization and Reaction: Post-War Evolutions and the Critique of Higher Learning in English-Speaking Canada, 1945–1970." *Journal of Canadian Studies* 36, no. 2 (2001): 130–63.
McGill University. *Annual Report, 1953–1954.*
McGill University. *Catalogue of Courses, 1953–1954.*
McGill University. *Catalogue of Courses, 1954–1955.*
Mellors, Peter. "Canada's Big Biblical Bargain." *Star Weekend Magazine* (26 November 1960): 10–11, 37.
"Members and Contributors." *Bulletin of the American Schools of Oriental Research* 133 (February 1954): 4–5.
Merryman, John H. "The Public Interest in Cultural Property." *California Law Review* 77, no. 2 (1989): 339–64.
- "The Nation and the Object." *International Journal of Cultural Property* 3, no. 1 (1994): 61–76.
- "Cultural Property Internationalism." *International Journal of Cultural Property* 12, no. 1 (2005): 11–39.
Messenger, Phyllis M., ed. *The Ethics of Collecting Cultural Property.* Albuquerque: University of New Mexico, 1989.
Meyer, Michael A. *Joachim Prinz, Rebellious Rabbi.* Bloomington: Indiana University Press, 2007.
Milik, Józef T. "Deux Documents Inédit du Désert de Juda." *Biblica* 38 (1957): 245–68.
- *Dix ans de découvertes dans le désert de Juda.* Paris: Cerf, 1957.
- "Le Travail d'édition des Manuscrits du Désert de Juda." In P.A.H. de Boer, ed., *Volume du Congrès: Strasbourg 1956. Vetus Testamentum Supplements*, G.W. Anderson et al., eds, no. 4. Leiden: E.J. Brill, 1957, 17–26.
- "Henoch au pays des aromates (ch. XXVII a XXXII): Fragments arameens de la grotte 4 de Qumran." *Revue biblique* 65, no. 1 (1958): 70–7.
- *Ten Years of Discovery in the Wilderness of Judaea.* John Strugnell, trans. Studies in Biblical Theology, no. 26. London: SCM Press, 1959.

Murphy-O'Connor, Jerome. "In Memoriam: Pierre Benoit, O.P." *Bulletin of the American Schools of Oriental Research* 268 (November 1987): 1–2.

Newman, Peter. *Bronfman Dynasty: The Rothschilds of the New World*. Toronto: McLelland and Stewart, 1978.

Nimmer, David. "Copyright in the Dead Sea Scrolls: Authorship and Originality." *Houston Law Review* 38, no. 1 (2001): 1–222.

Oren, Michael B. "A Winter of Discontent: Britian's Crisis in Jordan, December 1955–March 1956." *International Journal of Middle East Studies* 22, no. 2 (1990):171–84.

Orlinsky, Harry M. "Studies in the St. Mark's Isaiah Scroll." *Journal of Biblical Literature* 69, no. 2. (1950): 149–66.

– "The Dead Sea Scrolls and Mr. Green." In Harry M. Orlinsky, ed., *Essays in Biblical Culture and Bible Translation*. New York: Ktav, 1974, 245–56.

PACIFIC Exchange Rate Service. "Foreign Currency Units per 1 British Pound, 1948–2006." http://fx.sauder.ubc.ca (accessed 18 July 2007).

Patrich, Joseph. "Mird, Khirbet." In Lawrence H. Schiffman and James C. Vanderkam, eds, *Encyclopedia of the Dead Sea Scrolls*, vol. 1. Oxford: Oxford University Press, 2000, 563–6.

Pfann, Stephen J. "History of the Judean Desert Discoveries." In Emanuel Tov, ed., with collaboration of Stephen J. Pfann, *The Dead Sea Scrolls on Microfiche: A Comprehensive Facsimile Edition of the Texts of the Judean Desert. Companion Volume*. Leiden: E.J. Brill, 1993, 97–108.

Pilkington, Gwendoline. "A History of the National Conference of Canadian Universities 1911–1961." Ph.D. diss., University of Toronto, 1974.

Plenderleith, Harold James. *The Conservation of Antiquities and Works of Art: Treatment, Repair, and Restoration*. London: Oxford University Press, 1956.

Pope, Marvin H. "Report of the Director of the School in Jerusalem." *Bulletin of the American Schools of Oriental Research* 161 (February 1961): 4–8.

Pritchard, James B. "Industry and Trade at Biblical Gibeon." *Biblical Archaeologist* 23, no. 1 (1960): 23–9.

Prott, Lyndel V. and Patrick J. O'Keefe. *Discovery and Excavation*. In *Law and the Cultural Heritage*, vol. 1. London: Butterworths, 1984.

Puech, Émile. "Milik, József T." In Lawrence H. Schiffman and James C. Vanderkam, eds, *Encyclopedia of the Dead Sea Scrolls*, vol. 1. Oxford: Oxford University Press, 2000, 552–4.

– "Starcky, Jean." In Lawrence H. Schiffman and James C. Vanderkam, eds, *Encyclopedia of the Dead Sea Scrolls*, vol. 2. Oxford: Oxford University Press, 2000, 891–2.

Ramsey, Paul. "Princeton University's Graduate Program in Religion." *Journal of Bible and Religion* 30, no. 4 (1962): 291–8.

Reed, Stephen A. "Survey of the Dead Sea Scrolls Fragments and Photographs at the Rockefeller Museum." *Biblical Archaeologist* 54, no. 1 (1991): 44–51.

Reed, William L. "Annual Meeting of the Corporation." *Bulletin of the American Schools of Oriental Research* 137 (February 1955): 4–5.

Reich, Ronny. "Israel Antiquities Authority." In Lawrence H. Schiffman and James C. Vanderkam, eds, *Encyclopedia of the Dead Sea Scrolls*, vol. 1. Oxford: Oxford University Press, 2000, 391–3.

Reid, Donald M. *Whose Pharaohs? Archaeology, Museums, and Egyptian National Identity from Napoleon to World War I*. Berkeley: University of California Press, 2002.

Reif, Stefan C. "Cairo Genizah." In Lawrence H. Schiffman and James C. Vanderkam, eds, *Encyclopedia of the Dead Sea Scrolls*, vol. 1. Oxford: Oxford University Press, 2000, 105–8.

Renfrew, Colin. *Loot, Legitimacy and Ownership*. London: Duckworth, 2000.

Robinson, James M. "Commentary: Handling Future Manuscript Discoveries." *Biblical Archaeologist* 54, no. 4 (1991): 235–40.

Robson, Eleanor, Luke Treadwell, and Chris Gosden, eds. *Who Owns Objects? The Ethics and Politics of Collecting Cultural Artefacts*. Oxford: Oxbow, 2006.

Rowley, Harold Henry. *The Zadokite Fragments and the Dead Sea Scrolls*. New York: Macmillan, 1952.

— "The International Old Testament Conference in Copenhagen." *Vetus Testamentum* 3, no. 4 (1953): 423–8.

— "The Second International Old Testament Congress." *Vetus Testamentum* 6, no. 4 (1956): 443–7.

— *The Faith of Israel*. Philadelphia: Westminster Press, 1957.

Running, Leona G., and David N. Freedman. *William Foxwell Albright: A Twentieth-Century Genius*. New York: Two Continents, 1975.

Saʻad, Yusif. *The Palestine Archaeological Museum and the Dead Sea Scrolls*, Jerusalem: The Palestine Archaeological Museum, 1961.

Samuel, Athanasius Yeshue. *Treasure of Qumran: My Story of the Dead Sea Scrolls*. Philadelphia: Westminster Press, 1966.

Sanders, James A. *The Psalms Scroll of Qumrân Cave 11 (11QPs^a). Discoveries in the Judaean Desert*, vol. 4. Oxford: Clarendon Press, 1965.

Schiffman, Lawrence H. *Reclaiming the Dead Sea Scrolls: The History of Judaism, the Background of Christianity, the Lost Library of Qumran*. New York: Doubleday, 1995.

— "The Many Battles of the Scrolls." *Journal of Religious History* 26, no. 2 (2002): 157–78.

— "Inverting Reality: the Dead Sea Scrolls and the Popular Media." *Dead Sea Discoveries* 12, no. 1 (2005): 25–9.

Schiffman, Lawrence H., and George Brooke. "The Past: On the History of Dead Sea Scrolls Research." In Robert Kugler and Eileen M. Schuller, eds, *The Dead Sea Scrolls at Fifty*. Atlanta: Society of Biblical Literature, 1999, 9–20.

Schiffman, Lawrence H., Emanuel Tov, and James C. VanderKam, eds. *The Dead Sea Scrolls: Fifty Years After Their Discovery*. Jerusalem: Israel Exploration Society, 2000.

Schiffman, Lawrence H., and James C. Vanderkam, eds. *Encyclopedia of the Dead Sea Scrolls*. 2 vols. Oxford: Oxford University Press, 2000.

Schuller, Eileen M. "The 40th anniversary of the Dead Sea Scrolls." *Studies in Religion* 18, no.1 (1989): 61–5.

– *The Dead Sea Scrolls: What Have We Learned?* Louisville: Westminster John Knox, 2006.

Scott, Gavin. "Home for Christmas: Report from the North." *Harvard Crimson* (19 December 1956). http://www.thecrimson.com/article.aspx?ref=135598 (accessed 11 August 2007).

Scott, John. "The Dead Sea Scrolls: Some of the Oldest Manuscripts of the Bible Ever Found are Acquired by the University." *McGill News* 4 (Autumn 1954): 24–5, 52–4.

– "The Dead Sea Scrolls: Some of the Oldest Bible Manuscripts." *Canadian Jewish Congress Bulletin* (October–November 1954): 3.

Scott, Robert B.Y. "The Original Language of the Apocalypse." Ph.D. diss., University of Toronto, 1928.

– "The Living Interest of the Old Testament." In *Four lectures, delivered in 1949 by J.S. Thomson, R.H.L. Slater, W.C. Smith and R.B.Y. Scott, to inaugurate the Faculty of Divinity of McGill University*. Montreal: McGill University, 1950, 63–81.

– "More Treasure Trove: Dead Sea Region Discoveries," *United Church Observer*, (15 July 1953) 5, 28.

– "Acquisition of Dead Sea Scroll Fragments by McGill University." *Bulletin of the American Schools of Oriental Research* 135 (October 1954): 8.

– "Another Griffin Seal from Samaria." *Palestine Exploration Quarterly* 86, no. 2 (1954): 87–90.

– "Is Preaching Prophecy?" *Canadian Journal of Theology* 1, no. 1 (1955): 11–18.

– "The Dead Sea Scrolls." *Star Weekend Magazine*, 15 October 1955, 2–4, 40, 42.

– "The John Henry Birks Collection of Ancient Palestinian Manuscripts." *Canadian Journal of Theology* 1, no. 1 (1955): 51–2.

– *Treasure from Judæan Caves: The Story of the Dead Sea Scrolls*. Toronto: United Church Publishing House, 1955.

– "Christianity Not Born in a Vacuum." *The New Republic*, 9 April 1956, 22–4.

- "Review: *The Qumran Community, Its History and Scrolls*, by Charles T. Fritsch." *The Princeton Seminary Bulletin* 50 (1956): 44–5.
- "Methods and Objectives of Biblical Scholarship." Reprinted pamphlet, n.p., n.d. Originally published as "Biblical Scholarship; Like the Dead Sea Scrolls the Graduate Program in Religion Raises Questions for the Liberal Arts." *Princeton Alumni Weekly*, 15 April 1960, 10–15, 19.
- *Proverbs and Ecclesiastes*. The Anchor Bible, vol. 18. Garden City: Doubleday, 1965.
- "Special Report: What Ever Happened to McGill's Dead Sea Scrolls?" ARC 9 (1981): 55–8.
- Weights from the 1961–1967 Excavations. In A. Douglas Tushingham, *Excavations in Jerusalem 1961–1967*, vol. 1. Toronto: Royal Ontario Museum, 1985, 197–212.
- *Towards the Christian Revolution*. 1936. Reprint, Kingston, Ont.: R.P. Frye, 1989.

Sellers, Ovid R. et al. *The 1957 Excavation at Bet-Zur*. Annual of the American Schools of Oriental Research, vol. 38. Cambridge: American Schools of Oriental Research, 1968.

Shanks, Hershel. "Leading Dead Sea Scroll Scholar Denounces Delay." *Biblical Archaeology Review* 16, no. 2 (1990): 18–25.
- "Is the Vatican Suppressing the Dead Sea Scrolls?" In Hershel Shanks, ed., *Understanding the Dead Sea Scrolls: A Reader from the* Biblical Archaeology Review. New York: Vintage Books, 1993, 275–90.
- "Silence, Anti-Semitism, and the Scrolls." In Hershel Shanks, ed., *Understanding the Dead Sea Scrolls: A Reader from the* Biblical Archaeology Review. New York: Vintage Books, 1993, 264–74.
- *The Mystery and Meaning of the Dead Sea Scrolls*. New York: Random House, 1998.
- "Chief Scroll Editor Opens Up: An Interview with Emanuel Tov." *Biblical Archaeology Review* 28, no. 3 (2002): 32–5, 62.

Shanks, Hershel, ed. *Understanding the Dead Sea Scrolls: A Reader from the* Biblical Archaeology Review. New York: Vintage Books, 1993.

Shor, Pnina, and Lena Libman. "Conservation of the Dead Sea Scrolls." In Ellen Middlebrook Herron, ed., *The Dead Sea Scrolls: Catalog of the Exhibition of Scrolls from the Collections of the Israel Antiquities Authority, Public Museum of Grand Rapids*. Grand Rapids: William B. Eerdmans, 2003, 19–22.

Silberman, Neil Asher. *The Hidden Scrolls: Christianity, Judaism, and the War for the Dead Sea Scrolls*. New York: Riverhead Books, 1994.
- "Operation Scroll." In Karen D. Vitelli, ed., *Archaeological Ethics*. London: AltaMira Press, 1996, 132–6.

- "Department of Antiquities of Jordan." In Lawrence H. Schiffman and James C. Vanderkam, eds, *Encyclopedia of the Dead Sea Scrolls*, vol. 1. Oxford: Oxford University Press, 2000, 192–4.
- "Sukenik, Eleazar L." In Lawrence H. Schiffman and James C. Vanderkam, eds, *Encyclopedia of the Dead Sea Scrolls*, vol. 2. Oxford: Oxford University Press, 2000, 902–3.
- "Yadin, Yigael." In Lawrence H. Schiffman and James C. Vanderkam, eds, *Encyclopedia of the Dead Sea Scrolls*, vol. 2. Oxford: Oxford University Press, 2000, 999–1000.

Skehan, Patrick W. "A Fragment of the 'Song of Moses' (Deut. 32) from Qumran." *Bulletin of the American Schools of Oriental Research* 136 (December 1954): 12–15.
- "The Qumran Manuscripts and Textual Criticism." In P.A.H. de Boer, ed., *Volume du Congrès: Strasbourg 1956. Vetus Testamentum Supplements*, G.W. Anderson et al., eds, no. 4. Leiden: E.J. Brill, 1957, 148–60.

"Stanley Frost: A Cool Look at History." *McGill Reporter* 35, no. 10 (13 February 2003). http://www.mcgill.ca/reporter/35/10/kaleidoscope/ (accessed: 22 July 2007).

Strugnell, John. "In Memoriam – Roland Guérin de Vaux, O.P." *Bulletin of the American Schools of Oriental Research* 207 (October 1972): 3–5.
- "On the History of the Photographing of the Discoveries in the Judean Desert for the International Group of Editors." In Emanuel Tov, ed., with collaboration of Stephen J. Pfann, *The Dead Sea Scrolls on Microfiche: A Comprehensive Facsimile Edition of the Texts of the Judean Desert. Companion Volume*. Leiden: E.J. Brill, 1993, 123–34.
- "The Original Team of Editors." In Timothy H. Lim, Hector L. MacQueen, and Calum M. Carmichael, eds, *On Scrolls, Artefacts and Intellectual Property*. Journal for the Study of the Pseudepigrapha: Supplement Series, Lester L. Grabbe and James H. Charlesworth, eds, no. 38. Sheffield: Sheffield Academic Press, 2001, 178–92.

Sukenik, Eleazar L. *Megilot Genuzot*. 2 vols. Jerusalem: Mossad Bialik, 1948–50.
- *The Dead Sea Scrolls of the Hebrew University*. Jerusalem: Magness Press, 1955.

Sussman, Ayala, and Ronny Reich. *L'Toldot Muzaon Rockefeller B'Yirushalaim*. In Ely Schiller, ed., *Zev Vilnay's Jubilee Volume Part II*. Jerusalem: Ariel, 1987, 83–92.

Testuz, Michel. "Deux fragments inédit de la Mer Morte." *Semitica* 5 (1955): 37–40.

"The Oldest Decalogue." *Time* (29 September 1958). http://www.time.com/time/magazine/article/0,9171,821184,00.html (accessed: 14 November 2007).

Tov, Emanuel. *The Greek Minor Prophets Scroll from Nahal Hever (8HevXIIgr): The Seiyâl Collection I. Discoveries in the Judaean Desert*, vol. 8. Oxford: Clarendon Press, 1990.
- "Discoveries in the Judaean Desert." In Lawrence H. Schiffman and James C. Vanderkam, eds, *Encyclopedia of the Dead Sea Scrolls*, vol. 1. Oxford: Oxford University Press, 2000, 205–8.
- "The Publication of the Dead Sea Scrolls." In Timothy H. Lim, Hector L. MacQueen, and Calum M. Carmichael, eds, *On Scrolls, Artefacts and Intellectual Property*. Journal for the Study of the Pseudepigrapha: Supplement Series, Lester L. Grabbe and James H. Charlesworth, eds, no. 38. Sheffield: Sheffield Academic Press, 2001, 199–213.
- "Categorized List of the 'Biblical Texts.'" In Emanuel Tov, ed., *The Texts from the Judaean Desert: Indices and an Introduction to the Discoveries in the Judaean Desert Series. Discoveries in the Judaean Desert*, vol. 39. Oxford: Clarendon Press, 2002, 165–83.
- *Scribal Practices and Approaches Reflected in the Texts Found in the Judean Desert*. Leiden: E.J. Brill, 2004.

Tov, Emanuel, ed., with collaboration of Stephen J. Pfann. *The Dead Sea Scrolls on Microfiche: A Comprehensive Facsimile Edition of the Texts of the Judean Desert. Companion Volume*. Leiden: E.J. Brill, 1993.
- "The Texts from the Judean Desert and Their Negative Numbers." In *The Dead Sea Scrolls on Microfiche: A Comprehensive Facsimile Edition of the Texts of the Judean Desert. Companion Volume*. Leiden: E.J. Brill, 1993, 17–72.
- *The Texts from the Judaean Desert: Indices and an Introduction to the Discoveries in the Judaean Desert Series. Discoveries in the Judaean Desert*, vol. 39. Oxford: Clarendon Press, 2002.

Trever, John C. "The Discovery of the Scrolls," *Biblical Archaeologist* 11, no. 3 (1948): 45–57.
- *The Dead Sea Scrolls: A Personal Account*. Rev. ed. Grand Rapids: William B. Eerdmans, 1977.

Trompf, Garry W. "Introduction I: The Long History of Dead Sea Scrolls Scholarship." *Journal of Religious History* 26, no. 2 (2002): 123–44.

Tubb, Kathryn Walker. "Artifacts and Emotion." In Neil Brodie et al., eds, *Archaeology, Cultural Heritage, and the Antiquities Trade*. Gainesville: University Press of Florida, 2006, 284–302.

Tushingham, A. Douglas. "Report of the Director of the School in Jerusalem." *Bulletin of the American Schools of Oriental Research* 132 (December 1953): 41–5.
- *Excavations in Jerusalem 1961–1967*. vol. 1. Toronto: Royal Ontario Museum, 1985.

- "In Memoriam: Frederick Victor Winnett, 1903–1989." *Bulletin of the American Schools of Oriental Research* 279 (August 1990): 1–4.
Ulrich, Eugene. "Daniel Manuscripts from Qumran. Part 1: A Preliminary Edition of 4QDan^a." *Bulletin of the American Schools of Oriental Research* 268 (November 1987): 17–37.
- "Cross, Frank Moore." In Lawrence H. Schiffman and James C. Vanderkam, eds, *Encyclopedia of the Dead Sea Scrolls*, vol. 1. Oxford: Oxford University Press, 2000, 157–8.
- "Skehan, Patrick W." In Lawrence H. Schiffman and James C. Vanderkam, eds, *Encyclopedia of the Dead Sea Scrolls*, vol. 2. Oxford: Oxford University Press, 2000, 880.
Ulrich, Eugene, et al. *Qumran Cave 4.IX: Deuteronomy, Joshua, Judges, Kings. Discoveries in the Judaean Desert*, vol. 14. Oxford: Clarendon Press, 1995.
Ulrich, Eugene, et al. *Qumran Cave 4.X: The Prophets. Discoveries in the Judaean Desert*, vol. 15. Oxford: Clarendon Press, 1997.
Ulrich, Eugene, et al. *Qumran Cave 4.XI: Psalms to Chronicles. Discoveries in the Judaean Desert*, vol. 16. Oxford: Clarendon Press, 2000.
Van Beek, Gus W., ed. *The Scholarship of William Foxwell Albright: An Appraisal. Papers Delivered at the Symposium 'Homage to William Foxwell Albright', the American Friends of the Israel Exploration Society, Rockwell, Maryland, 1984.* Harvard Semitic Studies, vol. 33. Atlanta: Scholars Press, 1989.
VanderKam, James C., and Peter Flint. *The Meaning of the Dead Sea Scrolls: Their Significance for Understanding the Bible, Judaism, Jesus, and Christianity.* New York: HarperSanFrancisco, 2002.
Vermes, Geza. *Providential Accidents: An Autobiography.* Lanham: Rowman and Littlefield, 1998.
- "Access to the Dead Sea Scrolls: Fifty years of Personal Experience" In Timothy H. Lim, Hector L. MacQueen, and Calum M. Carmichael, eds, *On Scrolls, Artefacts and Intellectual Property*. Journal for the Study of the Pseudepigrapha: Supplement Series, Lester L. Grabbe and James H. Charlesworth, eds, no. 38. Sheffield: Sheffield Academic Press, 2001, 192–8.
Vitelli, Karen D., ed. *Archaeological Ethics*. Walnut Creek: AltaMira, 1996.
Vogt, Ernst. "'Pax Hominibus Bonae Voluntatis' Lc 2:14" ("Peace Among Men of God's Good Pleasure" Lk. 2:14). *Biblica* 34, no. 3 (1953): 427–9.
Wacholder, Ben Zion, and Martin G. Abegg. *A Preliminary Edition of the Unpublished Dead Sea Scrolls: The Hebrew and Aramaic Texts from Cave Four.* 4 vols. Washington, D.C.: Biblical Archaeology Society, 1991–96.
Warren, Karen J. "A Philosophical Perspective on the Ethics and Resolution of Cultural Property Issues." In Phyllis M. Messenger, ed., *The Ethics of Collecting Cultural Property*. Albuquerque: University of New Mexico, 1989, 1–26.

Wechsler, Tovia. "The 'Hidden Geniza' Once More or Mr. Trever *versus* Mr. Trever." *Jewish Quarterly Review* 41, no. 3 (January 1951): 247–50.
- "The Origin of the So Called Dead Sea Scrolls." *Jewish Quarterly Review* 43, no. 2 (October 1952): 121–39.
- "Wechsler, Tovia." In *Who's Who in Israel, 1966–67*, col. 653. Tel Aviv: Mamut, 1966.
- *Tsfunot baMasoret Yisrael*. Jerusalem: Ruben Mass, 1968.

Wilson, Edmund. "A Reporter at Large: The Scrolls from the Dead Sea." *The New Yorker* 31, no. 13 (14 May 1955): 45–121.
- *The Scrolls from the Dead Sea*. London: W.H. Allen, 1955.

Winnett, Frederic V. "Report of the Director of the School in Jerusalem." *Bulletin of the American Schools of Oriental Research* 156 (December 1959): 4–7.
- "Tribute: Gerald Lankester Harding 1901–1979." *Biblical Archaeologist* 43, no. 2 (1980): 127.

Wiseman, D.J. "Obituary: Sir Godfrey Driver." *Bulletin of the School of Oriental and African Studies* 39, no. 1 (1976): 160–3.

Wright, G. Ernest. "Archaeological News and Views." *Biblical Archaeologist* 12, no. 3 (1949): 64–8.
- "Archaeological News and Views." *Biblical Archaeologist* 16, no. 1 (1953): 17–20.
- "Report of the Representative on the Board of Trustees of the American School of Oriental Studies." *Journal of Biblical Literature* 76, no. 1 (1957): xvi–xviii.

Wolters, Al. "Copper Scroll." In Lawrence H. Schiffman and James C. Vanderkam, eds, *Encyclopedia of the Dead Sea Scrolls*, vol. 1. Oxford: Oxford University Press, 2000, 144–8.

Yadin, Yigael. *The Message of the Scrolls*. New York: Simon and Schuster, 1957.
- *The Temple Scroll: The Hidden Law of the Dead Sea Sect*. London: Weidenfeld and Nicolson, 1985.

Zeitlin, Solomon. "Where Is the Scroll of the Haftarot?" *Jewish Quarterly Review* 40, no. 3 (January 1950): 291–6.
- "When Were the Hebrew Scrolls 'Discovered' – in 1947 or 1907?" *Jewish Quarterly Review* 40, no. 4 (April 1950): 373–8.
- "More Hebrew Scrolls." *Jewish Quarterly Review* 43, no. 4 (April 1953): 406–8.
- "The Fiction of the Recent Discoveries near the Dead Sea." *Jewish Quarterly Review* 44, no. 2 (October 1953): 85–115.
- "The Antiquity of the Hebrew Scrolls and the Piltdown Hoax. A Parallel." *Jewish Quarterly Review* 45, no. 1 (July 1954): 1–29.
- "A Note on the Fiction of the 'Bar Kokba' Letter." *Jewish Quarterly Review* 45, no. 2 (October 1954): 174–80.

- "The Dead Sea Scrolls: 1. The Lamech Scroll: A Medieval Midrash. 2. The Copper Scrolls. 3. Was Kando the Owner of the Scrolls?" *Jewish Quarterly Review* 47, no. 3 (January 1957): 245–68.
- "Review: The Dead Sea Scrolls: Fantasies and Mistranslations." *Jewish Quarterly Review* 48, no. 1 (July 1957): 71–85.

Zias, Joseph. "Palestine Archaeological Museum." In Lawrence H. Schiffman and James C. Vanderkam, eds, *Encyclopedia of the Dead Sea Scrolls*, vol. 2. Oxford: Oxford University Press, 2000, 634–5.

Index

Index

1QapGen, 57
1QIsa^a, 57
1QpHab, 57
1QS, 57
4QMMT, 129
11QNew Jerusalem, 79
11QPs^a (11Q5): publication rights purchased by ASOR, 115
11QTargum of Job, 79; rights to publication purchased, 372n140

Abegg, Martin, 7, 321n21; controversy over early publications of DSS, 7
Afghanistan, antiquities, 18
al-Alami, Feidi, 21
Albareda, Joaquin Anselmo M., 232n256, 363n61
Albina, Najib Anton, 234n264, 350n223
Albright Institute of Archaeology, 333n40
Albright, William Foxwell, 8, 47, 54, 76, 82, 48, 49, 171, 171n105, 321n26, 322n33, 322n35, 343n152, 349n215, 358n312; on the authenticity and antiquity of the DSS, 48–9
All Souls Deuteronomy (4Q41/Deutⁿ), 99
All Souls Unitarian Church (New York), 5, 98–9, 108, 220n224
Allegro, John Marco, 5, 6, 12–13, 22–3, 28, 34, 36, 48, 69, 100, 123, 127–8, 178n126, 190n155, 190n158, 193n167, 201, 234n265, 256n325, 275n358, 320n8, 345n187, 355n278, 361n26, 371n130; advisor to Jordan regarding DSS, 380n6; controversial statements, 357n311; controversy over DSS, 75–6; criticism of, 380n8; *The Dead Sea Scrolls: A Reappraisal* (by J. M. Allegro), 226; efforts to exhibit DSS abroad, 375–376n188; letter concerning funding and DSS acquisition, 22–23; letter concerning PAM and publication of DSS, 124; scheme to purchase all the PAM scrolls to keep in Jordan, 101, 265
American Council of Learned Societies, 102

American Schools of Oriental
Research (ASOR), 8, 12, 15, 28–30,
32–3, 47, 53, 56–7, 74, 86, 92–4,
102, 115, 120, 130, 163n72–3,
164n76–7, 185, 210n201,
218n222, 237, 258n330, 259n331,
260n333, 261, 266n345, 296n424,
320n7, 322n35, 324n46, 330n11,
332n31, 333n40–1, 346n190,
347n199–200, 353n257; institutional membership for McGill University, 162–4; purchased publication rights to 11QPs^a, 376n189; Statement of ASOR Policy on Preservation and Protection of Archaeological Resources, 130; R.B.Y. Scott as visiting professor, 301
Ancient Library of Qumran, The (by Frank M. Cross), 12, 27
Antiquities, 114–15; cultural property law, 123–34, 377n192, 383n45, 383n48, 384n50; financial aspects, 116; national identity formation, 113, 375n175; ownership and controversy, 15, 18, 129–34, 326n74; problems in policy, 376n190; problems in the preservation of, 18; *See also* ASOR, Statement of ASOR Policy on Preservation and Protection of Archaeological Resources; cultural property; *Hague Convention for the Protection of Cultural Property in the Event of Armed Conflict*; International Centre for the Study of the Preservation and Restoration of Cultural Property; law; UNESCO, *Convention on the Means of Prohibiting and Preventing the Illicit Import, Export and Transfer of Ownership of Cultural Property*
Arab Legion, 82, 124
Arab nationalism, 82, 210n201, 225, 359n13; impact on situation of the Dead Sea Scrolls, 258. *See also* Nasser, Gamal Abdel
ARC: *The Journal of the Faculty of Religious Studies, McGill University*, xvi, 14, 121
Archaeological Museum of Amman, 126
ASOR. *See* American Schools of Oriental Research (ASOR)
Association of Universities of the British Commonwealth, 176n119
Aswan Dam, 113
Avigad, Nahman, 72–3, 94, 125, 262n335

Baghdad Museum, 328n82
Baigent, Michael, conspiracy theorist, 6
Baillet, Maurice, 190n155, 256n325, 353n256
Baltimore Hebrew College, 336n74
Bar Kokhba (Cochba) letter, 31, 335n63
Bar Som, interpreter for Boulos Gelph, 48
Barthélemy, Dominique, 144n24, 190n155
BBC Radio, John Allegro broadcasts, 75; H. H. Rowley broadcasts, 72, 178–9
Beatty, Edward, 327n79
Beaulieu, Paul André, Canadian ambassador to Lebanon, 111, 280n372, 287, 297n425; letter

regarding funding for acquisition of DSS, 112
Bechtel, Elizabeth Hay, funded the acquisition of Cave II mss for PAM, 79, 218n222, 359n6, 376n189
Beirut Museum, 90
Benoit, Pierre, 134, 190n155, 196n175, 325n56; described the work of DSS editorial team, 11
Bentley, William, 83, 200n179, 205n192, 206n193, 252n313, 360n22; letters, 223, 208
Biblical Archaeologist, 11, 125
Biblical Archaeology Review, 7
Biblical Archaeology Society, 7
Biran, Avraham, 125
Birks family, donors to McGill University, 46, 53, 71–3, 79, 87, 122, 159n66, 351n234
Birks, Elizabeth Leggo McConnel, wife of Henry, donor to McGill University, 44, 151n45, 152n48, 157–8
Birks, Henry Guifford, 39, 44, 129, 132, 151n45, 152–3, 157n62, 179, 180n132
Birks, John Henry Metcalf, 49, 60, 151n45, 152n48. *See also* John Henry Birks Collection of Ancient Palestinian Manuscripts; John Henry Birks Foundation
Birks, William Massey, 39, 151n45, 338n100
Boer, Pieter Arie Hendrik de, 225
Bogdanos, Matthew, military supervisor of Iraq Museum investigation, 18–19
British Commonwealth, 32
British Library, 215n214

British Mandate, 8, 21
British Museum, 36, 48, 50, 72, 88, 115, 127, 128, 145n29, 146n32, 167, 227, 227n244, 232, 346n195; aided conservation of DSS, 376n188; invited to send scholar for Dead Sea Scrolls editorial team, 56
British Overseas Airways Corporation, 197n177, 199n178
British School of Archaeology, 22, 330n11
British Society for Old Testament Study, 54, 175, 345n179
Bronfman, Allan, 264n337
Brooke, George, 379n218
Broshi, Magen, 125
Brown, Dan, 6
Brown, Judith, daughter of John Allegro, 13, 124, 256n325
Brown, Raymond, 266n345
Brown University, 320n7
Brownlee, William H., 115, 127; published 11QEzek, 376n189
Bulletin of the American Schools of Oriental Research (BASOR), 11, 53–4, 93, 164n77, 322n34; noted McGill University acquisition of Cave 4 fragments, 171
Burrows, Millar, 5, 29, 33, 47, 54, 76, 94, 171, 175, 320n7, 347n199, 358n312; director of ASOR, 8; *The Dead Sea Scrolls* (by. M. Burrows), 211

Cairo Genizah, 47, 342n140
Cairo Museum of Arab Art, 113
Cambridge University, 28

Canada, higher education in the post-WW II period, 17, 37–9, 45; national identity formation in post-WW II period, 31–2
Canadian Broadcasting Corporation, 53; R.B.Y. Scott lectures, 75
Canadian Department of External Affairs, 119–20
Canadian Friends of Hebrew University, 264n337
Canadian Jewish Congress, Adult Education Committee of the Eastern Region, 41, *Congress Bulletin*, 54
Canadian Journal of Theology, 168n94
Carson, Cindy, 19, 131
Catholic University of America, 127, 163n72, 353n257
CBC. *See* Canadian Broadcasting Corporation
Centre National de Recherches Scientifiques, 324n46
Chicago Tribune, 89
Christianity, DSS and controversy about, 75–7
Clokie, H. McDowall, 32
CNRS. *See* Centre National de Recherches Scientifiques
Colonialism, Britain and Canada, 31–2; Iraq, 18–19
Congregational College of Canada, 338n98
Cooper, W. Mansfield, 104
Copper Scroll (3Q15), 126–7, 143n20, 265n341
Cross, Frank Moore, 3, 9–12, 15, 27, 46, 51, 54–7, 60, 76, 89, 97–100, 127, 152n49, 163n72, 165–6, 172n106, 175, 190n155, 215n214, 221n226, 256n325, 258, 323–4n43, 324n46, 332n34, 340n118, 345n187, 346n193, 361n26, 382n24; on content of McGill Cave 4 acquisitions, 61, 253; description of DSS purchase arrangements, 27; description of rushed editorial work, 100; letter to R.B.Y. Scott regarding situation of DSS, 89–90; request for an article by R.B.Y. Scott, 172
cultural property, 114–15, 129–34, 328n82–3, 335n62; "cultural nationalism," 133; financial aspects, 116; and identity formation, 375n175; Jordanian nationalization of the DSS, 90–4, 292; law, 377n192, 383n45, 383n48, 384n50; object-oriented approach, 30; problems in policy, 376n190; repatriation of Polish cultural objects, 254n318; rights and ownership, 123–34, 326n74. *See also* Antiquities; ASOR, Statement of ASOR Policy on Preservation and Protection of Archaeological Resources; *Hague Convention for the Protection of Cultural Property in the Event of Armed Conflict*; International Centre for the Study of the Preservation and Restoration of Cultural Property; law; UNESCO, *Convention on the Means of Prohibiting and Preventing the Illicit Import, Export and Transfer of Ownership of Cultural Property*

Da Vinci Code, 6
Dajani, Awni Khalil, director, Jordanian Department of

Antiquities, 111–12, 115, 120, 124–5, 128, 278n366, 301–3, 364n66, 380n4; letters, 304
Danforth, William H., 63
Davies, G. Henton, 345n179
Davies, William David, 54, 175, 345n178
Dead Sea Discoveries, 14, 326n67
Dead Sea Scrolls (Cave 1): advertised in *Wall Street Journal*, 59; circumstances of discovery, 7, 21; Jordan's loss/Israel's acquisition of manuscripts, 114; purchased and sold by Athanasius Samuel, 57–9; purchased by Yigael Yadin, 58
Dead Sea Scrolls (Cave 11): acquisition and sale of manuscripts, 49, 96, 127, 349n215, 354n270; discovery, 79; funding for acquisition, 103; ownership of Cave 11 mss, 372n140; Psalms Scroll, 115; unpublished manuscripts (whereabouts unknown), 328n81
Dead Sea Scrolls (Cave 4): acquisition of additional Cave 4 fragments by McGill University, 69, 212–13; acquisition of manuscripts with funding from McGill University, 14, 27, 71–2, 98–9; Cave 4 manuscripts editorial team, 323–4n43, 324n46; concordance of Cave 4 texts, 346n189; description of Cave 4 manuscripts, 9; discovery of Cave 4 manuscripts, 143; fragments acquired by R.B.Y. Scott, 300n441; infra-red photographs of fragments sent to McGill University, 173; manuscript images, 62–6; McGill University's allotment, 68, 80–1, 90, 194, 308–18; plans to distribute manuscripts after editing, 104–6; plans to ship manuscripts to McGill University, 80; preservation of fragments, 214–15. *See also* John Henry Birks Collection of Ancient Palestinian Manuscripts

Dead Sea Scrolls on Microfiche, 13

Dead Sea Scrolls: academic study of religion and, 42; acquisition arrangements with Bedouin, 144, 156; acquisition of manuscripts by private collectors, 196n175, 327n81; acquisition, editing, and preservation of, 20, 26, 28, 195, 379n223; administrative pressures on editorial team, 100; Allegro advises Jordan to buy all and nationalize, 101; Canadian involvement in early study described, 29–33; completion of editorial work, 104; concern for integrity of collection as a whole, 133; conflict between Israel and Jordan over, 112–13; conservation and restoration efforts, 10–11, 21–2, 88, 100–1, 104, 127–9, 178–9, 215n214, 217, 226–30, 260, 376n188, 381n18; conservation problems, 9, 86, 363n57, 219n223, 371n139; conspiracies about, 6; controversies over editorial team, publication, and access, 6–7, 57, 68–9, 361n26; correspondence of the editorial team, 15; creation of international editorial team, 146; cultural property issues and, 131–4; dating of manuscripts, 319n2 (ch. 1), 341n136; debates about origin, date, and authenticity, 9,

46–7, 335n57, 342n145; early history of discovery, 11, 21; funding problems in acquisition of, 22, 25; historical reconstruction of scrolls community, 170; impact on study of Judaism and Christianity, 75–6, 170; impact on the text of the Old Testament, 152; institutional contributions to preservation, 189; insured, 196–7; John Allegro and controversy over, 75–6; Jordanian nationalization of the scrolls, 14, 90–4, 109–16, 123, 278–9n366; Jordanian policies regarding, 82–3, 90–1, 118, 233–55, 280–1, 354n275, 365–6n76; Jordanian politics and, 131–4; manuscripts in paleo-Hebrew script, 353n257; national identity formation and, 19; nature of contents and study, 259; nature of the biblical manuscripts, 166, 174; new documentary sources about early history, 13; of St Mark's Monastery, 47–8, 347n200, 348n205; politics and anti-Semitism, 346–7n195; preparations for storage during conflict, 86–7, 226; problems in historiography of, 12–14; propagandistic use by Arab language press, 374n163; publicity problems, 98–9; rights of ownership, access, and publication, 95–6, 103, 130–1, 287; scholastic prestige and, 145, 155, 197, 287; search for caves, 29–30, 217; study and publication of, 12, 66, 97–8, 104, 165–6, 189–90, 269–70, 381n19; study and publication problems, 10, 71, 84, 86–7, 99–103, 109, 126–7, 190n158, 231, 368n106, 370n120–1; taken over by Israel after Six-Day War, 125–6, 373n148; theft of fragments, 360n17; Vatican's perspective on, 354n272

Dead Sea Scrolls, The (by John Allegro), discussed, 12

Dead Sea Scrolls, The (by Millar Burrows), discussed, 29

Deep River Science Association, 232

Del Medico, Henri E., 85, 225, 361n35

Detweiler, A. Henry, 93, 366n84

Deutsche Forschungsgemeinschaft, 190n155, 353n256

Deutschen Evangelischen Instituts für Altertumswissenschaft des Heiligen Landes, 330n11

Dever, William G., description of aftermath of Six-Day War, 124–5

edh-Dhib, Mohammed, 21, 330n7

Ad-Difaa (Jordanian newspaper), 99

Dinur, Ben Zion, 358n312

Discoveries in the Judaean Desert, 98, 134; renamed after Six-Day War, 126

Dix ans de Découvertes dan le Désert de Juda (by Józef Milik), discussed, 12

Dix, William S., 217n221

DJD. See *Discoveries in the Judaean Desert*

Dominican School, 99

Douglas, Lewis Williams, 327n79

Drioton, Étienne, 113

Driver, Godfrey Rolles, 25, 46, 48, 85, 225, 331n23, 346n195

Dropsie College, 336n74, 341n137; meeting of DSS scholars on 10th anniversary of discovery, 358n312

DSS. *See* Dead Sea Scrolls
Duke University, 54, 127, 175, 324n48, 345n178
Duplessis, Maurice Le Noblet, 45, 164n77, 340n128
Dupont-Sommer, André, 85, 225, 362n36
Durham University, 345n179
al-Durra, Saeed, 236n269, 249n306, 364n66

École Biblique et Archéologique Française, 6, 8, 11–12, 23, 30, 52, 72, 108, 141, 155, 156n56, 170, 188, 225n238, 320n6, 324n46, 325n56, 330n11; advanced funds to purchase Cave 4 fragments, 209, 212, 216; funded study of Dead Sea Scrolls, 354n275
education, changes in post-war Canada, 37–9
Egypt, antiquities and political history, 113
Egyptian Antiquities Service, 113, 375n175
Egyptian Museum of Cairo, 113
Egyptian Society for Historical Studies, 50, 157n61, 159
Eisenman, Robert, 321n19; controversy over DSS publication, 6
Elgin Marbles, and cultural property issues, 129
Engnell, Ivan, 26
Erskine and American Church, 151n46
Essenes, 52, 75–7, 143n16, 169–70, 189
Ezekiel scroll (11QEzekiel), 127

Falastin, 110, 278n366
Farouk I, king of Egypt, 375n174

Fechner, Frank, 116
Fields, Weston, 26, 56–7, 84, 125, 324n50, 345n181
Fitzmeyer, Joseph, 86, 332n35
Flint, Peter, 7
Forestell, James Terence, 33, 336n73
Foulkes, Valerie, 128
Francis, Frank, director of British Musueum, 127–8, 376n188
Free Officers' Coup, 113
French Institute of Archaeology, 113
Frost, Stanley Brice, 11, 15, 17, 41–2, 95, 96, 100–2, 109–10, 112, 114, 116–21, 132, 156n57, 248, 250, 260n333, 266n343, 272–6, 327n76, 346n190; letters, 257–63, 265, 277, 282–90, 293–307; met with Jordanian director of antiquities and minister of education, 265; replaced R.B.Y. Scott at McGill University, 94; report of visit to Israel and Jordan, 266–8; trip to Israel, 262–4
Fulton, Alexander Strathern, 36, 338n87

Gardner, Bertie Charles, 239n280
Gazette (Montreal), 32, 41, 47–8, 53, 60, 115
Gelph, Boulos, 48
Ghureibah, Abdel Karim, director, Jordanian Department of Antiquities, 90, 236n269, 239n278, 244n288, 249n306, 364n66
Gibbon, Fitz, 129
Gitin, Seymour, 322n33
Globe and Mail, 210n201
Glubb, John Baggot, 82
Glueck, Nelson, 358n312
Golb, Norman, 41–2, 339n112

Green, Howard, Canadian secretary of state for external affairs, 117, 286n396

Hague Convention for the Protection of Cultural Property in the Event of Armed Conflict, 130; territorial attribution of cultural property, 132. *See also* Antiquities; ASOR, Statement of ASOR Policy on Preservation and Protection of Archaeological Resources; cultural property; International Centre for the Study of the Preservation and Restoration of Cultural Property; law; UNESCO, *Convention on the Means of Prohibiting and Preventing the Illicit Import, Export and Transfer of Ownership of Cultural Property*
Hamilton, Robert William, 329n5
Hammond, Philip C., 70, 353n261–62
Harding, Gerald Lankester, 4, 6, 8, 11–12, 14–15, 21–2, 25, 27–9, 34, 36, 45–7, 49–51, 55–7, 60–1, 65, 67–8, 70–1, 75, 79–80, 84–9, 91, 93, 102, 112, 116, 122, 129–31, 135, 140n2, 142n12, 143n18, 144n24, 145n28–30, 146n32, 149n41, 156–7, 160n67, 165, 169, 188–9, 195n173, 204n191, 300n441, 320n6, 320n13, 328n81, 329n5; dismissal as Director of Antiquities of Jordan, 64, 82–3, 224–5, 358–9n1; impact of dismissal on McGill, 84; letters, 140, 145–7, 153, 158, 161–2, 188, 209, 221; role in preservation of DSS, 347n197

Harvard Divinity School, 343n160
Harvard University, 15, 127, 248n302, 280n374, 324n43, 324n48, 346n190
Hashim, Ibrahim, Jordanian prime minister, 220n224
Hebrew Union College – Jewish Institute of Religion, 33, 41, 77, 336n74, 349n215, 357–8n312
Hebrew University, 21, 58, 72, 125, 143n15, 262–3, 262n335, 264n337, 322n28, 325n58, 362n50, 370n127; acquisition of DSS, 8
Heeney, Arnold Danford Patrick, 242n286, 246n294
Heichelheim, Fritz M., 336n70
Henniker-Major, John Patrick Edward Chandos, 278n366
The Hidden Scrolls (by Neil Asher Silberman), discussed, 13
higher education, in the post-WW II period, 338n95
HUC–JIR. *See* Hebrew Union College – Jewish Institute of Religion
Huntington Library, 7, 321n22
Hunzinger, Claus-Hunno, 69, 85, 190n155, 193n167, 195n173, 201, 225, 237, 345n187, 353n256; letter to R.B.Y. Scott concerning new finds, 69–70
Hussein bin Talal, king of Jordan, 82, 101, 113, 210n201

IAA. *See* Israel Antiquities Authority
International Association of Universities, 74, 213n212
International Centre for the Study of the Preservation and Restoration of Cultural Property, 88. *See also*

Antiquities; ASOR, Statement of
ASOR Policy on Preservation and
Protection of Archaeological
Resources; cultural property;
*Hague Convention for the
Protection of Cultural Property in
the Event of Armed Conflict*; law;
UNESCO, *Convention on the Means
of Prohibiting and Preventing the
Illicit Import, Export and Transfer
of Ownership of Cultural Property*
International Organization for
the Study of the Old Testament
(IOSOT), Copenhagen congress,
16, 23, 25, 27, 29, 34, 141, 165;
Strasbourg congress, 83–5, 203,
218, 223–5, 361n26, 361n29
IOSOT. *See* International Organization
for the Study of the Old Testament
(IOSOT)
Iraq, antiquities and cultural property
issues, 18
Isaiah Scroll, 322n35
Israel Antiquities Authority, xx, 7, 14,
134, 383n43; archives, 13. *See also*
Israel Department of Antiquities
and Museums
Israel Department of Antiquities and
Museums (IDAM), 129

Jacobs, Monty, 349n215
James, Frank Cyril, 17, 34, 35,
36–7, 39–40, 43–7, 51, 53, 56,
58, 60, 68, 70, 72–5, 87–8, 92–6,
122, 141n4, 142n12, 146n31,
159n66, 169, 172, 188, 232n254,
252–3, 255n320, 326n73, 327n79,
352n237, 362n49; letters, 157–8,
163–4, 175–6, 181, 185, 192,
199–200, 211, 213–14, 228,
230–1, 242–8, 262–4; press release
concerning McGill University's
acquisition of Cave 4 manuscripts,
52–3; trip to Israel, 72–3, 367n89
Jeremias, Joachim, 210n202
Jerusalem Post, 126
Jewish Chronicle, 349n215
Jewish community of Montreal, and
Dead Sea Scrolls, 41–2
Jewish Institute of Religion, 336n74.
See also Hebrew Union College –
Jewish Institute of Religion
Jewish National Fund, 264n337
Jewish Palestine Exploration Society,
330n11
Jewish Public Library (Montreal),
339n113
Jewish Quarterly Review, 47
John Henry Birks Collection (variously named): Cave 4 acquisitions
for McGill University, 49, 51, 63,
68, 70, 95, 157, 163, 168, 170,
172, 173, 176, 179–80, 182, 184,
186, 188, 193, 199–200, 231;
manuscript allotment list,
308–18
John Henry Birks Foundation, 60,
62, 64, 68, 77, 157, 169, 179,
180n131, 181, 201, 205n192,
212n207, 303; funded acquisition
of Cave 4 fragments by McGill
University, 154, 183; memorandum
regarding purchase of Cave 4 fragments for McGill University,
154–5; second donation for acquisition of additional Cave 4 fragments, 204–17
John Rylands Library, 226
Johns Hopkins University, 322n33,
322n35

Johnson, Ralph R., 44, 157n62, 184, 200, 205n192, 212n207
Johnston, Charles Hepburn, 92, 226n239, 278n366, 279
Johnston, George Fonds, 261
Jordan: policies on cultural property, 383–4n48; refusal to disperse DSS mss to foreign institutions, 233–55
Jordanian Department of Antiquities, 6, 8, 12, 26–7, 30, 43–4, 46, 51, 68, 84–5, 91, 96, 98–9, 101–3, 111, 116–17, 120, 124, 128, 320n6, 320n13, 329n3; decision regarding non-exportation of DSS to foreign institutions, 292; efforts to acquire looted DSS mss, 155; expenditures related to acquisition of DSS mss, 142; letter to all donor institutions requesting records of payment, 281–2
Jordanian Department of Finance, 111
Jordanian politics, impact on McGill University acquisition of Cave 4 fragments, 297–8
Jordanian-American Joint Fund for General Economic Development, 360n20

Kando. *See* Shahin, Khalil Iskandar (Kando)
Katzman, Avi, 134, 328n81
Kendrick, Thomas Downing, director of British Museum, 36–7, 346n195
Kenyon, Kathleen, 333n44, 353n261
Khirbet Mird, 144, 335n60
Khirbet Qumran, 4, 8, 11, 52; nature of the site, 352n240
King, Jaime Litvak, 376n190
Kiraz, Anton, 13

Koninklijke Nederlandse Akademie van Wetenschappen, 372n140. *See also* Royal Academy of Sciences of the Netherlands
Kraeling, Carl H., 28, 89–90, 93, 102, 238, 332n31; diplomatic role in regard to Dead Sea Scrolls, 366n85
Kuhn, Karl Georg, 85, 189n152, 225
Kutscher, Edward Y., 358n312

Lacau, Pierre, 113
law: appropriation of movable cultural objects, 18; cultural property, 7, 18, 116, 129–34, 326n74, 377n192, 383n45, 383–4n48, 384n50; difficulty in establishing ownership of cultural objects, 15; object-oriented approach to cultural property, 130. *See also* Antiquities; ASOR, Statement of ASOR Policy on Preservation and Protection of Archaeological Resources; cultural property; *Hague Convention for the Protection of Cultural Property in the Event of Armed Conflict*; International Centre for the Study of the Preservation and Restoration of Cultural Property; UNESCO, *Convention on the Means of Prohibiting and Preventing the Illicit Import, Export and Transfer of Ownership of Cultural Property*
Leigh, Richard, conspiracy theorist, 6
Leveen, Jacob, staff-member of British Museum, 56, 346n195
Levy, B. Barry, xx, 15, 339n113
Libman, Lena, 127
Library of Congress (United States), 145n29, 146n32, 338n86

Linsley, Thayer, 98
Louvre, Musée de, 375n175

Maclean's, article on the Dead Sea Scrolls, 232
Mahmud the Silwani, antiquities dealer, 69, 201
al-Majali, Hazza, 110, 278n366
Mallory, Lester DeWitt, 226n239
Manoog, Charles, 58–60, 172n107–8, 320n7, 348n207; correspondence regarding sale of scrolls by Athanasius Samuel, 172
Manual of Discipline, 73
Mariette, Auguste, 375n175
Marina, HRH the Duchess of Kent, 176
Massolin, Philip, 37
Mazar, Benjamin, 72, 73, 94, 262, 264n337, 370n127
McCormick Theological Seminary, 5, 89–90, 98–9, 105, 108, 116, 118, 220n224, 324n46; allotment of DSS manuscripts, 364n65; purchased DSS manuscripts, 14
McGill News, 54, 61, 65–6
McGill University, allotment lists of Cave 4 manuscripts, 81, 106–8, 200–1, 221–2; alternative plans for study of Cave 4 fragments, 293–5; argument over establishment of Faculty of Divinity, 39–41; arrangements for acquisition of Cave 4 fragments, 54, 140, 159, 182–3, 185–7, 191; conditions on purchase of Cave 4 fragments, 141–2, 176–7; conference on the Dead Sea Scrolls, 165; continued diplomatic efforts regarding the DSS Cave 4 mss, 120; difficulty obtaining purchased Cave 4 fragments, 101–2, 254–5; distribution and treatment of Cave 4 fragments, 255–7, 270–6; donor funding for purchase of Cave 4 fragments, 43–6, 49, 148–51; donor funds used for special library collection on Dead Sea Scrolls, 306; earliest formal acknowledgment of Cave 4 fragment purchase, 188; establishment of Faculty of Divinity, 17, 36; funding trouble in post-WW II period, 45; helped fund recovery and preservation of Cave 4 manuscripts, 11, 369n109; Institute of Islamic Studies, 41, 50, 157n61, 162, 259, 287, 343n160; institutional member of the American Schools of Oriental Research (ASOR), 94; invited to appoint a scholar to DSS editorial team, 55–6; legal claims to DSS Cave 4 mss, 117–18; letter to Jordanian Director of Antiquities, 240–2; nature of Cave 4 acquisitions, 194–5; papyrus fragments from Redpath Museum, 135, 136; preservation and storage of Cave 4 fragments, 214–15, 227–30, 260; press release on acquisition of Cave 4 fragments, 50–2, 169–70; prestige of Cave 4 fragments collection, 167, 260; purchase of Cave 4 fragments and international cultural property law, 129; purchase of Cave 4 fragments publicized, 168n94; record of purchase transactions for Cave 4 fragments, 284–5; Redpath Library, 87, 231; reimbursement for purchase price

of Cave 4 fragments, 120–1,
  295–307; relationship with
  Montreal Jewish community, 42;
  rights to Cave 4 fragments rejected
  by Jordan, 121–2, 233–55,
  278–81; second acquisition of
  Cave 4 fragments, 202–17; transportation of Cave 4 fragments,
  199, 270–6
McMaster University, 15
McMurray, Dorothy, 168
McNeill, William Everett, 38
Mellors, Peter, 103
Merryman, John Henry, 129–30,
  132–3
Meyer, Michael, 10
Milik, Józef T., 5, 12, 21, 30, 51,
  55, 76, 127, 165–6, 190n155,
  193n167, 196n175, 203n189,
  225, 237, 254n317, 256n325, 266,
  320n10, 323n43, 324n46, 324n48,
  345n187; report on DSS publication plans, 361n29
Mills, Sheldon Tibbets, 110–11,
  278n366
Moffet, William A., 7
Montreal Diocesan Theological
  College, 338n98
Montreal Museum of Fine Arts,
  151n46
Montreal Star, 32, 43, 45, 53, 74,
  121, 266n343
Mufti, Izziddin, Jordanian minister of
  finance, 301
al-Mulki, Fawzi, Jordanian prime
  minister, 240
Munro, Donald, 111–12
Musée Bible et Terre Sainte (Paris),
  fragment of Cave 4 Psalms manuscript, 196n175

Nahal Hever, 144n22
Nasser, Gamal Abdel('Abd al-Nasir),
  113, 114, 210n201, 375n174;
  influence on Jordanian politics,
  82
National Archaeological Museum
  (Amman), 381n17
National Council of Canadian
  Universities, 45
National Museum of Antiquities,
  Hebrew University, 322n28
Naveh, Joseph, 125
New Republic, 76
New York Times, 4, 8, 29, 53, 57, 71,
  89
New Yorker, 43, 75–6, 94
Nimer, Abdul Halim, Jordanian min-
  ister of education, 240
Nutrilite Foundation, funded pur-
  chase of Cave 4 fragments, 89, 98

O'Keefe, Patrick J., 132
Oberlin College, Graduate School of
  Theology, 12
Oriental Institute, University of
  Chicago, 333n44
Orlinsky, Harry Meyer, xix, 33,
  319n1 (Preface), 336n74, 337n75,
  343n152; assigned by Glueck
  to coordinate international DSS
  conference, 358n312; authenti-
  cated DSS manuscripts for sale by
  Athanasius Samuel, 349n215
Osborne, Cecil, 332n35
Ottoman Bank in Amman; storage
  site for Dead Sea Scrolls, 86, 97,
  236–7
Oxford University, 5, 25, 48, 108,
  220n224, 331n23, 362n42
Oxford University Press, 54

Oxtoby, Willard Gurdon, 55, 260n333, 266, 303, 346n190, 370n126

Palestine Archaeological Museum, 4, 11–12, 14, 22, 26–8, 36, 43, 46, 51–4, 56, 68, 71, 73, 79–80, 82–9, 92, 96, 98–102, 104, 106, 108–10, 115, 120–1, 129, 133, 135, 142n11, 142n13, 144n22, 156n56, 170, 326n72, 330n11; appeal to ambassadors as members of the board, 226; expenditures related to acquisition of DSS mss, 142; funding crisis, 103; nationalization by Jordan, 123, 380n4; records housed in IAA archives, 13; taken over by Israel after Six-Day War, 125, 380n11. *See also* Rockefeller Museum
Palestine Exploration Fund, 88
Palestine House, 328n85
Palestine Post, 8, 58
Palestinian Archaeology Department, 131
PAM. *See* Palestine Archaeological Museum
Pan-Arabism. *See* Arab nationalism
Parrot, A., 26
Pearson, Lester Bowles, 233n261
Pennington, Richard, McGill University librarian, 87, 228, 229n250
Pfann, Stephan J., 13, 72, 175n118, 178n126, 355n278, 380n5, 331n29
Phillips, Lazarus, 44, 147n35
Plenderleith, Harold James: advised conservation of DSS mss, 87–8, 127–8, 227, 363n51, 376n188

Politics, impact on disposition of Dead Sea Scrolls, 225, 233–55; impact on excavations in the Middle East, 209–210
Pontifical Biblical Commission, 336n73
Pontifical Biblical Institute (Rome), 71, 336n73
Pontifical Institute of Medieval Studies (Toronto), 33, 336n73
Pope, Marvin H., 259n331
Preliminary Edition of the Unpublished Dead Sea Scrolls: The Hebrew and Aramaic Texts of Cave Four, A, 7
Presbyterian College, 338n98
Princeton University, 4, 14, 56, 63–4, 69–70, 77, 79–80, 94, 135, 164n77, 179n130, 182, 185, 201–2, 207, 217n220–1, 218, 225, 280n374, 296n424, 337n79, 345n178, 346n190, 358n314; Graduate Studies Program in Religion, 62; possibility of acquiring DSS manuscripts, 217, 219–20
Pritchard, James, 48
Prott, Lyndel V., 132

Qimron, Elisha, 7
Quattan, Ibrahim, Jordanian minister of education, 297n429, 301
Queen's Theological College, 29
Queen's University (Kingston, Ontario), 38
Qumran Cave 12, 25

Rehnborg, Carl F., 89
Religion, study of, 39; study encouraged in post-WW II Canada, 17
Renfrew, Colin, 133

Rent, James, 336n73
Revue biblique, 11, 29, 174, 325n56
Revue de Qumrân, 11
Rifaʻi, Dja Bey, director of antiquities of Jordan, 101, 265n338, 267, 274
Rifai, Abdul Munim, Jordanian ambassador to Washington, 243n287
Robertson, Edward, 226n243
Robinson, James, 370n121
Rochman-Halperin, Arieh, 189n1551, 334n46
Rockefeller, John D., Jr., 100, 102, 269n348, 326n72, 332n31, 334n52
Rockefeller Foundation, 102, 109, 234n264
Rockefeller Museum (formerly Palestine Archaeological Museum), 15, 126, 155, 326n72, 334n52. See also Palestine Archaeological Museum
ROM. See Royal Ontario Museum
Rome, David, 339n113
Rowley, Harold Henry, 25–6, 34, 72, 85, 90–2, 178n128, 225–6, 235, 331n22, 345n179; comments on de Vaux's presentation at IOSOT, Copenhagen, 26; extract of broadcast talk on DSS, 178–179; *The Faith of Israel* (by H. H. Rowley), 234; letter of warning to R.B.Y. Scott, 238
Royal Academy of Sciences of the Netherlands, 203n188, 218n222, 354n270; funded acquisition of Cave 11 manuscripts for PAM, 79. See also Koninklijke Nederlandse Akademie van Wetenschappen

Royal Ontario Museum (ROM), 29, 210n201, 328n85
Runnals, Donna, 15, 135
Rusheidat, Shafiq, minister of education, Jordan, 236n270

Saʻad, Yusif, secretary of PAM, 30, 86, 99, 101, 109, 120, 189, 254n319, 266, 274, 277n362, 333n46
Samaria Papyri (Wadi ed-Daliyeh Papyri), 127
Samuel, (Mar) Athanasius Yeshua, 320n7, 325n58, 347n200, 348n205, 348n207; archbishop of the Syrian Orthodox Church, 8, 12–13; head of Syrian Jacobite Monastery of St Mark, 143n15; Metropolitan of Syrian Orthodox Church of Antioch in US and Canada, 21, 57; sale of Cave 1 manuscripts, 57–9, 172
Sanders, James A., 218n222, 376n189
Sandmel, Samuel, 41, 77, 357n311, 358n312
SBL. See Society of Biblical Literature
Schiffman, Lawrence, 127, 134, 370n120
Schuller, Eileen, 15, 48
Scott, John, 54, 61, 65–6
Scott, Kathleen Cordingley, R.B.Y. Scott's wife, 281n376, 298n431
Scott, Robert Balgarnie Young (R.B.Y.), 3–5, 16–18, 20, 24, 25, 27, 29, 32–7, 39–51, 53, 57, 60; correspondence used as source for history of DSS, 14; description of Cave 4 material to be purchased by McGill University, 30–1; died at age 88, 134; draft

letter to Jordanian Department of Antiquities, 240–2; interest in connecting academy and laity, 74; invited to join DSS editorial team, 56; letter to F. Cyril James requesting funds to purchase DSS Cave 4 mss, 34–5; letters, 140–5, 147–54, 159–63, 168, 171–80, 182–91, 200–2, 204–7, 213–15, 217–20, 222–7, 231–5, 238–9, 248–50, 254–5, 297–8, 305; media presence, 75–6; on Biblical Studies, 39–40; personal papers, xix–xxi, 17, 54; purchase of small Cave 4 fragments in Jerusalem, 195; report on visit to Jerusalem, 193–9; request for funds from F. Cyril James, 141–2; role in founding McGill Faculty of Divinity, 327n76; took position at Princeton University, 56, 63, 182; transferred responsibility to Stanley Frost, 96; trip to Jerusalem to study McGill Cave 4 collection, 176–7, 179–80, 185–6

Septuagint, 61

Shahin, Khalil Iskandar (Kando), 21, 26, 57, 69, 130, 156n59, 191n160, 329n3, 371n138

Shanks, Hershel, 7, 57, 324n50, 326n69

Sharett, Moshe, prime minister of Israel, 60

Shingiti, Sheikh M. (also Shangiti/ Shangity/Shauqiti), Jordanian minister of education, 101, 118–19, 265n339, 267, 274, 284n385, 286, 288n402, 293n412, 295n418; letters, 281–82, 291

Shor, Pnina, 127

Shrine of the Book, 125–6, 215n214

Silberman, Neil Asher, 13, 100, 325n63; on the ethics of the IAA, 377n192

Six-Day War, 10, 19, 124, 134, 326n72, 373n148; description of aftermath, 124–5

Skehan, Patrick W., 69, 76, 127, 163n72, 190n155, 193n167, 195n173, 203n189, 225, 256n325, 345n187, 353n257, 358n312, 382n25

Slater, Robert Henry Lawson, 248n302, 280

Smith, Arnold Cantwell, 287

Smith, Wilfred Cantwell, 41, 50, 60–1, 87, 157n61, 162, 171, 176–7, 246n293, 259, 287n401; established McGill University Institute of Islamic Studies, 343n160; report on visit to Jerusalem and PAM, 161, 165–7

Society of Biblical Literature (SBL), 86, 258n330

St Basil's Seminary (Toronto), 336n73

St Mark's Monastery, 47–8

Starcky, Jean, 76, 190n155, 193n167, 196n175, 256n325, 345n187, 356n302

Strasbourg University, Centre de Recherches d'Histoire des Religions, 84

Strugnell, John, 10, 12, 15, 76, 86, 97, 127, 134, 190n155, 193n167, 226n242, 254n317, 256n325, 266, 324n48, 325n56, 327–8n81, 334n52, 345n187, 362n42, 370n126, 382n26

Suez Canal Crisis, impact on the editing and study of DSS, 85–6, 92, 97,

125, 226n242, 231n253, 233n261, 238n274
Sukenik, Eleazar Lipa, 8, 12, 21, 58, 131, 143n15, 322n28, 325n58, 329n4, 343n152, 347–8n203, 362n50

Ta'amireh tribe, recovered DSS manuscripts, 21–2, 69, 141
Taha, Hamdan, 131
al-Talhouni, Bahjat, 292n411
Temple Emanu-El (Montreal), Reform Jewish congregation, 41, 77
Temple Scroll (11Q19), 348n210, 371n138
Thomas, George F., 182n141
Thomson, David L., dean of Graduate Studies at McGill, 53, 176n122, 179
Thomson, James Sutherland, dean of Faculty of Divinity, McGill University, 62, 87, 163n75, 181n137, 228, 229n250, 250n309, 327n76, 344n167
Time Magazine, 99
Times (London), 53, 76, 115, 189n154, 346n195
Toronto Daily Star, 32–3, 71, 74
Treasure from Judaean Caves: The Story of the Dead Sea Scrolls (by R.B.Y. Scott), 75
Trever, John C., 8, 47, 321n26, 322n35, 329n5, 347n199–200
Tushingham, Arlotte Douglas, , 29–32, 36, 83, 153n51, 155, 160, 165, 167n88, 210n201, 333n41, 333n44, 334n48, 334n52, 335n54–5; letter to G. Lankester Harding regarding his removal as Director of Antiquities, 83

Tutankhamen, 114

UNESCO (United Nations Educational, Scientific and Cultural Organization), 88, 114, 128, 130, 255n320; *Convention on the Means of Prohibiting and Preventing the Illicit Import, Export and Transfer of Ownership of Cultural Property*, 129; focused on patrimonial attribution of cultural property, 132. *See also* Antiquities; ASOR, Statement of ASOR Policy on Preservation and Protection of Archaeological Resources; cultural property; International Centre for the Study of the Preservation and Restoration of Cultural Property; *Hague Convention for the Protection of Cultural Property in the Event of Armed Conflict*; law
Union College (Vancouver), 23
Union Theological Seminary (New York), 258n330, 345n178
United Church Observer, 74
United Church of Canada, xx, 14, 23, 29, 95
United Nations Emergency Force, 233
United Theological College (UTC), 23, 62, 151n47, 180n132, 338n98; Birks Foundation provides funding for, 306
Université de Montréal, 327n78
University of Bonn, and purchase of DSS fragments by University of Heidelberg, 255n320
University of Bristol, 94
University of Chicago, 41, 332n31; Oriental Institute, 333n44

University of Göttingen, 210n202
University of Hamburg, 353n256
University of Heidelberg, purchased Cave 4 manuscripts and helped fund collection of DSS, 5, 6, 11, 14, 85, 91, 108, 116, 118, 121, 189, 225n237, 236–7, 255n320, 362n39
University of Jordan, 364n66
University of Leiden, 225n235
University of London, 248n301, 364n66
University of Manchester, purchased DSS manuscripts and helped fund collection of DSS, 5, 6, 11, 14, 25, 34, 72, 85, 90–2, 101, 104, 108, 113, 116, 118, 121, 127, 175, 178, 189, 226n243, 236–7, 326n68, 331n22, 355n276, 379n218
University of Pennsylvania, 327n79
University of Saskatchewan, 344n167
University of Toronto, 23, 29–30, 33, 327n78, 333n41, 333n44, 336n70
University of Uppsala, 26
University of Wales, 345n179

VanderKam, James, 7
Vanier, Georges Phileas, 258n329
Vatican: conspiracy about the DSS, 7; involvement in DSS deals, 226; perspective on impact of DSS on Christianity, 354n272
Vatican Library (Bibliotheca Apostolica Vaticana), purchased DSS manuscripts and helped fund collection of DSS, 5, 6, 11, 14, 71, 72, 85, 88, 90, 108, 113, 116, 118, 121, 178, 189, 213, 215n214, 232, 236, 354n271, 355n278, 363n61

Vaux, Roland de, 3–4, 6, 8, 11–12, 14–15, 22–3, 25, 26–30, 34, 36, 46–7, 50–2, 56–7, 65, 67–8, 70–2, 75–6, 79–80, 84–5, 87–8, 90–3, 95–7, 99, 188–9, 100–4, 108–11, 114–15, 122, 124, 126–8, 134, 141, 142n11, 143n18, 143n21, 144n24–5, 146n31, 155, 156n56, 160n66, 164–5, 170, 174, 186, 203n189, 215n214, 225, 248n300, 254n317, 255n320, 256n325, 277n362, 278–9, 320n6, 325n56, 332n29, 334n48, 358n312; honorary member of the Society of Biblical Literature and Exegesis (SBL), 210; letter supporting institutions regarding dispersal of DSS manuscripts, 104; letter to H. H. Rowley concerning ownership and study of the DSS, 91–2; letter to Jordanian government concerning dispersal of DSS manuscripts, 104–6; letters, 164–5, 202–3, 209–10, 216–19, 236–8, 249–52, 272, 278–9; request for financial aid in acquiring DSS Cave 4 mss, 16
Vogt, Ernst, 71, 72, 354n272, 354n275

Wacholder, Ben Zion, 321n21; controversy over early publications of DSS, 7
Wadi ed-Daliyeh Papyri (Samaria Papyri), 127
Wadi Murabba'at, manuscript finds, 135, 144, 190, 207n197, 325n56, 335n63, 337n79, 396n7
Wall Street Journal; advertisement for sale of DSS manuscripts, 59, 348n207

Washington National Gallery, 115
Washington Post, 6
Wechsler, Tovia, 47, 342n142–3
Wesleyan College, 338n98
West Bank, policies on cultural property, 383–4n48
Wharton School of Business, 327n79
Wiet, Gaston, 113
Wilson, Edmund, 43, 57, 74–7, 94, 339n115; impact on public, 357n311; importance for public discourse on DSS, 356n293; *New Yorker* article, 192
Winnett, Fred V., 29, 30–3, 47, 333n41
Wise, Michael O., 321n19; controversy over DSS publication, 6
World Council of Churches, 306n458
World War I, 36
World War II, 31, 37; impact on science and technology, 42; impact on higher education in post-war period, 16–17, 37–9, 45, 149n39, 327n78
Wright, G. Ernest, description of political problems involving the DSS, 86

Yadin, Yigael, 59–60, 73, 94, 125, 247, 262n335, 325n58, 348n209–10, 349n215, 362n50, 371n138; purchased Cave 1 scrolls from Mar Samuel, 58
Yale Divinity School, 320n7
Yale University, 8, 33, 54, 171, 175, 259n331, 347n199, 353n262

Zeitlin, Solomon, 47–8, 58, 70, 341n137, 343n152, 358n312
Zias, Joe, 131